Calvin and the Christian Tradition

John Calvin lived in a divided world when past certainties were crumbling. Calvin claimed that his thought was completely based upon scripture, but he was mistaken. At several points in his thought and his ministry, he set his own foundations upon tradition. His efforts to make sense of his culture and its religious life mirror issues that modern Western cultures face, and that have contributed to our present situation. In this book, R. Ward Holder offers new insights into Calvin's successes and failures and suggests pathways for understanding some of the problems of contemporary Western culture such as the deep divergence about living in tradition, the modern capacity to agree on the foundations of thought, and even the roots of our deep political polarization. He traces Calvin's own critical engagement with the tradition that had formed him and analyzes the inherent divisions in modern heritage that affect our ability to agree, not only religiously or politically, but also about truth. An epilogue comparing biblical interpretation with Constitutional interpretation is illustrative of contemporary issues and demonstrates how historical understanding can offer solutions to tensions in modern culture.

R. Ward Holder is a professor of theology at Saint Anselm College. A recipient of a National Endowment for the Humanities grant for this project, he has written, among other works, *John Calvin and the Grounding of Interpretation: Calvin's First Commentaries* (Brill, 2006) and edited *John Calvin in Context* (Cambridge University Press, 2020).

Calvin and the Christian Tradition

Scripture, Memory, and the Western Mind

R. WARD HOLDER

Saint Anselm College, New Hampshire

CAMBRIDGE
UNIVERSITY PRESS

CAMBRIDGE
UNIVERSITY PRESS

University Printing House, Cambridge CB2 8BS, United Kingdom

One Liberty Plaza, 20th Floor, New York, NY 10006, USA

477 Williamstown Road, Port Melbourne, VIC 3207, Australia

314–321, 3rd Floor, Plot 3, Splendor Forum, Jasola District Centre,
New Delhi – 110025, India

103 Penang Road, #05–06/07, Visioncrest Commercial, Singapore 238467

Cambridge University Press is part of the University of Cambridge.

It furthers the University's mission by disseminating knowledge in the pursuit of
education, learning, and research at the highest international levels of excellence.

www.cambridge.org
Information on this title: www.cambridge.org/9781316512944
DOI: 10.1017/9781009071413

© Cambridge University Press 2022

First published 2022

A catalogue record for this publication is available from the British Library.

Library of Congress Cataloging-in-Publication Data
NAMES: Holder, R. Ward, author.
TITLE: Calvin and the Christian tradition : scripture, memory, and
the Western mind / R. Ward Holder.
DESCRIPTION: Cambridge ; New York, NY : Cambridge University Press, 2022.
| Includes bibliographical references and index.
IDENTIFIERS: LCCN 2021970032 | ISBN 9781316512944 (hardback)
| ISBN 9781009071413 (ebook)
SUBJECTS: LCSH: Calvin, Jean, 1509-1564. | Tradition (Theology)
| Reformed Church – Doctrines – History. | Church history – 16th century.
| Civilization, Western – Christian influences. | BISAC: RELIGION / History
CLASSIFICATION: LCC BX9418 .H575 2022 | DDC 284/.2–dc23/eng/20220224
LC record available at https://lccn.loc.gov/2021970032

ISBN 978-1-316-51294-4 Hardback

In memory of Robert M. Kingdon, David C. Steinmetz,
and Irena D. Backus
Scholars whose work reminds me
that I stand on the shoulders of giants

Contents

Acknowledgments

When one sits down to reckon up the debts incurred in the writing of a book, there is a moment of pause, when the enormity of the debts one owes actually comes into focus. When the book has been over a decade in the making, that debt can grow out of all proportion, and one begins to feel as if no amount of thankfulness can repay the balance. But some stand out so much that even among the cloud of witnesses that have aided this effort, they must be recognized. It is in that spirit that I take up this task, while recognizing that this is only a token of the gratitude that I feel.

I must give thanks to the institutions that nurtured this project. First, to Saint Anselm College, which has been my intellectual home for the past two decades. The granting of two sabbaticals to work on this book, and a Summer Grant, has greatly speeded the process of writing. Beyond that, I am blessed by a set of colleagues who are generous with their time, both within and outside my department. Somehow, the Interlibrary Loan office at Saint Anselm College still cheerfully helps me along my way, seemingly forgetting the number of obscure requests that I submit. David Quinn is a gem, and the college is lucky to have him. Second, to the National Endowment for the Humanities that bestowed on me a Summer Grant that allowed me to address a set of questions early on in the writing that put the entire project on a better footing. Third, the Institute for Reformation History of the University of Geneva, where Irena Backus let me wander through their collection and took me over to the library of the university. Many of those early explorations proved unfruitful, but some produced more than I had hoped. Fourth and finally, to Cambridge University Press for taking this on – from Beatrice Rehl's enthusiasm for the project, to the editorial team who chose to accept the book, to the two unnamed scholars whose deep consideration of the book has made it so much more focussed, I owe all a huge debt of gratitude.

Second, I am blessed by a number of colleagues within the bounds of Calvin studies whose conversations with me over the years have provided a rich vein of ideas on which to ponder. Randall Zachman's good humor masked a sharp eye for detail and consequence; Karen Spierling, Jeff Watt, and Ray Mentzer reminded me that Calvin had a very specific historical context out of which his thought grew; Elsie Anne McKee was a wonderful example of scholarship and delving into what Calvin was actually doing in his life in Geneva, and Karin Maag represents everything one would want in a colleague who runs a research center – always willing to track down a reference or answer a question about a treatise, frequently with a caution about going too far with an idea. Bruce Gordon's generosity in listening while I asked short questions that became hour long conversations sharpened my thought innumerable times. In a way, this entire book is a response to a question he asked in 2011, "What do you mean when you say tradition?"

Third, as the project became a book, it was time to get the response from critical readers. David Whitford and Greta Kroeker read sections of the manuscript – I cannot imagine the final draft without their input. A special note of thanks goes to those who worked through the entire manuscript, Kathleen Comerford, Bruce Gordon, and Nate Antiel. The ways that their insights and questions have improved the final product are beyond all of my ability to count or measure. Their help improved this immeasurably, all the faults that remain are my own.

Finally, this book makes the argument that Calvin did not escape his own tradition because to do so was impossible. That reminds me that I stand in a rich tradition, most frequently on display at the Sixteenth Century Society and Conference annual meetings, but alive throughout the years in telephone calls, e-mails, Zoom meetings, Facebook posts, and chance encounters. Beyond all those already mentioned, I have been graced with the insights of Andrew Pettegree, Euan Cameron, Liz Lehfeldt, Jennifer Powell McNutt, Jon Balserak, Barbara Pitkin, Esther Chung-Kim, Rady Roldan-Figueroa, Christine Kooi, Brad Gregory, Mirjam van Veen, Jesse Spohnholz, Sujin Pak, Amy Nelson Burnett, Hal Parker, Ron Rittgers, Sabine Hiebsch, Jonathan Reid, Kay Edwards, Nick Terpstra, Peter Opitz, Amy Leonard, Bruce Janacek, Arnold Huijgen, Bill Naphy, Michael Bruening, Carlos Eire, Jill Fehleison, Steve Burnett, Ute Lotz-Heumann, and Ken Woo. All of these are part of the scholar-friends that make the work of scholarship a joy, as well as a vocation.

A Note on Translations

In general, I have used translations that are widely available in English, so as to make the work of retracing my steps easier for other scholars. I have endeavored to be clear in the notes what translations I was using. In a very few cases, I have adjusted the translation to clarify the points being made.

A Note on Language

Naming Christians who rejected the Church of Rome in the early modern period is not easy. "Protestant" was given to followers of Luther who protested at the Diet of Speyer in 1529, and was not a universal sixteenth-century term. Many, though definitely not all, used the term "evangelical," in various languages, to deny other terms such as heretic, schismatic, or Lutheran. In this work, I have chosen the term "evangelical" as a term to describe the theological and ecclesiastical world in which Calvin lived. However, in the epilogue, because it deals with twenty-first-century America, "evangelical" is used to describe a specific modern Christian movement. Though the words are the same, the meaning is not. Finally, when necessary, I have generally referred to the reforming movement in which Calvin found himself as "Reformed," rather than "Calvinist." Many scholars have pointed out that the tradition was broader than Calvin, that it preceded him, and it still continues centuries after his death.

Abbreviations

CO   Calvini, Ioannis. *Opera Quae Supersunt Omnia.* 59 volumes. Edited by Wilhelm Baum, Edward Cunitz, and Edward Reuss. Brunswick: C.A. Schwetschke and Son, 1895. Cited by volume and column number.

ICR   Calvin, John. *Institutes of the Christian Religion.* 2 volumes. Translated by Ford Lewis Battles, edited by John T. McNeill. Philadelphia, PA: Westminster Press, 1960. Cited by book, chapter, and paragraph number.

OS   Calvini, Ioannis. *Opera Selecta.* 5 volumes. 3rd ed. Edited by Peter Barth and Wilhelm Niesel. Munich: Christian Kaiser, 1967. Cited by volume and page number.

Introduction

Calvin and Tradition – A Window on the Western Mind

Tradition stands as an unexplored and misunderstood segment of humanity's memory, a moment of déjà vu for the collective unconscious that the twenty-first century strains to escape or resolve. Tradition remains so foreign to the modern mind that explorations of it are only taken up by philosophers, theologians, and cultural critics – in other words, by those members of society who do not seem to contribute to a kinetically and technologically driven world. Tradition is so outré that most cannot define it. Is tradition the ground and context that is the precondition for all thought and discourse? Is it instead the set of chains that precludes the possibility of true rationality? Even if a thinker manages to define what tradition is, the next step may be even more fraught with difficulty: determining its function within a society or institution.

But tradition did not always prove so elusive or fractured. For the medieval imagination, tradition provided the unquestioned assurance of the stability of the mental worlds of the three orders of medieval Europe, the clerical, knightly, and laboring orders.[1] During this time even significant innovations were understood through the spectacles of tradition.[2] It was assumed to provide a framework which could answer particular questions, and support what was, in retrospect, a narrow range of worldviews

---

[1] Georges Duby, *The Three Orders: Feudal Society Imagined*, translated by Arthur Goldhammer (Chicago: University of Chicago Press, 1980).

[2] Jo Ann McNamara, "Canossa and the Ungendering of the Public Man," in *Medieval Religion: New Approaches*, edited by Constance Huffman Berman (New York: Routledge, 2005), 92–110, argues that the reforms of the investiture that engendered the conflict between Gregory VII and Henry IV were always defended as being deeply rooted in the church's tradition.

that might be organized into a sociocultural synthesis.[3] There were always outliers to the Christian tradition – the Jews and Muslims were known to exist – though their presence could be seen to serve as particular examples of alterity or otherness that demonstrated the vastness of the reach of the hegemonic culture.[4] The general notion that tradition or custom provided a basic structure to society allowed many to appreciate and respect the weight or authority of tradition wherever they found it.

[3] See McNamara, "Canossa and the Ungendering of Man," in which she wrote, "Christian religion gave the emerging European civilization its unifying conceptual framework. The Church-state conflict that so long divided the European conscience tends to distract our attention from the basic harmony of their goals" (93).

[4] See David Nirenberg, *Communities of Violence: Persecution of Minorities in the Middle Ages* (Princeton: Princeton University Press, 1996); Mark R. Cohen, *Under Crescent and Cross: The Jews in the Middle Ages* (Princeton: Princeton University Press, 1994); M. Lindsay Kaplan, "Jessica's Mother: Medieval Constructions of Jewish Race and Gender in 'The Merchant of Venice,'" *Shakespeare Quarterly* 58 (2007): 1–30; David Nirenberg, "Conversion, Sex, and Segregation: Jews and Christians in Medieval Spain," *The American Historical Review*, 107(2002): 1065–93; Geraldine Heng, "England's Dead Boys: Telling Tales of Christian-Jewish Relations Before and After the First European Expulsion of the Jews," *MLN* 127, *Comparative Literature Issue: De Theoria: Early Modern Essays in Memory of Eugene Vance* (2012): S54–S85; Francesca Matteoni, "The Jew, the Blood and the Body in Late Medieval and Early Modern Europe," *Folklore* 119 (2008): 182–200; Deanna Klepper, "Historicizing Allegory: The Jew as Hagar in Medieval Christian Text and Image," *Church History: Studies in Christianity and Culture* 84 (2015): 308–44; Jeremy Cohen, ed., *From Witness to Witchcraft: Jews and Judaism in Medieval Christian Thought* (Wiesbaden: Otto Harrassowitz, 1996); Marina Torres Arce, "Swimming Against the Tide: The Entry of Jews in Spain. Religious Mobility, Social Control and Integration at the End of the Ancien Régime," in *Religious Diaspora in Early Modern Europe: Strategies of Exile*, edited by Timothy G. Fehler, Greta Grace Kroeker, Charles H. Parker, and Jonathan Ray (London: Pickering and Chatto, 2014), 19–29; Jonathan Ray, "Chaos and Community: 1492 and the Foundation of the Sephardic Diaspora," in *Religious Diaspora in Early Modern Europe*, edited by Fehler, Kroeker, Parker, and Ray, 153–66; Benjamin Braude, "The Sons of Noah and the Construction of Ethnic and Geographical Identities in the Medieval and Early Modern Periods" *William and Mary Quarterly* 54 (1997): 103–42; Josiah Blackmore, "Imaging the Moor in Medieval Portugal," *Diacritics* 36 (2006): 27–43; Stephen F. Kruger, "Medieval Christian (Dis)Identifications: Muslims and Jews in Guibert of Nogent," *New Literary History* 28 (1997): 185–203; Mark D. Meyerson, "The Survival of a Muslim Minority in the Christian Kingdom of Valencia (Fifteenth-Sixteenth Centuries)," in *Conversion and Continuity: Indigenous Christian Communities in Islamic Lands Eighth to Eighteenth Centuries*, edited by Michael Gervers and Jibran Bikhazi (Toronto: Pontifical Institute of Medieval Studies, 1990), 365–80; Kevin Ingram, ed., *The Conversos and Moriscos in Late Medieval Spain and Beyond*, vol. 1, *Departures and Change* (Leiden: Brill, 2009); Ronald E. Surtz, "Morisco Women, Written Texts, and the Valencia Inquisition," *The Sixteenth Century Journal* 32 (2001): 421–433; Mark D. Meyerson, *A Jewish Renaissance in Fifteenth-Century Spain* (Princeton: Princeton University Press, 2004); L. P. Harvey, *Muslims in Spain, 1500–1614* (Chicago: University of Chicago Press, 2005); James S. Amelang, *Parallel Histories: Muslims and Jews in Inquisitorial Spain* (Baton Rouge: Louisiana State University Press, 2013).

While the theologian or ecclesiastical figure might speak of tradition as if it were settled and easily available, the historian recognizes that tradition has never been as solid as its protectors imagined, nor so amorphous as its detractors claimed. Tradition has both a constructed character and a received nature. The Christian tradition had gone through many arguments about what orthodox belief and practice was; the early modern period was only one of a number of times across Christian history during which the certainty of the tradition was either questioned or challenged. The early church's arguments over the Trinity and Christology are two such instances, as was the medieval iconoclastic struggle. Yet priests, laypeople of high and low estate, and theologians have all acted, both explicitly and implicitly, as if the tradition was a firm foundation for religious and theological practice.

However, the early modern world is frequently viewed as a time when the question of tradition arose. The fractures which mark tradition as a matter of debate in the modern world begin in the late medieval period when confidence in the seamlessness of the cultural and ecclesiastical traditions began to fray.[5] Whether it was through political theory, with the criticisms of Dante (1314) and Marsilius of Padua (1324); ecclesiastical power struggles, in the threats to papal power represented by the Avignon Papacy (1309–76) and conciliarism (fourteenth–fifteenth centuries); or even theological discussion with the growth of late medieval threats to orthodox teaching by Ockham (d. 1347), Wycliffe (d. 1384), and Hus (d. 1415); the mentality of assumed confidence in a monolithic synthesis was gradually replaced by one that sought confidence in a variety of areas.[6]

---

[5] Mark Lotito claims that the process of setting historical foundations for validation of an empire or claim to power are at least as old as the Ottonian empire in the tenth century. He examines the use of the model of the Four Monarchies from Daniel as a guide to considering the tension between decline and permanence. See Lotito, *The Reformation of Historical Thought* (Leiden: Brill, 2019), 37–50.

[6] Dante Alighieri's *De Monarchia* (ca. 1314) argued for the necessity of a world ruler to ensure peace, as did Marsilius of Padua's *Defensor Pacis* (1324). The Avignon Papacy (1309–76) moved the papal court to Avignon, and weakened the claims of Rome as the heart of Christianity, and led straight into the Western Schism or Papal Schism, that lasted from 1378 to 1417, with two, and eventually three, different claimants to the papal throne. Conciliarism – authority by councils – was in part an answer to this situation, and the Council of Constance in 1417 ended the schism. John Wycliffe argued that only scripture was the true foundation of theology. Jan Hus argued for reforms, some following Wycliffe, and others in sacramental life – the Council of Constance lured him to the Council in order that he might speak with guarantee of safe passage, then reneged and executed him in 1417. William of Ockham, in considering whether the scripture or the pope was right in a disputed question about the Franciscan right to own property, argued that the pope was a heretic. All of these seriously undercut the power of the church, or the theological doctrines upon which it was built.

Actually, that makes the process seem too organic. Instead, there was a sometimes frantic search for the one true tradition.[7] This search both exposed the various differing foundations upon which the mental world had been built and created new foundations in the search for univocity. The crumbling of confidence only accelerated in the sixteenth and seventeenth centuries. Various evangelical theologians certainly took part in that attack, raising up a tension between the purity of the scriptures and the debased nature of human traditions. But the variety of cultural and political changes that swept across Europe over the long duration of the era of the Reformations tore at those foundations as well. When the Enlightenment's attack on heteronomy in the eighteenth century pressed hard against the bulwarks of tradition, the end seemed nigh.[8]

But the end did not come. The modern world has both received and constructed a rich and fractured inheritance of tradition. The gamut runs between two poles: The positive argues that tradition provides the basic necessities for rational undertakings – a position adopted by many philosophers of the interpretation of texts; the negative asserts that tradition prevents the possibility of truly free inquiry and knowledge that is worthy of the title – a position staked out by Enlightenment thinkers who argued that rationality must be totally free. Figures as different as Jesus of Nazareth, Tertullian, Augustine, Boethius, Peter Lombard, Martin Luther, John Calvin, Robert Bellarmine, Immanuel Kant, Friedrich Schleiermacher, Yves Congar, Hans-Georg Gadamer, Paul Ricoeur, and John Milbank have weighed in on the topic over the last two thousand years. But at the end of two millennia of the Christian era, in what frequently is called the Western post-Christian era, the answer to the question of the essence of tradition and its epistemological power remains uncertain.[9]

---

[7] Paul Tillich argued that the Reformation was an effort to find the true tradition, arguing that "There is no reformation without tradition." Tillich, *Systematic Theology III: Life and the Spirit, History and the Kingdom of God* (Chicago: University of Chicago Press, 1963), 182.

[8] Dating the Enlightenment is as controverted in scholarship as many other topics. For my purposes, the Enlightenment stretched from the early 1700s to 1789, the French Revolution, that for historians marks the beginning of modernity. Kant's essay, "Was Ist Aufklärung?" was published in 1784.

[9] This includes the doctrinal statements of the Roman Catholic Church. In the Dogmatic Constitution on Revelation, commonly known as Dei Verbum, the Church promulgated two sources of authority but then argued that functionally they were one. (10) *Dogmatic Constitution on Divine Revelation, Dei Verbum, Solemnly Promulgated by his Holiness Pope Paul VI, November 18, 1965*. While confessionally neat, this approach does not answer questions of what to do when scripture and tradition seem to exist in tension or contradiction.

Because of this fractured inheritance, and because of the fractious reception of it, the modern Western mind faces two problems. The first of these is a nebulous turn to tradition by a variety of thinkers that cannot always define what the tradition is or what its effect in political, religious, cultural, or philosophical speech should be. The second problem is that in the turn away from tradition – ostensibly supported by the reformers – communities of discourse create a variety of traditions to help interpret texts, to highlight what is important in life, and to argue against their opponents, all while denying that they use tradition at all. A deeper understanding of tradition would aid both problems.

In the following study, I wish to investigate tradition through a deep consideration of Calvin's engagement with and construction of a useful past, and its constitutive function in his thought. I have chosen Calvin because he is frequently taken as the representative par excellence of a strand of thought that denies the role of tradition in clear and biblically-based theology. Calvin is the Protestant's Protestant.[10] But that picture of Calvin actually tells us as much or more about the modern analytical mind than it does about Calvin's actual practices.[11] As late as the last decade of the twentieth century, a prominent Calvin scholar preparing an edition of one of Calvin's commentaries failed to consider the history of the period and confined his attention to Calvin's comments upon the scriptures without context, thereby signaling that Calvin's model of biblical interpretation was simply to follow the Word of God.[12] A more general investigation of the Reformation's interpretation of scripture, published in 2011, satisfied itself with the facile model of the Protestant

---

[10] An example comes from Marjorie O'Rourke Boyle's recent work, *The Human Spirit: Beginnings from Genesis to Science* (University Park, Pennsylvania: The Pennsylvania State University Press, 2018), in which Boyle takes up the question of what is meant by the human spirit. After finding Augustine and Aquinas more interested in dialectic than in the rhetoric of the scriptures, Boyle proceeds to treat Calvin, depending upon his scriptural prescription for those who would know God (204ff).

[11] Calvin himself has regularly suffered from both hagiographical accounts of his life and work, as well as vicious fables that were fabricated merely to besmirch his name. See J. R. Armogathe, "Les vies de Calvin au XVIᶜ et XVIIᶜ siècle," in *Historiographie de la Réforme*, edited by Philippe Joutard (Paris: Delachaux et Niestle: 1977), 45–59; and Jennifer Powell McNutt, "Calvin Legends: Hagiography and Demonology," in *John Calvin in Context*, edited by R. Ward Holder (Cambridge: Cambridge University Press, 2020); 383–392.

[12] *Ioannis Calvini Opera Exegetica, Commentarius in Epistolam ad Hebraeos*. Edited by T. H. L. Parker (Geneva: Droz, 1996), ix–xxxiv.

Reformation's foundation on the pure scriptures.[13] Casual views of Calvin by both the scholarly community and those who merely come across his name in an essay in the *New York Times Review of Books* consider him a proponent of *sola scriptura*.[14]

Calvin himself believed that he was leaving tradition behind for the firm foundation of the scriptures. He could wax eloquent about the manner that his Roman opponents had twisted the tradition for their own benefit. But his clear sense that his theological work was different from theirs caused him to believe that the relative difference between his work and theirs was actually absolute. That sometimes inaccurate sense of the foundations of his own thought would influence generations, and echo down to the present day in the way that moderns think about their heritage from the Reformation.

At heart, there is a paradoxical tension in Calvin's thought. John Calvin sought to ground his reforms and truth claims in the simple and uncluttered words of scripture, accepting it as a divine source. But John Calvin was a theological conservative who tried to maintain the true essence of medieval European Christianity as it had been passed down to him in liturgy, doctrine, and piety. Both of these statements capture the truth. In his first published exposition of scripture in 1540, Calvin could not escape the first page of the commentary without discussing both Augustine and Origen, two ancient authorities.[15] He depended upon the patristic witness both for conversation partners and authorities to help settle disputes in his commentaries, in the *Institutes*, and in his treatises. He accepted the ground of tradition on which to engage his opponents, and produced a number of arguments drawn from tradition in

---

[13] Timothy George, *Reading Scripture with the Reformers* (Grand Rapids: IVP Academic, 2011), 17–18.

[14] Cf., for example, Brad Gregory, who in his *The Unintended Reformation: How a Religious Revolution Secularized Society* (Cambridge: Harvard University Press, 2012), spends a significant number of pages on Luther and Calvin's efforts to establish a society on the pure dictates of scripture. "From the very outset of the Reformation, the shared commitment to *sola scriptura* entailed a hermeneutical heterogeneity that proved doctrinally contentious, socially divisive, and sometimes ... politically subversive." (92) Gregory finds that impulse corrosive to society in both the early modern and modern ages but does not see any particular reason to doubt the truth of that conception of what Luther and Calvin were attempting.

[15] T. H. L. Parker, ed., *Iohannis Calvini Commentarius in Epistolam Pauli ad Romanos* (Leiden: Brill, 1981), 11. "Quod Augustino placuisse hoc tantum nomine puto, ut argute philosophandi occasionem arriperet. Probabilior Origenis sententia, qui binominum fuisse indicate."

his positive constructive theological efforts and his negative polemics. In great part, Calvin's theology depended upon and arose from engagement with the tradition.

Another reason to choose Calvin is that the significance of Calvin's relationship with tradition transcends a mere exercise in Reformed dogmatics or early modern theological history. While understanding Calvin's thought for its own sake is a worthwhile exercise, the Genevan reformer's importance extends far beyond those bounds. First, Calvin stands as one of the symbolic figures of the beginning of modernity. Beside Martin Luther, Calvin's example continues to be used as a demonstration of the character of the age. Thanks to a superficial reading of Max Weber, the number of people who believe that Calvin is the author of capitalism and Puritanism is legion. Further demonstrating Calvin's permanent residence in the Western imagination, Bruce Gordon's biography of Calvin, timed to appear in bookstores on the five hundredth anniversary year of Calvin's birth in 1509, climbed bestseller charts.[16] Calvin continues to live in the Western imagination, and understanding his role in the arrangement of the mental furniture of the Western mind is an enticing goal.[17] Calvin has stood, much like the stone statue commemorating him in Geneva, as a figure demanding a choice between scripture and tradition for Christian faith. But the actual Calvin can be proven to depend upon tradition in greater and more profound manners than even he recognized.

This is true for a number of reasons. First, Calvin's field of battle for his chosen polemics and theological pronouncements was frequently set long before he prepared for conquest.[18] Such is the case, for instance, in the struggles over the presence of Christ in the Lord's Supper. Calvin was moved to intervene in that argument by a conflict between the Swiss and German evangelicals – which had been highlighted at the abortive Marburg Colloquy in 1529, an event that occurred while Calvin was still a Catholic. But the issue was hardly new in the early modern era: Paschasius Radbertus, Ratramnus, and Berengar of Tours had explored

---

[16] Bruce Gordon, *Calvin* (New Haven: Yale University Press, 2009).

[17] See, for instance, Bruce Gordon's *John Calvin's Institutes of the Christian Religion: A Biography* (Princeton: Princeton University Press, 2016). Gordon states that "The *Institutes* and its author have inspired and horrified men and women from the 1530s until our day for Calvin's book is immensely powerful" (xv–xvi).

[18] On the topic of the purpose of early modern polemic, see Amanda Eurich, "Polemic's Purpose," in *John Calvin in Context*, edited by R. Ward Holder.

the manner of the real presence much earlier – Radbertus and Ratramnus as early as the ninth century.[19] This pattern could be demonstrated for any number of theological topics the Genevan reformer took up. Calvin was not famed for his inventive mind that generated a variety of truly new concepts.

Second, Calvin accepted the true religion that he received from the church's tradition.[20] He made this clear in a variety of ways. Calvin rejected the idea that an uninstructed believer could approach the scriptures and simply find true doctrine. He even went so far as to suggest that the teaching of the true religion was separable from the interpretation of scripture.[21] Calvin was not a proto-Alexander Campbell, the cofounder of the Restoration Movement in American Christianity beginning in 1809, who sought to define Christianity by its dependence upon the scriptures.[22] In great part, Calvin sought to reform the church that the centuries of tradition had delivered to him. He did not attempt to take Christianity back to the first generation, nor did he start with a clean slate. His effort at reform of the church involved him in identifying an orthodoxy that

[19] Owen M. Phelan, "Horizontal and Vertical Theologies: 'Sacraments' in the Works of Paschasius Radbertus and Ratramnus of Corbie," *Harvard Theological Review* 103 (2010): 271–89; Charles M. Radding and Francis Newton, *Theology, Rhetoric and Politics in the Eucharistic Controversy, 1078–1079: Alberic of Monte Cassino against Berengar of Tours* (New York: Columbia University Press, 2003); Pascaline Turpin, "'Ceci est mon corps, ceci est mon sang': comment le haut Moyen Âge lit-il la Cène?," *Mélanges de Science Religieuse* 71 (2014): 41–51.

[20] Calvin believed he had found this summary of Christianity he called "the true religion" in the writings of the fathers, and was shepherding it forward to his audiences. He does not seem to have recognized his own creative influence, through choosing which sources would be authoritative, and navigating those instances when the patristic witness offered no consensus. He used the term in the commentary on Romans.

[21] Calvin, Commentary on Romans, 4. Parker, Ad Romanos, 4.

[22] Nathan Hatch has argued that the democratic tendencies of the new country affected the polity of the Second Great Awakening churches. See his *The Democratization of Christianity* (New Haven: Yale University Press, 1989). Peter Verkruyse has maintained that the rhetoric of Alexander Campbell was significant in his career and sets out the different roles that allowed him to respond to the changing needs of the Stone-Campbell churches. See *Prophet, Pastor, and Patriarch: The Rhetorical Leadership of Alexander Campbell* (Tuscaloosa: University of Alabama Press, 2005). J. Caleb Clanton considers Campbell's religious philosophy, especially his rejection of natural theological arguments for the existence of God, and his answer in revealed religion. See *The Philosophy of Alexander Campbell* (Knoxville: University of Tennessee Press, 2013). For more on Campbell's exegesis, see Thomas H. Olbricht, "Exegetical and Theological Presuppositions in Nineteenth-Century American Commentaries on Acts," in *Scripture and Traditions: Essays on Early Judaism and Christianity in Honor of Carl R. Holladay*, edited by Patrick Gray and Gail R. O'Day (Leiden: Brill, 2008), 359–86.

he believed the church had allowed to fall into disuse, and defending it through recourse to history and authorities as well as scripture.

While presenting an exercise in understanding Calvin, this project seeks to offer a significant contribution to the investigation of tradition and its function in the mentality of the Western mind. Moreover, the investigation could well begin to uncover the roots of why analysts have customarily been so quick to dismiss any function of tradition in Calvin's thought, and thus grant readers a mirror into the ways that the modern mind seeks to classify, categorize, and harness the past. This exercise will begin with an exploration of one of the greatest barriers to discussing tradition: The twentieth and twenty-first-century Western mind does not truly know what tradition is.[23] Genealogically, this makes sense, as the modern world appropriates both the wealth of traditions from the classical, medieval, Renaissance, and early modern experience, and the deep suspicions of tradition that come from the various rationalistic revolutions, especially the Enlightenment and the scientific revolution.[24] The classical world exercised an enormous sway over the manner in which medievals considered both the sensible and ideal worlds.[25] In turn, the medieval

---

[23] Perhaps the most famous Roman Catholic effort at understanding tradition, Yves Congar's *Tradition and Traditions*, is introduced in one of its modern translations by an introduction that bluntly states, "Tradition is widely misunderstood and widely vilified." Yves Congar, OP, *Tradition and Traditions: The Biblical, Historical, and Theological Evidence for Catholic Teaching on Tradition*, translated by Michael Naseby and Thomas Rainborough (New York: Simon and Schuster, 1997), xix.

[24] This is not to say that the Enlightenment stands alone. The Scientific Revolution sought to overcome the influence of accepted truths to free the mind to consider the experimentally demonstrable. Further, Thomas S. Kuhn has argued in his *The Structure of Scientific Revolutions* (Chicago: University of Chicago Press, 1962), that far from a process of predictable progress that reflects the accumulation of scientific knowledge, science progresses by erratic jumps defined by paradigm shifts. But to shift one's paradigm always requires the destruction of the tradition that one knows. For a fascinating application of Kuhn's thesis in Catholic moral theology, see Mark S. Massa, SJ, *The Structure of Theological Revolutions: How the Fight Over Birth Control Transformed American Catholicism* (Oxford: Oxford University Press, 2018).

[25] The literature on this is vast. A small sampling suggests the influence. See Werner Jaeger, *Paideia: The Ideals of Greek Culture*, 3 vols., translated by Gilbert Highet (Oxford: Oxford University Press, 1939-1945); Jean LeClercq, *The Love of Learning and the Desire for God: A Study in Monastic Culture* (New York: Fordham University Press, 1961); Beryl Smalley, *The Study of the Bible in the Middle Ages* (South Bend: University of Notre Dame Press, 1964); Irena Backus, *The Reception of the Church Fathers in the West: From the Carolingians to the Maurists*, 2 vols. (Leiden: Brill, 1997); Eugenio Refini, *The Vernacular Aristotle: Translation as Reception in Medieval and Renaissance Italy* (Cambridge: Cambridge University Press, 2008).

world wielded a similar force upon the early modern mind.[26] The early modern world, almost unknowingly bound by the hegemony of the mentalities of the medieval world, directed its attention to the classical world and the riches to be found there.[27]

But the path that was marked by the importance and authority of tradition did not march unimpeded into the modern world. The power of the Enlightenment, or *Aufklärung*, spread its mantle over Western thought. Building upon the advances of the Scientific Revolution that had largely sought to avoid entanglement with questions of religion, the Enlightenment shattered those polite dividing walls. Immanuel Kant would write that the goal of enlightenment was release from self-incurred tutelage. Further, he particularly pointed this release chiefly at religion because he believed that the powers of his day had no desire to act as guardians in the matters of art and science.[28] This revolutionary way of conceiving the place of both religion and the authority of historical communal practices touched all of Western rationality. Hans-Georg Gadamer's later diagnosis of the hegemony of Enlightenment models of rationality has proved correct.[29] The Enlightenment was a revolution, one that convulsed familiar patterns of thought without providing a sufficient number of explicit models as replacements.

Faced with this new mental landscape, intellectual culture could and did develop in myriad ways. Scientific discoverers forged new pathways

[26] Again, this represents only a small sample. See Marcia Colish, *Medieval Foundations of the Western Intellectual Tradition, 400–1400* (New Haven: Yale University Press, 1997); M. D. Chenu, *Nature, Man, and Society in the Twelfth Century: Essays on New Theological Perspectives in the Latin West*, translated by Lester K. Little (Chicago: University of Chicago Press, 1968); Erika Rummel, *The Humanist-Scholastic Debate in the Renaissance and Reformation* (Cambridge: Harvard University Press, 1995); Rummel, *Biblical Humanism and Scholasticism in the Age of Erasmus* (Leiden: Brill, 2008).

[27] A small illustration of this tendency can be seen in the following titles: Eugene F. Rice, *Saint Jerome in the Renaissance* (Baltimore: Johns Hopkins University Press, 1988); Arnoud Visser, *Reading Augustine in the Reformation: The Flexibility of Intellectual Authority in Europe, 1500–1620* (Oxford: Oxford University Press, 2011); A. N. S. Lane, *John Calvin: Student of the Church Fathers* (Grand Rapids: Baker 1999); David C. Steinmetz, *Luther and Staupitz: An Essay in the Intellectual Origins of the Protestant Reformation* (Durham: Duke University Press, 1980); Karla Pollmann and Willemien Otten, eds., *The Oxford Guide to the Historical Reception of Augustine*, vol. 1 (Oxford: Oxford University Press, 2013); Hilmar Pabel, *Herculean Labors: Erasmus and the Editing of St. Jerome's Letters in the Renaissance* (Leiden: Brill, 2008).

[28] Immanuel Kant, "What is Enlightenment?" in *Immanuel Kant, Philosophical Writings* (New York: Continuum, 1999), 462, 466.

[29] Hans-Georg Gadamer, *Truth and Method*, 2nd revised ed., edited and translated by Joel Weinsheimer and Donald G. Marshall (New York: Continuum, 2004), esp. 174–83.

that disregarded biblical warrants.[30] Art sought to describe the human experience that did not heed the strictures of the traditions of piety. Political thought derived ever more from concepts of realpolitik that recognized the greatest value in techniques that provided desired results rather than particular goods that endured. Modernity spun in dozens of directions, and fewer of these were bound by a close adherence to the traditions of the Christian ages.

Confronted with this new reality, Christian thinkers needed to devise methods of traversing the changed and ever changing landscape. Catholic thinkers tended to argue for the superiority of neo-scholastic models of rationality and argumentation.[31] Protestants attempted a variety of models. Some drew from Romanticism, which could not be critiqued by a purely rational approach; others concentrated upon biblical metaphor; still others sought to expand the biblical witness by claiming its inerrancy or infallibility. Arriving in the modern period, Protestantism supplied two different dominant models of biblical witness: Bultmann's project of demythologization and Barth's demand for the primacy of revelation. Bultmann was not only cognizant of the wider cultural context, but he also required that the Bible be read through it.[32] Barth simply denied the significance of cultural relevance, insisting that believers surrender themselves to the dominion of revelation. Such a confusion of impulses led to the stance where the foremost American Christian theologian could say in the midst of the twentieth century that the cross and resurrections were neither literal nor meaningless without being able to define what he meant.[33]

---

[30] Thus, Darwin's investigations represented at least a methodological shift from those of the seventeenth- and early-eighteenth-century astronomers, who sought to find the truths of the scripture written in the creation. See Kenneth J. Howell, *God's Two Books: Copernican Cosmology and Biblical Interpretation in Early Modern Science* (South Bend: Notre Dame University Press, 2002).

[31] See Francis Schüssler-Fiorenza and John P. Galvin, *Systematic Theology: Roman Catholic Perspectives* (Minneapolis: Augsburg Fortress Press, 1991), 30–35. See also the works of Josef Pieper, especially *The Four Cardinal Virtues: Prudence, Justice, Fortitude, Temperance* (South Bend: University of Notre Dame Press, 1991); and *Leisure, the Basis of Culture* (San Francisco: Ignatius Press, 2009).

[32] Rudolf Bultmann, "New Testament and Mythology," in *New Testament & Mythology and Other Basic Writings*, selected, edited, and translated by Schubert M. Ogden (Philadelphia: Fortress Press, 1984), 3. He wrote: "But it is impossible to repristinate a past world picture by sheer resolve, especially a mythical world picture, now that all of our thinking is irrevocably formed by science."

[33] Reinhold Niebuhr, *The Nature and Destiny of Man: A Christian Interpretation.* v. 1 Human Nature. 1941. v. 2 Human Destiny. 1943 (Louisville: Westminster John Knox Press, 1996), 1.275.

Small wonder that confessional Christian historians, whether Protestant or Catholic, might grasp those truths that they knew were certain: that the Protestant reformers had relegated tradition to the ash-heap of theological history long before the Enlightenment had demanded it. Even smaller wonder that cultural critics would look upon the fractured Christian history of dependence upon the authority and power of tradition and the biblical witness without a clear stance on how the biblical text was to be handled, and criticize both as insufficiently serious.[34]

But the story does not end there. The modern mind is heir to multiple strands of influence. The same worldview that seeks to command nature through the process of experimentation and implicitly recognizes no rationality beyond its own reason also explicitly acknowledges the enduring power of ideals that define a society, or a community, or a religion, or even a research program.[35] This basic tension has led to a variety of directions in modern thought. There has been an effort to demonstrate the impossibility of exhibiting the foundations of rational investigation, especially in the work of figures such as Karl Popper who contributed to the concept of critical rationalism.[36] In neopragmatism, Richard Rorty argued against the possibility of any foundational concepts.[37] Robert Nozick explored the concept that rationality itself was a Darwinian adaptation that was never supposed to work without a number of axiomatic "givens," items that were accepted rather than proved.[38] Ethicist Jonathan Haidt attacked foundations of both philosophical epistemology and religion by proposing that morals were simply formed by the communities that formed the individual.[39] All of these efforts sought either to

[34] The modern critiques of the fundamental intellectual foundations of Christian thought and practice are both common and significant. The best known are the New Atheists, sometimes known as the "Four Horsemen and One Horsewoman of the Non-Apocalypse," that included Christopher Hitchens (d. 2011), Sam Harris, Richard Dawkins, Daniel Dennet, and Ayan Hirsi-Ali. See John Gray, "What Scares the New Atheists," *The Guardian*, March 3, 2015. www.theguardian.com/world/2015/mar/03/what-scares-the-new-atheists, accessed May 11, 2020; and Borden W. Painter, Jr., *The New Atheist Denial of History* (New York: Palgrave, 2014).

[35] See especially Thomas S. Kuhn's *The Structure of Scientific Revolutions*. Kuhn's major thesis is that science does not progress through a predicted evolution, but instead a series of radical revolutions that each reject that which came before.

[36] See especially his *The Open Society and Its Enemies* (London: Routledge, 1945).

[37] Richard Rorty, *Contingency, Irony, and Solidarity* (Cambridge: Cambridge University Press, 1989).

[38] Robert Nozick, *The Nature of Rationality* (Princeton: Princeton University Press, 1993).

[39] Jonathan Haidt, *The Righteous Mind: Why Good People Are Divided by Politics and Religion* (New York: Pantheon Books, 2012).

do away with the dependence on non-existent foundations or made the fact of their absence a feature of modern life to be embraced, rather than feared. But all of these were, in one manner or another, efforts to deal with the conflict between models of rationality that sought to be founded purely and empirically and those that accepted a number of axioms that included streams of tradition.

This study seeks to understand the divided character of the Western mind and Calvin's contribution to that situation. Both are important. I do not wish to explore "Calvin against himself."[40] However, it is fair to examine historical figures and ask two questions: "What were they doing?" and "What did they believe they were doing?" These two investigations rarely lead to exactly the same answers. Calvin was a man of his time, attempting to be a biblical humanist and evangelical pastor. That dynamic alone meant that he was endeavoring to break the French Catholic mold into which he was born. But how successful could he be in that effort? Further, context remains a crucial element in our understanding of Calvin's thought.[41] What appeared to Calvin to be an abandonment of tradition because of its difference from customary models of theology and ecclesiastical practice may seem very different from the vantage point provided by the passage of several centuries.[42] It is imperative in this study both to grasp what Calvin was doing and what he believed he was doing, and thus to see how an unresolved tension between scriptural foundation and orthodox tradition characterized his thought.

Calvin lived in a divided and dividing world. He sought to maintain contact with the Christian world in which he had been raised even while reforming it through a biblical-interpretive effort. This complex aim placed him in a situation of tension between two epistemological sources. While in the worldview of the early modern period he was attempting to reduce the dependence upon and use of tradition, his success was a relative rather than absolute accomplishment. Calvin used, was formed by, and gave credence to tradition. He parsed it carefully, accepting a certain notion that was historically coherent, and rejecting the Roman idea of

[40] Suzanne Selinger, *Calvin Against Himself: An Inquiry in Intellectual History* (Hamden, Connecticut: Archon Books, 1984). Selinger's book suggests that significant areas of Calvin's thought represented unresolved tensions.

[41] See the variety of articles in *John Calvin in Context*, edited by R. Ward Holder. As one of my basic points is that Calvin could not extract himself from his historical context, I will return to these articles frequently.

[42] Yves Congar noted several instances where Calvin had room for the witness of tradition. Congar, *Tradition and Traditions*, 153.

tradition that both gave it equality with scripture of revelatory power and locked that power in the hands of the episcopacy.

It is also important to examine the present situation. The modern or postmodern world has received Calvin's influence, but that reception has been active – in deciding what was worthy of engagement, and passive – in accepting impulses it did not even fully realize. This project will look at a variety of disciplines – sociology, theology, history, psychology, politics, and philosophy – to try to capture the gestalt of the modern Western mind that allows significant insights into the way we consider both our intellectual ancestors and the influence that tradition carries in our own lives in the present.

Tradition, memory, history, custom: All seek in one manner or another to articulate the claim that the past has upon the present. Whether in the prose of Joyce, whose Stephen Dedalus claimed "History is a nightmare from which I am trying to awake," or in the confident piety of a theologian who knew his claim to the faith of the historical church kept him from error, these terms acknowledge the ongoing power of events and ideas long past to contend with us.[43] The ancients studied history for patterns of leadership, citizenship, and morality. That ancient trend continues into the present as twenty-first-century politicians and evangelical pastors claim that America was founded as a Christian country.[44] Whether persuasive or not, the fact that other politicians and pastors pick up the gauntlet and argue about origins demonstrates the shared grasp that the past has upon us.[45]

William Faulkner famously wrote that, "The past is never dead. It's not even past.[46] People have been quoting him ever since, even though the exact quotation is sometimes mauled. Remembering holds us – gives friends something about which to speak, allows us to recognize those from deep in the past, even creates the possibility of intellectual work. Yet the modern world has a tendentious relationship with the past. The Holocaust memorials, with their multilingual calls of "Never Again," demand that memory hold us in thrall. But the twenty-first-century rise

---

[43] James Joyce, *Ulysses* (New York: Random House, 1961), 34.

[44] See the discussion in John Fea, *Was America Founded as a Christian Country?: A Historical Introduction*, rev. ed. (Louisville: Westminster John Knox, 2016).

[45] Joseph Ratzinger argued that "intellect is memory" in "Anthropological Foundation of the Concept of Tradition," in *Principles of Catholic Theology: Building Stones for a Fundamental Theology*, translated by Frances McCarthy (San Francisco: Ignatius Press, 1987), 86–87.

[46] William Faulkner, *Requiem for a Nun* (New York: Random House, 1951), 73.

of Holocaust denial demonstrates the fragility of that bond. Human communities forget, either through indulgence in their ill-spent leisure or through political will. Philosophers point out that memory dictates what is written down in histories.[47] "Working through the past" is a catchphrase that suggests the ability to escape the past and its claims upon the present, but this is an impossible task, for the past is still very much alive.[48]

Though alive, the past frequently escapes our memory, our grasp, and our control. Maurice Halbwachs wrote of childhood memory and its puissance in his consideration of memory.[49] We can know the significance of history by examining the loss of memory, the slide from a shared stock of stories and legends and truth claims from the past to a technical subject fit only for the specialist. Pierre Nora wrote of the problems of memory for a people and a nation.[50] Nora points out the phenomenon of a lost memory, which does not exercise either a sacred or national function. Rather than providing the warmth of shared bonds of materiality, kinship, and community, such memory falls into academic history. From there, how far can it be to the realm of manufactured history?[51] Going further, he theorized about the possibility of "lieux de mémoire," items which have no referents in reality, but only exist as pure signs.[52]

---

[47] Pierre Nora, *Zwischen Geschichte und Gedächtnis* (Berlin: Verlag Klaus Wagenbach, 1990), 29. "In diesem Gemenge ist es das Gedächtnis, das diktiert, und die Geschichte schreibt auf."

[48] Theodor W. Adorno, "The Meaning of Working Through the Past," in *Critical Models: Interventions and Catchwords*, translated by Henry W. Pickford (New York: Columbia University Press, 2005), 89.

[49] Maurice Halbwachs, "The Reconstruction of the Past," in *On Collective Memory*, edited, translated, and with an introduction by Lewis A. Coser (Chicago: University of Chicago Press, 1992), 46.

[50] Pierre Nora, *Zwischen Geschichte und Gedächtnis* (Frankfurt am Main: Fischer Taschenbuch Verlag, 1998), 20. Quoted in Siegfried Wiedenhofer, "Tradition-History-Memory: Why Do We Need a Complex Theory of Tradition?" translated by John Cochrane, in *Tradition and Tradition Theories: An International Discussion*, edited by Thorsten Larbig and Siegfried Wiedenhofer (Munich: Lit, 2006), 377.

[51] Jesse Spohnholz notes exactly such a manufactured tradition in his *The Convent of Wesel: The Event that Never Was and the Invention of Tradition* (Cambridge: Cambridge University Press, 2017). A less spectacular example comes from Jonathan Strom's *German Pietism and the Problem of Conversion* (University Park: Penn State University Press, 2017). Strom notes that though August Hermann Francke's conversion became the paradigmatic form of conversion in later pietism, that later popularity hid the fact that Francke's conversion was almost completely unknown in the decades after his death.

[52] Pierre Nora, *Realms of Memory: Rethinking the French Past*, translated by Arthur Goldhammer, in 3 vols. (New York: Columbia University Press, 1996), I.19–20.

John O'Malley set out the problem with his customary succinctness: "[H]ow do we deal with our rich past so that we remain faithful to it, yet do so in a manner that renders it engaging and life-giving?"[53] He interpreted Vatican II (1962–5) as asserting that the basic task of the church is one of ministry. As ministry must change according to the contexts and times in which it occurs, Vatican II justified a reading of the "history of Christianity that makes a more generous allowance for the discontinuities in that history than has often been verified, especially in Catholic circles."[54] This form of reading opens new possibilities to the believing community or individual believer, both for thinking about the past and contemplating the future.

Tradition acts partly as collective human kinetic memory, the distilled value of a repeated act or ceremony that guides present choices, values, and worldviews. Adorno wrote, "It recalls the continuity of generations, what is handed down by one member to another, even the heritage of handicraft. The image of handing down expresses physical proximity, immediacy – one hand should receive from another."[55] Human communities know this implicitly, though that recognition in becoming explicit frequently creates epistemological, social, and authoritative questions. Tradition has the power to anticipate and even in some fashion create the future, setting the community on a particular path.[56] This is true in both colloquial and academic communities. "Although 'tradition' is one of the most frequently used terms in educated and academic discourse, it remains a relatively imprecise basic term of cultural theory, and as such is used to mean a variety of things."[57] Writing on tradition, T. S. Eliot claimed that, "It cannot be inherited, and if you want it you must obtain it by great labour. It involves, in the first place, the historical sense, which we may call nearly indispensable to any one who would continue to be a poet beyond his twenty-fifth year; and the historical sense involves a

---

[53] John W. O'Malley, SJ, "Tradition and Traditions: Historical Perspectives," *The Way* 27 (1987): 163.

[54] O'Malley, "Tradition and Traditions," 167.

[55] Theodor W. Adorno, "On Tradition," in *Telos*, 94 (1992): 75. Originally published as "Über Tradition," in "Inselalmanach auf das Jahr 1966." Collaborative translation based on text in Theodor W. Adorno, *Gesammelte Schriften* (Frankfurt a/M: Suhrkamp Verlag, 1977), Vol. X, Pt. 1, 310–320.

[56] Ivana Noble, "The Tension between an Eschatological and a Utopic Understanding of Tradition: Tillich, Florovsky, and Congar," *Harvard Theological Review* 109 (2016): 401.

[57] Wiedenhofer, "Tradition-History-Memory," 379.

perception, not only of the pastness of the past, but of its presence."[58]
The presence of the past, its life that inspires the present, is inescapable.
Hans-Georg Gadamer's consideration of tradition presented a dialogical
model through which the tradition could make claims upon the present. Further, he argued that tradition was the necessary condition for
knowledge, rather than a barrier to finding it.[59] Tradition has taken up
an enormous place in the language – family traditions, theological traditions, scientific traditions. The list can be expanded almost ad infinitum.
For an age dedicated to the present and future, the escape from the past
still seems nigh on impossible.

Related questions arise. Are customs traditions?[60] Are all repeated
actions of individuals and communities traditions? What is a tradition
generally, and is the theological tradition a species of that larger genus?
These questions arise in part because of the lack of specificity of language
in colloquial speech around these topics. Tradition is important because
it provides human communities epistemological markers to assign value
to their present. Whether a political, cultural, or religious tradition, cultures agree that traditions are significant but do not have the language to
discuss them. That which has been done in the past makes a claim on the
present. Contemporary communities constantly decide what to jettison
and what to retain from their past. This is a dynamic process where there
are no rules or consistently-applied arguments that can be made for the
new or the tried and true. That is why social groupings argue about the
correct adherence to tradition.

In its Latin base, the verb *tradere* means to hand over or hand down,
to transmit. That fact implies the community aspect – for the verb to be
enacted there must already be someone who has received and is willing to
give and another who will receive. The range of the gift given or transmit-
ted is extraordinarily broad: hence the number of "traditions" that colloquial speech notes. It can be a simple lesson, the gift of culture, or the
gift of faith from one's religion that mimics the divine gift of revelation

---

[58] T. S. Eliot, "Tradition and the Individual Talent," 1919, published in *The Sacred Wood: Essays on Poetry and Criticism* (London: Methuen, 1920). I thank Nate Antiel for draw-ing my attention to the ways that the discussions of Calvin and theology are mirrored in literary criticism generally, and Eliot especially.

[59] Gadamer, *Truth and Method*, 277–84.

[60] For a parallel consideration of ritual, see Victor Turner and Edith Turner, *Image and Pilgrimage in Christian Culture* (New York: Columbia University Press, 1978), esp. Appendix.

to humanity.[61] In all of these significations, the tradition carries forward allowing the giver and the recipient to participate in the continuation of the existence and influence of the gift. When we are speaking of traditions, we are considering the roots of how social groups cohere.

But implicit in the model of transmission is the notion of change and thus of critique. We noted earlier the notion of tradition as cultural kinetic memory, but just as a therapist can work with a patient to improve, so too we must recognize that not every bit of received wisdom will survive critique. We can imagine this in the idea of a master craftsman who takes on an apprentice. Certainly that apprentice will receive the tradition of weaving or blacksmithing or medicine. But just as surely, at the end of his apprenticeship, he will be a journeyman, able to make his own choices. Should he wish to be a true master of the craft, he must go beyond the patterns he received, re-forming them in ways both subtle and extreme. That is to say, the reception of the *tradita* (the material passed on), cannot be, and never has been, passive. The simple choice of authorities to follow demonstrates the active role in reception. A further step involves the interpretation of the sources, the necessity of arguing for a particular interpretation from a possible field of meanings.[62] Whether in brewing beer or training horses or caring for the sick or teaching Christian doctrine, the reception must be critical.

The collection of this study's evidence will demonstrate several points. The first is that John Calvin used the theological tradition as a necessary constitutive element in his thought. He accepted both the parameters of his theological explorations and the substance of his arguments from the tradition, sometimes consciously but often not. Second, in his somewhat tortured engagement with the Western Christian theological tradition, Calvin provides a distant mirror of the postmodern problematized fascination with tradition. In seeking a more certain and less malleable source of authority as the foundation for Christian doctrine, Calvin prefigures the modern search for intellectual foundations that are truly substantial. Finally, the combination of these elements leads to a historiographical addendum: The difficulty of grasping Calvin's utilization of and devotion

---

[61] Wiedenhofer, "Tradition-History-Memory," 380.

[62] Harold Bloom argued that "a reading, to be strong, must be a misreading, for no strong reading can fail to insist upon itself." (287) While Bloom illustrates the furthest degree of this arc, he makes the point. The reading of the tradition itself must critique, and reject other readings. Bloom, "The Necessity of Misreading," *The Georgia Review* 29 (1975): 267–88.

to the tradition is as much a function of the modern inability to accept the realities of the lack of foundations of our explorations as it is the varied record that Calvin left. An epilogue will exhibit the value of this consideration of foundation and tradition, and examine the modern or postmodern Western mind. Far from seeing ourselves as those who have left Calvin behind in the premodern dustbin and progressed to a new and better stage, we will find that this dilemma sits at the heart of some of our greatest difficulties.

Calvin lived in a historical epoch of division, where Protestant and Catholic, evangelical and Anabaptist, lay and clergy, scholastic and humanistic, and a host of other choices defined the character of early modern life. To deal with that turmoil, the reformer of Geneva attempted both adherence to tradition and to a humanistic model of biblical interpretation. He never resolved that tension, instead bestowing it on the Reformed tradition and on the wider Western intellectual and ecclesiastical traditions. This study will seek to demonstrate that he made these choices, why he did so, and what the ramifications were. Equipped with that knowledge, the modern thinker will be better able to work through the issues of our own day, many of which stand as monuments to Calvin's influence.

I

What Is Tradition?

John Calvin desired to engage the rich tradition of Christianity in a troubled and turbulent world and to demonstrate that the new religious movement he had joined was only a purified form of the ancient church, adapted to the uses and context of the sixteenth century. Calvin argued that he was returning to the orthodox tradition of the fathers. To accomplish this, he argued that the scriptural principle would guide his work: He would found everything upon the clear Word of God. But his effort at maintaining the true or purified orthodoxy enmeshed him in forces of tradition.[1] In demonstrating that his doctrine was simply the church's doctrine, Calvin became involved in discussions of what traditional words, constructs, power structures, and liturgical patterns meant. This struggle would characterize all his theological career and make his work extraordinarily dependent upon tradition.

Calvin embarked on this effort, at least in part, because of the historical character of his age. Barbara Pitkin wrote that "[t]he meaning and normativity of the past was one of the most pressing intellectual and practical issues of the age in which Calvin ... lived; the outbreak of repeated religious warfare in France and elsewhere only rendered that issue more urgent."[2] He had learned his lessons of context well at the feet of the humanist masters. To understand a text properly, one had to understand the history surrounding it. This was true for the Bible, for the

---

[1] For the sake of the flow of the argument, this study uses "orthodoxy" and "the orthodox tradition" synonymously.

[2] Barbara Pitkin, *Calvin, the Bible, and History: Exegesis and Historical Reflection in the Era of Reform* (Oxford: Oxford University Press, 2020), 199.

writings of the fathers and medieval theologians, and for texts composed in his own day. He would take those lessons of history and apply them to the tradition – rejecting a hierarchically defined sense of tradition in favor of one expressed by history. The linked understanding of history and tradition were important for Calvin, and so are crucial for our understanding of him.[3] In this chapter, we will explore the theological tradition in its various senses and the contemporary meanings of tradition.

THE THEOLOGICAL TRADITION

The theological tradition exists as a substantial part of the complex of traditions. Siegfried Wiedenhofer suggests that this stems from the history of the Christian faith, where tradition came to be recognized as a fundamental concept as early as the second century.[4] Heiko A. Oberman agrees that the Christian tradition began early.[5] But the theological tradition comprises more than those items passed down, whether texts, doctrinal constructs, or liturgical artifacts. John M. Headley asserted that the Christian tradition differs from Christian traditions, the former being a theological concept, the latter historical realities that matured over time.[6] While that is a helpful distinction, it is too neat – the historical record does not always align with such a clear distinction.[7] There are a number of historical trajectories that analysts loosely identify as traditions, and while not as defined as the Catholic magisterial tradition, they are no

---

[3] Euan Cameron noted that, in his historical style, Calvin was more modern than some of his contemporaries who sought to build a transparent scheme of divine providence. Instead, he saw that the "Hebrew Scripture referred to a very remote period, and that the past was the past." See Euan Cameron, "Calvin the Historian: Biblical Antiquity and Scriptural Exegesis," in *Calvin and the Book: The Evolution of the Printed Word in Reformed Protestantism*, edited by Karen E. Spierling (Göttingen: Vandenhoeck & Ruprecht, 2015), 80.

[4] Siegfried Wiedenhofer, "Tradition-History-Memory: Why Do We Need a Complex Theory of Tradition?," in *Tradition and Tradition Theories: An International Discussion*, edited by Thorsten Larbig and Siegfried Wiedenhofer (Münster: LIT Verlag, 2006), 375–98, at 380.

[5] Heiko A. Oberman, "*Quo Vadis, Petre?* Tradition from Irenaeus to *Humani Generis*," *Scottish Journal of Theology* 16 (1963): 225–255.

[6] John M. Headley, "The Reformation as Crisis in the Understanding of Tradition," *Archiv für Reformationsgeschichte* 78 (1987): 6.

[7] An example is that Headley accepts the substance of Luther's attacks upon Henry VIII as illustrative of Luther's theology of tradition. But his work does not seriously engage Luther's sacramental theology, that maintained far more of the medieval liturgical and doctrinal traditions than did Zwingli's.

less significant.[8] For instance, we sometimes speak of the tradition that a historian mentions when she writes of the "exegetical tradition" that Erasmus, Luther, Calvin, and Bucer inherited at the beginning of the sixteenth century. That tradition, and its corollaries such as the "doctrinal tradition," or "Augustinian tradition," or "liturgical tradition," is actually a historical trajectory that can exercise great or insignificant influence over the thinker who receives it and works in the present day, answering the questions that earlier interpreters had identified and advancing or critiquing them. These historical trajectory traditions partially define the worldview or *mentalité* of an era; they are the elements of what it is possible to think at a certain time.[9] As such, they are enormously important, both for our understanding of Calvin and for the understanding of any culture and its appropriation of the past.

Another possible meaning of tradition is the Catholic theological tradition as defined by the magisterium. This was the predominant view in Calvin's lifetime and theological career, and it remains a specific case today. It exercised a hegemonic influence in the early modern period for a great number of believers and theologians, and it still exercises a particular influence of both antiquity and utility in today's ecclesiastical spheres and in wider conversations. This sense of tradition would seem to have the advantage of a far greater specificity and definition than the historical trajectory traditions because it specifies defined producers and conservators. However, any implied certitude is an illusion: The concept of tradition, even magisterial tradition, has itself changed over time.

A further example of the critical reception that is so crucial to a living tradition that influenced the hierarchy shows itself in the various Augustinianisms in the medieval era.[10] Augustine's legacy was in demand

---

[8] By Catholic magisterial tradition, or hierarchical tradition, or the early modern Catholic tradition, I am referring to that complex of authority that Catholic theologians and canonists defended as part of revelation, and the reason that the church and perhaps the pope were infallible.

[9] Lucien Febvre (*The Problem of Unbelief in the Sixteenth Century: The Religion of Rabelais*, translated by Beatrice Gottlieb [Cambridge, MA: Harvard University Press, 1982]) suggested that true atheism in the sixteenth century was impossible. But see also Ethan Shagan's criticism of Febvre in *The Birth of Modern Belief: Faith and Judgment from the Middle Ages to the Enlightenment* (Princeton: Princeton University Press, 2018), 95–128.

[10] Eric Leland Saak, "The Reception of Augustine in the Later Middle Ages," in *The Reception of the Church Fathers in the West: From the Carolingians to the Maurists*, edited by Irena Backus (Leiden: Brill, 1997), 661–700. See also David C. Steinmetz, *Luther and Staupitz: An Essay in the Intellectual Origins of the Protestant Reformation* (Durham, NC: Duke University Press, 1980), 13–15.

in the medieval world. Varied – and even contradictory – thinkers such as Bernard of Clairvaux (d. 1153), Peter Lombard (d. 1160), Hugh of St. Victor (d. 1141), Thomas Aquinas (d. 1274), and Gregory of Rimini (d. 1358) have claimed the mantle of the bishop of Hippo, though each received Augustine's texts through his own ideals, or through the *mentalité* his socio-historico-cultural moment afforded him.

Finally, there is the notion of tradition popularized by hermeneutics, the science of interpretation. The hermeneutical function of tradition was propagated especially by the work of twentieth-century philosopher Hans-Georg Gadamer and those whom he affected. This model shapes the work of historians, philosophers, textual critics, and theologians. Gadamer's insight established that any particular act of understanding, whether literary, philosophical, or artistic, stood within a tradition that made sense of the choices that it made. The three different senses of tradition – historical trajectory, Catholic theological tradition, and hermeneutic function – can be used simultaneously by a thinker, but they are usefully considered separately.

In part because of this multivalence, the theological tradition is both hard to grasp and to investigate.[11] The investigator of tradition must engage in two deep excavations, historical and sociological/cultural. The combination of these two are necessary components of a full examination of the fractured inheritance the modern Western mind has received in the complex series of considerations of this concept. To make this easier, this book will first concentrate upon the theological traditions inherited by the early modern period of the sixteenth century and then, in later chapters, turn to those of Calvin. These insights can then be more broadly applied to a variety of cultural and political situations and will offer some suggestive illustrations in the Epilogue.

TRADITION AND HISTORY FROM THE REFORMATIONS TO MODERNITY

From the beginnings of the Christian tradition and Tertullian's plaintive query "What has Athens to do with Jerusalem?" to Peter Lombard's organization of theological topics by a series of quotations from the fathers, to the Christian humanists' return to the sources, the Reformation world was heir to a rich and confusing convention of recourse to historical trajectory

---

[11] Wiedenhofer, "Tradition-History-Memory," 375–98.

traditions and the Catholic theological traditions. The historical research
on this topic appears clear and somewhat obvious. Finding out what Calvin
meant by "tradition," insofar as he dealt with it at all, is a historically oriented task. Calvin was born into the Christian movement that was fifteen
centuries old, and Western Christianity had already fostered a demonstrable development of doctrine and practice. Calvin himself dealt openly with
both the historical trajectory of tradition into which he was born as well
as the Catholic magisterial doctrinal tradition. Though some thinkers were
ready to argue for a model of tradition that supported a never-changing,
semper eadem character, or some modification thereof, others in the early
modern era discerned a significant amount of change in doctrine, discipline, and liturgy since the apostolic period.[12] This never-changing theory
was an early theory of tradition, most frequently attributed to Vincent of
Lerins, a fifth-century monk who had written that orthodoxy was that
which was believed always, everywhere, and by all. This rule came to be
called the "Vincentian canon."[13] The work of early theologians prior to
the first ecumenical council at Nicaea in 325 CE differed from those who
followed it, and explicit references to an unwritten tradition that stood
beside the scriptures were rare.[14] The medieval doctors shifted even further. Finding out what "tradition" referred to remained a contextually
fraught task throughout the medieval era, so that by the sixteenth century
the model had proved untenable in several instances.[15]

---

[12] Cardinal Jacopo Sadoleto, in his 1539 letter to the Genevans, proffered just such
a theory, arguing that written records only permitted one to be certain as far back
as 1,300 years. John C. Olin, ed., *A Reformation Debate: Sadoleto's Letter to the
Genevans and Calvin's Reply* (San Francisco: Harper Torchbook, 1966), reprinted
frequently. CO 5.369–416. For this reference, see Olin, *A Reformation Debate*, 40–41.
CO 5.378.

[13] Vincentius of Lerins, *The Commonitorium of Vincentius of Lerins*, edited by Reginald
Stewart Moxon (Cambridge: Cambridge University Press, 1915).

[14] Basil of Caesarea, *De Spiritu Sancto* (PG 32, 188a; EP, 954). Quoted in O. P. Yves
Congar, *Tradition and Traditions: The Biblical, Historical, and Theological Evidence
for Catholic Teaching on Tradition*, translated by Michael Naseby and Thomas Rainborough (New York: Simon and Schuster, 1997), 47.

[15] It is also necessary to set out what this study is not attempting to do. This effort is not an
attempt to catalogue Calvin's citations and allusions to the fathers and medievals. Others have done that – see especially R. J. Mooi, *Het Kerk-en Dogmahistorisch Element
in de Werken van Johannes Calvijn* (Wageningen: H. Veenman, 1965); A. N. S. Lane,
John Calvin: Student of the Church Fathers (Grand Rapids: Baker Book House, 1999);
and Johannes van Oort, "John Calvin and the Church Fathers," in *The Reception of
the Church Fathers in the West: From the Carolingians to the Maurists*, edited by Irena
Backus (Leiden: Brill, 1997), 661–700. This study is far more interested in what Calvin
did with the thought of the orthodox theologians he inherited – and how he used it.

In the second half of the twentieth century two important though brief historical studies took up the nature of tradition in the Reformation. In 1963, Heiko A. Oberman wrote his *"Quo Vadis, Petre? Tradition from Irenaeus to Humani Generis."*[16] John Headley returned to the question with "The Reformation as Crisis in the Understanding of Tradition."[17] Both concentrate upon Luther and his consideration or rejection of tradition. Further, both argue that the struggle in the Reformation is not between scripture and tradition, but either between two differing theories of what tradition is, or between two different ideals of authority.

Oberman's work began with the theory that the early Christian tradition and scripture coinhere, and that the fathers rejected any sense of an extrascriptural tradition.[18] This notion did not last unchallenged, however, as thinkers such as Basil the Great and Augustine introduced the concept of an extra-biblical oral tradition. Vincent of Lerins' fifth-century canon of orthodoxy in the *Commonitorium* stated that the Catholic church must hold to that which has been believed everywhere, always, and by everyone.[19] Oberman argued that this might well have been aimed at Augustine. In any case, out of this came the situation that lasted through the medieval period. There were two senses of tradition, Tradition I, which tied tradition to the scriptures, and Tradition II, which posited an extra-biblical oral tradition.[20]

This was the true division, according to Oberman – not scripture vs. tradition, but Tradition I vs. Tradition II. Oberman illustrated this by a consideration of Luther's theology, especially his output from 1522 and after. The Council of Trent was the finalization of the church of Rome's acceptance of Tradition II.[21] Though Oberman was arguing on the basis of Luther's theology, there is much to recommend his framework for Calvin, especially in terms of what Calvin believed he was doing.

Headley also took up the senses of tradition, though he did not give them the nomenclature that Oberman had already established. Instead,

16 Oberman, "*Quo Vadis, Petre?*," 225–55; rpt. as chap. 12 of *The Dawn of the Reformation* (Edinburgh: T. & T. Clark, 1986).
17 Headley, "The Reformation as Crisis," 5–23.
18 Oberman, "*Quo Vadis, Petre?*," 227.
19 "In ipsa item catholica ecclesia magnopere curandum est ut id teneamus quod ubique, quod semper, quod ab omnibus creditum est...." *Commonitorium* II.3; edited by Reginald S. Moxon (Cambridge, 1915), 10; quoted in Oberman, "*Quo Vadis, Petre?*," 236.
20 Oberman, "*Quo Vadis, Petre?*," 238.
21 Ibid., 244. Oberman went further into the development of these conceptual schemes, positing a Tradition III that characterized the modern Catholic church, but that is beyond the scope of this chapter.

Headley argued that tradition in the singular was a theological concept not subject to the forces of history. "Indeed the concept of tradition proper has nothing at all to do with a unified historical development nor with any accumulation of practices over time both of which disfigure and pervert the concept."[22] Tradition derived this character because it must remain bound to scripture which is a witness to Christ. While Headley did not adopt Tradition I vs. II, he clearly posited something similar in the division between tradition and traditions. In Headley's reconstruction of the problem of authority in the early modern period, Luther used a form of tradition that reintegrated the power of the Holy Spirit with Christ the Word. This allowed him to prune the "extravagant foliage of the medieval church."[23]

Both Oberman and Headley are correct in pointing out the necessity of historians coming to grips with the ways that tradition was used in the religious struggles of the early modern world. Further, both note, with different language, the different meanings that the term "tradition" occupied in the sixteenth century. However, there are problems with their reconstructions of the historical record. First, while Oberman assumes that the reformers were all Tradition I, or at least the Lutherans were, that will prove not to be the case, either in their polemics, or in the manner of their liturgies. Headley, on the other hand, in arguing that tradition was always and only Tradition I (without that nomenclature), provides a model unrecognizable in the late medieval and early modern world.

The era of the Reformations is a watershed moment in the history of the Western recourse to tradition. Luther, Calvin, Knox, Cranmer, Zwingli, and Bullinger all attacked the authority of tradition. This attack seemed to create two models of theological consideration of tradition. On the one hand was Rome, with its claim to an ecclesiastical and hierarchical tradition, unchanging for over 1,000 years.[24] Against this was put the thought of the reformers who were willing to sacrifice all for the purity of the scriptures.[25] The contrast is stark, straightforward, and

---

[22] Headley, "The Reformation as Crisis," 6.

[23] Ibid., 22.

[24] This claim of *semper eadem* is noted and discussed in John O'Malley S. J.'s "The Hermeneutic of Reform: A Historical Analysis," *Theological Studies* 73 (2012): 517–46. An excellent example of this claim comes from Jacopo Sadoleto's letter to the Genevans of 1539, where he balances 1,300 years of consent against the weight of the innovations of twenty-five years of crafty men. Olin, *A Reformation Debate*, 40–41; CO 5.378.

[25] Timothy George, *Reading Scripture with the Reformers* (Grand Rapids: IVP Academic, 2011), 17–18, has the reformers returning to "the pure teachings of the Scriptures."

far-reaching. The consequences reach beyond the areas of ecclesiastical order and theological rectitude to influence general theories of epistemology and rationality.

But that portrait is too simple, too shaded in primary colors. Though several reformers attacked the recourse to tradition as a significant source of doctrinal or spiritual authority, many magisterial reformers quickly found that the theological tradition proved too tempting in its polemic and constructive value to be completely ignored. Whether the historian is considering Lutherans, the Reformed, Anabaptists, or Anglicans, seeing the Reformations as a series of purely primitivistic religious movements following some form of an ideal that sought to gain the greatest purity from closeness to the wellspring's source fails to understand their intellectual underpinnings, their social and cultural embeddedness, and the worship styles in which the movements engaged. Even as they eschewed parts of the Roman ecclesiastical tradition, especially some of the ecclesiological developments, many reformers found themselves embracing other aspects of tradition.[26]

The Reformations changed everything.[27] Calls were made for the scriptural principle, but tradition and historical memory played their roles as well. Luther argued against the infallibility of councils because councils had disagreed with each other. However, he would also fiercely protect the accustomed understanding of the eucharist and attack the Swiss as sacramentarians. The Augsburg Confession began with its most traditional material, with references to the Nicene Creed, original sin, and the Apostles' Creed. Melanchthon published *Carion's Chronicle* to argue the Holy Roman Empire's freedom from papal interference.[28] A group of scholars would create the *Magdeburg Centuries*, a massive work that even other Lutherans worried would smear their reputations.[29] Heinrich Bullinger wrote histories specifically to settle disputed questions, such as his *Concerning the Origins of Error*, a 1539 treatise that examined the

---

[26] James Stayer offers an alternative typology of the Reformations in his "The Contours of the Non-Lutheran Reformation in Germany, 1522–1546: The Distinction between Bible-Centered Meeting Places and the Altar-Centered Churches," *Church History and Religious Culture* 101 (2021): 167–74.

[27] Whether those changes were positive or negative remains, at least in part, a matter of perspective. Brad Gregory's view is certainly negative, giving only the grace that these outcomes were unintended. See his *The Unintended Reformation: How a Religious Revolution Secularised Society* (Cambridge, MA: Harvard University Press, 2012).

[28] Mark A. Lotito, *The Reformation of Historical Thought* (Leiden: Brill, 2019).

[29] Ibid., 244–45.

origins in the Middle Ages of doctrinal errors in the eucharist and other doctrines.[30] He would write a *History of the Reformation in Zurich* that served as much as a defense of Zurich's religious choices as it did its history.[31] John Knox wrote *A History of the Reformation in Scotland* as an argument for the Scottish Reformed church's legitimacy.[32] The quest to forge the true history based on the right memories was significant throughout the era.

The issues of history and tradition were not reserved to Lutherans and the Reformed. In the fifteenth century, the humanist scholar Lorenzo Valla demonstrated that the Donation of Constantine was a counterfeit. Luther's study of Valla's exposé of the Donation's origins infuriated him and contributed to his antipathy for the papacy.[33] The existence of such a document makes clear that adherents of Rome also saw the need to strengthen claims of tradition. The Catholic author Cesare Baronius wrote his *Ecclesiastical Annals* beginning in 1588 at the request of Philip Neri, as much to answer Protestant claims as to document history.[34] John Foxe's *Acts and Monuments of these Latter and Perillous Days, Touching Matters of the Church*, more popularly known as Foxe's *Book of Martyrs*, fused both tradition and (hagiographical) history to make English Protestants the true heirs of the early martyrs of Christianity.[35] Even Anabaptists were not above polemically useful remembrances.[36] The struggle between various types of foundation, even in areas of religious faith, are endemic to the Western mind, whether Protestant, Catholic, or anything else.

[30] Christian Moser, "Heinrich Bullinger's Efforts to Document the Zurich Reformation: History as Legacy," in *Architect of Reformation: An Introduction to Heinrich Bullinger, 1504–1575*, edited by Bruce Gordon and Emidio Campi (Grand Rapids: Baker Academic Publishing, 2004), 201–14.

[31] Moser, "Heinrich Bullinger's Efforts to Document the Zurich Reformation," 204–14.

[32] See Jane Dawson, *John Knox* (New Haven: Yale University Press, 2015). David D. Hall argued that the Church of Scotland constructed their identity based on the immediate glorious past of 1560–1567. See David D. Hall, *The Puritans: A Transatlantic History* (Princeton: Princeton University Press, 2019), 105.

[33] David M. Whitford, "The Papal Antichrist: Martin Luther and the Underappreciated Influence of Lorenzo Valla," *Renaissance Quarterly* 61 (2008): 26–52.

[34] See Hubert Jedin, *Kardinal Caesar Baronius: der Anfang der katholischen Kirchengeschichtsschreibung im 16. Jahrhundert* (Münster: Aschendorff, 1978); and Cyriac Pullapilly, *Caesar Baronius: Counter-Reformation Historian* (South Bend: University of Notre Dame Press, 1975).

[35] See David Loades, ed., *John Foxe and the English Reformation* (Brookfield, VT: Scolar Press, 1997).

[36] See Geoffrey Dipple, *Just as in the Time of the Apostles: Uses of History in the Radical Reformation* (Kitchener: Pandora Press, 2005).

AFTER THE REFORMATIONS

The aftermath of the Reformations did not prove that a newly pristine biblicism or rationalism had been discovered. In the first place, evangelical thinkers sought to maintain the essential Christian faith which they believed was available in the scriptures, even though the reformers accepted many points that had been established in ecumenical (universal) councils. Further, in the fight to demonstrate that they were not merely innovators, reformers considered it crucial that their confessions could make claims to hold the historic faith.[37] Protestant theologians also found that the theological tradition was too useful both for considering the mistakes of their opponents and for helping shape their own theological constructs. Finally, the early reformers especially Luther, soon became traditional authority figures in their own rights, with the later members of the confessions taking great pains to maintain fealty to their thought, and to punish those who fell too far astray.[38]

The thesis of confessionalism demonstrates the power of ecclesiastical traditions in the early modern period. While one can argue that the Lutherans, Anglicans, the Reformed, or Roman Catholics were setting aside prior traditions, it is obvious that they were going to great lengths to establish new traditions.[39] We see the argument made that culture was irretrievably changed, but seem unwilling to recognize what that meant

[37] See Rebecca Giselbrecht, "Trinitarian Controversies," in *John Calvin in Context*, edited by R. Ward Holder (Cambridge: Cambridge University Press, 2019), esp. 273–77. Sara Georgini made the case that as the eighteenth-century New Englanders wrote their histories, it was an "idealized memory of Puritans" that undergirded their thought. Sara Georgini, *Household Gods: The Religious Lives of the Adams Family* (Oxford: Oxford University Press, 2019), 19ff.

[38] An excellent case is the polemic of Joachim Westphal against Calvin's eucharistic doctrines in the early 1550s. There is no doubt that Westphal was certain that Calvin taught the wrong doctrines, especially those that denied the corporeal presence of the body of Christ in, with, and under the elements. But just as strong was Westphal's defense of Luther's doctrine, a theological endeavor that was fraught with elements that defined Luther's thought as definitive for the Lutheran tradition. See also Bjørn Ole Hovda, *The Controversy over the Lord's Supper in Danzig 1561–1567: Presence and Practice – Theology and Confessional Policy* (Göttingen: Vandenhoeck & Ruprecht, 2018). Hovda argues throughout that Luther's death created a vacuum of authority, which the Gnesio-Lutherans solved by making Luther himself a source of valid tradition.

[39] See among others Bodo Nischan, "Confessionalization and Absolutism: The Case of Brandenburg," in *Calvinism in Europe, 1540–1620*, edited by Andrew Pettegree, Alistair Duke, and Gillian Lewis (Cambridge: Cambridge University Press, 1996), 181–204; Robert M. Kingdon, "Confessionalism in Calvin's Geneva," *Archiv für Reformationsgeschichte* 96 (2005): 109–16; Heinz Schilling, "Luther, Loyola, Calvin und die europäische Neuzeit," *Archiv für Reformationsgeschichte* 85 (1994): 5–31.

for the intellectual underpinnings of early modern societies.[40] The various Protestant communities – whether confessions, churches, or biblical communities of discourse – sought the comfort of lived traditions and hardened their traditions as they lived.

The great rupture in this effort at religious and rational epistemology was the Enlightenment.[41] It is difficult to imagine the enormity of the shockwaves that accompanied the impact of the Enlightenment's sustained attack on tradition and external authority for the Western mind. For some, obviously, that was immensely freeing. For others, the effect was just the opposite. The ideals that Kant put forward in his 1784 essay "What is Enlightenment?" could and did erode confidence in efforts at religious and secular epistemology as easily as it enabled thinkers to make new attempts at attaining knowledge.[42] Some would see this concentration upon the purity of the rational element as too narrow and sought to supplement the rational model with other elements. Friedrich D. E. Schleiermacher's turn to Romantic elements while maintaining contact with the rationalistic models illustrated both the promise and difficulty of such an enterprise.[43]

Karl Barth's bombshell in the playground of the theologians was another moment when the theological tradition was shaken to its core.[44] Now it was the liberal theological movement that suffered the slings and arrows of an enraged pastor. But it is not possible to grasp the tectonic shift that Barth's commentary on Romans effected with its publication in 1919 until one grants that a new tradition had taken root. Barth demanded a paradigm shift that would not be fully described for decades,

---

[40] See Jill Fehleison, *Boundaries of Faith: Catholics and Protestants in the Diocese of Geneva* (Kirksville: Truman State University Press, 2011); and Margo Todd, *The Culture of Protestantism in Early Modern Scotland* (New Haven: Yale University Press, 2002).

[41] Ethan Shagan locates the seeds of this problem of historical faith and belief far earlier in the work of Fausto Paolo Sozzini or Faustus Socinus (d. 1604), but I disagree because of the noted impact of the Enlightenment that cannot be demonstrated in Sozzini's time. See Shagan, *The Birth of Modern Belief*, 188–95.

[42] See Immanuel Kant, "What Is Enlightenment?," in *Basic Writings of Kant* (New York: Modern Library, 2001), 133–42.

[43] See especially his *On Religion: Speech to Its Cultured Despisers*, originally published in 1799, and *The Christian Faith*, originally published in 1821–1822.

[44] The reference is to Karl Adam's comment in Das Hochland, 1926. Das Hochland was a Catholic cultural journal (*Kulturzeitschrift*). Adam was commenting on the publication of Barth's *Commentary on Romans*. See Wim A. Dreyer, "Karl Barth's Römerbrief: A Turning Point in Protestant Theology," *Studia Historiae Ecclesiasticae* 43 (2017): www .researchgate.net/publication/322775281_Karl_Barth's_Romerbrief_A_turning_point_ in_Protestant_Theology, accessed August 31, 2020.

and then by a philosopher of science, not a theologian.[45] Barth assaulted the idealism of liberal theology – by then a tradition in its own right – and urged a return to the scriptures. But that return to the scripture was itself wrapped up in a particular set of traditions, even as it formed a new tradition that still stands as one of the dominant forms of Christian thought in the modern West.

The examples of figures within the history of Christianity attacking the tradition while establishing the foundation of a new tradition through use of the tradition's materials can be multiplied beyond all worthwhile consideration. Many were formed around a core issue of the tension between tradition and text, whatever words were used to describe that struggle.

THE CONTEMPORARY MEANING OF TRADITION

Considering the place of tradition in the twentieth and twenty-first centuries may, at first glance, seem odd for a deep study of a sixteenth-century thinker. But the argument of this study is that Calvin was not able to escape the tradition into which he was born and raised, not through moral or intellectual failing, but because to do so is impossible. If such is the case, then modern or postmodern thinkers must consider the world in which we stand, and the traditions we have inherited. To do otherwise would be to suggest that we can find a place outside our own historical context and received tradition from which to view the past with a clinical and sterile consideration, beyond the infecting influences of anything other than the facts of the past. Surely, such a stance is impossible.

The positive definition and consideration of tradition remained, through the middle of the twentieth century, almost entirely the province of Roman Catholic thinkers. While Yves Congar deserves his reputation in the front rank of theologians of tradition, this consideration was common to many of the thinkers of the *nouvelle théologie* school. While delving into the church's tradition of interpreting the scripture,

---

[45] T. S. Kuhn, *The Structure of Scientific Revolutions* (Chicago: University of Chicago Press, 1962). Gadamer rejected the "neutrality of science," and saw significant hermeneutical elements in the application of science. While his early work posited "science" in a positivistic manner that many natural scientists rejected, he appreciated Kuhn's rejection of the linear progression of science. See Lawrence K. Schmidt, "Gadamer and the Philosophy of Science," in *Hermeneutics and Phenomenology: Figures and Themes*, edited by Saulius Geniusas and Paul Fairfield (London: Bloomsbury, 2018), 149–62, esp. 151–54.

Henri de Lubac also made significant advances in considering the nature of tradition.[46] But that formerly purely Roman Catholic bailiwick became a site for Protestant doctrinal consideration through a variety of avenues. Most important for this study is the consideration of the investigations of philosophical hermeneutics. The work of figures such as Gadamer and Paul Ricoeur were enormously important in this regard. While this started with investigations in university settings, theologians of various confessions have come to recognize the importance of these ideas for the modern task of theology. The Protestant voices in this discussion were frequently debating the meaning of tradition without fully understanding the variety of senses and serious complex of significations that their Roman Catholic conversation partners brought to the exchange. The ongoing engagement brought a far more sophisticated consideration of the topic than had been the case in previous ages when ecumenism could not take as full a scope as was possible after Vatican II.

PHILOSOPHICAL HERMENEUTICS AND TRADITION

Tradition has assumed a greater explicit role in modern theological dialogue than in Western theological discourse prior to the twentieth century. Thinkers from all confessions have been hard at work in considering the way that tradition functions, and the way it should function, in theological complexes. Roman Catholics are joined by Lutherans, the Reformed, Southern Baptists, and even by card-carrying Evangelicals.[47] Yet the problem is not getting theologians to think about

---

[46] See his *The Sources of Revelation* (New York: Herder & Herder, 1968).

[47] A brief and quite incomplete listing of the past few years analysis would include Najeeb George Awad, "Should We Dispense with Sola Scriptura? Scripture, Tradition and Postmodern Theology," *Dialog: A Journal of Theology* 47 (2008): 64–79; Hans Boersma, "Anchored in Christ: Beyond the Scripture-Tradition Divide," *Christian Century* 128 (February 8, 2011): 26–31; John W. De Gruchy, "Transforming Traditions: Doing Theology in South Africa Today," *Journal of Theology for Southern Africa* 139 (2011): 7–17; O'Malley, "The Hermeneutic of Reform," 517–46; Terrence Tilley, *Inventing Catholic Tradition* (Maryknoll: Orbis Books, 2000); John Thiel, *Senses of Tradition: Continuity and Development in Catholic Faith* (Oxford: Oxford University Press, 2000); John Webster, "Purity and Plenitude; Evangelical Reflections on Congar's *Tradition and Traditions*," *International Journal of Systematic Theology* 7 (2005): 399–413; Kevin Vanhoozer, *First Theology: God, Scripture, and Hermeneutics* (Downers Grove: IVP, 2002); and D. H. Williams, "The Patristic Tradition as Canon," *Perspectives in Religious Studies* 32 (2005): 357–79.

tradition so much as generating something like a consensus on a definition or signification of the term. To do that requires some excavation. So we turn to one of the sources of the modern recourse to tradition, philosophical hermeneutics.[48]

The history of Western philosophy since the Enlightenment is littered with efforts at a consistent or even useful hermeneutic. While especially true for the Christian scriptures, it is also at play for the broadest possible issues – the West became uncertain what texts mean or how they mean what they do. Friederich D. E. Schleiermacher, Wilhelm Dilthey, Martin Heidegger, Edmund Husserl, and Rudolf Bultmann, to name only a few thinkers, have attacked the problem in a variety of ways.[49]

Gadamer clarified that it was the Enlightenment itself that was at the core of the problem.[50] With its critique of all forms of authority, the Enlightenment did not only strip away the power of hierarchy and tradition. Taken to its logical conclusion, the Enlightenment's critique eviscerates one of the most widely respected theories of textual meaning, that of authorial intent. Speaking to this, Gadamer wrote:

The recognition that all understanding inevitably involves some prejudice gives the hermeneutical problem its real thrust. In light of this insight it appears that historicism, despite its critique of rationalism and of natural law philosophy, is based on the modern Enlightenment and unwittingly shares its prejudices. And there is one prejudice of the Enlightenment that defines its essence: the fundamental prejudice of the Enlightenment is the prejudice against prejudice itself, which denies tradition its power.[51]

---

[48] This consideration of hermeneutic theory in the twentieth century is meant only as a brief overview. To delve deeply into the discussions of Gadamer and Ricoeur alone would preclude the possibility of ever reaching a discussion of Calvin.

[49] See Anthony C. Thiselton's summary in *New Horizons in Hermeneutics: The Theory and Practice of Transforming Biblical Reading* (Grand Rapids: Zondervan, 1992).

[50] Gadamer's mark on hermeneutics and tradition theory has spawned a significant literature dedicated to understanding his work. See Csaba Olay, "Die Überlieferung Der Gegenwart Und Die Gegenwart Der Überlieferung. Heidegger Und Gadamer Über Tradition," *International Yearbook for Hermeneutics* 12 (January 1, 2013): 196–219; Bernd Auerochs, "Gadamer Uber Tradition," *Zeitschrift Für Philosophische Forschung* 49, no. 2 (April 1, 1995): 294–311; Martin Nosál, "The Gadamerian Approach to the Relation Between Experience and Language," *History and Theory* 54 (2015): 195–208; Georgia Warnke, "Experiencing Tradition versus Belonging to It: Gadamer's Dilemma," *The Review of Metaphysics* 68 (2014): 347–69.

[51] Hans-Geog Gadamer, *Truth and Method*, 2nd rev. ed., translated by Joel Weinsheimer and Donald G. Marshall (New York: Continuum, 1991), 270.

Literally, Gadamer argued that the radical skepticism about all foundations of thought except rationality itself had made interpretation impossible.[52]

In linking human finitude and historicity to the necessity of prejudice, Gadamer flew in the face of the entire Enlightenment criticism of tradition. For Gadamer, the Enlightenment was the culprit, not in questioning the authority of traditions, but in suggesting that self-grounding rationality was the standard by which all other human accomplishments and statements of truth should be judged.[53] Gadamer's great work, *Truth and Method*, set out not to create the procedure by which texts would be interpreted, but instead to "clarify the conditions in which understanding takes place."[54]

The Enlightenment held out the possibility of and demand for humans to establish all ideals from the principle of rationality alone, without the aid of external authorities or traditional influence. This was a form of an argument about the existence of a self-grounding or unequivocally foundational rationality. But that ideal comes with certain problems. It is not self-evident. It does not survive the adoption of radical skepticism. And it may not truly exist.[55]

---

[52] For Gadamer, this insight was universal. Gadamer believed that the scientific positivism that was ineluctably attached to Enlightenment thinking rendered the search for truth impossible because the modern scientific method had substituted a method for interpretation. One of the early reviewers of Gadamer stated that he was challenging beliefs that had long gone out of fashion. Schmidt, "Gadamer and the Philosophy of Science," 150. But Gadamer's thought did not remain static, and he went beyond these early discussions. He argued that "[w]hat makes modern scholarship scientific is precisely the fact that it objectifies tradition and methodically eliminates the influence of the interpreter and his time on understanding." Hans-Georg Gadamer, *Hermeneutik I: Wahrheit und Methode. Grundzüge einer Philosophischen Hermeneutik* (1960), 1986, vol. 1, *Gesammelte Werke* (Tübingen: J.C.B. Mohr [Paul Siebeck], 1986), 338; Gadamer, *Truth and Method*, 333, quoted in Schmidt, "Gadamer and the Philosophy of Science," 151.

[53] Gadamer concentrated upon the interpretation of the classic and explored its implications for the exegesis of scripture, especially in his Hermeneutics, Religion, and Ethics, translated by Joel Weinsheimer (New Haven: Yale University Press, 1999). See also Jens Zimmerman, "Phenomenology, Hermeneutics, and Religion: Restoring the Fullness of Knowing," in *Hermeneutics and Phenomenology: Figures and Themes*, edited by Saulius Geniusas and Paul Fairfield (London: Bloomsbury, 2018), 163–74; those insights have been applied beyond the fields of philosophy and religion. An excellent example is given by Francis J. Mootz, III, who edited *Gadamer and Law* (Farnham: Ashgate, 2007). Articles in that collection took up issues of how hermeneutics would affect jurisprudence, constitutional interpretation, and even legal theory.

[54] Gadamer, *Truth and Method*, 295.

[55] For an extended argument on the difficulties with this approach, difficulties that add up to an impossibility, see Robert Nozick, *The Nature of Rationality* (Princeton: Princeton University Press, 1993).

The Enlightenment's effort to free humanity from self-imposed chains drove the epistemic project into a cul-de-sac from which it is impossible to be extricated. While certain thinkers have sought to celebrate this problem as the new freedom from having to find justifications for life choices or patterns of thought, they have not been able satisfactorily to answer critics who pointed out the dangers of neopragmatism.[56] These critics attacked the pragmatic turn with questions about the nature of societies, social interactions, and the nature of the good.

Gadamer turned his attention to "both the nature of understanding and the social relational nature of communication."[57] In Gadamer's thought, one comes to understanding through a process that would include a conversation or dialogical exercise. Gadamer expanded this model of engagement with the other to include the conversation partner of an historical text.[58] He argued for a "historically-effected consciousness."[59] Gadamer thought that history had a far greater function in the lives of humans than we normally recognize. Modern humanity does not see this because of the effects of the Enlightenment. In his eyes, a significant change in the ways that humans perceived the philosophical, religious, and aesthetic traditions began in the late eighteenth century. This change caused these traditions to lose their authoritative power and to become objects of research instead.[60]

He argued that the highest type of hermeneutical experience was the "openness to tradition characteristic of historically-effected consciousness."[61] This consciousness made several things possible. The tradition, in Gadamer's thought, offered the thinking present subject with an actual conversation partner, rather than a simple automaton that could be used for whatever purpose the present subject assigned it. This conversational relationship allowed the tradition to make claims upon the present. Gadamer argued that "[t]o be situated within a tradition does not limit the freedom of knowledge but makes it possible."[62] This means that the

---

[56] Richard Rorty, *Contingency, Irony, and Solidarity* (Cambridge: Cambridge University Press, 1989).

[57] Robert Evans, *Reception History, Tradition and Biblical Interpretation: Gadamer and Jauss in Current Practice* (London: Bloomsbury T&T Clark, 2014), 3. The following discussion is dependent on Evans' consideration of Gadamer's thought, though not that of Jauss.

[58] Evans, *Reception History, Tradition and Biblical Interpretation*, 3.

[59] Gadamer, *Truth and Method*, 361.

[60] Anders Odenstedt, *Gadamer on Tradition-Historical Context and the Limits of Reflection* (New York: Springer, 2017), 33.

[61] Gadamer, *Truth and Method*, 361.

[62] Ibid.

historical traditions actually engage in a dialogical process with those interpreting them – the creator and created in a circle of reciprocity. This tradition was not a hegemonic compulsion; far from it. Instead, Gadamer believed that "the fact is that in tradition there is always an element of freedom and of history itself. Even the most genuine and pure tradition does not persist because of the inertia of what once existed. It needs to be affirmed, embraced, cultivated. It is, essentially, preservation, and it is active in all historical change. But preservation is an act of reason, though an inconspicuous one."[63] We shall return to this insight at a later stage in the study.

In Gadamer's work, the historically effected consciousness became basic to the understanding of the past, as well as the interpretation of texts. In fact, much of his work tore down the idea of a wall between the interpretation of the past and the reading of texts. Instead, Gadamer suggested that understanding and interpretation of history, art, classics, and the Bible had far more in common with each other than the predominant Western culture had previously seen or understood. For the German philosopher, the problem was not in the external influences that affect the interpreter. Far more, the problem was the search for a perfect method, the effort to gain guarantees of the foundationally correct interpretations.[64] Gadamer's whole work can be seen as a rejection of such a conception of interpretation.

Other thinkers took up the hermeneutical question of tradition. The New Testament scholar Peter Stuhlmacher would write of the "horizon of the church's faith and experience," and argue that biblical "texts can be fully interpreted only from a dialogical situation defined by the venture of the Christian existence as it is lived in the church."[65] This worked well with the thought of Ricoeur, who argued that all knowledge is mediated through language. As he considered the historical subject, Ricoeur placed it in the category of *Geschichte*, normally translated as "history," which is more broadly the flow of life within history, or

[63] Ibid., 293. Quoted in Antonio Calcagno, "The Force of the Embodied Individual: De Beauvoir and Gadamer on Interpretive Understanding," in *Relational Hermeneutics: Essays in Comparative Philosophy*, edited by Paul Fairfield and Saulius Geniusas (London: Bloomsbury, 2018), 41.

[64] See Merold Westphal, *Whose Community? Which Interpretation? Philosophical Hermeneutics for the Church* (Grand Rapids: Baker Book House, 2009), 85–86.

[65] Peter Stuhlmacher, *Historical Criticism and Theological Interpretation of Scripture*, translated by Roy A. Harrisville (Philadelphia: Fortress Press, 1977), 88–89.

rather the current of linkage within time.[66] Ricoeur argued that the community of readers, sometimes called the textual community, were opened up in their engagement with the text to a new world – but that world itself created a new sense for the community – one that could be called tradition.

Ricoeur believed, like Gadamer, that hermeneutics was broader than the interpretation of texts – rather, hermeneutics involved the interpretation of symbols that point toward language as the creative reservoir from which intersubjective meaning is produced.[67] Further, the French philosopher offered a model of hermeneutics as appropriation – an act of "making one's own what was initially alien."[68] For Ricoeur, all philosophy was hermeneutics, for in the "continual exegesis of all the significations that come to light in the world of culture," humans could find the path to the self.[69] That insight pointed out his sense that the hermeneutical task was essentially a reflexive or self-reflective endeavor. The interpreter sought to gain insight into him or herself as much as a greater understanding of the text or symbol that was engaged.

Thus, the value of the hermeneutical effort, as presented by philosophical hermeneutical work of the twentieth century, naturally became clear in both theological and religious studies at the end of the twentieth and beginning of the twenty-first centuries. This was true both for the consideration and interpretation of the texts of history, and for the sense of the claims of history itself makes on the modern world. Systematic and historical efforts have begun to take advantage of these insights. One of the aims of the present study is to apply such perceptions to the understanding of Calvin's sense of tradition and its place in the broader sense of his theology.

---

[66] Paul Ricoeur, "Hermeneutics and the Critique of Ideology," in *The Hermeneutic Tradition: From Ast to Ricoeur*, edited by Gayle L. Ormiston and Alan D. Schrift (Albany: SUNY Press, 1990), 326.

[67] Maureen Junker-Kenny, *Religion and Public Reason: A Comparison of the Positions of John Rawls, Jürgen Habermas, and Paul Ricoeur* (Berlin: Walter de Gruyter, 2014), 185.

[68] Paul Ricoeur, *Hermeneutics and the Human Sciences*, edited and translated by J. B. Thompson (Cambridge: Cambridge University Press, 1981), 159. Quoted in George H. Taylor, "Understanding as Metaphoric, Not a Fusion of Horizons," in *Gadamer and Ricoeur: Critical Horizons for Contemporary Hermeneutics*, edited by Francis J. Mootz, III and George H. Taylor (London: Continuum, 2011), 110.

[69] Paul Ricoeur, "Existence and Hermeneutics," in *The Philosophy of Paul Ricoeur: An Anthology of His Work*, edited by Charles E. Reagan and David Stewart (Boston: Beacon Press, 1978), 106.

CONCLUSION

It has become popular to consider tradition as a category in discussing
and analyzing the theologies of the early modern period.[70] Perhaps as a
backlash against the triumphant confessional historiographical tendencies of the middle of the twentieth century that saw Roman Catholicism
as maintaining tradition while Protestant reform grasped the purity of
the scriptures, tradition became an important topic to consider in the
theological tasks of all early modern theologians.[71] However, it is becoming clear that even as we have turned our attention to tradition and have
been rewarded with a clearer and more defensible portrait of the theological landscape in the early modern period, the very number of studies
with their accompanying differing methodologies and assumptions have
begun to raise the question of the meaning of tradition.

The question does not answer itself. But if we take seriously the work
of various scholars who have demonstrated the dependence of various
reformers upon patristic sources, answering the question too simply runs
the risk of missing the point. Too often, the analysis of an early modern
thinkers' allusions to patristic and medieval sources masquerades as tradition. It cannot be that simple. Early modern thinkers were faced with a
truly new situation, a set of options that the tide of history had not presented for a millennium. Theologians, whether Catholic or Anabaptist,
Lutheran or Reformed, had to consider the nature of the truth claims
and their foundations. Would they base everything on scripture and the

---

[70] I too have been a contributor to that tendency. See R. Ward Holder, "The Reformers and
Tradition: Seeing the Roots of a Problem," *Religions* 8 (2017): 1–11. But other studies
have impacted the historiographical tendency of the early modern academy. See, among
others, Irena Backus, ed., *The Reception of the Church Fathers in the West: From the
Carolingians to the Maurists* (Leiden: Brill, 1997); Irena Backus, *Historical Method and
Confessional Identity in the Era of the Reformation (1378–1615)* (Leiden: Brill, 2003);
Dipple, *Just as in the Time of the Apostles*; Leif Grane, Alfred Schindler, and Markus
Wriedt, eds., *Auctoritas Patrum: Contributions on the Reception of the Church Fathers
in the 15th and 16th Centuries* (Mainz: Verlag Philipp von Zabern, 1993); Scott Hendrix,
Tradition and Authority in the Reformation (Aldershot: Variorum, 1996); Matthijs Lam-
berigts and Leo Kenis, eds., *L'Augustinisme à l'ancienne Faculté de théologie de Louvain*
(Louvain: Peeters; Leuven University Press, 1993); Karl Reuter, *Das Grundverständnis
der Theologie Calvins: unter Einbeziehung ihrer geschichtlichen Abhangigkeiten* (Neu-
kirchen-Vluyn: Neukirchener Verlag des Erziehungsvereins, 1963); David Steinmetz,
"Luther and Staupitz: The Unresolved Problem of the Forerunner," in *Ad Fontes Lutheri:
Essays in Honor of Kenneth Hagen's Sixty-fifth Birthday*, edited by Timothy Maschke,
Franz Posset, and Joan Skocir (Milwaukee: Marquette University Press, 2001), 270–80.
[71] Raymond A. Mentzer, "The Deconfessionalization of the Reformations," *The Sixteenth
Century Journal* 50 (2019): 43–48.

individual's interpretation? Would the church's – or Christianity's – history matter? Working through these questions that faced the early modern thinkers, and seeking to find their solutions to them, is the best way to understand the influence of and engagement with tradition.

I propose that the answer to this question is to go back to the basics, with a study that takes the question seriously and is willing to use a variety of methodologies. To that end, this study will analyze Calvin's definition of tradition. To summarize, we will see that Calvin defined tradition both negatively and positively. He rejected the ideas that tradition was the possession of the hierarchy, and that tradition could subvert the clear teaching of scripture. Positively he argued that tradition should ideally be apostolic, that it would be clearly available to any who studied historical sources, and that it should only deal with matters of order. We must now consider his use of tradition, and his theology of tradition. This task will outline Calvin's conscious use of fathers and "the tradition," whatever he called it, to introduce a greater specificity to the word tradition as we engage that complex term.

The task of this study will be twofold. First, what did Calvin believe about the various traditions that came down to him as a French Christian living in the early modern period? I will examine how Calvin used tradition in the theological, polemical, and exegetical works he wrote. I will examine whether his use of the traditions changed significantly according to his audience. Did Calvin employ a different theological methodology when writing to French vernacular audiences than he did when his readers were learned in Latin? Further, did Calvin change his patterns of use of the tradition when discussing his thought with Lutheran, or Catholic, or Anabaptist colleagues and foes? Similarly, did he change between genres? Did Calvin use varied techniques of application of the Christian traditions when writing commentaries, or treatises, or the *Institutes*, or was his appeal to the tradition broadly the same? Finally, what was tradition, for Calvin? Did he accept the Roman definitions of that construct, or did he transform them?

Second, what did Calvin's set of choices mean for the Reformed tradition, for Western Christianity, and for the modern world? Did he create a second model of doctrine, radically different from the Roman paradigm that appealed to scripture and tradition? Did the confessional community that was formed after him and that frequently bears his name accept his sense of the relationship of doctrine to the scriptures? After examining Calvin's sense of tradition, I will discuss the influence he exerted upon

Reformed Christianity and the modern world and the way that influence still works today.

Tradition is significant because of its function in memory and rationality. While there is a broad variety of meanings attached to tradition, the modern mind finds itself between two poles. On the one hand, it seeks the foundational pillar for its rationality, which is frequently posed as a text. For theologians it is scripture – for lawyers the constitution and for literary critics the classic. But the drive for a written clarity is balanced by a situatedness that remains a reflection of a historical moment, one that cannot deny the set of historical circumstances surrounding the richness of this time. Both impulses war against the fortress of unbound rationality that Kant suggested. Both are reflected in Calvin's thought, a mirror of our own.

2

Calvin, Tradition, and Exegesis

Chapter 1 traced the notions of tradition that had been significant in Calvin's day and that continued into the present. This chapter examines Calvin's exegetical works to accomplish two tasks. First, it is important to see how Calvin dealt with the tradition. The examination of his engagement with exegetical and doctrinal traditions and his discussions of hierarchical tradition will allow a sense of Calvin's theology of tradition to take shape. Second, in this chapter we begin to consider whether his engagement with the tradition spanned the various genres of his work. Calvin's works covered the breadth of theological production in the early modern period, and as this study seeks to establish his theory of tradition, it will also be important to ascertain whether that theory functioned in all the genres of his work, or only in a select few, and the reasons for that. In this chapter, we begin with Calvin's biblical work.

SCRIPTURE COMMENTARIES

Calvin was one of the great interpreters of scripture in the sixteenth century. In part, this was simply because of his production. He published more commentaries or lectures on biblical books than Zwingli, Melanchthon, Bucer, Luther, and Bullinger. He commented upon most of the New Testament, skipping only Revelation and II and III John. He then turned to the Old Testament, beginning with Isaiah, before proceeding to write on Genesis, the Psalms, the Twelve Minor Prophets, Daniel, Jeremiah, Lamentations, and Exodus-Deuteronomy; this last Calvin published as a harmony.[1] In 1564, the year of his death, Calvin's lectures on Joshua were published. The commentary on the first twenty chapters of Ezekiel was published posthumously in 1565.[2]

While Calvin published many commentaries on the New Testament, not all of his interpretive works on the Old Testament were true commentaries. In fact, of the works on the Old Testament, that label only fits his Mosaic Harmony, the Psalms, and Joshua; the rest of his Old Testament explications were transcriptions of his lectures. These lectures were given regularly and were addressed to the young men of Geneva who sought an education.[3] These young men would have been joined by pastors and others who wished to hear Calvin lecture; expertise in Latin, Greek, and Hebrew was a prerequisite. This prodigious productivity presents a challenge in considering a representative sample of Calvin's work. I have selected two of Calvin's New Testament commentaries, those on Romans and II Corinthians, and two of his interpretive works on the Old Testament, his lectures on Genesis, and his lectures on Daniel. The selection represents both testaments, and his earlier and later work, Romans from 1540, II Corinthians from 1547, Genesis from 1554 and republished in edited form in 1563, and Daniel in 1561.

ROMANS COMMENTARY

In 1540, while living in Strasbourg, Calvin presented the literary and theological world with his first commentary on scripture, a genre that would define him as significantly as any other during his lifetime. The Romans commentary rolled off the press at the shop of Wendelin Rihel in 1540.[4] While the move back to Geneva and attendant duties would keep Calvin

---

[1] The *Harmony of the last Four Books of Moses* truly was innovative, and a project that Calvin knew differed from other treatments of the law. See Raymond A. Blacketer, "Calvin as Commentator on the Mosaic Harmony and Joshua," in *Calvin and the Bible*, edited by Donald McKim (Cambridge: Cambridge University Press, 2006), 30–52. See also Raymond A. Blacketer, *The School of God: Pedagogy and Rhetoric in Calvin's Interpretation of Deuteronomy* (Dordrecht: Springer, 2006).

[2] For background, see Donald McKim, ed., *Calvin and the Bible* (Cambridge: Cambridge University Press, 2006).

[3] T. H. L. Parker, *Calvin's Old Testament Commentaries* (Edinburgh: T. & T. Clark, 1986), 15.

[4] R. Ward Holder, "Calvin as Commentator on the Pauline Letters," in *Calvin and the Bible*, edited by Donald McKim (Cambridge: Cambridge University Press, 2006), 224–56. See also T. H. L. Parker, *Commentaries on Romans 1532–1542* (Edinburgh: T. & T. Clark, 1986).

from publishing further Pauline commentaries for another six years, this first commentary would mark a significant step in Calvin's writing career.[5] Calvin began with the Pauline epistles and did not follow the New Testament's canonical order as he did not begin with the synoptic gospels. Instead, it is far more likely that he believed Paul, and Romans in particular, provided the key to interpreting the scriptures and the Christian life rightly.[6]

As I have noted elsewhere, perhaps one of the more important and surprising features of Calvin's commentaries in general – and his Romans commentary in particular – was his constant reference to the church's traditions, both doctrinal and exegetical.[7] Those readers who have been easily swayed by the term *sola scriptura* must either ignore Calvin's actual manner of treating the biblical material or are soon disabused of this facile mnemonic.[8] Calvin was fully aware that he was working as a theologian and exegete of the church, an institution with fifteen centuries

---

[5] David Steinmetz, "Calvin among the Thomists: Exegesis of Romans 9," in *Biblical Hermeneutics in Historical Perspective*, edited by Mark Burrows and Paul Rorem (Grand Rapids, MI: Eerdmans, 1991), 198–214. Steinmetz argues that Calvin's exegesis is as often traditionally motivated as it is contextually.

[6] See Gary Neal Hansen, "Door and Passageway: Calvin's Use of Romans as a Hermeneutical and Theological Guide," in *Reformation Readings of Romans*, edited by Kathy Ehrensperger and R. Ward Holder (Edinburgh: T. & T. Clark, 2008), 77–94. T. H. L. Parker has argued that Calvin's choice of the Pauline epistles as his first commentaries was not a random choice but purposeful, reflecting Calvin's sense of the aim or *scopus* of scripture and the key to understanding it. Calvin himself wrote that there were many commentaries on Romans from ancient and modern interpreters, but that this made sense, because "Et sane nusquam melius collocare suam operam poterant: quando siquis eam intelligat, aditum sibi quendam patefactum habet ad totius Scripturae intelligentiam": T. H. L. Parker, ed., *Iohannis Calvini Commentarius in Epistolam Pauli ad Romanos* (Leiden: Brill, 1981), 2 (hereafter cited as Calvin, Ad Romanos, with page number); ("They could indeed have had no more suitable object on which to bestow their labours, for if we understand this Epistle, we have a passage opened to us to the understanding of the whole of scripture": John Calvin, *The Epistle of Paul the Apostle to the Romans*, translated by Ross Mackenzie, in Calvin's New Testament Commentaries, edited by David W. and Thomas F. Torrance, vol. 8 (Edinburgh: Oliver and Boyd Ltd., 1960) (hereafter cited as Calvin, Romans Comm., with page number).

[7] R. Ward Holder, *John Calvin and the Grounding of Interpretation: Calvin's First Commentaries* (Leiden: Brill, 2006), especially chap. 3.

[8] John Thompson noted the rejection of tradition as a too common fallacy about the Reformation's exegesis. "Although the exegesis of the Reformation era has often been characterized as having shaken off traditional views in favor of the unadorned Word of God, the reality is rather different. Sixteenth-century commentators were constantly in conversation with their patristic, medieval, and rabbinic predecessors, and many of these traditional views survive, albeit often in new forms." Thompson, *Writing the Wrongs: Women of the Old Testament among Biblical Commentators from Philo through the Reformation* (Oxford: Oxford University Press, 2001), 69. Further, Calvin was not alone among the reformers

of history.[9] His access to the sources of that tradition is a constant question for modern analysts, with numerous commentators weighing in with finely tuned studies. This practice of Calvin's may have stemmed from an effort to avoid innovation for its own sake as well as an effort to offer the pure teachings of religion.[10] Further, he regularly lauded positions that had the patina of antiquity, and he denigrated faddish newness.[11]

Calvin would demonstrate this habit throughout his commentaries.[12] It was a practice that reflected a deep appreciation for the church's tradition across time and was integral to his exegesis, from his very first effort at biblical commentary. In the Romans commentary, Calvin attacked the question of the name of Paul through recourse to tradition. As is known from the history of exegesis school's work, Calvin's choice to take up that question was hardly original, but already marked his continuation within a well-established tradition of commenting upon Romans.[13] Calvin began

in taking this stance. Heinrich Bullinger, would go so far as to state "In so far as the Holy Fathers have not digressed from this kind of interpretation, I have not only recited them as interpreters of the Scriptures but have venerated them as elected tools of God." Quoted in Fritz Büsser, "Bullinger as Calvin's Model in Biblical Exposition: An Examination of Calvin's Preface to the Epistle to the Romans," in *In Honor of John Calvin, 1509–64*, edited by E. J. Furcha (Montreal: Faculty of Religious Studies, McGill University, 1987), 74.

[9] Karlfried Froehlich, in his "The Fate of the *Glossa Ordinaria* in the Sixteenth Century," *Die Patristik in der Bibelexegese des 16. Jahrhunderts*, edited by David C. Steinmetz (Wiesbaden: Harrassowitz Verlag, 1999), has noted that Erasmus himself had access to and probably uncritically quoted printed versions of the *Glossa ordinaria*. However, though Froehlich is able to demonstrate varying levels of dependence upon the *Glossa* in the work of reformers such as Bucer and Bullinger, this is impossible at this time in Calvin's work. "For Calvin and the Geneva theologians after his death, the *Glossa ordinaria* had ceased to play a role, *any* role as an accepted source of patristic exegetical material, or even as a source in its own right" (37).

[10] Olivier Millet noted Calvin's knowledge of the patristic sources and his sense that they are the first source of ideas of theological and historical argumentation for the church: *Calvin et la dynamique de la parole: Etude de rhétorique réformée* (Paris: Librairie Honoré Champion, 1992), 168.

[11] An example can be seen in Calvin's comments upon Romans 7, where he makes clear that he is following the "corrected" view of the later Augustine on the divided self. See David C. Steinmetz, "Calvin and the Divided Self of Romans 7," in *Calvin in Context*, 2nd ed. (Oxford: Oxford University Press, 2010), 108–19.

[12] This was an effort to grasp the tradition of the church. For an example of this, see Elsie McKee's "Les Anciens et lInterpretation de 1 Tm 5, 17 chez Calvin: Une Curiosite dans l'Histoire de l'Exegese," *Revue de Theologie et de Philosophie* 120 (1988): 411–17, which points out the way in which Calvin's interpretation does draw upon the twofold elder that is a common theme in the prior exegetical tradition.

[13] Gwenfair Walters Adams, *Romans 1–8 (Reformation Commentary on Scripture)*, edited by Scott Manetsch (Downers Grove, IL: IVP Academic, 2019). See also *Philip Melanchthon Commentary on Romans*, 2nd English ed., translated by Fred Kramer (St. Louis, MO: Concordia Publishing, 2010); and Parker, *Commentaries on Romans 1532–1542*.

by noting those who have seen special significance in the name Paul. Then he considered those who suggested that the name Paul was given to Saul to mark his conversion to following Jesus Christ, and he referenced Augustine's acceptance of this theory. "Augustine, I imagine, approved of this hypothesis simply because it provided him with the opportunity of some subtle argument in his discussion."[14] Calvin preferred the solution offered by Origen, that Paul had two names.[15] But it is important to note that the reformer did not proceed past his consideration of the first word of the letter to the Romans without recourse to the tradition.

Calvin continued his consideration of the Christian orthodox theologians alongside scripture at Romans 1.31. He noted that "[s]ince Paul holds that want of mercy is a proof of the depravity of human nature, Augustine, in arguing against the Stoics, concludes that mercy is a Christian virtue."[16] He explicated Romans 6.5 through a consideration of Chrysostom's solution, though Calvin went further.[17] In Romans 10.2, Calvin used both Augustine and Lactantius to argue for the necessity of following the Word of God.[18] It is significant that, in his first commentary on scripture, Calvin set out a pattern of commenting that demanded a consideration of the orthodox tradition, as well as a dividing between the correct tradition and the fallacious. Certainly, at times the reformer criticized points from the exegetical tradition, and sarcastically ridiculed those whose opinions he felt were unworthy. But that practice was an effort to serve the orthodox interpretive tradition. Calvin's exegetical practice regularly included the setting out of the exegetical traditions of the church, which were either to be accepted or critiqued. He believed that the important terms in a given passage had a history shaped by the church's struggle with that text – a struggle revealed in the interpretations of the fathers and later commentators. Though Calvin wrote disparagingly of "traditions" even within the commentaries, he

---

[14] Calvin, Romans Comm. 13. See also Calvin, Ad Romanos, 11. (Ending the quotation with that portion of the translation that fits the 1540 edition, without the later expansion.) That Augustine was pleased with this idea, was so that he could seize the occasion for clever philosophizing. "Quod Augustino placuisse hoc tantum nomine puto, ut argute philosophandi occasionem arriperet."

[15] Romans Comm. 13. Ad Romanos 11. "Probabilior Origenis sententia, qui binomiun fuisse indicat."

[16] Romans Comm. 38. Ad Romanos 36. "Quia misericordiae defectum inter signa depravatae humanae naturae ponit: hinc colligit Augustinus adversus Stoicos, misericordiam esse virtutem Christianam."

[17] Romans Comm. 124. Ad Romanos 123.

[18] Romans Comm. 221. Ad Romanos 222.

was consciously in conversation with a living historical discourse on the meaning of the scriptural text.

II CORINTHIANS COMMENTARY

Calvin published his commentary on II Corinthians in 1547 in French and a year later in Latin. This commentary is the only one of the Pauline commentaries in which the French version preceded the Latin, and historians suspect that the unique publication history is related to the history of the manuscript.[19] Calvin had established a relationship with Wendelin Rihel in Strasbourg, who had printed Calvin's first two commentaries, Romans and I Corinthians, but in 1541 Calvin had moved back to Geneva. It is likely that he maintained the printing relationship both out of bonds of friendship and obligation.[20] Rihel's press was not significant, and he did not have all the type that Calvin might have liked.[21] In any case, in July 1546, Calvin sent his only copy of the manuscript to Rihel in Strasbourg. After a month had passed without word from Strasbourg, Calvin began to worry that the manuscript had been lost.[22] The Genevan pastor was beside himself. In the middle of September, Calvin learned that Rihel had received it but did not rush it to press. Jean-François Gilmont argues that the temporary loss of the manuscript for the II Corinthians commentary and subsequent delay were only part of the reason for Calvin shifting his publications from Rihel to Jean Gerard in Geneva. Gilmont claimed that the reason for Calvin taking the manuscript back was the Schmalkaldic War that impeded the Strasbourg booksellers' freedom of movement.[23] In January 1547 Jean Gerard of Geneva printed a French version, with a Latin edition coming from the same printer in 1548.

This was the third commentary Calvin completed, as he began his commenting with the Pauline epistles. In this commentary, the Genevan reformer frequently made recourse to the exegetical and orthodox doctrinal traditions.[24] He regularly considered the options of the

---

[19] See Andrew Pettegree, "Calvin and Luther as Men of the Book," in *Calvin and the Book: The Evolution of the Printed Word in Reformed Protestantism*, edited by Karen E. Spierling (Göttingen: Vandenhoeck & Ruprecht, 2015), 17ff.

[20] Jean-François Gilmont, *John Calvin and the Printed Book*, translated by Karin Maag (Kirksville, MO: Truman State University Press, 2005), 182.

[21] Ward Holder, "Calvin as Commentator on the Pauline Epistles," 228–30.

[22] Pettegree, "Calvin and Luther as Men of the Book," 16.

[23] Gilmont, *John Calvin and the Printed Book*, 182.

[24] David C. Steinmetz has devoted much of his work to the analysis of Calvin's interpretation of scripture in its proper historical focus. See especially his *Calvin in Context*.

patristic exegetes. Calvin's favorites from the patristic tradition are readily available in the II Corinthians commentary. Considerations of John Chrysostom's exegesis far outstrip those of Augustine. While Calvin considered Chrysostom the greater biblical interpreter, his favorite doctrinal source among the fathers of the church was easily Augustine. But in his commentary on II Corinthians, Chrysostom is considered in four times as many passages as Augustine, a ratio that is quite rare in Calvin's commentaries.[25]

Calvin did not unequivocally accept the received tradition and could attack the exegetical tradition harshly. A particular case can be seen in his consideration of Origen's interpretation of II Corinthians 3.6, "the letter kills, but the Spirit gives life." Calvin wrote:

This passage has been distorted and wrongly interpreted first by Origen and then by others, and they have given rise to the most disastrous error that Scripture is not only useless but actually harmful unless it is allegorized. This error has been the source of many evils. Not only did it open the way for the corruption of the natural meaning of Scripture but also set up boldness in allegorizing as the chief exegetical virtue. Thus many of the ancients without any restraint played all sorts of games with the sacred Word of God, as if they were tossing a ball to and fro.[26]

This is the Calvin that the traditional historiography leads the reader to expect. Incensed by the license to allegorize, and the ideal of moving further and further away from the plain sense of scripture (*germanum Scripturae sensum*), the Genevan prepared himself to throw off the shackles of the human tradition and prepare for the clear light of God's word. However, a close examination of the commentary finds a very different Calvin, one who frequently used the interpretations of the fathers

---

[25] See A. N. S. Lane, "Calvin's Use of the Fathers and the Medievals," in *John Calvin: Student of the Church Fathers* (Grand Rapids, MI: Baker Book House, 1999), 54–57, where he demonstrates that Augustine is cited far more than Chrysostom in the 1559 *Institutes*.

[26] John Calvin, *The Second Epistle of Paul the Apostle to the Corinthians*, translated by T. A. Smail, in Calvin's New Testament Commentaries, edited by David W. and Thomas F. Torrance, vol. 10 (Edinburgh: Oliver and Boyd Ltd., 1960), 45, commenting on II Cor. 3.7. Hereafter cited as II Corinthians Comm. with page number. See also Helmut Feld, ed., *Ioannis Calvini Commentarii in Secundam Pauli Epistolam ad Corinthios* (Geneva: Librairie Droz, 1994), 58. Hereafter cited as Secundam ad Corinthios with page number. "Hic locus ab Origene primum, deinde ab aliis perperam detortus fuit in adulterinum sensus. Unde sequutus est valde perniciosus error, quod putarunt Scripturae lectionem non vanam modo., sed noxiam quoque fore, nisi ad allegorias traheretur. Hic error fons fuit multorum malorum. Neque enim modo permissa fuit licentia germanum Scripturae sensum adulterandi, sed quo quisque audacior fuit in eo genere, eo excellentior havitus fuit Scripturae interpres. Ita impune luserunt multi ex veteribus sacro Dei verbo non secus ac pila versatili."

and regularly cited them with approval. Even when not considering them affirmatively, though, Calvin frequently used their example as a model from which to build his own interpretation.

One significant set of cases involves Calvin's use of the tradition to open up his own closely linked interpretation of the text. Readers see this at II Corinthians 2.11. Calvin uses Chrysostom's interpretation to move toward his own, which was fairly close. He wrote: "For one of Satan's worst tricks is to deprive us of all consolation and then swallow us up in an abyss of despair. This is how Chrysostom interprets the passage. I prefer to relate it to Paul and the Corinthians."[27] Chrysostom saw this as a universal message; Calvin related it to the Corinthian experience. But that marks only a small difference, since Calvin regularly linked the lessons for the Corinthians to his own audience.

A similar example comes from II Corinthians 4.2. In interpreting "the secret things of shame," Calvin noted that Chrysostom believed Paul meant the vain show through which his opponents were arrogantly setting themselves up. He used that position to move to his own, a reference to all the pretenses by which Paul's opponents might defile the purity of the gospel.[28] In point of fact, neither interpretation is as simple as saying that Paul had put away shameful things so as to be more able to preach the gospel message.

Another significant set of examples can help demonstrate the variety of Calvin's engagements with the tradition. The passage on II Corinthians 11.1 provides an excellent model for Calvin's practice of using the patristic model to open a pathway toward his own slightly different interpretation. Calvin wrote:

I have taken "bear with me" to be an imperative whereas Chrysostom makes it an affirmative statement, for the Greek word is ambiguous and either rendering will suit well enough. But since the reasons that he adds are designed to induce

---

[27] II Corinthians Comm. 31. Secundam ad Corinthios, 41. "Est enim illa pessima Satanae circumventio, quum escussa omni consolatione, quasi desperationis abysso, nos absorbet; atque ita exponit Chrysostomus. Ego tamen ad Paulum et Conthios referre malo."

[28] II Corinthians Comm. 51–52. "By 'the hidden things' or 'the secrets of shame' some understand the shadows of the Mosaic law and Chrysostom takes this to mean the vain show in which his opponents were vaunting themselves. My own view is that the expression refers to all the pretenses by which they were adulterating the pure and innate comeliness of the Gospel." Secundam ad Corinthios, 68. "Per latebras dedecoris vel occultamenta nonnulli umbras Legis Mosaicae intelligunt, Chrysostomus ostentationem, qua se venditabant. Ego fucos omnes intelligo, quibus adulterabant puram et nativam Euangelii pulchritudinem."

the Corinthians to bear with him and later he will again take them to task for conceding him nothing, I have followed the Vulgate.[29]

This is not to say that Calvin never used the prior exegetical tradition in a negative fashion. He did this frequently. Sometimes, it was to correct a common direction in the traditional comment upon the scripture. More often, however, Calvin's negation of an answer from the tradition served as a framework within which to offer his own answers to interpretive questions. A pertinent example comes at v. 13 of the first chapter of II Corinthians. Calvin points out the translation difficulty of Ἀναγινώσκειν (to read, to recognize), and ἐπιγινώσκειν (to discover, to acknowledge). He supplies the Latin verb *agnoscere*, and references Bude's *Commentarii Linguae Graecae*, saying that Budaeus had noted this.[30] Calvin then notes that Ambrose had translated the Greek in an unsuitable manner, thereby opening the door for Calvin's translation that clarified the text.[31]

---

[29] II Corinthians Comm. 139. Secundam ad Corinthios, 173. "Ubi reddidi «sufferte», in modo imperativo, Chrysostomus affirmative exponit. Et certe Graeca vox est anceps, et sensu uterque satis congruit. Verum quoniam rationes, quas subiicit, huc tendunt, no molestum sit Corinthiis eum sufferre, et iterum postea cum illis expostulabit, quod sibi nihil concedant, sequutus sum Veterem interpretem."

[30] Secundam ad Corinthios, 23, n.46.

[31] II Corinthians Comm. 17. "Ἀναγινώσκειν in Greek means sometimes 'to read' and sometimes 'to recognize' and ἐπιγινώσκειν means sometimes 'to discover' and sometimes the same as the Latin verb agnoscere, 'to acknowledge' e.g. in the legal phrase 'to acknowledge a child', as Budaeus has also noted. Thus ἐπιγινώσκειν is stronger than ἀναγινώσκειν. A person may 'recognize' something, that is, be privately convinced of it in his own mind, and yet not 'acknowledge' it, that is, give open expression to his acceptance of it. We may now examining Paul's words. Some render them, 'We write nothing but what you read and acknowledge', but that is very dull and quite unsuitable. Ambrose changes it to read, 'You do not only read but also acknowledge', but that is clearly an impossible translation of the words. The interpretation I offer is plain and natural and the only difficulty in understanding it us the confusion caused by the different meanings of the words. In short, I take Paul's meaning to be that the Corinthians already know and can indeed bear witness to all that he is saying. The first word is *recognoscere*, which means to be convinced of a thing by experience, and the second is *agnoscere* which means to give open assent to the truth." Secundam ad Corinthios, 23. "ἀναγινώσκειν Graicis nunc 'legere', nunc 'recognoscere' significat, ἐπιγινώσκειν nunc 'cognoscere', nunc quod Latini proprie dicunt 'agnoscere', sicut apud iurisconsultos: 'agnoscere partum'. Quot etiam Budaeus annotavit. Hoc modo ἐπιγινώσκειν plus est quam ἀναγινώσκειν. Recognoscit enim, hoc est: tacito animi sensu convictus verum esse intelligit, qui tamen non agnoscit, hoc est: suo consensus libenter comprobat. Nunc expendamus verba Pauli. Alii legunt: 'Non alia scribimus, quoam quae legitis et agnoscitis.' Quod palam est esse nimis frigidum, ne dicam ineptum. Nam quod Ambrosius ita mitigate: 'Non modo legitis, sed etiam agnoscitis' nemo est qui non videat a verbis esse omnino alienum. Sensus autem, quem affero, planus est ac sponte fluit. Neque alia ratio hactenus impedivit lectores, quominum ipsum perciperent, quam

Another example in this set, which seems negative until fully examined, appears in Calvin's comment upon II Corinthians 5.3.[32] Here, Calvin considered the question of whether this was a repetition or two distinct moments of God clothing believers. Calvin notes that Chrysostom and others had suggested that this was a rhetorical repetition and used that to argue instead that the first clothing was the sanctification of the Spirit while the second, after death, referred to the saints' being clothed with immortality and glory.[33]

Finally, Calvin frequently used the exegetical tradition as a source-book with which to agree and from which to create his own interpretations. A good example comes from II Corinthians 11.20.[34] Calvin often privileged the contextual meaning, but in this case he overruled it. He wrote:

There are three possible meanings here. He might be ironically reproaching the Corinthians, because they could bear nothing on account of their delicacy; he might be charging them with negligence that they surrendered themselves to such a shameless servitude to the false apostles; or he might be referring, as if he were another person, to charges made against him without any justification, as if he had usurped a right of tyrannical domination over them. The second sense has the support of Chrysostom, Ambrose and Augustine and is commonly accepted. This one does suit the context best. However, to me the third interpretation is just as good. Indeed we see how time and again he was slandered by the evil, as though he were a domineering tyrant—which he certainly was not. As the other meaning is more received, however, I have no objection that it should be accepted.[35]

---

quod diversa verbi significatione decepti clausos oculos habuerunt. Summa est, quod Paulus alia se in medium proferre negat, quam quae nota sint et comperta Coninthiis, imo de quibus reddituri sibi sint testimonium. Prius est 'recognoscere', quum rem ita habere experiential convicti sunt. Secundum est 'agnoscere', quum veritati subscribunt." Calvin incorrectly accepts Ambrose as the author, when it is Ambrosiaster.

[32] "if so being that being clothed again we shall not be found naked."

[33] II Corinthians Comm. 67. Secundam ad Corinthios, 88–89.

[34] I have covered some of this material in my earlier work, *John Calvin and the Grounding of Interpretation: Calvin's First Commentaries* (Leiden: Brill, 2006), chap. 3.

[35] II Corinthians Comm, 148–49. Secundam ad Corinthios 184–85. "Triplex potest esse sensus: vel quod ironice Corinthios perstringat, quia nihil ferre queant, ut solent delicati; vel quod socordiae eos insimulet, quod pseudoapostolis se in pudendam servitutem addixissent; vel quod referat quasi in aliena persona, quod odiose de ipso praedicabatur, acsi tyrannicum imperium sibi adversus eos usurparet. Secundus sensus Chrysostomo, Ambrosio, Augustino placet, adeoque communiter receptus est. Equidem optime congruit contextui. Quanquam mihi tertius non minus arridet. Videmus enim, ut passim a malevolis traductus fuerit, quasi impotenter dominaretur. A quo tamen longissime aberat. Sed quoniam alter ille est receptior, non repugno, quin valeat."

Calvin presented a powerful counterexample to his own preference. In Chrysostom, Ambrose, and Augustine, he was dealing with three of his favorite theologians whose orthodoxy was unimpeachable. Further, the Genevan interpreter noted that the fathers' interpretation fit the context best – a canon of humanistic exegesis that he rarely neglected. Calvin recognized the weight of their testimony and allowed that his favored meaning could be declined in favor of theirs.

Calvin's comment on II Corinthians 4.6 provides another example. Calvin offered four interpretations. He offered his own opinion in concurrence with Chrysostom, which is the fourth, but also commended Ambrose's different solution, and allowed the readers to use their own judgment.[36] Calvin posed a number of options, noted those approved by the patristic authorities, and allowed readers to use their own judgment. Certainly, Calvin wished his reader to follow his interpretation. However, the very placing of the other options within the commentary, as well as the fact that they are not denigrated, left the field of appropriate

---

[36] II Corinthians Comm. 57, Secundam ad Corinthios 74–75. "I see that it is possible to explain this passage in four different ways. First, God has commanded light to shine from the darkness, that is, by the ministry of humans who according to their nature are darkness, he has brought the light of his gospel to the world. Second, God in the place of the Law which was obscured in shadows, has caused the light of the Gospel, so has brought light out of darkness. Those who like clever arguments could easily accept such explanations. However, anyone who inspects this thing more closely will know that these do not express the Apostle's meaning. The third follows, which is that of Ambrose. When all was covered in darkness, God kindled the light of his Gospel. Humans were sunk in the darkness of ignorance when suddenly God shone forth to them by his Gospel. The fourth explanation is Chrysostom's, who thinks that Paul makes an allusion here to the creation of the world, in this way. God, who by His Word created light, as if out of darkness, has now spiritually illuminated us when we were buried in darkness. This analogy (*anagoge*) between light that is visible and corporeal and light that is spiritual has more grace and there is nothing forced in it. The preceding interpretation is not badly put. Everyone may use his own judgment." "Video hunc locum quadrifariam posse exponi. Primo sic: Deus iussit lucem e tenebris splendescere, id est hominum ministerio, qui suapte natura tenebrae sunt, lucem Euangelii sui mundo protulit. Secundo sic: Deus in locum Legis, quae obscuris umbris erat involuta, fecit Euangelii lucem succedere, atque ita e tenebris lucem eduxit. Qui argutias amant, facile istas expositiones admitterent. Sed qui propius rem inspexerit, agnoscet non congruere menti Apostoli. Sequitur tertia, quae est Ambrosii: Quum omnia tenebris operta essent, Deus lumen Euangelii sui accendit. Demersi enim erant homines in ignorantiae tenebris, quum illis subito Deus per Euangelium affulsit. Quarta est Chrsysostomi, qui putat allusisse Paulum ad mundi creationem, hoc modo: Deus, qui verbo suo lucem creavit quasi ex tenebris erutam, idem nunc spiritualiter nos illuminavit, quum essemus in tenebris sepulti. Haec anagoge lucis visibilis et corporeae ad spiritualem plus habet gratiae et in ea nihil est coactum. Proxima tamen non male quadrat. Fruatur quisque suo iudicio."

interpretations very much open. Further, Calvin did not rhetorically stress his desire for his position, only writing against one of the options.

Calvin noted patristic authorities as frequently as he could. In the text itself, he noted Ambrose (whom he frequently confused with Ambrosiaster), Augustine, Chrysostom, Origen, Basil, Hilary, and Cyprian. The only early modern author who received regular mention was Erasmus. But as previously noted, it is not enough simply to count citations. Calvin betrayed himself as depending upon an extra-scriptural standard. Interpreting II Corinthians 1.20, Calvin used the standard of a "fuller teaching" (sensum pleniorem), to argue for a particular reading between two variant Greek textual possibilities. After choosing the "Quare et per ipsum sit amen" (Wherefore also through Him is the amen), reading he preferred, he offered his reasoning.[37]

I confess that the other reading is more usually chosen. However, it is flat, and I have no doubt in preferring that which contains fuller teaching and is more aptly suited to the context. For Paul is admonishing the Corinthians of their duty that to respond with their amen after they have been taught in the simple truth of God.[38]

This was not a unique case. In II Corinthians 4.4, he asserted that "[t]here is some doubt whether 'the gospel of the glory of Christ' stands for 'the glory of the gospel,' according to the Hebrew idiom, or rather 'the Gospel in which Christ's glory shines.' This second reading, because it is fuller, is preferable."[39] "Fuller" is a standard that looks to an extrinsic sense of the meaning that should be in the text. Calvin was arguing that those significations that fit the orthodox thought of the church should be preferred. But such a standard was always colored by the tradition.

---

[37] II Corinthians Comm. 22, Secundam ad Corinthios 30–31. "**Wherefore also through Him is the amen.** Here the Greek manuscripts are not in agreement. Some have them joined together in one, 'All the promises of God that exist are through him and through him amen to the glory of God through us.' The other reading, which I have followed, is more expedient and contains a fuller meaning." "*Quare et per ipsum sit amen.* Hic etiam Graeca exemplaria non consentiunt. Quaedam enim habent uno contextu: 'Quotquot sunt Dei promissiones, per ipsum sunt etiam, et per ipsum amen, Dei ad gloriam per nos'. Verum diversa lectio, quam sequutus sum, magis est expedita et sensum pleniorem continet."

[38] II Corinthians Comm. 22–23, Secundam ad Corinthios 31. "Diversa lectio fateor magis est usitata. Sed quia frigida est, hanc praeferre non dubitavi, quae pleniorem doctrinam continet; deinde ad contextum longe est aptior. Officii enim Corinthios admonet Paulus, ut suum amen respondeant, postquam in simplici Dei veritate fuerunt edocti."

[39] II Corinthians Comm. 55, Secundum ad Corinthios 73. "Dubium est, an Euangelium gloriae Christi posuerit pro glorioso Euangelio, secundum phrasin Hebraicam, an vero pro Euangelio, in quo lucebat Christi gloria. Hoc secundum, quia est plenius, magis amplector."

GENESIS COMMENTARY

In 1554, Calvin first published his commentary on Genesis; he would publish a revised version of it with the *Harmony on the Last Four Books of Moses* in 1563.[40] Calvin attempted to present the Hebrew *veritas*, arguing that ignorance of the Hebrew language had led other interpreters astray. This was the case in his interpretation of the genealogy in Genesis 46.8. He noted that the number provided in Acts 7.14 differed from that in Genesis, and explained this difference by arguing that the scribes who were responsible for copying the scriptures were ignorant of Hebrew.[41] Calvin's own facility with Hebrew was far from exemplary, but better than the great majority of Christian interpreters of the Old Testament in his era.[42]

Calvin's Hebrew did allow him to consult several aids to reading and interpreting the text of Genesis. Anthony Lane and H. F. van Rooy have traced the sources that Calvin used.[43] Lane argues that the time pressures

---

[40] Randall C. Zachman, "Calvin as Commentator on Genesis," in *Calvin and the Bible*, edited by Donald McKim (Cambridge: Cambridge University Press, 2006), 1–29.

[41] John Calvin, *Genesis*, translated by John King (Carlisle, Pennsylvania: Banner of Truth Trust, 1847, 1965), 391. Hereafter cited as Genesis Comm. with page numbers. "But that the error is to be imputed to the transcribers, is hence apparent, that with the Greek interpreters, it has crept only into one passage, while, elsewhere, they agree with the Hebrew reckoning. And it was easy when numerals were signified by marks, for one passage to be corrupted. I suspect also that this happened from the following cause, that those who had to deal with the Scripture were generally ignorant of the Hebrew language; so that conceiving the passage in the Acts to be vitiated, they rashly changed the true number." Calvini Opera, vol. 23, columns 13–622. Hereafter cited as CO with column numbers. CO 23.562 "Quod autem imputandus sit error librariis, inde constat, quia apud graecos interpretes tantum in unum locum obrepsit: alibi autem cum hebraica supputatione conveniunt. Facile autem fuit, ubi notis signantur numeri, corrumpi locum unum. Hinc etiam factum fuisse suspicor, quia hebraicae linguae fere ignari erant qui tractabant, scripturam, ut locum in actis vitiatum esse putantes, perperam verum numerum mutarint."

[42] See Max Engammare, "Joannes Calvinus Trium Linguarum Peritus? La Question de L'Hebreu." *Bibliothèque d'Humanisme et Renaissance* 58 (1996): 35–60. Engammare writes, "Quant á l'hébreu biblique, il est indéniable que Calvin le connaissait relativement bien. La majorité des traductions données au début d'un sermon sont tout á fait fideles. Le lendemain d'un jour oú un texte a été mal traduits, la traduction est même excellente. Je ne peux pas chasser de moi le soupçon que, Calvin se rendant compte des difficultés qu'il avaitt rencontrées, son humilité et son intelligence, bref sa conscience professionnelle le poussaient á mieux se préparer, pendant quelques jours."

[43] A. N. S. Lane, "Did Calvin Use Lippoman's *Catena in Genesim*?" in *John Calvin: Student of the Church Fathers* (Grand Rapids, MI: Baker Book House, 1999), 191–204, and "The Sources of the Citations in Calvin's Genesis Commentary," in *John Calvin: Student of the Church Fathers* (Grand Rapids, MI: Baker Book House, 1999), 205–38. See also H. F. van Rooy, "Calvin's Genesis Commentary – Which Bible Text Did He Use?": in *Our Reformational Tradition. A Rich Heritage and Lasting Vocation*, edited by B. J. van der Walt (Potchefstroom: Potchefstroom University for Higher Education, 1984), 203–16.

upon Calvin as he prepared the Genesis lectures were significant, and that he would have had relatively few aids directly to hand.[44] While Calvin endeavored to make use of the best tools available to him for the interpretation of the Hebrew scriptures, he was not an innovator. David Steinmetz has analyzed Calvin's engagement with the exegetical tradition, finding that he frequently was bound by the exegetical choices and issues that came directly from the tradition.[45] Further, Calvin's work on the Genesis commentary, came during a period of extraordinary productivity, the work could not be the product of measured leisure.[46] Several studies have given the picture of a scholar without leisure, who sought to lecture for the good of the church, rather than because he had time to prepare.[47] All of these factors coalesced when Calvin approached Genesis.

Calvin considered Moses to be the author, inspired by the Holy Spirit, of the entire Pentateuch. However, he rejected a literal and simplistic view of the scripture's meaning, and recognized moments when Moses was writing in an accommodated manner.[48] Calvin argued that Genesis was written to inform humanity of five connected points. These were that humanity was placed in the world God created to adore their creator and enjoy his works. Second, all creation was made for humanity, so that humans would be grateful to their generous creator. Third, humans were created to contemplate higher things, especially eternal life, as they had been created in God's image. Fourth, humanity fell into sin in Adam, losing all the gifts given to Adam and earning eternal death. Fifth and finally, God promises humanity its restoration in Christ and preserves the church by God's providential care so that there will always be a community of faith on earth that worships God.[49] Calvin considered Genesis to have been written to edify believers.[50]

In Calvin's interpretation of Genesis, we see many of the same patterns familiar from II Corinthians. Calvin did shift from opening a chapter with a few verses on which he would comment, to opening the chapter

[44] Lane, "The Sources of the Citations in Calvin's Genesis Commentary," 233–34.

[45] David C. Steinmetz, "Calvin as an Interpreter of Genesis," in *Calvin as Protector of the Purer Religion*, edited by Wilhelm Neuser and Brian Armstrong (Kirksville, MO: Sixteenth Century Journal Publishers, 1997), 53–66, compares Calvin's, Luther's, and Denis the Carthusian's interpretation of Genesis 32.24–32.

[46] Zachman points out the enormous production Calvin was maintaining in the early 1550s. See Zachman, 1–2.

[47] As noted, Lane makes this point explicitly, and Zachman does implicitly. See also Max Engammare, *On Time, Punctuality and Discipline in Early Modern Calvinism*, translated by Karin Maag (Cambridge: Cambridge University Press, 2009), chaps. 1–2.

[48] Zachman, 6. On accommodation in Calvin, see n. 54.

[49] Zachman, 11.

[50] Zachman, 21. Holder, *Calvin's First Commentaries*, 81ff., and passim.

with a translation of the entire chapter into Latin. But otherwise, the philological and contextual manner of interpretation was similar to his earlier interpretive works. He continued to engage the orthodox exegetical tradition in order to open up his own closely related interpretations of the text. Calvin overwhelmingly turned to Augustine, Jerome, and the Vulgate to decipher the meaning of Genesis. In considering chapter 1.26, God's statement to "make humanity in our image and likeness," Calvin noted that there were many interpreters who differentiated between image and likeness. He then turned to Augustine, calling on him by name:

But Augustine, beyond all others, speculates with excessive refinement, for the purpose of fabricating a Trinity in man. For in laying hold of the three faculties of the soul enumerated by Aristotle, the intellect, the memory, and the will, he afterwards out of one Trinity derives many. If any reader, having leisure, wishes to enjoy such speculations, let him read the tenth and fourteenth books on the Trinity, also the eleventh book of the "City of God." I acknowledge, indeed, that there is something in man which refers to the Father, and the Son, and the Spirit: and I have no difficulty in admitting the above distinction of the faculties of the soul: although the simpler division into two parts, which is more used in Scripture, is better adapted to the sound doctrine of piety; but a definition of the image of God ought to rest on a firmer basis than such subtleties. As for myself, before I define the image of God, I would deny that it differs from his likeness.[51]

Calvin used Augustine's consideration of the social analogy of the Trinity to open up his own discussion of the faculties of the soul, how these were suggested in the image and likeness of God. In so doing, he also demonstrated a knowledge of the theological tradition – and directed his readers to *On the Trinity* and *The City of God*. This was more than an endorsement, almost an exhortation to tradition for Calvin's readers.[52] But after that commendation of the doctrinal tradition, Calvin returned to his own position, that image and likeness mean the same thing.

Another example of this tendency occurs in his discussion of the size of the ark of Noah in 6.14. Some critics had suggested that the

---

[51] Genesis Comm. 93. CO 23. "Caeterum Augustinus prae aliis nimium argute philosophatur, ut trinitatem in homine fabricet. Nam quum tres animae facultates recenseantur ab Aristotele, intellectus, memoria, voluntas: illud arripiens, ex una trinitate multas postea derivat. Eiusmodi speculationibus si quis otiosus lector oblectare se velit, legat librum 10. de Trinit, et 14. item de Civit. Dei libro 11. Fateor quidem esse in homine aliquid quod Patrem, et Filium, et Spiritum referat: illam quoque facultatum animae distinctionem non aegre admitto: etsi brevior partitio, nempe bimembris, quae scripturae magis usitata est, ad solidam pietatis doctrinam aptior est: sed definitio imaginis Dei plus habere firmitatis debet quam in talibus argutiis. Ego priusquam imaginem Dei definiam, a similitudine differre nego."

[52] I thank Nathan Antiel for bringing this aspect to my attention.

measurements given suggested too small a boat for the animals of the world. Calvin wrote:

For, formerly, certain profane men ridiculed Moses, as having imagined that so vast a multitude of animals was shut up in so small a space ... Origen solves this question, by saying that a geometrical cubit was referred to by Moses, which is six times greater than the common one; to whose opinion Augustine assents in his fifteenth book on the 'City of God,' and his first book of 'Questions on Genesis.' ... But what was then the measure of the cubit I know not; it is, however, enough for me, that God (whom, without controversy, I acknowledge to be the chief builder of the ark) well knew what things the place which he described to his servant was capable of holding.[53]

Calvin noted that the difficulties that Origen and Augustine were addressing were real. This was not a case of patristic authorities being overly clever or reasoning sophistically. However, Calvin believed that Moses himself regularly accommodated his speech in the Pentateuch.[54]

---

[53] Genesis Comm. 256–57. CO 23.123. "Nam olim profani quidam homines suis sannis Mosen vexarunt, quod tam angusto spatio ingentem animalium turbam inclusam finxisset; cuius pars tertia vix quatuor elephantos caperet. Hanc obiectionem solvit Origenes, cubitum geometricum a Mose notari dicens, qui sextuplo maior est quam vulgaris: in cuius sententiam descendit Augustinus libro de Civitate Dei 15 et lib. 1. Quaestionum in Genesin. Fateor equidem quod obtendunt, Mosen qui edoctus fuerat in omni scientia Aegyptiorum, non fuisse geometriae expertem : ... geometrica subtilitate usum esse. Certe capite primo non disseruit argute de astris, ut philosophum decebat, sed populariter ex rudium adspectu potius quam ex re ipsa, solem et lunam duo luminaria magna vocavit. Ita ubique perspicere licet, usitatis nominibus res omnis generis fuisse ab eo designatas. Caeterum quis tunc fuerit cubiti modus ignoro : quia mihi sufficit non latuisse Deum (quem sine controversia primarium arcae fabrum agnosco) quarum rerum capax esset locus quem servo suo descripsit."

[54] There is a large literature on accommodation in Calvin. In 1952, Edward Dowey spent a chapter discussing it, Dowey, *The Knowledge of God in Calvin's Theology*. 3rd ed. (Grand Rapids, MI: Wm. B. Eerdmans, 1994), 3–7. Only two years earlier, François Wendel noted the use, but did not discuss accommodation as an independent issue; *Calvin: Origins and Development of His Religious Thought*, translated by Philip Mairet, (Durham, NC: Labyrinth Press, 1987, originally published 1950), 229–30. By 1962, H. Jackson Forstman was terming accommodation as "perhaps [his] most widely used exegetical tool." *Word and Spirit*: Calvin's Doctrine of Biblical Authority, (Stanford, CA: Stanford University Press, 1962), 13. The most widely cited study of Calvin's use of accommodation in English is that of Ford Lewis Battles, "God Was Accommodating Himself to Human Capacity," *Interpretation* 31 (1977): 19–38. Olivier Millet has weighed in by dedicating a section of his magisterial volume, *Calvin et la dynamique de la parole: Etude de Rhétorique réformée* (Geneva: H. Champion, 1992), 247–56, where he concludes that for Calvin, the accommodation of God is an omnipresent phenomenon, without which special revelation is not able to be understood. Stephen Benin has considered the history of accommodation in Jewish and Christian thought in *The Footprints of God: Divine Accommodation in Jewish and Christian Thought*,

His style would remain simple, unlike the erudition of highly specialized geometry. That left Calvin with the problem of how the ark could have been big enough to hold the necessary cargo, which he solved with a turn to God's power. These are only two examples of many.[55]

Calvin also gave important context to his own consideration of the interpretive task through his use of the patristic sources. One of his favorite sources for contextual considerations in the Genesis commentary was the Vulgate. This was the case in Genesis 2.23. Calvin noted that in translating אשה, the Latin was problematic. He wrote, "A deficiency in the Latin language has compelled the ancient interpreter (the Vulgate) to render אשה (ishah) by the word virago. It is, however, to be remarked, that the Hebrew term means nothing else that the female of the man."[56] Calvin gave a reason for his separation from the most common and widely read translation of the last thousand years, the Vulgate, and in doing so blunted any criticism for innovating for the sake of newness. Another example came from Genesis 3.11, where God chastizes Adam for his disobedience. Calvin noted that Vulgate translation had introduced a question into the form of God's examination of Adam. "What the Vulgate translates, 'Unless it be that thou has eaten of the tree,' is rather an interrogation. God asks, in the language of doubt, not as if he were searching into some disputable matter, but for the purpose of piercing more acutely the stupid man."[57] Calvin used the Vulgate's wording

---

(Albany, NY: SUNY Press, 1993). Vincent Bru's "La notion d'accommodation divine chez Calvin: Ses implications theologiques et exegetiques." *La Revue Reformee* 49 (1998): 79–91, considers the various ways in which accommodation is essential to the relationship between God and humanity. Finally, David F. Wright has considered accommodation in Calvin in several articles. See his "Calvin's Pentateuchal Criticism: Equity, Hardness of Heart, and Divine Accommodation in the Mosaic Harmony Commentary." *Calvin Theological Journal* 21 (1986): 33–50; "Accommodation and Barbarity in John Calvin's Old Testament Commentaries." *Understanding Prophets and Poets: Essays in Honor of George Wishart Anderson*, 413–27, edited by A. Graeme Auld, (Sheffield: Journal for the Study of the Old Testament Press, 1993); and most recently in his "Calvin's Accommodating God." *Calvinus Sincerioris Religionis Vindex*, edited by Wilhelm Neuser and Brian Armstrong, (Kirksville, MO: Sixteenth Century Journal Publishers, 1997), 3–20. Finally, in 2006, my *John Calvin and the Grounding of Interpretation: Calvin's First Commentaries* (Leiden: Brill, 2006), included a section, 45–50.

55 Further good examples could be found at Genesis 3.6 and 17.12.

56 Genesis Comm. 135. CO 23.50 "Latini sermonis inopia coegit interpretem reddere אשה viraginem. Notandum tamen est, hebraicam vocem nihil aliud sonare quam feminam viri."

57 Genesis Comm. 163. CO 23.67 "Ubi vulgaris translatio habet: Nisi quod de arbore, potius interrogatio est. Dubitanter autem inquirit Deus, non quasi de re ambigua, sed quo stupidum hominem acrius pungat,"

to enter into a personification of the deity to see the logic in the divine actions. This is a common occurrence for Calvin's use of the Vulgate.[58]

Of course, there are also some devastating critiques of voices from the tradition. Origen was a favorite whipping boy for Calvin, who linked him inextricably to the drive for allegorizing which he stated was characteristic of all medieval biblical interpretation. Thus, it is no surprise to see Calvin lambaste Origen in his comment on Genesis 2.8: "We must, however, entirely reject the allegories of Origen, and of others like him, which Satan, with the deepest subtlety, has endeavoured to introduce into the Church, for the purpose of rendering the doctrine of Scripture ambiguous and destitute of all certainty and firmness."[59] For Calvin, this departure from the plain sense of scripture had been a key fault in the medieval church. He could be just as harsh in relation to other patristic sources. In commenting on Genesis 2.18, Calvin attacked Jerome for his stance against marriage.[60] In interpreting Genesis 21.8, Calvin criticized Augustine for his too-subtle reasoning about the timing of Abraham's feast; this was a frequent theme in Calvin's estimation of the North African bishop.[61] Calvin's otherwise generous assessment of Augustine did not extend to his sense of the meaning of scripture's words – far too frequently, he saw him departing from sound interpretations with flights of fancy.

For all his criticism of the orthodox exegetical tradition, Calvin could and did give frequent praise. He used the tradition not only to open

[58] Other examples come at Genesis 2.24, 3.3, 8.6, and 8.21. It is an interesting point that Calvin in the Genesis commentary is far more likely to be positive or contextual when he uses the terms for the Vulgate – such as "Vulgate," or "ancient interpreter," – than when he names Jerome by name.

[59] Genesis Comm. 114. CO 23.37 "Allegoriae autem Origenis et similium prorsus repudiandae sunt: quas pessima astutia in ecclesiam invehere conatus est Satan, ut ambigua esset scripturae doctrina, nec quidquam certi vel firmi haberet."

[60] Genesis Comm. 128–29. "Not only have heathen writers defined that to be a happy life which is passed without a wife, but the first book of Jerome, against Jovinian, is stuffed with petulant reproaches, by which he attempts to render hallowed wedlock both hateful and infamous. To these wicked suggestions of Satan let the faithful learn to oppose this declaration of God, by which he ordains the conjugal life for man, not to his destruction, but to his salvation." CO 23.46 "Nec solum profani homines definierunt beatam esse vitam procul uxore degere: sed prior Hieronymi liber contra Iovinianum, petulantibus conviciis refertus est, quibus exosum conatur et infame reddere sanctum coniugium. His pravis Satanae suggestionibus opponere discant fideles hanc Dei sententiam, qua hominem coniugali vitae, non in eius exitium, sed in salutem destinat."

[61] Genesis Comm. 541. "The subtle reasoning of Augustine, that the day of Isaac's weaning was celebrated, in order that we may learn from his example, no more to be children in understanding, is too constrained." CO 23.299. "Quod argute philosophatur Augustinus, celebrari diem ablactationis Isaac, ut discamus eius exemplo non amplius esse pueri sensu, nimis coactum est."

interpretive space for his own solutions that were different, but also as solutions in their own right. The tradition helped form his own thought, and the fathers were presented frequently as authorities to be accepted. Such was the case in Calvin's comment upon Genesis 23.2, Abraham's weeping over Sarah when she died. Calvin questioned whether Abraham had wept too much. But then he wrote, "And yet, what Moses soon after subjoins, that he rose up from his dead, is spoken in praise of his moderation; whence Ambrose prudently infers, that we are taught by this example, how perversely they act, who occupy themselves too much in mourning for the dead."[62] Calvin agreed with the bishop of Milan, and used that agreement to attack, if somewhat obliquely, the cult of the saints and Roman liturgical practices that surrounded death.

Calvin used Genesis 13.1, the authority of Augustine, and the story of Abraham's departure from Egypt with all his wealth, to denounce those who believe that wealth removed any hope of salvation. The Genevan reformer wrote:

Yet many fanatics repel rich men from the hope of salvation; as if poverty were the only gate of heaven; which yet, sometimes, involves men in more hindrances than riches. But Augustine wisely teaches us, that the rich and poor are collected together in the same inheritance of life; because poor Lazarus was received into the bosom of rich Abraham. On the other hand, we must beware of the opposite evil; lest riches should cast a stumbling-block in our way, or should so burden us, that we should the less readily advance towards the kingdom of heaven.[63]

This is a fascinating passage for the many twists and turns it displays in Calvin's interpretation. First, Calvin used Augustine to wield the New Testament, and the parable of the rich man and Lazarus from Luke 16.19–31 to interpret the passage from Genesis. This is not surprising, as both Augustine and Calvin held to a model of the unity of the scriptures. What is surprising is the parable's message itself – the passage is normally taken as a condemnation of wealth. In fact, Luke has Abraham, who is comforting Lazarus, deliver the denunciation of the rich man, who had

---

[62] Genesis Comm. 578. CO 23.322. "Et tamen quod paulo post subiicit Moses, eum surrexisse a mortuo suo, ad laudem moderationis pertinet: idque Ambrosius prudenter expendit, hoc exemplo nos doceri, perverse eos facere, qui se in mortuis lugendis nimium occupant."

[63] Genesis Comm. 368. CO 23.189. "Multi tamen phanatici, divites procul repellunt a spe salutis: ac si sola paupertas coelorum esset ianua: quae tamen pluribus impedimentis interdum homines involvit quam divitiae. Scite autem Augustinus qui divites pauperibus aggregari admonet a Deo in eandem vitae haereditatem: quia Lazarus pauper in sinum divitis Abrahae receptus fuerit. Rursus cavendum est ab altero vitio, ne scilicet remoram iniiciant divitiae, vel nos aggravent quominus expediti pergamus in regnum coelorum."

already received his good things. But Calvin, through Augustine and the exegetical tradition, transformed that message and turns away from the rich man to concentrate upon the manner in which wealthy Abraham and poor Lazarus enjoyed heaven together.

A particularly strong example of Calvin's building on the tradition comes in his comment on Genesis 3.6. He rhetorically posed the question of how soon the fall followed the act of creation. Calvin noted that there was not sufficient material available in the scriptures to merit a firm answer, but that it seemed from Moses' narration of the story that the time period between creation and fall was short. Calvin wrote:

If Adam had lived but a moderate space of time with his wife, the blessing of God would not have been unfruitful in the production of offspring; but Moses intimates that they were deprived of God's benefits before they had become accustomed to use them. I therefore readily subscribe to the exclamation of Augustine, "O wretched free-will, which, while yet entire, had so little stability!" And, to say no more respecting the shortness of the time, the admonition of Bernard is worthy of remembrance: "Since we read that a fall so dreadful took place in Paradise, what shall we do on the dunghill?"[64]

Here is an example of Calvin's turning aside from the question at hand to consider separate topics raised by the entire passage. In examining Adam's fall, Calvin cannot help critiquing the doctrine of free-will, and he turns to his favorite source, Augustine. But he builds directly on that Augustinian foundation with another favorite, Bernard of Clairvaux. Bernard's point was not on the topic of the freedom of the will, but the difficulty of living the Christian life in the present fallen circumstances. So Calvin achieved both a doctrinal and a moral teaching through appeals to his favorite vein of the tradition.

Calvin continued many of his interpretive habits, both theoretical and instrumental, in his lectures on Genesis. Among those were a deep conversation with the tradition, and a choice to accept its conclusions far more often than not. Even when Calvin seemed to be rejecting the tradition, he repeatedly called upon the patristic source to allow for his own closely related interpretive preference. Certainly, Calvin could and did attack Origen for the practice of allegory. But the simplicity and lack of specificity with which he did so suggests that Calvin had not read

---

[64] Genesis Comm. 156–57. CO 23.63. "Facile igitur Augustini exclamationi subscribo; O miserum liberum arbitrium, quod adhuc incolume tam parum habuit firmitatis. Atque ut taceamus de brevitate temporis, illa Bernardi admonitio memoratu digna est: Quum tam horribile praecipitium in paradiso accidisse legamus, quid nos facturi sumus in sterquilinio?"

deeply in medieval uses of the quadriga, and that this was a set piece of polemic that would arise at opportune moments. Far more frequent were his laudatory comments about Augustine, as well as the Vulgate. Calvin's rhetoric nourished a fruitful engagement with the church's tradition.

LECTURES ON DANIEL

Calvin published his lectures on Daniel in 1561. These lectures were far from a commentary, they were transcriptions of Calvin's lectures that he gave between June of 1559 and April of 1560.[65] These lectures were quite different from a commentary. Jean Budé, one of Calvin's students, noted that he and others who heard Calvin's lectures felt that it would be a great loss if only the relatively few in the audience would ever hear Calvin's interpretation. So he endeavored, along with other students, to record the lectures. The transcriptions were collated and taken to Calvin, who reviewed them, and then they were printed.[66] The printer, Jean Crespin, included a preface that gave a detailed description of this manner of arriving at the final text.[67] In fact, the title page of the first edition of the Lectures on Daniel bore the inscription acknowledging the labors of Jean Budé and Charles Jonvillier.[68] So in the lectures, rather than a commentary written in the quiet of one's study, we have lecture notes, prepared by others, rather than Calvin himself.

In Wilcox's reconstruction of Calvin's lecture habits, depending upon Budé and Nicolas Colladon, Calvin would only approach the audience with a copy of the Hebrew scripture, and no further notes. He began with a reading of the Hebrew, then translated it into Latin. He then worked through the text in an expository fashion. Budé himself noted that Calvin's style was bare and simple, accommodated to the needs of his hearers.[69] Calvin himself noted his own uncertainty about the value of publishing his lectures. He wrote, "If I can hardly succeed in being slightly useful to the Church by compositions well worked over, how foolish I should be to claim a place for my spoken words among my published works."[70] Calvin recognized the very different characters of

---

[65] Wilcox, "Calvin as Commentator on the Prophets," in *Calvin and the Bible*, edited by Donald McKim (Cambridge: Cambridge University Press, 2006), 111.

[66] Wilcox, 108–09.

[67] Quoted in Wilcox, 109; CO 42.189–190, "Ioannes Crispinus Christianis Lectoribus."

[68] Wilcox, 109.

[69] Quoted in Wilcox, 115.

[70] Translated in Wilcox, 117; CO 42.183–184.

the lectures and the commentaries, and that difference should be basic to one's consideration of them.

Given the circumstances of the creation of the Daniel lectures, one could expect that Calvin would include no engagement with the ortho-dox exegetical and doctrinal traditions. Armed with a copy of the Hebrew and Aramaic of Daniel, having no prepared notes, and facing a large audience, many of whom were being equipped for the ministry in France, the reformer might have been prudent to avoid discussions of tradition.[71] But instead, he maintained his normal model of reference to the tradition. We see this in Daniel 4.1–3. Calvin wrote, "Hence, without doubt, King Nebuchadnezzar bore witness to his repentance when he celebrated the God of Israel among all people, and when he proclaimed a punishment to all who spoke reproachfully against God. Hence this passage is often cited by Augustine against the Donatists."[72] At first, this seems like a very slight tip of the cap to the tradition, Calvin noted that Augustine cited this passage in a struggle for him. However, even though Calvin's turn to Augustine seemed perfunctory, the depth of his consideration of the Donatists was not. Calvin accused them of granting themselves impu-nity while disturbing the church, and then turning to a doctrine of tol-eration.[73] The Donatists sought only license under the cover of religious toleration after they committed their crimes. Calvin stressed, "With the view then of vomiting forth their poison, they strive eagerly for freedom from punishment, and deny the right of inflicting punishment on heretics and blasphemers."[74] Calvin used Augustine to move quickly from the crimes of the Donatists into the fusion of the powers of the state and the church that characterized the medieval and early modern European

---

[71] Wilcox notes that a letter written by Beaulieu to Guillaume Farel in 1561 contains an estimate of over 1,000 listeners in the audience for Calvin's lectures. Wilcox, 114; CO 19.10.

[72] John Calvin, *Commentaries on the Book of the Prophet Daniel*, translated by Thomas Myers, originally printed for the Calvin Translation Society in two volumes (Grand Rapids, MI: Baker Book House, 1979), vol. 1.245. Hereafter cited as Daniel Comm., with volume and page numbers. Calvini Opera volume 40, columns 517–722 and vol-ume 41, columns 1–304. Hereafter cited as CO, with volume and column number. CO 40.649. "Ergo hoc extra controversiam est, testatum fuisse regem Nebuchadnezer suam poenitentiam quum celebravit deum Israelis apud omnes populos: deinde quum poenam proposuit omnibus qui contumeliose loquerentur adversus Deum. Ideo saepe hic locus citatur ab Augustino contra Donatistas.

[73] Daniel Comm. 1.245–246; CO 40.649–650.

[74] Daniel Comm. 1.246. CO 40.649. "Ut ergo liceat ipsis evomere virus suum, tantopere litigant pro impunitate, et negant poenas de haereticis et blasphemis sumendas esse."

church.[75] Instead of praising the breakaway church of the Donatists for their claim of religious toleration, Calvin instead found a clear support in Daniel for the cooperation of ecclesiastical and political powers.[76]

This was a significant moment in French political theology. Calvin's lectures on Daniel stretched from the June of 1559 to April of 1560. In November of 1559, Calvin wrote to the "brethren of France," counseling them to a patient confidence in God's providence.[77] The French king, Henry II, had died of the complications from a jousting accident on 10 July 1559. Calvin probably hoped that Henry's son, Francis II, would adopt a religious policy that was more tolerant of French Reformed Christians, known as Huguenots. As Margolf notes, that was not what came to pass; instead, "Henry II's death catapulted France into an extended period of political, religious, and social upheaval that encompassed the second half of the sixteenth century."[78] Calvin, and the Huguenots whom he inspired, were suspected by French Catholics who made up the majority of the French population of rebellion against both secular and religious authority.[79] Calvin, by rejecting the Donatist call for toleration for heterodox religious believers, was aligning his theology and that of his followers with the dominant political theology of the early modern period. That doctrine taught that it was the duty of the prince of a realm to provide for the maintenance of the true religion. That care extended to the extermination of heretics, who were viewed as a cancer on the body politic, which was coequal with the corpus Christianorum. Calvin demonstrated that his concerns were not with the Donatists of the fourth and fifth centuries, but modern political realities, when he linked their efforts to those of Sebastian Castellio.[80] He wrote, "Such is that dog Castellio and his companions, and all like him, such also were the Donatists; and hence, as I have mentioned, Augustine cites this testimony

---

[75] The classic treatment is R.I. Moore, *The Formation of a Persecuting Society: Authority and Deviance in Western Europe, 950-1250* (Cambridge: Cambridge University Press, 1987).

[76] See David M. Whitford, "Robbing Paul to Pay Peter: The Reception of Paul in Sixteenth Century Political Theology," in R. Ward Holder, ed., *A Companion to Paul in the Reformation* (Leiden: Brill, 2009), 573–606.

[77] Quoted in Diane C. Margolf, "The French Wars of Religion," in *John Calvin in Context*, edited by R. Ward Holder (Cambridge: Cambridge University Press, 2019), 50.

[78] Margolf, 50.

[79] Margolf, 51–53.

[80] Sebastian Castellio (1515–1563), was a teacher who sought to be appointed as a preacher in Geneva. When being examined, he questioned the canonical status of the Song of Songs. That and his differences with other pastors on the interpretation of scripture prevented his appointment. He took umbrage at Calvin, and would later write two treatises against the persecution of heretics, using Calvin as his chief example of religion gone wrong.

in many places and shows how ashamed Christian princes ought to be of their slothfulness, if they are indulgent to heretics and blasphemers, and do not vindicate God's glory by lawful punishments."[81] Calvin's assertion adopted the dominant tradition of the close alignment of the prince's power with the church's interests, and rejected any hint of heterodox or heretical pleas for toleration. By linking the Donatists to his enemy Castellio, Calvin strengthened his rhetorical adoption of orthodoxy.

Calvin's next significant consideration of the orthodox tradition appears at Daniel 7.13, where the vision presents one who is "like the son of man."[82] Calvin wrote that this could not mean anyone but Christ.[83] But then the question arose, why did Daniel write "like" the son of man? The reformer noted that such a construction could be twisted into the heresy of the Manichees, who did not accept the existence of Christ's human body. He blamed the Manichees for twisting Paul's use of the kenotic hymn in the epistle to the Colossians, even though that was not the apostle's intent. But for Daniel, Calvin's solution was that the prophet wrote this way because Christ had not yet, in the course of history, taken his humanity.[84] For support for his position, Calvin turned to both Irenaeus and Tertullian. Irenaeus wrote that Christ's appearance in Daniel was a "prelude." Tertullian stated that the Son of God put on a "specimen of his humanity."[85] Faced with a biblical passage that seemed to open the door to a heretical interpretation, Calvin turned to orthodox fathers of impeccable authority.

Calvin turned again to Augustine in his discussion of Daniel 9.20. Calvin's point in the explication of the verse was that Daniel had confessed his own sin and that of the people of Israel.[86] The reformer's goal

---

[81] Daniel Comm. 1.246. CO 40.649–650. "Talis est canis ille Castalio, eiusque sodales, et si qui sunt alibi similes: tales etiam tunc fuerunt Donatistae. Et ideo, quemadmodum iam attigi, Augustinus pluribus locis citat hoc testimonium: et ostendit pudendam esse ignaviam christianis principibus, si indulgeant haereticis et blasphemis, et non asserant legitimis poenis Dei gloriam."

[82] The *New Revised Standard Version* renders this as "one like a human being," which does not present the issues Calvin sought to explicate, but preserves the traditional translation in the footnotes.

[83] Daniel Comm. 2.40–41. CO 41.60. "Dixi non posse aliter sumi hunc locum, quam de Christo."

[84] G. Sujin Pak notes that Calvin "believed that careful attention to the prophets' histories enabled the present-day church to better perceive God's will and gain the godly wisdom of teachers." See her *The Reformation of Prophecy: Early Modern Interpretations of the Prophet & Old Testament Prophecy* (Oxford: Oxford University Press, 2018).

[85] Daniel Comm. 2.41. CO 41.60. "quemadmodum etiam Irenaeus dicit hoc fuisse praeludium: utitur verbo illo. Tertulianus etiam dicit, Tunc praelusit filius Dei humanitati suae."

[86] Daniel 9.20.

in doing so was to illustrate the point that even the holiest of humans have sinned and fallen short of God's glory and keeping God's law. Calvin then enlisted Augustine, writing, "Hence Augustine with much wisdom often cites this passage against the followers of Pelagius and Coelestius."[87] Augustine's orthodoxy was beyond question, so Calvin's turn to him fortified Calvin's own orthodoxy.

In Calvin's turn to Augustine, the French Reformer took a passage about Daniel's prayer during which the angel Gabriel came and delivered to him wisdom and understanding, and made it about the sinfulness of all humans, even the most pure. That provided the interpretive room for Calvin to arrive at his point that human righteousness is found through the confession of sins so that God might make the sinners pure.[88] This explanatory model turns to the New Testament, when Christ directs his followers to petition the Lord to "forgive us our debts."[89] Both the children of Israel and the later believers in Christ should see their greatest chance at righteousness in confessing their own sinfulness, and depending upon the Lord for righteousness. This was a hallmark of evangelical theology, both Lutheran and Reformed, and Calvin's ability to see it in Daniel strengthened both his claims about justification and his dependence on Augustine.

These are not all the passages that consider the fathers and the way they considered the way to interpret the scriptures.[90] But they give a strong sense of how Calvin, even faced with lecturing on the Bible without notes, with scant time to prepare, and with other calls upon his time and energy, continued to engage the orthodox exegetical and doctrinal traditions for his consideration of the Bible. It is clear that the lecture format caused Calvin to diminish the instances of his engagement with the fathers and medievals. But it is just as clear that he continued to frame his interpretations within the structure of historic orthodoxy.

CONCLUSION: CALVIN, EXEGESIS, AND TRADITION

Calvin's commentaries on scripture, far from presenting the "pure scripture alone," present a lively conversation with the exegetical and doctrinal traditions of the early and sometimes even the medieval church.

---

[87] Daniel Comm. 2.189. CO 41.163. "Ideo Augustinus prudenter hunc locum toties citat contra Pelagianos, et contra Coelestinos."

[88] Daniel Comm. 2.190. CO 41.163.

[89] Matthew 6.12; Luke 11.4.

[90] Other examples would include Calvin's explication of Daniel 9:24–25, and Daniel 11.37.

Calvin used the tradition to help him determine the correct questions to answer in his interpretations. He sought to engage the voices of the patristic authorities, to make room for his own thought, to craft his own interpretive answers, and to provide authority and the imprimatur of orthodoxy to his interpretations.

This is not to say that Calvin always turned to the orthodox tradition, or that he always agreed with it. His attacks on Origen make clear that the practice of allegorization had hurt the church's message. He regularly took Augustine to task for his too-philosophical considerations. In rare instances, he produced works that barely took up the orthodox tradition by name, such as his Joshua commentary of 1564. Far more common would be the example of Genesis, which had a large number of explicit considerations to the patristic sources and an even greater number of sources Calvin did not explicitly mention. When Calvin had time to sit down in his study to prepare lectures or commentaries, the various books and collections of the orthodox tradition were never far from his elbow.

Calvin not only used the orthodox theological tradition, but also did so frequently, and across the breadth of his biblical interpretive works. In both commentaries and lectures, he took up the theological tradition both to frame his arguments and as an appropriate battlefield on which to attack his opponents. His use of the exegetical and doctrinal traditions to explicate the scriptures suggests that he believed that using it was a basic part of the interpreter's task. Calvin's efforts at interpretation sought to define the historical context of a passage, and his consideration of the orthodox tradition was basic to that endeavor.[91]

Of course Calvin did not always turn to the tradition. At times, his works could avoid the material entirely. Such is the case with the commentary on Joshua, published in the last year of Calvin's life.[92] Calvin made no explicit references to sources from the tradition in that work. Arguments can be made for the reasons that he did so. Perhaps the strain of ill health and the attempt to deliver one last work to the printer during his life made him make uncharacteristic choices. Perhaps Calvin was confined to his bed and did not have his usual access to other works – though this is unlikely, as many studies have pointed out that Calvin frequently quoted from memory. What does stand out is how infrequently Calvin

---

[91] G. Sujin Pak notes Calvin's historicizing tendencies in her *The Judaizing Calvin: Sixteenth-Century Debates over the Messianic Psalms* (Oxford: Oxford University Press, 2010).

[92] Calvin, Commentary on Joshua, CO 25.417–570.

produced works that did not engage the orthodox theological tradition in a variety of manners.

While Calvin occasionally avoided explicit reference to the tradition, in general, he turned to the orthodox theological traditions systematically in his various writings. He did this for a number of reasons – to add authority to his arguments, to deprive his polemical foes of the imprimatur of a patristic source or of the general patristic witness, to have theological conversation partners, to work out the intricacies of his own positions on particular doctrines, and to demonstrate the evangelical or Genevan location within the historic Christian faith.

Calvin utilized a variety of techniques in engaging the orthodox theological traditions. First, and easiest to demonstrate, Calvin frequently cited or made allusion to the patristic tradition. Second, and still easy to establish, were Calvin's considerations of the decisions of the church. These instances were also frequent. Further, when agreeing with the historical patterns of the church's discipline that were not easily supported by scripture, Calvin rarely if ever saw the need to proffer a reason for his choice. This could be calling an opponent by the name of an ancient heresy that had been anathematized by a council, or by working within frameworks that had become normalized through the church's history. Third, and far more difficult to establish, Calvin used the prior tradition as a guide to those questions that were important to answer in both commenting upon scripture and in considering piety and the Christian life. The work of the history of exegesis school has revealed conclusively that one of the significant questions in considering an exegete's work is to see what prior theologians he had read. This is broader than the practice of commenting upon scripture, and requires deep genealogical work on any theologian's corpus. Finally, Calvin tended to use the orthodox fathers as historians – sources to establish what practices had been common or noteworthy in their day. In this manner, he worked out a practice of creating a history of the church that rejected innovation for its own sake and, instead, maintained a fealty to the tradition that had been handed down through the centuries.

3

Calvin, Tradition, and Polemics

Across his career, John Calvin wrote in most of the popular religious styles.[1] He wrote sermons and treatises, commented and lectured on scripture, blasted away at his opponents, and wrote a summary guide to scripture and theology that he continually rearranged and expanded in its Latin form until 1559, when it reached its final version. I have argued in Chapter 2 that he used the tradition in a variety of manners in his exegetical works. But what about those polemical attacks on various opponents? Did Calvin maintain a notion of the usefulness and necessity for the use of the tradition across the various opponents he confronted? Certainly, it seems logical that Calvin would use more traditional material in his debates with Catholic authors than with those representatives of the Radical Reformation or Lutheran authors. So this section will consider representative samples from his polemics.[2]

Calvin wrote a number of treatises across his career. Sometimes these made a particular point of doctrine more clear for his readers. At other times, his treatises answered the attacks of critics or attacked those he believed violated the faith on a particular point of doctrine. It is a frequent practice in Calvin studies to attempt to differentiate between

---

[1] Francis Higman, "La Littérature Polémique Calviniste au XVIᶜ Siècle," in *Lire et Découvrir: La Circulation des Idées au Temps de la Réforme* (Geneva: Librairie Droz, 1998), 437–48.

[2] Amanda Eurich, "Polemic's Purpose," in *John Calvin in Context*, edited by R. Ward Holder (Cambridge: Cambridge University Press, 2019), 215–23. See also Francis Higman, "I Came Not to Send Peace, but a Sword," *Lire et Découvrir: La Circulation des Idées au Temps de la Réforme* (Geneva: Librairie Droz, 1998), 419–33.

polemical and doctrinal treatises – those where he did verbal battle and those where he sought to be a teacher. But a close examination of his treatises reveals that this is an effort at finding a clear point of distinction within a continuum. Calvin was not a systematic theologian in the sense of working out his theological system from a particular doctrine or metaphysical framework. However, he was an ordered theologian, who sought to find the best order of teaching so as to reach his students. Calvin never wrote a polemical work that did not also teach, and his efforts at communicating the evangelical religion included frequent attacks on those whom he believed failed to reach the standard to which he thought God was calling.

Across his career, Calvin responded to challenges from thinkers from a variety of confessional communities: Catholics, Lutherans, and even Radicals. It is important to note two points. First, Calvin's writings could serve dual purposes. By way of example, a treatise responding to Lutheran concerns on the Lord's Supper both explained his interpretations and critiqued those who disagreed. This was in many ways the continuation of a medieval practice of vernacular texts aimed at educating the laity or unskilled priests.[3] Second, we will see him use a variety of techniques in his engagement with the tradition, much as he did in his biblical interpretive work. It will be important to define more clearly whether Calvin's use of tradition was aimed at a particular confessional group. Were that to prove to be the case, one might then be drawn toward the thesis that Calvin's use of tradition was motivated in great part or even wholly by polemical concerns and had little to do with the formation of his own thought, to say nothing of the construction of his doctrines. But we will see that this was not the case. Instead, there was a surprising stability in Calvin's turn toward tradition.

ANABAPTISTS

Very early in his theological career, Calvin came to see Radical Reform as enormously problematic for the cause of evangelical religion or, as he termed it, true religion. The young French scholar began to write his

---

[3] See Francis Higman, "The Reformation and the French Language," in *Lire et Découvrir: La Circulation des Idées au Temps de la Réforme* (Geneva: Librairie Droz, 1998), 337–52; and Higman, "Theology for the Layman in the French Reformation, 1520–1550," in *Lire et Découvrir*, 87–106.

Psychopannychia in 1534, though it would not be published until 1542.[4] This early stage of the production of the work preceded the publication of Calvin's first edition of the *Institutes of the Christian Religion* in 1536. The extent of Calvin's early grasp of Anabaptism or Radical Reform is difficult for the historian to determine. The attempt to define the Anabaptist movement doctrinally and ecclesiologically despite his relative lack of substantive knowledge of the radical religion at the time of the composition of *Psychopannychia* and the first edition of the *Institutes* served his effort at proffering an apologetic to Christian governments suspicious of the larger reform movements. The Anabaptists or radicals offer a significant analytical opportunity because Calvin still used the orthodox tradition, even though many of the Radical Reformers were likely to make claims about the priority of scripture over the church's belief – especially when some believed that the church had gone desperately astray.

Psychopannychia – 1534, 1542

Calvin's *Psychopannychia* was drafted in its original form in 1534.[5] This work was written against the doctrine of the sleep of the soul, a belief that some Radicals may have held.[6] Calvin argued they believed in the

---

[4] *Psychopannychia* is still not well studied. Among the few works are Hans Scholl, "Karl Barth as Interpreter of Calvin's Psychopannychia," in *Calvinus Sincerioris Religionis Vindex: Calvin as Protector of the Purer Religion*, edited by Wilhelm H. Neuser and Brian G. Armstrong (Kirksville: Sixteenth Century Essays and Studies, 1997), 291–308; and Timothy George, "Calvin's *Psychopannychia*: Another Look," in *In Honor of John Calvin, 1509–1564*, edited by E. J. Furcha (Montreal: McGill University Press, 1987), 297–329; George W. Tavard, *The Starting Point of Calvin's Theology* (Grand Rapids: Eerdmans, 2000); Brian C. Brewer, "'Those Satanic Anabaptists': Calvin, Soul Sleep, and the Search for an Anabaptist Nemesis" in *Calvin and the Early Reformation*, edited by Brian C. Brewer and David M. Whitford (Leiden: Brill, 2020), 125–54.

[5] Wulfert de Greef, *The Writings of John Calvin: An Introductory Guide*, expanded edition, translated by Lyle D. Bierma (Louisville: Westminster John Knox Press, 2008), 151–52.

[6] Ford Lewis Battles suggested that the choice of taking on the topic of the sleep of the soul was motivated by an apologetic issue of demonstrating that the evangelicals did not hold this heretical belief, that he asserted was more broadly believed in France than in other realms touched by the evangelical reforms. Battles, "Introduction," in *Institutes of the Christian Religion, 1536 Edition* (Grand Rapids: Eerdmans, 1975), xli. Brian Brewer has argued that Calvin simply did not understand Anabaptist belief and was unintentionally arguing against a straw man. See his "'Those Satanic Anabaptists': Calvin, Soul Sleep, and the Search for an Anabaptist Nemesis," in *Calvin and the Early Reformation*, edited by Brian C. Brewer and David M. Whitford (Leiden: Brill, 2020), 125–54.

sleep of the soul between death and the final resurrection at the end of time. Calvin had sent the manuscript to Wolfgang Capito in Strasbourg, early enough for Capito to advise against immediate publication. Capito's main concern was that Calvin should gain a deeper knowledge of scripture on this doctrine.[7] Bucer was also at first opposed to publication, but later changed his mind. The effect of this unique writing and publication history of *Psychopannychia* is that Calvin wrote the treatise in 1534 and revised it in the early 1540s when it was published.[8] As such, it represents one of his earliest theological offerings, but one that is unclear as to its editing history.[9]

Catholics and Evangelicals agreed on very little in the 1520s and 1530s, but one uniting belief was that radical religion was too dangerous to the *corpus Christianorum* to permit its existence. When Catholic voices argued that all evangelical believers, whether Lutheran, Zwinglian, or English, were in fact allied with Radical Reform, they hit on a politically and militarily important stratagem.

Thus, Calvin's responses to radical religion gave an early and urgent set of reactions to this set of confessions. Though Calvin probably did not have significant knowledge of radical religion until he lived in Strasbourg in the late 1530s, he sought to define the doctrine of the sleep of the soul doctrinally and ecclesiologically. His work at defending the true religion and his efforts to demonstrate that evangelical magisterial religion was not radical or Anabaptist, and his effort to establish that Anabaptism was not a true form of the Christian religion were all important aspects of his efforts to write apologetically to Christian governments.

Calvin noted that this idea of the sleep of the soul was ancient, citing Eusebius' *Ecclesiastical Histories* and Augustine's *Book of Heresies*.[10] He further pointed out that this had not remained in the distant past, but had

---

[7] CO 10.45–46. The letter from Capito to Calvin is undated, but the editors of the CO assign it to an early time, and certainly Calvin did not publish the *Psychopannychia* until much later.

[8] See de Greef, *The Writings of John Calvin*, 151–52. De Greef also noted that Capito believed that the confused situation of the church in the early 1530s called for more evangelical preaching.

[9] Tavard, *The Starting Point of Calvin's Theology* (Grand Rapids: Eerdmans, 2000).

[10] John Calvin, "Psychopannychia: Or a Refutation of the Error Entertained by some Unskillful Persons Who Ignorantly Imagine that in the Interval Between Death and the Judgment the Soul Sleeps," in *Selected Works of John Calvin: Tracts and Letters* vol. 3, edited by Henry Beveridge and Jules Bonnet, translated by Beveridge (Grand Rapids: Baker Book House, 1983), 413–90. Hereafter cited as Psychopannychia (415). CO 5.171.

rankled the theology faculty of the University of Paris.[11] He wrote against "the nefarious herd of Anabaptists," because of their "noxious stream," and provided a typology for their error.[12] First, the Anabaptists achieved some knowledge of Christian commonplaces; but, wishing to seem wise, they defended their fantasies. At some point, they turned to scripture in order to find support for their errors. However, they perverted, adulterated, and corrupted what they found to distort it to their own view.[13] This was a crucial logical and rhetorical move for Calvin. He denied that the scriptures were self-interpreting. This was wholly compatible with the concerns he would come to express in the various prefaces to the *Institutes*, the preface to his commentary on Romans, and the preface to the unfinished edition of Chrysostom. Without guidance, readers would at best wander to and fro within the forest of the scriptures. At worst they would twist scripture's meaning out of context.[14] This helps to explain Calvin's frequent recourse to the patristic witnesses and the use of his appeal to their authority. Eusebius, Ambrose, Augustine, Hilary, Basil, Chrysostom, Tertullian, and others help Calvin to delineate the correct understanding of scripture from the failure of the Anabaptists.

The argument depended upon the interpretation of scripture, and that only made sense given the audience against whom the treatise was written. Some of the Radical Reformers had repudiated a number of orthodox teachings, claiming to be led only by scripture.[15] Throughout the treatise, Calvin attacked the Anabaptists on the basis of their failure to understand the scripture and repeated his recourse to scripture again and

---

[11] Psychopannychia, 415, Jean Gerson (1363–1429), is Calvin's source. CO 5.172. "Et aliquanto post tempore, Ioannem episcopum romanum, quem schola parisiensis ad palinodiam adegerit."

[12] The full title in 1542 was "Vivere apud Christum non dormire animis sanctos, qui in fide Christi decedunt. Assertio." See CO 5.165–232. The common term "Psychopannychia" was a part of the title in the second printing, in Strasbourg in 1545: "Psychopannychia qua refellitur quorundam imperitorum error qui animas post mortem usque ad ultimum iudicium dormire putant. Libellus ante septem annos compositus nunc tamen primem in lucem aeditus." For a consideration of the text, see George H. Tavard's *The Starting Point of Calvin's Theology* (Grand Rapids: Eerdmans, 2000). Psychopannychia, 416. CO 5.173–74.

[13] Psychopannychia, 417. CO 5.174–75.

[14] See R. Ward Holder, *John Calvin and the Grounding of Interpretation: Calvin's First Commentaries* (Leiden: Brill, 2006), esp. 3–9.

[15] Though it would not attain a broad consensus at this time, an example can be found in the Schleitheim Brotherly Union, or Schleitheim Confession of 1527. The seven articles make frequent reference to the scriptures, but never cite the patristic or medieval tradition.

again. He noted that humans were made in the image of God, which was repeatedly set forth in scripture.[16] He answered the testimony of apocryphal writers with evidence from the canonical scriptures.[17] Even so, Calvin did not avoid coming to grips with the patristic witness. While at times he criticized the orthodox writers for their mistakes, he was unwilling to surrender their influence to the Anabaptist cause. This was clearly the case when he denied his opponents' interpretation of Augustine's consideration of the rich man and Lazarus in *Genesi ad Literam*.[18] Interestingly, he frequently considered agreement with the trajectory of the orthodox fathers as the test for the orthodoxy of his own interpretations. While Calvin absolutely held for the authority of scripture in this early effort, he would not surrender the authority of tradition to his opponents and preserved its weight for the orthodox Evangelicals he sought to protect and defend.

The *Psychopannychia* focuses on a dense theological topic – answering the question of what happens to souls between the death of the body on earth and the resurrection of the body on the day of final judgment. The problem had troubled theologians for centuries, and Calvin apparently knew that Pope John XXII had maintained and taught a heretical belief on the topic that he had been forced to recant.[19] This seems to be exactly the type of tract wherein one would expect to find a dense thicket of patristic sources. But such is not the case. In all, Calvin cites the fathers by name nineteen times in the treatise, which takes up sixty-one columns in the *Calvini Opera*. This number does not include Calvin's suggestion that his opponents are Apollinarians, and counts as a single instance an example when Calvin explicitly cites Ambrose, Gregory, Tertullian, Irenaeus, Origen, Cyprian, and Jerome together as supporters of his position.[20] Perhaps Calvin used comparatively fewer patristic references in the work because it was a treatise against Anabaptists. As Anabaptists did not place a high value on sources outside the scriptures, it would make sense that his arguments rested on biblical passages.[21]

---

[16] Psychopannychia, 423. CO 5.180.
[17] Psychopannychia, 425. CO 5.182.
[18] Psychopannychia, 431. CO 5.187.
[19] CO 5.171–72.
[20] CO 5.187.
[21] Psychopannychia, 414. He wrote that he had received some notes from a friend who had taken down their ideas, or accumulated in some way that he did not know. CO 5.170. "Tantum ab amico notulas quasdam accepi: quibus perscripserat quae vel ex ore loquentium excipere illi cursim licuerat, vel undecunque colligere."

Since counting references does not suffice, theological and historical analysis remains. There are several points known about *Psychopannychia* that are rarely drawn together. First, Calvin must have been writing this around 1534; he names Orleans in his dedication. Second, there were a number of pressing theological topics on which Calvin might have attacked the Anabaptists, such as their belief in the necessity of believer's baptism or their unwillingness to accept the rulings of the civil magistrate. Calvin could have especially turned to the issue of the rebellion of the Kingdom of Münster, which occurred throughout 1534 and the first half of 1535.

But instead, Calvin took on the sleep of the soul. This was an abstruse theological topic, never destined to become part of a pamphlet or broadsheet. Calvin defined the problem with Anabaptism as doctrinal, rather than an issue of discipline or piety. Framed in that manner, he accepted the orthodox belief that souls did not sleep between death and the final coming of Christ and argued accordingly. It was not as if the Anabaptist side of the case did not have biblical texts that gave warrant. Calvin noted several, especially Job 14.7–12 and I Corinthians 15.56. But he hardly gave any time or space to I Thessalonians 4.13–14, which stated, "But we do not want you to be uninformed, brothers and sisters, about those who have fallen asleep, so that you may not grieve as others do who have no hope. For since we believe that Jesus died and rose again, even so, through Jesus, God will bring with him those who have died." Calvin was certain this did not apply, but that certainty could only come through the orthodox framework he accepted.

At the end of Calvin's introduction to the treatise, he penned an attack on the theological methodological errors of the Anabaptists that would have made any Catholic polemicist proud. He wrote,

They are called, and would wish to be thought Christians, because they have got a slight knowledge of some commonplaces; and as they would be ashamed to be ignorant of anything, they with the greatest confidence, as if from a tripod, give forth decisions upon all things. Hence so many schisms, so many errors, so many stumbling blocks to our faith, through which the name and word of God are blasphemed among the ungodly. At length, (this is the head of the evil!) while they proceed obstinately to defend whatever they have once rashly babbled, they begin to consult the oracles of God, in order that they may there find support to their errors. Then, good God! what do they not pervert, what do they not adulterate and corrupt, that they may, I do not say bend, but distort it to their own view? As was truly said by the poet, "Fury supplies armour."

Is this the way of learning – to roll the Scriptures over and over, and twist them about in search of something that may minister to our lust, or to force them into subjection to our sense? Nothing can be more absurd than this, O pernicious pest![22]

Immediately taking oneself ignorantly to the scriptures was a recipe for disaster, Calvin wrote. This should not be surprising, as he would say this throughout his career.[23] Calvin demanded that doctrine be orthodox. He may have occasionally defined orthodoxy differently from his Catholic counterparts, but there can be little doubt that faced with a choice of true innovation and conservative reformulations of traditional teachings, Calvin would choose the latter.

Brief Instruction – 1544

Calvin's next treatise against the Anabaptists was his *Brief Instruction for Arming All the Good Faithful Against the Errors of the Common Sect of the Anabaptists*, published in 1544.[24] Calvin wrote the treatise in response to the request of his old friend Guillaume Farel. The treatise itself was dedicated to the ministers of Neuchâtel.[25] Farel sent Calvin a letter in early 1544 warning that the Anabaptists were becoming more active, and sending him a copy of the *Confessio Schlattensis* – a French translation of the Schleitheim Confession.[26] The work was largely that of

[22] Psychopannychia, 417–18. CO 5.174–75. "Christiani videri volunt, et dicuntur: quia aliquot capita locorum communium delibarunt. Et quum nescire aliquid pudeat, de omnibus confidentissime, quasi ex tripode, respondent. Hinc rursum tot schismata, tot errores, tot fidei nostrae scandala. Qua occasione nomen ac verbum Dei blasphematur inter impios. Tandem (quod est caput mali) dum obstinate tueri pergunt quod semel temere effutiverunt: tum oracula Dei consulunt, ex quibus errorum suorum patrocinia quaerant. Ibi, Deus bone, quid non invertunt? quid non depravant atque corrumpunt? ut ad sensum suum, non dico inflectant, sed vi incurvent. Scilicet vere dixit poeta, 'Furor arma ministrat.' Haeccine est discendi via? versare ac volutare scripturas, ut libidini nostrae serviant? ut sensui nostro subiiciantur? quo nihil est stolidius. O sonticam pestem."
[23] Holder, *John Calvin and the Grounding of Interpretation*, passim and especially Chapter 1.
[24] "Brieve instruction pour armer tous bons fideles contre les erreurs de la secte commune des Anabaptists," CO 7.49–142. It is available in a translation by Benjamin Wirt Farley, in *Treatises Against the Anabaptists and Against the Libertines* (Grand Rapids: Baker Book House, 1982), 11–158. Hereafter, Brief Instruction, with page number.
[25] De Greef, *The Writings of John Calvin*, 153.
[26] The Schleitheim Confession, or Schleitheim Brotherly Union, had been adopted by believers in adult baptism at a synod meeting in 1527. For German text, "Brüderlich Vereinigung etlicher Kinder Gottes, siben Artikel betreffend," in *Flugschriften aus den ersten Jahren der Reformation*, ed. Otto Clemen (Leipzig: Halle, 1907–11), vol. 2, part 3. It is widely seen as mainly the work of Michael Sattler, who was executed along with his wife soon after the synod accepted the confession. For more detail, see Williams, *The Radical Reformation*, 3rd ed. (Kirksville: Truman State University Press, 2000), 288–97.

Michael Sattler, who had been prior of the Benedictine monastery of St. Peter's near Freiburg.[27] Sattler had left the monastery and found a wife. He joined the Anabaptists in 1525, not long after the beginning of the movement with the baptism of Georg Blaurock in Zurich in January of that year. But the next two years were difficult for the fledgling movement, with the execution of Felix Manz in Zurich and the death of Conrad Grebel. The synod took place at Schleitheim, a small city in the Swiss canton of Schaffhausen, near the border of the Empire.[28]

The Schleitheim Confession took the form of seven articles, or core beliefs, of the Swiss Brethren. These were the rejection of infant baptism; employment of the ban (forced exclusion from the community for sinful behavior); breaking bread together but with no others; separation from the world; the right for the congregation to elect pastors when a shepherd should flee or die; rejection of the sword – or any use of military force; and rejection of oaths.[29] While it was not immediately accepted as the "confession" of the Anabaptists, it grew in popularity throughout the 1530s. In taking this on, Calvin avoided the question of whether radicals really believed what he charged – an open question for his *Psychopannychia*. Calvin considered and answered each of the seven articles, and then concluded with two further topics. The first was an examination of the incarnation and condemnation of the "celestial flesh" doctrine that had been popularized by Melchior Hofmann. The second was a summary of *Psychopannychia*'s attack on the sleep of the soul. Perhaps signaling Calvin's desire for a wider audience, the treatise was written in French.

Calvin began with a recognition that even in his own day the group he called Anabaptists were split. He believed that the first group accepted scripture as evangelicals did. These would have been the Swiss Brethren, those who followed Michael Sattler's teaching, or to follow Williams' typology, Evangelical Anabaptists. On the other hand, Calvin asserted that the other group was a labyrinth that did not accept the authority of the scriptures except when it suited them. These he termed the Libertines.

[27] *Brief Instruction*, 14.
[28] For background on the Schleitheim Confession, see George Huntston Williams, *The Radical Reformation*, 3rd ed. (Kirksville: Truman State University Press, 2000), 288–94. The "employment of the ban" was a disciplinary tactic. Should a member of the community refuse correction for some sin, he or she would be "banned," kept away from contact with the believers until the disciplinary amendment was made.
[29] See John Howard Yoder, *The Legacy of Michael Sattler* (Scottdale, PA: Herald Press, 1973), 34–43.

Calvin noted the methodology of the Anabaptists, who accepted the Bible in much the same way as the Evangelicals.[30] This differed, in his opinion, from the Libertines.[31] So Calvin explained that he would write a treatise against the Anabaptists and another against the Libertines. He pointed out that in his day, Anabaptism was not a clearly defined confession. But since they had created a summary of their doctrine in the Seven Articles (*sept articles*), Calvin would speak to them through that framework.[32] He set out the doctrinal method of the Anabaptists as biblical, though he believed that they seduced their audience through this pretext.[33]

Because of this doctrinal position of the Anabaptists, Calvin very rarely took up the tradition explicitly in the *Brief Instruction*. Instead, the treatise contains a set of biblical passages that are interpreted differently from the method of the Schleitheim Articles. Calvin did not provide a method by which readers could decide which interpretation was better, though he did note that this was important, because even the devil had armed himself with the words of scripture.[34] However, in many cases his interpretation of the scripture depended heavily and explicitly on the orthodox tradition. A good example comes from the article on baptism. The *Confessio Schlattensis* asserted: "Baptism ought to be given to those who have been instructed in repentance, who believe that their sins have been blotted out by Jesus Christ, and who want to walk in His resurrection. Consequently it ought to be administered to those who request it for themselves, not for

---

30 Actually, Calvin wrote, "as we do." Brief Instruction, 39. CO 7.53. "...comme nous."

31 Mirjam van Veen has written the most recent consideration of Calvin, the Anabaptists, and the Libertines. She notes that in both of his treatises, Calvin proceeded in a similar fashion. "Calvin's polemical treatises against the libertines and Anabaptists follow a regular pattern. The texts open with a description of the insignificance of Calvin's opponents. They continue with an outline and a refutation of the libertine, or Anabaptist, doctrines. The two polemics conclude with Calvin's declaration that he is right. The entire body of the text is marked by invectives, ranting against the silliness and moral worthlessness of the Anabaptists and libertines. On asserting that his opponents are not worthy of refutation, Calvin goes on to say that the sects have led many simple people astray. He explains that his main objective is to give readers information about the false doctrines of these sects and to arm them with the shield of the Holy Scriptures." (22) See Veen, "Supporters of the Devil: Calvin's Image of the Libertines," *Calvin Theological Journal* 40 (2005): 21–32.

32 Brief Instruction, 41. CO 7.54.

33 Brief Instruction, 42. "Now inasmuch as there is no fairer guise for seducing poor Christians, who are zealous to follow God, than to quote God's Word, the Anabaptists, against whom we are currently writing, always preface their remarks by this pretext." CO 7.55. "Or, pource qu'il n'y a nulle plus belle couleur, pour seduire les povres Chrestiens, qui ont zele de suyvre Dieu, que de pretendre sa parolle, les Anabaptistes, contre lesquelz nous escrivons maintenant, ont tousiours ceste preface en la bouche."

34 Brief Instruction, 42. CO 7.56.

infants, as is done in the pope's kingdom."[35] Calvin's refutation asserted that infant baptism was neither recent, nor were its origins traceable to the papal church. He argued: "For I say that it has always been a holy ordinance observed in the Christian church. There is no doctor, however ancient, who does not attest that it has always been observed since the time of the apostles."[36] Calvin's opening salvo in his polemic cannot stand without a consideration of the history of the church's sacramental practice, buttressed by the authority of the orthodox doctors.

Calvin was not on firm historical ground when he wrote this. His argument that this practice of infant baptism had "always" been practiced since the time of the apostles either disregarded or was ignorant of the sermons that took the form of exhortations to baptism for those who were delaying their baptisms until old age.[37] Augustine himself was not baptized as an infant, as the *Confessions* makes clear. Modern studies of the history of the practice of infant baptism place this practice sometime in the late second century, which could not be stretched to include the time of the apostles.[38] Here, though Calvin had set his method of depending upon scripture, he still turned to the orthodox tradition. Calvin could not successfully parry one of the thrusts of Schleitheim without relying on tradition. Such was not an isolated occurrence. In defying the Anabaptist practice of the ban, Calvin noted the Cathars and the Donatists. "These, whether of the first or second, held to the same fantasy as do the poor dreamers today, looking for a church in which one could find no fault. Therefore they separated themselves from all of Christianity in order not to be in any way soiled by the imperfections of others."[39] Calvin did not

---

[35] Brief Instruction, 44. CO 7.56–57. "Le Baptesme doit estre donné à ceux qui sont enseignez à penitence, croyans que leurs pechez sont effacez par Iesus Christ, et qui veulent cheminer en la resurrection d'iceluy. Pourtant on le doit distribuer à ceux qui le demandent par euxmesmes, non pas aux petis enfans: comme on a faict au Royaume du Pape."

[36] Brief Instruction, 44–45. CO 7.57. "Car ie dy que ce a esté une saincte ordonnance tousiours gardée en l'Eglise Chrestienne. Qu'ainsi soit, il n'y a docteur bi ancien, qui ne confesse que tousiours on en a usé des le temps des Apostres."

[37] Everett Ferguson, *The Early Church at Work and Worship, Vol. 2, Catechesis, Baptism, Martyrdom and Eschatology* (Cambridge: James Clark and Company, 2014), 125. Ferguson notes the sermons of Basil of Caesarea, *Exhortation to Baptism*; Gregory of Nazianzus, *Oration 40*; and Gregory of Nyssa, *Against Those Who Delay*.

[38] Everett Ferguson, *The Early Church at Work and Worship, Vol. 2, Catechesis, Baptism, Martyrdom and Eschatology* (Cambridge: James Clark and Company, 2014), 155–65.

[39] Brief Instruction, 70. CO 7.76–77. "Iceux, tant les premiers que les secondz, ont esté en une mesme phantasie que sont à present ces povres resveurs, de chercher une Eglise en laquelle il n'y eust que redire. Pourtant se sont separé de toute la Chrestienté, pour n'estre point souillés par les imperfections des autres."

maintain his stance upon scripture, but turned to the church's history of dealing with schismatic bodies.

Near the end of the treatise, in his short summary of *Psychopannychia*, Calvin turned to the orthodox fathers again. He noted that he had set out sufficient materials in scripture for those who did not reject them, and noted that the ancient doctors also supported it. He quoted Tertullian, Irenaeus, Chrysostom, Augustine, and Bernard.[40] Calling it the perpetual teaching (*la doctrine perpetuelle*), that believers immediately after death receive joy and consolation, Calvin assailed the slim historical record that agreed with the Anabaptists, most especially John XXII.

Calvin's use of the tradition to answer Anabaptists was consistent, even when hidden beneath a methodological choice. Calvin regularly turned to the orthodox tradition, both for ecclesiastical help in demonstrating a false historical notion that the church back to the time of the apostles knew of nothing but infant baptism and in bolstering his doctrinal arguments. Extraordinarily, this was the case even though Calvin knew that those who followed the teachings of the Schleitheim Brotherly Union were unlikely to be swayed by arguments from the church's history or the orthodox tradition.

Against the Fantastic and Furious Sect of the Libertines – 1545

While Calvin had promised to write two treatises in his *Brief Instruction*, one each against the Anabaptists and Libertines, the treatment of the Libertines waited until 1545 to see the light. As was the case with the treatise against the Anabaptists, it was originally published in French; Nicolas des Gallars published a Latin translation of it in 1546.[41] Calvin noted that he had been asked to write against the Libertines by good believers.[42] Exactly who the Libertines were remains unclear to historians. Benjamin Kaplan suggests that two strains of piety predominated in libertinism, one Protestant and the other spiritualist. But he states that finally, Dutch libertinism was not a coherent system of belief.[43] Allen Verhey argues that Calvin did know the Libertines, especially

---

[40] Brief Instruction, 139–40. CO 7.125–26.
[41] De Greef, *The Writings of John Calvin*, 155, n. 9.
[42] See letters from Valérand Poullain and Guillaume Farel, CO 11.711–14, and CO 11.750–51.
[43] Benjamin Kaplan, "Remnants of the Papal Yoke: Apathy and Opposition in the Dutch Reformation," *Sixteenth Century Journal* 25 (1994): 653–69.

some of their leaders, such as Quintin Thieffry, also known as Quintin of Hainaut, Claude Perceval, and Anthony Pocquet; Verhey thinks Calvin likely had them in mind in writing the treatise. Calvin would have especially known Pocquet, as he had visited Geneva in 1542 to ask Calvin for a recommendation.[44] Mirjam van Veen argues that Calvin provided a distorted view of libertines, not because of receiving incorrect information, but because of the polemic style he used. She wrote: "Calvin's portrait of the libertines fits with contemporary stereotypes on heretics and was largely based on old-church and medieval polemics against them."[45] Her point is well made in light of Calvin's statement. "However, strictly speaking, heretics are not only like thieves or wolves, but are much worse. For since they corrupt the holy Word of God, they are like poison, murdering poor souls under the pretext of grazing them and providing them with good pasturage."[46] Van Veen asserts that Calvin's model of argumentation depends on early and medieval Christian models.

Calvin began his attack by arguing that at its core, libertinism had been a heresy since the time of the apostles. He then added that the rest of it was similar to the teachings of the Valentinians, the Cerdonites, and the Manichees.[47] The Valentinians were a loosely organized group of gnostic Christians who followed the teachings of Valentinus (*c.* 100–*c.* 160), who taught salvation was achieved through a secret knowledge. The core of his teachings are vague, as they were suppressed and are known mostly from his critics, Tertullian and Irenaeus.[48] Cerdon was the teacher of Marcion, and scholars know very little about Cerdon's teachings apart from Marcion, so by labeling them "Cerdonites," Calvin was basically attacking the Libertines for Marcionism. Marcion had taught a form of dualism and rejected the Old Testament and much of the New

---

[44] Allen Verhey, "Calvin's Treatise 'Against the Libertines,'" Introduction by Allen Verhey, translated by Robert G. Wilkie and Allen Verhey. *Calvin Theological Journal* 15 (1980): 190–219.

[45] Veen, "Supporters of the Devil," 23.

[46] *Against the Fantastic and Furious Sect of the Libertines Who are Called Spirituals*, in *Treatises Against the Anabaptists and Against the Libertines*, translated and edited by Benjamin Wirt Farley (Grand Rapids: Baker Book House, 1982), 188. Hereafter cited as Against the Libertines. CO 7.150. "d'autant qu'en corrompant la saincte parolle de Dieu, ilz sont comme empoisonneurs, meurtrissans les povres ames, soubz ombre de les paistre et leur presenter bonne viande."

[47] Against the Libertines, 190. CO 7.153.

[48] See Tertullian, Adversus Valentianos; and Irenaeus, Adversus Haereses.

Testament.[49] The Manichees were another heretical sect, who sought to make converts among Christians – the young Augustine famously converted to Manicheism.[50] Calvin's use of these well-established heretical frames set his task out clearly – that in dealing with Libertinism, Calvin was attacking heresy. Though Calvin went more deeply into the consideration of these heresies later in the treatise, he never made an argument as to why they were heretical. Instead, Calvin simply pronounced the church's decision. He relied on the orthodox doctrinal and ecclesiastical tradition. Calvin was writing in 1545, a time long after the claim that ecumenical and other church councils could err had been made.[51] What van Veen termed the "heresy stereotypes" and "existing clichés" were Calvin's frequent tools.[52] But these make no sense without a foundational acceptance of the catholic tradition and the truth of the received religion.

Beyond that structure, Calvin avoided open discussions of the patristic and medieval authorities in the treatise. His sole example was a quotation of Augustine, to argue that the highest understanding of the Christian life was to acknowledge one's imperfections and to confess one's weakness to God.[53] Calvin may have felt that the most basic form of correction, the argument from scripture, was the most effective to answer the problem of the Libertines. In any case, beyond descriptions

---

[49] On Marcion, see *Marcion und seine kirchengeschichtliche Wirkung/Marcion and his impact on church history : Vorträge der Internationalen Fachkonferenz zu Marcion, gehalten vom 15.-18. August 2001*, edited by Gerhard May, Katharina Greschat, and Martin Meiser (Berlin: Walter de Gruyter, 2002); the still-relevant Adolf von Harnack, *Marcion: das Evangelium vom fremden Gott* (Leipzig: J.C. Hinrichs, 1921); translated by John E. Steely and Lyle D. Bierma, *Marcion: The Gospel of an Alien God* (Durham: Labyrinth Press, 1990); and Heikki Räisänen, "Marcion," in Antti Marjanen and Petri Luomanen, eds., *A Companion to Second-Century "Heretics"* (Leiden: Brill, 2005), 100–24.

[50] On Manicheism, see Michel Tardieu, *Manichaeism*, translated by M. B. DeBevoise (Champagne: University of Illinois Press, 2008); Kurt Rudolph, *Gnosis: The Nature and History of Gnosticism*, translated by R. Wilson (San Francisco: Harper & Row, 1983); Majella Franzmann, *Jesus in the Manichaean Writings* (Edinburgh: T. & T. Clark, 2003).

[51] For a study of Calvin's consideration of councils, see James R. Payton, Jr., "Calvin and the Legitimation of Icons: His Treatment of the Seventh Ecumenical Council," *Archiv für Reformationsgeschichte* 84 (1993): 222–41.

[52] Veen, "Supporters of the Devil," 31.

[53] Against the Libertines, 169. "Nevertheless, as Saint Augustine says, the greatest perfection is to acknowledge and confess how imperfect one is and to confess without end one's weaknesses to God." CO 7.205. "Cependant, comme dit sainct Augustin, leur plus grande perfection est, de recongnoistre et confesser combien ilz son imparfaictz, et de confesser tousiours leurs infirmitez devant Dieu."

and allusions to classical heresies and heretics, the treatise against the Libertines offers an example of Calvin turning to the tradition the fewest number of explicit times. However, it also contained a basic argument that could not be made without tradition – that the decisions of the historic orthodox church regarding heresy should remain firm in the contemporary church.

NICODEMITES

Having considered various polemics against the Anabaptists and Libertines, it is important to consider Calvin's attacks on the Nicodemites. Nicodemite was a name given by several theologians in the early modern period to those who found themselves wanting to hide their true faith so that they could continue to live in Catholic realms.[54] The term derived from the example of Nicodemus in John's gospel, who came to see Jesus at night. By 1540, Calvin had been faced with a question arising from evangelical believers in Catholic countries.[55] Simply put, what should believers in the true gospel do about being seen and participating at Catholic worship services? This may have been a particularly sensitive question for Calvin, as one of his biographers suggested that he had himself dissembled early in his adult religious life.[56] Obviously, the importance of these ceremonies had been understood by all parties for some time, at the very least from the Diet of Augsburg in 1530.[57] To attend, to participate in cultic acts, was to proclaim the religion of Rome and the truth of the Catholic faith. On the other hand, to choose openly and explicitly to avoid participation was not a choice lightly made. Rather, it was fraught with peril for those who made it – opening the individual or family to suspicion, investigation, and possibly questioning by the authorities.

---

[54] For background on the Nicodemites in the early modern period, see Kenneth Woo, "Nicodemism and Libertinism," in *John Calvin in Context*, edited by Ward Holder, 287–95; and Francis Higman, "Calvin Polémiste," in *Lire et Découvrir: La Circulation des Idées au Temps de la Réforme* (Geneva: Librairie Droz, 1998), 403–18.

[55] Calvin would never call these Catholic countries, reserving the term "catholic" for positive ideals, and preferring terms such as "popish," or "Romish," or "Roman." But for the purposes of this consideration, I will anachronistically use the term "Catholic."

[56] Bruce Gordon, *Calvin* (New Haven: Yale University Press, 2009), 40.

[57] At which Charles V required the protesting princes to join in the Corpus Christi procession, a request that Philip of Hesse and others refused.

Religious dissembling was therefore common in the early modern period.[58] From Spanish false conversos or Moriscos, to French Reformed who attended Mass, to a Roman Catholic priest who directly left his parish to serve as pastor to the Anabaptist movement, we see time and again the phenomenon of worshipers whose internal participation in outward ceremonies can either be questioned or frankly called dissembling.[59] This may have even been the most common position among those who lived under the majority rule of those with a different faith.[60]

While Calvin was not unaware of these realities and the possible devastating consequences of religious minority profession, he was not inclined to ignore the theological and identity issues that religious dissembling presented. In his role as a doctor of the church, Calvin took up the

[58] This is related to but different from the doctrine of equivocation, frequently attached to the Jesuits, that Shakespeare noted in Macbeth. See Frank L. Huntley, "Macbeth and the Background of Jesuitical Equivocation," *PMLA* 79 (1964): 390–400; Archibald Edward Malloch, "Father Henry Garnet's Treatise of Equivocation," *Recusant History* 15 (1981): 387–95; William O. Scott, "Macbeth's – and Our – Self-Equivocations," *Shakespeare Quarterly* 37 (1986): 160–74; Susan Wabuda, "Equivocation and Recantation During the English Reformation: The 'Subtle Shadows' of Dr. Edward Crome," *Journal of Ecclesiastical History* 44 (1993): 224–42; Andrew Muttitt, "John Calvin, 2 Samuel 2:8–32 and Resistance to Civil Government: Supreme Equivocation or Mastery of Contextual Exegesis?" *KOERS – Bulletin for Christian Scholarship* 82 (2017): 1–10.

[59] For a discussion of Spanish suspicions of false conversion among the Moriscos, see Henry Kamen, *The Spanish Inquisition: A Historical Revision* (New Haven: Yale University Press, 1998); and Ronald E. Surtz, "Morisco Women, Written Texts, and the Valencia Inquisition," *Sixteenth Century Journal* 32 (2001):421–33. Surtz finds that Morisco women were instrumental in maintaining Arabic texts and a strong connection to the Islamic tradition. Mary Elizabeth Parry found widespread religious dissembling in her "Between Muslim and Christian Worlds: Moriscas and Identity in Early Modern Spain," *Muslim World* 95 (2005): 177–98. Hilda Nissimi compared various identity and religious groups and forced conversions, and the lack of success of these forced conversions, in her "Religious Conversion, Covert Defiance and Social Identity: A Comparative View," *Numen* 51 (2004): 367–406. Henning Juergens has noted the existence of the "Exules Christi" among the Gnesio-Lutherans in his "Intra-Protestant Conflicts in 16th Century Poland and Prussia – The Case of Benedict Morgenstern," in *Calvin and Luther: The Continuing Relationship*, edited by R. Ward Holder (Göttingen: Vandenhoeck & Ruprecht, 2013), 143–164. French Reformed Christians are the subject of the Nicodemite tracts; for the sake of space I will not consider the secondary literature. Menno Simons tells that he had stopped believing in transubstantiation as early as 1529 (conservatively), but continued to conduct masses until he left Witmarsum in early 1536 to pastor the Anabaptists.

[60] By majority rule, I am not suggesting early modern democracies, but pointing out that dangers came not only from princes, but also from the outraged religious sensibilities of the majority religion. It has been popular to absolve rulers of blame by pointing out that in several religiously motivated atrocities, the sovereign had not actually ordered the massacres.

issue from the perspective of doctrine and pastoral realities.[61] Pastorally, Calvin did not fulfill his mythic role as a brutal dictator; in fact he was quite the opposite, couching his words in the language of Christian counsel and noting the difficulty of giving advice in such a perilous situation. In 1543, Calvin published a "Small Treatise" in French that consisted of two letters to those in France suffering from a crisis of conscience.[62] He wrote that "it is a difficult thing to counsel a Christian acting in a place of captivity and servitude and without the ability to give glory to God and to live according to the law of his word. For it is not an easy thing to discover what course one should hold to in an abyss."[63] But eventually, Calvin determined that it was crucial to the faith and life of believers and the church either to flee a realm where the true worship of God is not permitted or to profess God and bear the consequences.

Excuse à Messieurs les Nicodémites – 1544

The most significant treatise Calvin wrote against the Nicodemites was his *Excuse à Messieurs les Nicodémites*, published in 1544.[64] This is Calvin's clearest tract on the issue of "Nicodemism," and contains his clear argument that the term "nicodemism" is inappropriate.[65] He stated this because Nicodemus ultimately came to the fullness of faith.[66] The *Excuse à Messieurs les Nicodémites* is deceptively easy to analyze for explicit references to the orthodox tradition. They do not exist. Calvin

---

[61] Calvin divided the ministry into four roles. These were elder, deacon, preacher, and doctor. A doctor had the responsibility for teaching Christian doctrine in the broadest sense, transcending local and national boundaries. Calvin saw himself as both a preacher and a doctor.

[62] De Greef, *The Writings of John Calvin*, 120.

[63] CO 6.579. "...ce m'est une chose difficile, de donner conseil à une personne chrestienne, comme elle se doit gouverner en un lieu, où on est detenu en captivité et servitude, tellement qu'on ne puisse donner gloire à Dieu, et vivre selon la reigle do sa parolle. Car ce n'est pas chose aisée, de trouver quelle voye on doit tenir en un abisme." On Calvin's idea of the abyss, see William Bouwsma, *Calvin: A Sixteenth Century Portrait* (Oxford: Oxford University Press, 1988).

[64] De Greef, *The Writings of John Calvin*, 122. For a modern translation, see "Apology of John Calvin, to Messrs The Nicodemites Upon the Complaint That They Make of His Too Great Rigour (1544)," translated by Eric Kayayan, *Calvin Theological Journal* 29 (1994): 346–63.

[65] Calvin's other treatments of Nicodemism came in his *Petit Traicté* of 1543 and his 1562 *Response á un certain Holandois*. See Mirjam van Veen, *Ioannis Calvini: Scripta Didactica et Polemica, Volumen I* (Geneva: Librairie Droz, 2005). This volume contains the response to Coornheert, the *Response à un Certain Holandois*.

[66] John 19.39–42.

seemed to avoid the overt mention of the patristic and medieval authorities that so frequently seem to swarm on pages of the *Institutes*. Clearly, Calvin did not always turn to the assistance of the orthodox tradition. However, the *Excuse* provides another case where merely counting citations does not suffice. Calvin set out to answer the Nicodemites by considering the nature of religion itself. In every moment of doing so, Calvin accepted a medieval model of the idea of religion. Religion would be found in civil realms, openly affirmed by the duly constituted authorities. Those who did not wish to participate fully and wholeheartedly should either speak out against the false church, or they should flee. Calvin did not attempt a more innovative model of thinking about the church and its relationship to the power of the prince, either for himself or for those whom he attacked.

The Nicodemite writings demonstrate that Calvin did not always resort to the orthodox tradition in the same manner. In these, he rarely if ever made explicit allusion to the fathers and medievals, though there are numerous moments when one might see that Calvin was calling on ideas that had come from specific sources. But beyond those, Calvin did not abandon the models of church and realm that were so familiar to him. He worked out his models of Christian truth-telling and obedience to God in the same type of societal setting in which he had learned Christianity. This represents an important note – that even when Calvin stopped using the fathers and medievals explicitly, he maintained his frame of reference that had been forged in a society saturated with their ideas.

CATHOLICS

John Calvin grew up in a world of French Catholicism. There were stories told of his touching a fragment of the head of St. Ann as a child, and the support for his education depended upon the economy of the ecclesiastical world.[67] He was steeped in the "robust communal orientation" that permeated people's lives.[68] Throughout his life of commenting upon the scriptures he would allude to and at times even prefer the Vulgate

---

[67] Pak notes Calvin receiving two livings or benefices, in 1521 and 1527. Gordon notes that Calvin surrendered his livings in 1534, presumably because his beliefs were incompatible with Catholicism. G. Sujin Pak, "John Calvin's Life," in *John Calvin in Context*, edited by Ward Holder, 9. Gordon, *Calvin*, 40.

[68] Raymond A. Mentzer, "French Christianity in the Early 1500s," in *John Calvin in Context*, edited by Ward Holder, 23.

translation of the scriptures that had been the Bible for his early life. This life of Catholicism influenced his work. As scholars have noted for other famous converts, frequently the new convert looked back upon his prior life and religious commitments with some form of contempt.[69] This was certainly the case with Augustine, one of Calvin's greatest theological influences. Therefore, it is no surprise that the majority of Calvin's early polemic attacked Roman religion. Except for the early effort at writing against Radicals in *Psychopannychia*, Calvin's early theological efforts were entirely written to, or for, or even against Catholics. This is especially true when one considers the 1536 edition of the *Institutes* to be the "apologetic" version, making it a very long treatise to members of the church of Rome.

Lausanne Disputation – 1536

Calvin finished the first edition of the *Institutes* in 1535. The next year, he was harangued by Guillaume Farel into taking a ministerial post in Geneva. In October of that year, Farel and Pierre Viret had Calvin accompany them to a public religious colloquy in Lausanne, set through Bern's invitation.[70] On October 5, a priest accused the Reformers of denigrating the authority of the fathers and of innovating in their doctrines. Calvin replied that the charges were groundless: The Protestants were willing to be judged as audacious and arrogant beyond all measure if they held such great servants of God in contempt. He also pointed out that the Evangelicals regularly read the patristic authors, though they did not obey them as authorities.[71] The Evangelicals, he said, "have always held them to belong to the number of those to whom such obedience is not due, and whose authority we will not so exalt, as in any way to debase the dignity of the Word of our Lord, to which alone is due complete obedience in the Church of Jesus Christ."[72] In this single paragraph, Calvin

---

[69] See Robin Lane Fox, *Augustine: Conversions to Confessions* (New York: Basic Books, 2015).

[70] De Greef, *The Writings of John Calvin*, 136–37.

[71] John Calvin, "Two Discourses on the Articles," in *Calvin: Theological Treatises*, edited and translated by J. K. S. Reid (Philadelphia: Westminster Press, 1954), 38. CO 9.877. Hereafter "Two Discourses on the Articles," with page number.

[72] Calvin, "Two Discourses on the Articles," 38. CO 9.877–78. "Mais ce que nous les avons tousiours cependant au nombre de ceux aux quelz nest pas deue obeissance et ne exaltons pas tellement leur autorité que elle puisse amoindrir ou aucunement abaisser la dignité de la parolle du seigneur, laquelle seule avec entiere obeissance doibt estre estimee en leglise de Iesu-christ."

adroitly avoided the charge of innovation, and turned back to the necessity of obedience to scripture.

Calvin continued to fortify his point with biblical arguments, noting God's commands to Peter, citing Isaiah 33, and enlisting James to his cause. He then began to produce extemporaneous patristic testimonies from memory to support his argument. He cited Cyprian, Tertullian, Pseudo-Chrysostom, and of course Augustine. Calvin showed a particular knowledge of Augustine, and spent the greatest amount of time on the North African doctor's support for the evangelical side.[73]

Calvin maintained his stance from the previous year's *Institutes* in the Lausanne Disputation: The Evangelicals were not innovators and took great care to revere the patristic witness, but did not allow that reverence to be elevated to an inappropriate level of authority that ought to be reserved for scripture. Significantly, however, Calvin had also changed. Where he had gone almost whole chapters of the *Institutes* without recourse to the early church theologians, it was clear that he was continuing to read them, committing the substance of their arguments to memory. Instead of arguing that it was unimportant to maintain fealty to the fathers, Calvin took the more nuanced route that preserved the Protestant connection to the early church doctors, while simultaneously stating the sufficiency of scripture's witness.

Epistolae Duae – 1537

Calvin wrote a pair of letters to Catholic friends that were published in Basel as *Epistolae Duae* in 1537. The first letter was to Calvin's friend Nicolas Duchemin, who had been his friend for years.[74] Duchemin had been appointed to an ecclesiastical post and had expressed to Calvin his concern about being involved in Catholic practices that he knew some had deemed to be polluting. Calvin's response was his first foray against Nicodemism, though he did not use the term in the letter. While the letter had almost no consideration of patristic sources, the one instance that it did provide suggested Calvin's orientation both toward the church of Rome and the orthodox tradition. Calvin quoted a passage from Augustine from a sermon where he hailed the example of Cyprian.

---

73 Calvin, "Two Discourses on the Articles," 39–42. CO 9.879–81.
74 De Greef, *The Writings of John Calvin*, 134–36.

Augustine had written that after Cyprian was condemned to death, he was offered his life if only he would abjure the Christian faith. This offer was made to him while he was facing all the instruments of torture and execution that would be brought against him.[75] Calvin brought before Duchemin the tradition of martyrdom, so strong in North Africa, and explicated it to prove his point. Beyond the Augustine quotation, there is almost no allusion to the patristic witness in the letter.

The second letter in the collection was written to Gérard Roussel, who had been a member of the Circle of Meaux, gathered around Guillaume Briçonnet, the bishop who had the favor of Marguerite of Navarre, the queen of Navarre and sister to the king of France, François I. Prior to François' being taken captive at the Battle of Pavia in 1525, the circle had exercised considerable power for reform, though almost none of its members converted to Protestantism. The king's capture and removal from French theological politics allowed conservative forces, especially the theology faculty at the University of Paris, to clamp down, and the circle had broken up in that same year.[76] Over a decade later, Roussel had been appointed the bishop of Oloron. Calvin wrote to him, speaking of their long friendship. He urged Roussel to leave the position behind because it forced him to bring souls to Mass, which could not help but endanger them. This letter had even less of the patristic substance that had graced the letter to Duchemin. Throughout its discussion of the office of bishop, the letter depended upon exegetical arguments.

Calvin's Reply to Sadoleto – 1539

Calvin next took up the polemic against Catholicism in his debate with Cardinal Jacopo Sadoleto, the bishop of Carpentras. Sadoleto had written a letter to the magistrates, council, and citizens of Geneva, dated March 18, 1539.[77] The letter sought to invite the Genevans to leave the schismatic movement that had been brought about by the efforts of

---

[75] Calvin, "On Shunning the Unlawful Rites of the Ungodly," in *Selected Works of John Calvin*, edited by Beveridge and Bonnet, 3.364, CO 5.242.

[76] Gordon, *Calvin*, 16.

[77] The standard translation is available in John C. Olin, ed., *A Reformation Debate: Sadoleto's Letter to the Genevans and Calvin's Reply* (San Francisco: Harper Torchbook, 1966), reprinted frequently. CO 5.369–416. Hereafter cited as Olin, with page number.

certain crafty men in an attempt to sow the wicked seeds of discord.[78] Even in his opening, Sadoleto rested his argument upon the difference between the desires of the crafty leaders ("homines astutos") and the way of the people's fathers and ancestors and the perpetual feelings of the Catholic church ("a via patrum maiorumque suorum, et a perpetua catholicae ecclesiae avertisse sententia").

Sadoleto reasoned with the Genevans that the one reason to put faith and hope in Christ was to obtain eternal salvation for their souls.[79] And the most certain way to acquire a certain hold on Christ was through the church, a church that had been purified through tribulations so that her fidelity attained the highest favor with God.[80] Therefore, the only safe way forward, one that the Genevans had left through the deceptions of their impious leaders, was to adopt a form of faith in the church. The medieval theologians had termed this implicit faith, the belief in something because of the authority of the church.

Sadoleto arrived at his conclusion with a kind of anticipation of Pascal's wager.[81] He wrote:

The point in dispute is whether is it more expedient for your salvation, and whether you think you will do what is more pleasing to God, by believing and

---

[78] Olin, 30. CO 5.370–71. "Etenim postquam fuit ad aures meas delatum, homines quosdam astutos, inimicos christianae unitatis et pacis, id quod in aliis antea nonnullis fortissimae gentis Helvetiorum oppidis et pagis iam fecissent, item in vobis et civitate vestra malae discordiae semina iecisse, Christique fidelem populum a via patrum maiorumque suorum, et a perpetua catholicae ecclesiae avertisse sententia, omniaque dissidiis et seditionibus implesse (qui tamen mos proprius eorum semper est, qui autoritate ecclesiae oppugnanda novas sibi potentias et novos honores quaerunt) testor Deum omnipotentem, eum ipsum qui nunc intimis meis cogitationibus praesens adest, me et indoluisse graviter, et duplici quadam misericordia affectum fuisse: quum ex una parte viderer mihi audire gemitum plorantis matris nostrae ecclesiae et lamentantis, quae tot et tam dilectis filiis uno tempore esset orbata: ex altera, vestris, o carissimi, incommodis et periculis commoverer."

[79] Olin, 32. CO 5.371–72. "Atque, ut inde initium capiamus, unde maxime opportunum esse ducimus: ego, fratres carissimi, sic existimo, me et vos, et reliquos praeterea omnes qui in Christo spem et fidem suam posuerunt, id ea una de causa ita facere et fecisse, quo salutem sibi atque animabus suis, non hanc mortalem et cito interituram, sed illam sempiternam et immortalem quaererent, quae in coelo solum vere obtineri, in terris autem nullo modo potest."

[80] Olin, 37. CO 5.375. "Quae ideo omnia et a praepotente Deo permissa, et a fortibus illis viris, Christi vere cultoribus suscepta, tolerata, decertataque sunt, ut per omne experimentorum et probationum genus plurimis veluti malleis excusa, multo igni purgata, tantis sanctorum aerumnis atque laboribus conflata, consolidata, expressa, et maximam apud Deum gratiam fidelitatis suae ecclesia obtineret, et summam apud homines autoritatem."

[81] Named for Blaise Pascal (1623–62), who in his *Pensées* argued from probability that it made sense to believe in God because the possibility of eternal rewards outweighed the possibility of finite sacrifices.

following what the Catholic Church throughout the whole world, now for more than fifteen hundred years, or (if we require clear and certain recorded notice of the facts) for more than thirteen hundred years approves with general consent; or innovations introduced with these twenty-five years, by crafty or, as they think themselves, acute men; but men certainly who are not themselves the Catholic Church?[82]

This representation of Catholic history and the nature of the church fascinates because of what it assumes. Sadoleto presumed a doctrine of implicit faith, that one who does not understand doctrine should simply accept the teachings of the church, and a quasi-doctrine of *semper eadem*, that the Catholic church had always believed what it presently believed. This constancy is guaranteed because the one Spirit of Christ, which unites the church, negates the possibility of dissension.

Calvin was approached by the Genevan Small Council to write a reply, after Pierre Viret declined to do so – and though at that moment he was banned from the city, he seemed eager to do so. He wasted no time: Sadoleto's letter is dated March 18, and Calvin's reply was dated September 1. Given Calvin's temperament, the insults were probably enough to move him to write, though he claimed that he was motivated by a concern to defend his ministry.[83] Calvin's analysis of Sadoleto's charges found two basic indictments: The Genevans had left behind the truth of God and had deserted the church.[84] These were not the only tasks he took up – Calvin attacked Sadoleto on a variety of subjects, including proclaiming that believers should take such a mercenary approach to the deity as to be primarily concerned for the salvation of their souls. Instead,

---

[82] Olin 40–41. CO 5.378. "Quam remita agam et proponam, quasi habeam vos adhuc deliberantes, necdum animi certos, quorum potius aut voluntatibus obsequi, aut consiliis credere debeatis. Disceptatio est, utrum vestrae saluti magis expediat, gratiusque Deo vos facturos existimetis, si ea credideritis eritisque sequuti, quae ecclesia catholica cunctum per orbem terrarum annos iam mille et quingentos amplius, aut (si claram certamque rerum gestarum memoriam et notitiam quaerimus) annos iam amplius mille et trecentos, magno consensu comprobat: an haec quae vafri homines, atque, ui sibi ipsi videntur, acuti, adversus tot saeculorum usum et contra perpetuam ecclesiae autoritatem, his annis quinque et viginti innovaverunt: qui certe ipsi catholica non sunt ecclesia."

[83] Olin, 53. CO 5.388.

[84] Olin, 57. CO 5.391. "Quod Genevenses nostra praedicatione edocti ab illa errorum colluvie, in qua demersi fuerant, ad puriorem evangelii doctrinam se contulerunt, defectionem a Dei veritate; quod a pontificis romani tyrannide se vindicarunt, ut paulo meliorem ecclesiae formam apud se constituerent, discessionem ab ecclesia esse dicis."

true piety should recognize that the prime motive for human existence is to illustrate the glory of God.[85]

Then Calvin took up the issue of the definition of the church. He noted that the clearest mark of the church was the word of the Lord, and he went on to offer his own definition of the church:[86]

Now if you can bear to receive a truer definition of the Church than your own, say, in future, that it is the society of all the saints, a society which, spread over the whole world, and existing in all ages, yet bound together by the one doctrine and the one Spirit of Christ, cultivates and observes unity of faith and brotherly concord. With this Church we deny that we have any disagreement.[87]

What is fascinating (if not flabbergasting) about this definition is that the "one doctrine and Spirit of Christ" has to take the place of the scripture. Calvin's emphasis on the doctrine and Spirit of Christ was logically separate from the pure teachings of scripture.

Having defined the church, Calvin took up the questions of the Genevans' desertion of the church and the truth. Calvin noted the historical character of the allegation, denied the charge, and argued to the contrary that the Genevan agreement with antiquity was closer than Rome's. He contended that their effort had been to renew the ancient form of the church ("vetusta ecclesiae").[88] Calvin then gave his sense of the downfall of the church. He wrote: "[A]ll we have attempted has been to renew that ancient form of the Church, which at first sullied and distorted by illiterate men of indifferent character, was afterward flagitiously mangled and almost destroyed by the Roman Pontiff and his faction."[89] Calvin did not repeat the claim of anti-Christ that Luther made

---

[85] Olin 58. CO 5.391. "Sive autem, ut omnem de te dubitationem tolleres, testari voluisti te de gloriosa apud Deum vita serio cogitare; sive censuisti tam longa eius commendatione excitandos vellicandosque esse eos ad quos scribebas (nolo enim divinare quid tibi consilii fuerit), id tamen parum est theologicum, hominem ita sibi ipsi addicere, ut non interim principium hoc illi vitae formandae praestituas, illustrandae Domini gloriae studium."

[86] Olin 60. CO 5.392–93. "ubi hic verbum Domini, maxime perspicua nota illa, quam ipse Dominus, in ecclesia designanda, toties nobis commendat?"

[87] Olin 61–62. CO 5.394. "Nunc si definitionem ecclesiae tua veriorem recipere sustines, dic posthac, societatem esse sanctorum omnium, quae per totum orbem diffusa, per omnes aetates dispersa, una tamen Christi doctrina et uno spiritu colligata, unitatem fidei ac fraternam concordiam colit atque observat. Cum hac esse nobis quidquam dissidii negamus."

[88] Olin 62. CO 5.394.

[89] Olin, 62. CO 5.394. "...sed nihil aliud conari quam ut instauretur aliquando vetusta illa ecclesiae facies, quae primo ab hominibus indoctis, et non optimis, deformata et foedata, postea a pontifice romano et eius factione flagitiose lacerata et prope deleta est."

in 1521, but his identification of those responsible for the distortions in the church was clear.[90]

Calvin then proceeded over and over to argue that the ancient church's practice and doctrine aligned more closely with those of the Evangelicals. In those cases where it did not, Calvin did not surrender the field but simply denied that the practice of the early church was the same in content as that of contemporary Rome.[91] He was adamant that Rome had changed doctrines and practices, long after the patristic age. Such was the case when Calvin took up the issue of auricular confession. He called it the "law of Innocent," referring to Pope Innocent III (r. 1198–1216).[92] It was Innocent who had called the Fourth Lateran Council, held in 1215; that council demanded that every believer would confess and receive the eucharist at least annually. By pointing out that the canon from this council was "neither commanded by Christ nor practiced by the ancient Church," Calvin attacked the notion of antiquity and the nature of the Roman tradition.[93] Throughout, Calvin consciously sought to deny the testimony of the ancient church and the patristic witness to Sadoleto. He wrote: "That I may altogether disarm you of the authority of the Church, which, as your shield of Ajax, you ever and anon oppose to us, I will show, by some additional examples, how widely you differ from that holy antiquity."[94] Calvin then turned to the issue of the form of the ministry, the doctrine of the Lord's Supper, and the worship of images.

---

[90] Luther arrived at a much more strident point much earlier. See David Whitford, "The Papal Antichrist: Martin Luther and the Underappreciated Influence of Lorenzo Valla," *Renaissance Quarterly*, 61/1 (2008): 26–52.

[91] Such a case comes in his discussion of penance. Olin 70. Calvin noted: "The ancient Church, I admit, had its satisfactions, not those, however by which sinners might atone to God and ransom themselves from guilt, but by which they might prove that the repentance which they professed was not feigned, and efface the remembrance of that scandal which their sin had occasioned. For satisfactions were not regularly prescribed to all and sundry, but to those only who had fallen into some heinous wickedness." CO 5.399. "Habuit, fateor, vetus ecclesia suas satisfactiones: non illas tamen, quibus Deo litarent peccatores, seque a noxa redimerent, sed quibus, et quam profitebantur resipiscentiam non esse fictam approbarent, et eius offensionis, quae ex eorum peccato excitata erat, memoriam delerent. Non enim quibuslibet, sed iis modo, qui in grave aliquod flagitium prolapsi erant, solenni ritu praescribebantur."

[92] Olin 71. CO 5.400. "Innocentii legem."

[93] Olin 72. CO 5.400. "...neque Christi mandato, nec veteris ecclesiae instituto fuisse traditam."

[94] Olin 73–74. CO 5.402. "Atque ut ecclesiae autoritatem, quam, veluti Aiacis clypeum, subinde nobis opponis, aliquando tibi prorsus excutiam: nonnullis adhuc propositis exemplis indicabo, quanto intervallo a sancta illa antiquitate differatis." "Shield of

Calvin completed his defense of the evangelical position by taking up Sadoleto's implicit and explicit argument for the infallibility of the church. He linked that argument to a claim of tradition's power and sought to deny it. Calvin wrote that the church must be founded on scripture to have a certain foundation.

Calvin attacked the church's claim of infallibility because of its connection to the Holy Spirit. In place of this claim, he sought to place the foundation of the believer and the church upon the testimony of the scripture. Calvin knew that this would not always supply a consensus that would demonstrate the truth of the Vincentian canon and provided a proleptic response to that line of attack. But the lack of universal consensus did not, in Calvin's opinion, mean relativism in terms of truth or loss in respect to salvation.[95] He argued that error was possible, but it would not lead to destruction as long as the foundation of the Word remained. In this case, Calvin argued for a model of scripture as the foundation, but his own actions did not strictly follow his own canon.

The Bondage and Liberation of the Will – 1543

In early 1543, Calvin published a treatise in response to the polemic of a Dutch theologian, Albert Pighius.[96] This work was titled *Defensio Sanae et Orthodoxae Doctrinae de Servitute et Liberatione Humani Arbitrii*, commonly known as *The Bondage and Liberation of the Will: A Defence*

Ajax" is a favorite epithet of Calvin's between 1539 and 1547, always being used to describe a falsely presumed impenetrable argument. Calvin used the term again, in much the same fashion, in his *Acts of the Council of Trent with Antidote*, CO 7.411.

[95] Calvin was not alone in turning to some form of the Vincentian canon in the early modern period. The Lutheran theologian Georg Calixt explicitly suggested that he had envisioned his theory of the *consensus quinquesaecularis* on the basis of Vincent's Commonitorium. See Andreas Merkt, *Das Patristische Prinzip: Eine Studie zur Theologischen Bedeutung der Kirchenväter* (Leiden: Brill, 2001), 102ff.

[96] Pighius, or Pigge in German, attacked Calvin on a number of grounds that are not germane to our discussion. One of these was his belief that the consensus of the church was sufficient to carry the day. Mütel writes: "So bekennt Pigge in der *Hierarchiae ecclesiasticae assertio*, dass der Glaube der Universalkirche als Wahrheitserweis genügt. In gleicher Argumentationsstruktur bekennt er in *De libero arbitrio*, dass, selbst wenn er Calvin argumentativ nicht widerlegen könnte, die Lehren der Kirche, der *consensus patrum* und schliesslich der Konsens aller Menschen die letzlich entscheidende Widerlegung von Calvins Thesen seien." Matthias Mütel, *Mit den Kirchenvätern gegen Martin Luther? Die Debatten um Tradition und auctoritas patrum auf dem Konzil von Trient* (Leiden: Ferdinand Schöningh, 2017), 79.

of the Orthodox Doctrine of Human Choice against Pighius.[97] This treatise contained more patristic citations than any other work of Calvin's
excepting the *Institutes.*[98] Both Pighius and Calvin recognized Augustine
as the greatest battleground in this particular war over the authority
of the fathers. There are six books in Calvin's reply to Pighius, corresponding to the first six books of Pighius' *De Libero Hominis Arbitrio
et Divina Gratia, Libri Decem* (Of the Free Choice of Man and Divine
Grace, Ten Books).[99] The whole of Calvin's third book is taken up with
the issue of Augustine's meaning and authority, but books four and five
are also liberally sprinkled with polemic about Augustine's meaning. The
crucial issue was context. Calvin wrote that Pighius had accused him of
taking a number of passages from Augustine out of context and of mis-
understanding them.[100] Calvin examined six passages that he had drawn
from Augustine, and believed that he had successfully defended his case
that he had not done so.[101]

The key difference between Pighius and Calvin revolved around
Augustine's work against Pelagianism. Pelagius (*c.* 360–420) was a
British monk who had read Augustine's *Confessions* and was worried that the North African bishop was giving so much over to God
in the Christian life that there was nothing left for Christian morality.

---

[97] Ioannis Calvini: Scripta Didactica et Polemica, Volumen III, *Defensio Sanae et Orthodoxae Doctrinae de Servitute et Liberatione Humani Arbitrii*, edited by A. N. S. Lane,
assisted by Graham Davies (Geneva: Droz, 2008), hereafter Defensio, with book and
page numbers. I was also assisted in this work by the prior publication of *The Bondage
and Liberation of the Will: A Defence of the Orthodox Doctrine of Human Choice
against Pighius*, edited by A. N. S. Lane, and translated by Graham Davies (Grand
Rapids: Baker, 1996), hereafter BLW, with page numbers.

[98] A. N. S. Lane, "Calvin and the Fathers in his *Bondage and Liberation of the Will*," in
John Calvin: Student of the Church Fathers (Grand Rapids: Baker 1999), 151. In fact,
Lane asserts that it contains more patristic citations than any three of Calvin's works,
excluding the *Institutes*.

[99] Albert Pighius, *De Libero Hominis Arbitrio et Divina Gratia, Libri Decem* (Cologne:
Melchior Novesianus, 1542).

[100] Defensio, 3.157. "Primum, abruptas me nec intellectas ex Augustino sententias citare
causatur."

[101] The six passages are taken from 1) the letter to Anastasius, Letter 145, NPNF 495–96.
PL 33, Letter 146; 2) *The Perfection of Righteousness*, NPNF vol. 5, 155–76. The text
in question is 4.9 – see Appendix B. PL 44, ninth breviate; 3) The Enchiridion, NPNF
3.229–76; PL 40; 4) and *Against Two Letters of the Pelagians*, NPNF 5.373–434;
PL44; 5) *Rebuke and Grace*, NPNF 5.471–91; PL 44; 6) *Against Julian*, Against Julian,
FoC 35.83; PL 44.

Pelagius had argued in a widely circulated letter that "since perfection is possible for man, it is obligatory."[102] He worried about the line in Augustine's *Confessions*, "Command what you will, and give what you command."[103] To Pelagius, this sounded like a blurring of moral responsibility with moral agency. Augustine, much like his later acolyte Calvin, did not accept criticism easily. He immediately saw a greater system of thought than probably Pelagius had even considered, and attacked, charging that Pelagius was asserting that humans could move unaided toward God and salvation, not needing prior grace.[104] This Pelagian controversy would affect much of Augustine's thought from 413 until his death in 430.[105] What is significant for our consideration of the Pighius-Calvin debate is that after the fall of Rome in 410, Augustine turned his attention to the question of the human will and its relationship to God's grace with an intensity he had not previously given. Not surprisingly, Augustine's anti-Pelagian writings frequently support Calvin on issues having to do with the relative freedom or bondage of the human will. Further, Calvin argued that his point had not been to decide the issue of the freedom of the will on the basis of Augustine, but only to demonstrate from Augustine's own corpus what the North African father meant when he called human choice "free."[106]

Calvin also argued with Pighius about the periodization, or the categorization, of Augustine's work.[107] Pighius asserted three sections of Augustine's works were germane to the discussion of the freedom of the will. The first group contained works written against the Manichees, prior to the anti-Pelagian writings.[108] The second group consisted of the anti-Pelagian writings.[109] The third group did not have the polemical cast that in Pighius' opinion stained the second section, because they were not written hotly against heretics but were instead a bare explication of the

---

[102] Pelagius to Demetrias, quoted in Peter Brown, *Augustine of Hippo: A New Edition with an Epilogue* (Berkeley: University of California Press, 2000), 342.

[103] Augustine, *Confessions*, translated and edited by Henry Chadwick (Oxford: Oxford University Press, 1991), Book 10. Also Brown, *Augustine of Hippo*, 343.

[104] Brown, *Augustine of Hippo*, 345–46.

[105] Brown, *Augustine of Hippo*, esp. 340–411.

[106] Defensio, 3.159–60; BLW 89.

[107] See Lanes' footnote 18, BLW 90, noting that for Pighius, there was a sense of the character of the works, not only the time at which they were written.

[108] Pighius, Folio 38a, Defensio, 381.

[109] Pighius, Folio 38a–b, Defensio, 381.

orthodox truth of the faithful.[110] Calvin accepted Pighius' categorization, although he made it a periodization, with the first group being
pre-Pelagian writings, the second being anti-Pelagian, and the third
post-Pelagian controversy.[111] Calvin made two caveats. First, he immediately attacked Pighius' characterization of the anti-Pelagian writings
as being less helpful because of their polemical cast. Both Calvin and
Pighius knew that these texts would prove most helpful to Calvin's side
of the argument, and Calvin accused Pighius of simply wanting to reduce
the authority of these.[112] Second, Calvin noted that he believed he could
make his case on the basis of the later books – meaning those written
after the Pelagian controversy – as they were better than those Augustine
wrote as a young man.[113] Calvin and Pighius adopted particular mutually
exclusive tactics of argumentation. Both agreed that Augustine was the
battleground. But each wanted to slant the field in his favor – Pighius by
suggesting that the anti-Pelagian Augustine was not fully to be trusted
because of the heat of his rancor against the heretics; Calvin by preferring
older Augustine to the younger.

Two significant points of interest arose in this argument. First, there
was the historical issue, both in the historical claims made and in the evaluation modern analysts might make of the historical ability of the two
antagonists. Both Pighius and Calvin made a claim based in the events
of Augustine's life, rather than a purely doctrinal assertion. Pighius
wished to lessen the impact of the doctrine of the anti-Pelagian writings
while maintaining the authority of Augustine. He chose not to make the
more straightforward doctrinal argument that Augustine's doctrine of
the bondage of the human will represented in this period of his work
stood at odds with the consensus of Catholic teaching over the recent
centuries. Instead, Pighius chose a more courteous solution that sought
to leave Augustine's authority unsullied – that the North African bishop

---

[110] Pighius, Folio 38b, Defensio 381. "Alia sunt quae eadem de re scripsit, non eiusmodi
conflictationis calore & pugna adversus haereticos, sed sedata meditataque nudae veritatis explicatione, orthodoxis & fidelbus." Pighius was not the only Catholic writer to
make this point. Christoph Burger points out that Erasmus came to a similar conclusion. "Nach Erasmus' Urteil wurde Augustin im Streit mit Pelagius, bedingt durch die
polemische Situation, ungerechter als zuvor in seiner Beurteilung der Leistungsfähigkeit
des freien Willens:" Christoph Burger, "Erasmus' Auseinandersetzung mit Augustin im
Streit mit Luther," in *Auctoritas patrum: zur Rezeption der Kirchenväter im 15. und 16.
Jahrhundert* edited by Leif Grane, Alfred Schindler, and Markus Wriedt (Mainz: Verlag
Philipp von Zabern, 1993), 13.

[111] Defensio 160, BLW 90.

[112] Defensio 160, BLW 90.

[113] Defensio 160, BLW 90.

said things less clearly and with more rancor than he would have had he not been pushed to do so by heretics.

Having chosen history, Pighius' historical method presents both strengths and weaknesses. He gained access to the primary documents that he was quoting and called on a wide range of Augustine's texts. Though he was not above using quotes that misled, his normal usage of Augustine's words was fair and judicious.[114] However, he did not display the critical facility to identify that an important source was pseudonymous, instead eagerly using the *Hypognosticon* as authentically Augustine's.[115] Further, he seemed unaware of some of the North African councils, and ignored the Second Council of Orange, though it had received papal approval by Boniface II in 531.[116]

Considering Calvin's use of history, the evidence offers a confusing set of impressions of Calvin as both adept and clumsy, or more likely adroit and intentionally obscure. At times, his feats of historical accuracy were remarkable.[117] Calvin correctly identified that *Hypognosticon* was not authored by Augustine.[118] He rather skillfully marshaled evidence from the councils of the church to throw back at Pighius.[119]

---

[114] Defensio 181, BLW 109.

[115] Erasmus had denied Augustine's authorship of the Hypognosticon in his treatise *Hyperaspistes II*, written as a response to Luther's *De Servo Arbitrio* and published by Froben in 1527. Erasmus criticized Luther for seeing it as a genuine work of Augustine's and, moreover, on his side. This confusion on Luther's part may have contributed to Pighius' acceptance of the work as genuine. For modern scholarship on the Hypognosticon, see the *Clavis Patrum Latinorum: Qua in Corpus Christianorum Edendum Optimas quasque Scriptorum Recensiones a Tertulliano ad Bedam* (Steenbrugis: Abbot of St. Peter, 1995), which does not list the work among Augustine's authentic works; and the article on its authorship by J. E. Chisolm, "The Pseudo-Augustinian Hypomnesticon against the Pelagians and Celestinians," vv. 20–21, *Paradosis* (1980).

[116] Lane notes that Peter Crabbe's Concilia omnia is likely Calvin's source, and that it contained this material. See his "Introduction," in Defensio, 51.

[117] For more on Calvin and history, see James R. Payton, "Calvin and the Legitimation of Icons: His Treatment of the Seventh Ecumenical Council," *Archiv für Reformationsgeschichte* 84 (1993): 222–41; "History as Rhetorical Weapon: Christian Humanism in Calvin's Reply to Sadoleto, 1539," in *In Honor of John Calvin, 1509–64*, edited by E. J. Furcha (Montreal: Faculty of Religious Studies, McGill University, 1987), 96–132; "Calvin and the Libri Carolini." *Sixteenth Century Journal* 28 (1997): 467–80; and Irena Backus, *Historical Method and Confessional Identity in the Era of the Reformation (1378–1615)* (Boston, Leiden: Brill, 2003), esp. 63–117.

[118] Defensio 178, BLW 107.

[119] See G. R. Evans, *Problems of Authority in Reformation Debates* (Cambridge: Cambridge University Press, 1992), 243. After noting a number of examples of collections of acts and decrees of councils in the sixteenth century, she notes: "One result of this insecure scholarly base was that it was not easy for anyone in the sixteenth century to arrive at a balanced and informed picture of what constitutes a Council and what its function is."

However, even though Calvin possessed historical ability, his method at times left much to be desired. Calvin exhibited a preference for the older Augustine, and for reading the earlier Augustinian corpus through the lens of the more mature Augustine at several points. He greatly depended on the *Retractationes*, which were a summary of Augustine's writings that the bishop had compiled in 426–427, and that included his mature reflections on his works.[120] Calvin commonly answered Pighius' quotations from the earlier treatises with quotations from the form given in this later work.[121] This was the case in his discussion of Augustine's three early treatises.[122] Calvin's use of sources later than those Pighius raised showed a historical and theological failing. Calvin recognized the older Augustine as more supportive, and only read the early Augustine through the lens of the older Augustine's reflections upon his earlier work. But Calvin's predilection for the older Augustine at times crossed the line from preference into prejudice, from a defensible choice to an undefended reflex. Calvin responded to citations from *De Libero Arbitrio*, *De Duabus Animabus*, and *De Vera Religione*, wholly on the basis of the *Retractatationes*.[123] These three treatises are early. Augustine probably wrote *De Libero Arbitrio* between 388 and 395, *De Duabus Animabus* in 391 and 392, and *De Vera Religione* from 389–391.[124] Augustine did attempt to "regularize" the doctrine of *De Libero Arbitrio* in his *Retractationes I.ix*, but he quotes himself quite unevenly and somewhat unconvincingly.[125]

---

[120] Peter Brown noted that when Augustine wrote his *Retractationes*, he was writing to mature Catholic Christians who would appreciate the path his life's journey took. Thus, the work is arranged chronologically. But Brown also pointed out that Augustine's historical framework was that of a man facing the 430s, and that the concerns of the fight with Pelagius, rather than the Manichees, occupied his mind. See Brown, *Augustine of Hippo*, 433–34.

[121] Defensio 161, BLW 91. Lane points out that Pighius raises an objection from *De Libero Arbitrio*, but Calvin always clearly answers him from *Retractiones*, never showing independent knowledge of *De Libero Arbitrio*. See also Defensio 163, n31, BLW 93, n39.

[122] Defensio 161, 163; BLW 91, 93. Defensio 166, BLW 95. Defensio 167, BLW 97.

[123] Augustine, De Libero Arbitrio 3.18.50, PL 32. Defensio 164; BLW 94. Augustine, *De Duabus Animabus* 10.14, PL 42, NPNF 4.102–03. Defensio, 166; BLW 95. Augustine, *De Vera Religione* 14.27–28, PL 34. Defensio 167; BLW 97. Cf. Lane's note, Defensio 161 n32.

[124] Dates from Brown, *Augustine of Hippo*, chronological table B, 64.

[125] J. H. S. Burleigh, ed., *Augustine: Earlier Writings* (Philadelphia: Westminster Press, 1953), 102–217. Burleigh writes: "In controverting the Manichees with largely Platonist weapons Augustine had exposed his flank to the Pelagians. Pelagius himself was happy to be able to quote from the *De Libero Arbitrio* in support of his own views" (107).

At this point of his argument, Calvin abandoned the historical field to his opponent. Calvin consistently rejected even the use of the earlier treatises, regularly answered Pighius from the *Retractationes*, and occasionally did so in a manner as to suggest that Pighius simply was refusing to turn the page of his copies of the treatises.[126] However, Calvin's rhetorical stratagem backfired. In attempting to ridicule Pighius for not turning the page, Calvin introduced the question of reading for polemical purpose. This proved to be a disastrous tactic for Calvin; he was the far more guilty party in this case – and by choice. Calvin was almost certainly using Erasmus' edition of the *Augustini Opera*, published by Chevallon in Paris in 1530–31.[127] The edition is bound in ten volumes.[128] But the *Retractationes* is bound together with both *De Vera Religione* and *De Libero Arbitrio* in that printing.[129] Calvin had recourse to the original sources to answer Pighius; and his choice to avoid using them must be seen as a polemical or theological choice, not an issue of access, and certainly sundered the humanistic canon of returning to the sources. For those who have seen Calvin's use of history in a primarily polemical fashion, this example provides corroboration.

The second point of difference between Pighius and Calvin appears in their different evaluations of the utility of the history of engagement with heresy. Pighius clearly saw the charged engagement with Pelagianism as deleterious to the sober and unruffled reflection upon the truths of the faith. This passion led Augustine to say those things that might not otherwise have been said.[130] Calvin agreed that heresies harm the church.

---

[126] Calvin stated, "Respondeo: cur non vertit paginam ubi reperiet quod stultum hunc eius clamorem compescat?" Defensio 163. BLW 93, "I reply: why does he not turn the page, where he will find something to curb this foolish uproar of his?"

[127] Ioannis Calvini: Scripta Didactica et Polemica, Volumen III, *Defensio Sanae et Orthodoxae Doctrinae de Servitute et Liberatione Humani Arbitrii*, edited by A. N. S. Lane, assisted by Graham Davies (Geneva: Droz, 2008), 50. See also his "Calvin and the Fathers in his Bondage and Liberation of the Will," in *John Calvin: Student of the Church Fathers* (Grand Rapids: Baker Book House, 1999), 160–62.

[128] *D. Aurelii Augustini Hipponensis Episcopi, Omnium Operum*. In 10 vols. Paris: Claude Chevallon, 1531. In Yale Divinity School Library.

[129] Actually also in the 1543 edition printed by Froben in Basel. Calvin certainly could not have used that edition. But comparing the earlier Parisian edition with Froben's suggests that the ordering of Augustine's works within the edition was not frequently changed, if ever.

[130] Calvin himself would use such a tool in his commentary on I Corinthians 7.1, discussing the problems with Jerome's interpretation. Commentary on I Corinthians 7.1, CO 49.401. See my *John Calvin and the Grounding of Interpretation: Calvin's First Commentaries* (Leiden: Brill, 2006), 127.

However, he found that the Pelagian heresy was unique in its helpful influence. Calvin wrote:

[T]he Pelagian heresy was much more of a help than a hindrance. For it aroused the spirit of this holy man to purify the church from that pagan philosophy about free choice which was by then generally prevalent, so that he might restore to the grace of God its proper honour. That was hidden and, as it were, half-buried by the false view of human ability which had then seized the minds of the masses.[131]

Calvin saw this particular heresy, or rather the effort to eradicate it, as wholly salubrious to the church.

While Calvin would continue to engage in arguments over the doctrines of the freedom of the will and predestination, he would not do so with Pighius, who died in 1542, before Calvin's reply to him was actually published. Calvin certainly did argue from scripture. But his argument with Pighius and the way he went about it betrayed a desire to maintain Augustine's support for the evangelical side that surpassed simple historical accuracy. In fact, Calvin abandoned historical accuracy in his effort to maintain a particular tradition that he believed had been set out by the most orthodox of fathers and surrendered the context that he accused his opponent of failing to understand. While a number of hypotheses could be posed, the simplest is that Calvin was willing to go to extraordinary lengths to maintain the support of tradition for an important part of his doctrinal complex.

ARTICLES OF THE FACULTY OF SACRED THEOLOGY OF PARIS, WITH ANTIDOTE – 1544

In 1544, Calvin took it upon himself to respond to the brief set of articles that the faculty of theology at the University of Paris had set out in 1543.[132] They had drawn up twenty-five articles that represented a

---

[131] Defensio 171, BLW 100. "Quin potius dicere soleo, haereses omnes alias plurimum incommodasse Ecclesiae, Pelagii vero haeresim multo plus profuise quam obfuisse, quod huius sancti viri spiritum excitaverit ut a profana illa de libero arbitrio philosophia (quae tunc vulgo invaluerat) Ecclesiam repugaret, ut suum gratiae Dei honorem, falsa humanae virtutis opinione (quae tunc multitudinis animos occupaverat) oppressum et quasi semisepultum, restitueret."

[132] De Greef, *The Writings of John Calvin*, 146. Articuli a facultate sacrae theologiae Parisiensi determinati super materiis fidei nostrae hodie controversis. Cum antidoto. John Calvin, "Articles by the Theological Faculty of Paris," in *Selected Works of John*

thoroughgoing rejection of evangelical teaching. The articles had the support of King François I and became a subscription test for theological students at Paris.[133] Calvin began with an attack on the nature of the theological method employed, arguing for a form of *sola scriptura*. Through a catena of scripture passages, Calvin arrived at his conclusion: "Therefore, whenever any controversy arises, the proper course is not to settle or decide it by the will of man, but to set it at rest by the authority of God only."[134] Calvin quoted Paul in Ephesians 6.17 that no other sword but the Word of God was necessary to defeat Satan.[135] However, Calvin provided a foretaste of things to come when he included, "In the admirable words of Augustine, 'When an obscure matter is under dispute, no aid being offered by clear and certain passages of sacred Scripture, human presumption, which gains nothing by leaning to either side, ought to restrain itself.'"[136] Calvin could not have written a more early modern Roman Catholic statement had he tried. He gave the exact argument that authorities at Trent would give for the insufficiency of scripture alone, that sometimes it did not offer a clear and certain passage. Calvin's effort was to turn that to restraint in matters of doctrine, and maintaining a healthy wariness of teaching doctrine that could not be grounded on scripture. But he provided a clear ideal that, at times, scripture alone was insufficient.

This model of the fusion of scripture and tradition in argumentation began in Calvin's response to the first article, which argued that baptism was necessary for salvation.[137] Calvin derisively answered that the Paris theologians wrote this in order to establish the efficacy of baptisms performed by women. It is likely that he had in mind the baptisms performed

---

Calvin, edited by Beveridge and Bonnet, 1:69–120; CO 7.1–44. Hereafter cited as Articles of Paris, with volume and page number.

[133] De Greef, *The Writings of John Calvin*, 146.

[134] Articles of Paris 1.73. CO 7.6. "Proinde si quid controversiarum inciderit, non hominum arbitrio transigi aut decidi, sed una Dei autoritate componi, aequum est."

[135] Articles of Paris 1.73; CO 7.6.

[136] Articles of Paris, 1.73; CO 7.6–7. "Praeclare enim Augustinus: ubi de re obscura disputatur, non adiuvantibus scripturae divinae certis clarisque testimoniis, cohibere se debet humana praesumptio, nihil faciens alteram in partem declinando."

[137] Articles of Paris 1.73. "We must believe, with sure and firm faith, that to all, even infants, Baptism is necessary for salvation, and that by means of it the grace of the Holy Spirit is given." CO 7.7. "Certa et firma fide credendum est baptisma omnibus etiam parvulis ad salutem necessarium esse: ac per ipsum dari gratiam spiritus sancti."

by midwives.[138] But Calvin did not immediately resort to a chain of New Testament citations to build the notion that it was invalid for women to baptize. Instead, he retorted that "the Council of Carthage declared, without any exception, that women must not presume to baptize."[139] Calvin continued the building of scripture and tradition in his consideration of the sacrament of penance. The theologians had argued that "It is not less certain that to adults, and those having the use of reason, after the commission of mortal sin, penitence is necessary; which penitence consists in contrition, and in sacramental confession, to be made audibly to a priest, and likewise in satisfaction."[140] Calvin could and did argue that the Spirit of God called believers to a repentant life, and gave scriptural warrant for that.[141] Further, Calvin denied the existence of a scriptural passage that demanded auricular confession to a priest, and cited the decree of Innocent III as evidence that this requirement did not exist prior to the Fourth Lateran Council in 1215.

The main quality of Calvin's responses was a fusion of carefully chosen passages from scripture and texts from orthodox authorities. Far from being an anti-tradition jeremiad, Calvin turned again and again to the fathers and orthodox medievals. Considering justification by works, Calvin quoted Augustine, Bernard, and Basil of Caesarea.[142] Arguing

---

[138] Kevin Madigan notes the prevalence of midwives baptizing in *Medieval Christianity: A New History* (New Haven: Yale University Press, 2015), chapter 18. See also Kathryn Taglia, "Delivering a Christian Identity: Midwives in Northern French Synodal Legislation, c. 1200–1500," in *Religion and Medicine in the Middle Ages*, edited by Peter Biller and Joseph Ziegler (Rochester: York Medieval Press, 2001), 77–90. Taglia's work demonstrates that so many synods and councils took this practice up that historians should assume it was commonplace. She concluded, "This examination of the synodal and conciliar legislation of northern France during the late Middle Ages shows that midwifery in the period was neither a gathering of ignorant women in need of professional medical enlightenment nor a cabal of female medical practitioners who were being systematically oppressed by a hostile Christian church. It seems likely from the ways in which the Church set out to professionalize this group that they were recognized for holding the necessary medical knowledge to assist in births according to the medical norms of the time. The legislation also clearly demonstrates that midwives were becoming increasingly recognized as an important part of pastoral care, required both to recognize emergency births as they occurred and to be able to perform emergency baptisms as the situation required." (87)

[139] Articles of Paris 1.74. CO 7.7. "Utcunque sit prohibitum in concilio Carthaginensi, quod mulieres baptizare non praesumant, sine aliqua exceptione."

[140] Articles of Paris 1.77. CO 7.10. "Nec minus certum est adultis et ratione utentibus, post peccatum mortale admissum necessariam esse poenitentiam: quae in contritione et confessione sacramentali vocaliter sacerdoti facienda, similiter et satisfactione consistit."

[141] Ezekiel 18.31; Jeremiah 4.4; Isaiah 1.16; Isaiah 58.6; Joel 2.13; Romans 6.6; etc.

[142] Articles of Paris, 1.82, CO 7.13.

against transubstantiation, Calvin cited Irenaeus, Cyprian, Fulgentius, and Augustine.[143] Contending that the articles of faith from the church that are not supported by scripture do not bind consciences, Calvin cited Augustine and Chrysostom.[144]

Calvin persisted with his joint attack through both scripture and tradition. The article on free will became a discussion of the interpretation of Augustine, with a detour into Ambrose and Cyprian.[145] The refutation of the article on justification by works returned to Augustine, supported by Bernard and Basil of Caesarea.[146] When considering transubstantiation, Calvin drew on Irenaeus, the Council of Nice, Cyprian, Fulgentius, and Augustine.[147] This was Calvin's pattern throughout the articles and their antidotes. He would normally begin with a scriptural passage and then proceed to interpretations of the fathers that supported his position. In adopting such a manner, he revealed how crucial he truly believed the apostolic witness and its imprimatur to be. By the end of the treatise, it was clear that Calvin did not intend to ground his entire argument on the foundation of the scriptural principle. He either did so because he wished to argue that the orthodox believers had never held certain positions or because it was simply too important to cloak his theology in the authority of the fathers – either solution is possible.

ACTS OF COUNCIL OF TRENT WITH ANTIDOTE – 1547

Calvin would continue to attack the Catholic positions over the rest of his career. He took up the idea of tradition again in his *Acts of the Council of Trent with Antidote*, published in December 1547.[148] The point of the frankly polemical text was to set forth Trent's model of the church and discipline, and to compare it with that of the Evangelicals.

---

[143] Articles of Paris, 1.84, CO 7.15.

[144] Articles of Paris, 1.105–06, CO 7.33.

[145] Articles of Paris, 1.75–77; CO 7.8–9.

[146] Articles of Paris, 1.82; CO 7.13. "Constituimus ergo cum Augustino, non secundum merita nostra, sed secundum Dei misericordiam firmam esse promissionem salutis. Item cum Bernardo, meritum omne nostrum esse miserationes Domini: vel, ut clarius loquamur, concludimus, post Basilium Magnum, hanc esse perfectam et integram gloriationem in Deo, quando propriae iustitiae inopes nos agnoscimus, sola autem fide in Christum iustificari."

[147] Articles of Paris, 1.84–85; CO 7.15.

[148] Some of this material has been published in my "Of Councils, Traditions, and Scripture: Calvin's Antidote to the Council of Trent," in *Calvinus Pastor Ecclesiae. Papers of the Eleventh International Congress on Calvin Research*, edited by Herman Selderhuis and Arnold Huijgen (Göttingen: Vandenhoeck and Ruprecht, 2016), 305–17.

The emphasis on ecclesiology and the practical instrument of ecclesiology, discipline, presents an extraordinary insight into Calvin's developing thought on tradition. In his polemic against the articles from the Council of Trent, Calvin clearly signaled his explicit acceptance of a particular idea of a doctrine of tradition. The tradition could remove nothing from the doctrine of the faith nor add anything to it; rather, tradition only could be applied to external rites having to do with decorum or discipline when used as a source in the absence of scripture. Second, tradition had to be an apostolic tradition ("deinde probare necesse habebunt, traditionem esse apostolicam"). This ideal allowed Calvin to use the tradition for his own purposes, within the parameters he had established.

Calvin began with the issue of the authority of councils. He noted that the very name of a sacred council (*sacri concilii*) was held in honor among both the ignorant and those of sound judgment. But Calvin saw a different honor. Without arguing against the authority of councils, Calvin sought a model by which clear thinkers would inquire before assent.[149] He noted that some believed that all councils that had been duly called must be judged inerrant, because they are led by the Holy Spirit.[150] Calvin chose not to take Luther's route of logic employed against Eck at Leipzig – that since various councils have contradicted each other, it is impossible that they are all inerrant. Instead, Calvin turned to Augustine:

How much wiser is Augustine who, from his singular modesty, indeed bestows no small honour upon Councils, and yet ceases not to observe the moderation which I have described. Writing against the Arian, Maximinus, he says: "I ought neither to adduce the Council of Nice, nor you that of Ariminium, as if to prejudge the question. I am not determined by the authority of the latter, nor you by that of the former. Founding on the authority of Scripture not peculiar to either, but the common witness of both, fact contends with fact, plea with plea, reason with reason." So much liberty does this holy man concede

---

[149] John Calvin, Articles of the Council of Trent, with Antidote, in *Selected Works of John Calvin*, vol. 3, edited by Beveridge and Bonnet, 17–188. Hereafter cited as Articles of Trent, with volume and page number. Articles of Trent, 3.30. CO 7.379. "Qui vero sunt saniores, sensim quidem et modeste, sed tamen inquirere sibi ante permittunt, quam plane assentiantur." Calvin pursued a similar form of inquiry prior to assent for scriptural interpretation as well.

[150] Articles of Trent, 3.30. CO 7.379. "Sed reclamant, quibus certo persuasum est, aut qui saltem aliis persuadere volunt, concilium, qualecunque sit, modo rite sit indictum, non posse errare: quia a spiritu sancto regatur. Volunt igitur, oraculi instar, absque controversia recipi, quidquid inde prodierit."

to himself and others, that he will not allow the Council of Nice to operate as a previous judgment, unless the truth of the case be plainly established from Scripture.[151]

The polemic usefulness of Calvin's strategy cannot be denied. He mustered a patristic witness of faultless authority, who judged the validity of conciliar decisions by the authority of scripture. Calvin could have made a direct appeal to scripture and dispensed with any consideration of councils. That was not the paradigm he chose. By taking up the problem in this manner, Calvin was leaving the door open, perhaps perpetually, for the qualified authority of councils and the authority of the orthodox tradition.

Calvin's turn to the authority of antiquity did not end with his opening salvos. He had commenced with his consideration of the authority of councils in order to take a swipe at Trent. This attack did not cease there – Calvin noted that Trent was called at an extraordinarily apposite moment. But he claimed that the council would not work because of the ways that the pope had set it up to support those abuses already in place. Even there he noted that "it is plain that both the doctrine and the whole administration of the Papacy are so much at variance with the majority of ancient Councils, that nothing more opposite can be imagined."[152] Here, Calvin was getting at what was the crux of the matter for him, ecclesiology and ecclesiastical authority. While Calvin could and did wax indignant about the bishops and theologians who were working for the church, he saved his greatest invective and his greatest concern for the pope. Calvin noted that even if all the theologians were the best and most acute, and the relatively small representation of the council could be pardoned, Trent still could not be authoritative. Calvin wrote: "For

---

[151] Articles of Trent, 3.30. CO 7.379. "At quanto Augustinus prudentior? qui pro singulari quidem sua modestia, non mediocrem conciliis honorem defert: illam tamen, quam dixi, moderationem non propterea retinere desinit. Nam adversus Maximinum Arianum scribens : Neque ego synodum Nicenam, inquit, nec tu Ariminensem debes, tanquam praeiudicaturus, afferre. Nec ego huius autorite, nec tu illius detineris. Scripturarum autoritatibus, non quorumcunque propriis, sed utrisque communibus testibus, res cum re, causa cum causa, ratio cum ratione certet. Tantum sibi et aliis libertatis sanctus vir concedit, ut ne ad praeiudicium quidem valere Nicenum concilium velit, nisi causae veritate ex scripturis bene perspecta."

[152] Articles of Trent, 3.32. CO 7.381. "Qui vero sunt saniores, sensim quidem et modeste, sed tamen inquirere sibi ante permittunt, quam plane assentiantur. Nam et quaestiones hodie agitantur, hactenus nunquam rite discussae: et palam est, quum doctrinam, tum vero universam papatus administrationem ita dissidere a plerisque conciliis veteribus, ut nihil magis adversum fingi queat:"

nothing is determined there save at the nod of the Roman Pontiff."[153]
For Calvin, the pope's authority over the council's decrees meant that it
was his and not the council's authority that brought forth the decrees.
The importance of this is not that Calvin disagreed with the doctrine of
the first session of the Council of Trent. What is significant is the point
to which he returns again and again. The doctrine and discipline of the
church was at stake, and Calvin used the patristic witness, his sense of
the orthodox tradition, and scripture to battle the Roman position. He
always sought to build multiple authorities into his answers, and thus
admitted the validity of multiple sources of authority.

Calvin continued his wider engagement with tradition in an argument
about what the apostles did with their lives. He noted that they had been
content with the rule of the Lord and had not sought to chain anyone
by laws and traditions.[154] The remark seemingly was made in passing as
Calvin set out the apostolic basis of the evangelical lifestyle. But again, he
was arguing about the nature of ecclesiastical discipline. Calvin was balancing the traditions that sought to bind clerics to celibacy (with disastrous consequences), dietary laws, and the necessity of certain prayers.[155]
Here, the issue was tradition against scripture.

Calvin at that point demonstrated his own freedom from and lack of
a true university education in theology. Surprisingly, he did not turn to II
Timothy 3.16–17 to refute Trent. This was a common text to cite throughout the medieval period, both in commentaries upon Peter Lombard's
Sentences and in later works. The text was considered a prooftext both
for the authority of scripture and for the nature of the divine science.[156]
Had Calvin sat through a doctorate in theology, it is more likely that he
would have supplied this idea as almost a reflex action. But instead, he
chose to fight the battle through the wisdom of the tradition.[157]

---

[153] Articles of Trent, 3.35. CO 7.384. "Nihil enim illic, nisi ex unius Romani pontificis
nutu, statuitur."

[154] Articles of Trent, 3.45. CO 7.392. "Qualis igitur apostolorum fuit vita? quibus igno-
tusfuit caelibatus, pro quo dimicant papistae: sub quibus nulla fuit unquam votorum
mentio: qui nullam in ciborum delectu necessitatem imposuerunt conscientiis : qui contenti ea regula, quam Dominus praescripserat, nullos unquam legum aut traditionum
laqueos iniicere tentarunt."

[155] Articles of Trent, 3.45. CO 7.392.

[156] See Alexander of Hales Summa Theologica I.1.4a ca. 1231; Thomas Aquinas Summa
Theologiae 1.1.1 c. 1265–73; Duns Scotus' Ordinatio (commentary on Sentences) I.1.4
c. 1300; see also works of Henry of Ghent, Petrus Aureoli and William of Ockham.

[157] Calvin also did not quote Titus 1.9, "He (the bishop) must have a firm grasp of the
word that is trustworthy in accordance with the teaching; so that he may be able both

Calvin then attacked the canon that the delegates to Trent set out, concerning their inclusion of the Apocrypha among the canonical books of scripture. Again, he did not oppose the judgment of Rome with the doctrine of revelation or a demand from scripture. He refrained, he said, from saying anything more than pointing out that Trent did this against the consent of the primitive church.[158] Calvin then cited Jerome and quoted Ruffinus as his support on the issue. Calvin noted Augustine, to point out that even those who included these books did so with a caveat.[159] Calvin used the pattern of the fathers as a corrective to the model of the actions of the delegates to Trent. Instead of making an argument based on the authorship of the scriptures by particular writers, or the apostolic and spiritual qualities of the books, or the evidence from the original languages, Calvin turned immediately to the practice of the ancient church. Further, Calvin turned to the exact model that the decree set forth – he went to the example of the orthodox fathers ("orthodoxorum patrum exempla secuta") in revering some books as the scriptures and withholding that reverence from others.[160] This was a crucial building block to establish. In his argumentation, Calvin frequently sought to determine a different reading of the tradition, complete with recourse to particular authorities.

In his treatise on the Council of Trent, Calvin set forth his acceptance of a circumscribed Roman tradition doctrine. Tradition could neither add nor subtract from the doctrine of faith, and was concerned with issues of discipline in the absence of scripture. Second, for the Roman adherents to make a claim of tradition, they would have to prove the item in question was an apostolic tradition ("deinde probare necesse habebunt, traditionem esse apostolicam").[161] Obviously, his opponents could not accept this version, and Calvin certainly intended to emphasize that. But we must note that this ideal allowed Calvin himself to use the tradition for his own purposes within the parameters he had established. In fact, he regularly went beyond the guidelines he established.

---

to preach with sound doctrine and to refute those who contradict it," another favorite medieval text that better suited his purpose.

[158] Articles of Trent, 3.70. CO 7.413. "De libris omnibus in canonem promiscue receptis non dicam aliud, nisi praeter ecclesiae veteris consensum id fieri."

[159] The Jerome comment is not cited, nor is Ruffinus. The Augustine citation is to the *De Doctrina Christiana*, 2.8.13, where Augustine does list the books of the Apocrypha, but also notes the problem that not all books are received by all the churches. 2.8.12.

[160] Articles of Trent, CO 7.408.

[161] Articles of Trent, CO 7.413.

Adultero-German Interim – 1549

Only two years later, Calvin returned to attack tradition again in his *Adultero-German Interim*, published in 1549.[162] This was Calvin's response to the Augsburg *Interim* of 1548, and Calvin's scorn for it was as withering as that of any Lutheran.[163] The Augsburg *Interim* was a settlement imposed by the Holy Roman Emperor, Charles V. He had defeated the Protestant princes at the Battle of Muhlberg in April 1547 and forced acceptance of an "interim" solution until the work of the Council of Trent could be finalized and the "religious question" settled for good.[164] The *Augsburg Interim* consisted of twenty-six articles that set several requirements for those territories controlled by the emperor. The *Interim* demanded seven sacraments, allowing only that laity could continue for the time being receiving both the bread and the wine at the eucharistic celebration in places that had adopted that practice. Belief in transubstantiation, the cult of the saints, purgatory, and various Catholic traditional disciplines were required. Protestant ministers who had married were allowed to keep their wives, but only until Trent had pronounced a final resolution on that question. The great majority of Protestant theologians and pastors rejected it, though notably Philip Melanchthon accepted it on the grounds that most of those points that Protestants rejected were actually points of *adiaphora*, matters of indifference.[165] Charles V attempted to force the German princes to accept it,

---

[162] Published in 1549, CO 7.545–686. Interim Adultero-Germanum: Cui Adiecta Est Vera Christianae Pacificationis Et Ecclesiae Reformandae Ratio. John Calvin, *The Adultero-German Interim, Selected Works of John Calvin*, vol. 3, edited by Beveridge and Bonnet, 189–357. Hereafter cited as Adultero-German Interim, with volume and page number.

[163] The German translation of the work was published in Magdeburg in 1549; De Greef suggests that it was translated by Flacius Illyricus. This version left out a portion of the original, and appended a criticism of Calvin that his concept of infant baptism was Pelagian (De Greef, *The Writings of John Calvin*, 150). In 1550, Calvin published an appendix responding to the charge, his Appendix Libelli adversus Interim adultero-germanum CO 7.675–86.

[164] For a brief review of the Augsburg Interim, see Kathleen M. Comerford, "The Council of Trent and the Augsburg Interim," in *John Calvin in Context*, edited by R. Ward Holder, 190–97. For more expansive accounts, see Irene Dingel, *Politik Und Bekenntnis: Die Reaktionen Auf Das Interim Von 1548* (Leipzig: Evangelische Verlag-Anst, 2006); and David M. Whitford, *Tyranny and Resistance : The Magdeburg Confession and the Lutheran Tradition* (St. Louis: Concordia Pub. House, 2001).

[165] Irene Dingel has collected some of the source documents, edited with Jan Martin Lies and Hans-Otto Schneider, in *Der Adiaphoristische Streit (1548–1560)* (Göttingen: Vandenhoeck & Ruprecht, 2012).

and many hedged, although Philipp of Hesse (whom Charles had captured and imprisoned) accepted. The result was increased religious tension, the exact opposite of Charles V's intention.

Calvin began his attack by supplying the text of the *Interim*, and followed this with his "True Manner of Attaining Peace for Christendom and of Reforming the Church." In discussing Rome's claim for the authority of the church, Calvin discerned a threefold argument – that the church discriminates between true and false scriptures, the church has the right of interpreting the scriptures, and the church's tradition has the force of oracles.[166] Here, Calvin rehearsed his point that accepting this kind of formulation of ecclesiological authority was tantamount to granting that Rome was right, that the Evangelicals should surrender. He wrote: "Where these foundations have been laid, it is plain that the power of which God has been robbed is transferred to horns and mitres. Be their conduct what it may, provided they are adorned with an episcopal title, they constitute the church."[167] Calvin's vitriolic argument was, essentially, that what was at stake was both the nature of the church and the exercise of authority within the church.

Calvin continued by an argument *ad absurdum* – did this license allow bishops to interpret scripture at will, to create new articles of faith, and to impose laws upon the conscience?[168] If so, what was left for God? Turning aside from Calvin's hyperbolic effort, the fear of an unfettered use of unwritten tradition which allowed humans to create whatever doctrines and disciplines they wished is implied. Again, Calvin the humanist sought clarity. What was the limit upon the ability of the hierarchy to formulate novel doctrines and disciplines? Was there any such limit? If not, what was the point of examining the fathers or the Bible?

But Calvin included an interesting sidenote in his destruction of the Roman model of unwritten traditions. He noted that his opponents adduced "a plausible example in the Baptism of Infants; but as there is no fiction too gross or childish to be vended in the Papacy under the name of

---

[166] Adultero-German Interim, 3.266. CO 7.612. "Nota est illa triplex cantilena: esse penes ecclesiam discernere veras scripturas ab adulterinis: eandem habere ius interpretandi: eius traditionem oraculorum vim habere."

[167] Adultero-German Interim, 3.266. CO 7.612. "His iactis fundamentis palam est, ereptum Deo imperium ad lituos et infulas transferri. Qualiscunque sit eorum caterva, qui modo episcopali titulo sint ornati, [pag. 108] ecclesiam constituit."

[168] Adultero-German Interim, 3.266. CO 7.612. "Porro, immensum est quod illis licebit, si arbitrio suo interpretentur scriptuiam, si fidei articulos fabricent, leges imponant conscientiis. Quid igitur Deo fiet reliquum?"

Tradition, whosoever has not the caution to keep out of this trap, voluntarily entangles himself in all kinds of superstition."[169] What attracts our attention is what Calvin gave up – the defenders of Rome have a plausible example in pedobaptism, as coming from the tradition of the church. They argued this on the basis of the lack of specific New Testament scriptural witness to any instance of infant baptism. This was a classic problem for magisterial Reformers, as David Wright notes: "Infant baptism was the weightiest constitutive feature of the old church that the magisterial Reformers perpetuated on the basis of tradition rather than explicit scriptural authority."[170] Calvin immediately attempted to withdraw his acceptance of its plausibility. He wrote:

I do not, however, concede to them that pedobaptism had its origin in the tradition of the church. It certainly appears to be founded on the institution of God, and to have derived its origin from circumcision. It would have little foundation if it depended only on the will of man. Accordingly, we must hold it as a universal rule, that no sacrament is legitimate unless it be from God and not from men.[171]

This quotation directly follows the other. But it is more than a little curious. Historically, we know that infant baptism is not part of the apostolic custom. Augustine, Calvin's favorite among the patristic authors, was baptized because he fell sick as a youth long after his infancy. While circumcision might be a type of baptism, it clearly was not baptism. Calvin demonstrated both an understanding of how this procedure might well be founded, at least in part, in ecclesiastical practice rather than upon scriptural warrant, and a wariness about attributing something so central as a sacrament solely to the tradition.[172]

---

[169] Adultero-German Interim, 3.268–69. CO 7.614. "Plausibile quidem exemplum adducunt in baptismo parvulorum, sed quum nullum sit tam crassum aut puerile commentum, quod non traditionis nomine vendlitetur in papatu, omni superstitionum genere ultro se implicat, quisquis ab hac captione sibi non cavet."

[170] David F. Wright, "George Cassander and the Appeal to the Fathers in Sixteenth-Century Debates about Infant Baptism," in *Auctoritas patrum*, edited by Grane, Schindler, and Wriedt, 259.

[171] Adultero-German Interim, 3.269. CO 7.614. "Tametsi, ne hoc quidem illis concedo, ex ecclesiae traditione fluxisse paedobaptismum, quem certo constat, in ipsa Dei institutione esse fundatum, et a circumcisione habere suam originem. Parum enim haberet firmamenti, si hominum tantum arbitrio staret. Adeoque haec tenenda est universalis regula, non esse legitimum sacramentum, nisi quod a Deo est, non ab hominibus."

[172] Calvin would continue to fight this issue out in the *Institutes*, in 1539, arguing that the Anabaptists were incorrect, and that there was no writer, however ancient, who did not believe in the apostolic origin of pedobaptism. *ICR*, IV.xvi.8.

Infant baptism presents us with a significant example of Calvin's acceptance of and argument for the church's tradition. As early as 1539, Calvin had set out that infant baptism was obviously of divine decree, since there could not be a sacrament that humans had set out. But he knew he was conflating two issues. First, there is the issue of the sacramental character of baptism – and very few theologians were arguing that baptism did not enjoy divine sanction. The second issue was infant baptism, and obviously this was a very different issue, about which there were serious disagreements by 1539. Calvin depended upon the Roman tradition to substantiate the validity of infant baptism because there were no New Testament texts to which he could turn. Further, he turned again to the tradition with a clumsy call upon all the ancients as his defenders when he wrote "There is not one writer among the ancients who does not know this."[173] However, both Tertullian and Gregory of Nazianzus had clearly taught a preference for the later baptism.[174] Calvin's citation of the patristic authorities here lacks the specificity that he sometimes preferred. But in any case, Calvin's whole argumentative weight is founded upon the tradition of the church in the absence of the clear scriptural witness. Calvin stated that the origins of infant baptism had to be scriptural, but he did not follow that principle in the process of making his arguments.

After considering baptism, Calvin turned to the more basic issue of tradition, returning to his project of constructing a workable theory of tradition subordinated to scripture. He wrote: "The true church of Christ never passed any laws save such as might conduce to maintain order, cherish concord and invigorate discipline."[175] Calvin placed the entirety of tradition's authority within ecclesiastical discipline, broadly speaking. This was the same position he had staked out in his debate with Sadoleto a decade earlier. He did not allow matters of faith or doctrine to be supplied by tradition alone, though clearly Calvin allowed orthodox tradition to regulate the manner of the application of scriptural doctrine.

---

[173] CO 2.982. "Siquidem nullus est scriptor tam vetustus qui non eius originem ad apostolorum saeculum pro certo referat."

[174] Tertullian, *De Baptismo*, 18, and Gregory of Nazianzus, Oration 40, *De Baptismo*. Tertullian's treatise was included in the edition of Tertullian edited by Beatus Rhenanus and published by Johann Froben in Basel in 1521; Calvin certainly could have known it. For Gregory of Nazianzus, things are easier – Calvin quoted Oration XL in the 1539 edition of the *Institutes*, both in Greek and Latin. See *Institutes*, I.xiii.17. CO 2.104.

[175] Adultero-German Interim, 3.269. CO 7.614. "Leges non alias unquam tulit vera Christi ecclesia, nisi quae ad retinendum ordinem, ad fovendam concordiam, ad tuendam disciplinam facerent. Tales nemo sobrius non fatebitur, et iure ferri, et ab omnibus piis servandas esse. Nec vero de eo contendimus."

Calvin then further restricted the field of tradition's authority by identifying two mistakes or evils that had to be avoided. He asserted: "But
it is necessary to provide against two evils, if we wish the church to be
safe."[176] The first was the loss of Christian freedom. Even though Christ
had abrogated divine laws in order to release believers from bondage, the
faithful had been oppressed by new human laws.[177] In Calvin's eyes, this
was done to subject souls to constant torture as the various rules entailed
duties that were not even possible ("observatio impossibilis"). The second evil Calvin diagnosed in the use of tradition was that "The laws
which the tyrants recommend under the name of the Church they term
spiritual, as being destined to rule the conscience."[178] That crossed from
the realm of discipline and good order into the domain of doctrine.
Calvin drew the line there. Further, Calvin applied this principle in a
zero-sum game: Whatever was credited to the human authority would
be taken away from divine authority. Calvin decried this: "Have done
then with that prevaricating obedience which breaks the bridle of God in
order to strangle us with the cords of men!"[179] For humans to have even
ecclesiastical authority without the express or implied basis of scripture,
in the realm of doctrine, was to remove it from God's hands.

Calvin demonstrated a clear engagement with scripture and tradition
across his career in dealing with theologians who had remained in the
church of Rome. The *Epistolae Duae* stand as remarkable outliers, otherwise, Calvin turns to the tradition time and again to make his points and
to stake his claim as a minister of the church that was the true descen-
dant of the church of the apostles. Calvin's theology not only reserved a
place for tradition, but it actually necessitated its use. Even when writing against Catholics, when analysts expect to find Calvin's attacks at
their most trenchant, he reserved a place for the use of the theological,
exegetical, and ecclesiastical traditions. Calvin was not formulaic in
his methodology, so one should not expect a short set of quotations or
allusions in every treatise. But the ongoing language of appeals to the

---

[176] Adultero-German Interim, 3.269. CO 7.614. "Sed duobus malis subvenire necesse est,
si volumus salvam esse ecclesiam."

[177] Adultero-German Interim, 3.269. CO 7.615. "Qui enim Dei leges abrogavit, ut nos a
servitute laxaret, novis profecto hominum legibus nos premi noluit. Factum est tamen."

[178] Adultero-German Interim, 3.270. CO 7.615. "Leges, quas sub ecclesiae nomine com-
mendant tyranni, spirituales vocant: ut quae regendis conscientiis sint destinatae."

[179] Adultero-German Interim, 3.270. CO 7.615. "Atqui, tantundem abrogatur imperio
Dei, quantum hominibus tribuitur. Valeat ergo praevaricatrix ista obedientia, quae Dei
fraenum abrumpit, ut nos hominum laqueis strangulet."

tradition, use of the tradition to demonstrate the facts of the past, and engagement with the tradition to forge Calvin's doctrinal positions, all show his ongoing engagement with the orthodox theological tradition. Calvin proposed a use of tradition that was guided by the apostolic witness, and could only add to the deposit of faith items of good order. But his practice was much deeper, engaging the substance of doctrine and liturgical practice.

LUTHERANS

In January 1545, John Calvin wrote a letter to Martin Luther, asking for his support and advice about the issue of Nicodemism in France. The letter was entrusted to Philip Melanchthon, who chose not to share the letter with Luther, because he realized Luther viewed Calvin as part of the party of "sacramentarians," those who followed the teachings of Zwingli about the Lord's Supper.[180] Luther believed that the presence of Christ in the sacrament was "in, with, and under" the elements of bread and wine, thus preserving the literal meaning of "this is my body" (Matthew 26.26–28) Zwingli had taught that this passage was figurative in meaning, and that the presence of Christ in the sacrament was spiritual. The Colloquy of Marburg's 1529 effort to knit together a pan-Protestant league through Swiss and German reconciliation and the building of mutual bonds had failed.

Calvin had not always occupied a position seemingly opposed to Luther and Lutheranism. At the beginning of his pastoral career, Calvin was so enamored of Luther that he was willing to call him an apostle. In his first published theological work, the 1536 *Institutes*, Calvin almost seemed to have Luther's *Small Catechism* open as he wrote.[181] The first four sections of Luther's *Small Catechism* explicate the Ten Commandments, the Creed, the Lord's Prayer, and the sacraments. Calvin followed that pattern exactly. The young Calvin's thought was extremely influenced by Luther. Even in polemic against a Lutheran pastor, Joachim Westphal, a Wittenberg-trained theologian who was ministering in Hamburg, Calvin would write that he revered Luther's memory.[182]

---

[180] Gordon, *Calvin*, 169.

[181] For this section, see Alexandre Ganoczy, *The Young Calvin*, translated by David Foxgrover and Wade Provo (Philadelphia: Westminster Press, 1987), chap. 14.

[182] *Defensio sanae et orthodoxae doctrinae de sacramentis eorumque natura vi fine usu et fructu, quam pastores et ministry Tigurinae ecclesiae et Genevensis antehac brevi consensionis mutuae formula complexi sun tuna com refutatione probrorum quibus eam indocti et clamosi homines infamant.* CO 9.18, Beveridge 2.224.

However, Calvin and Swiss theology were becoming odious in Lutheran realms even before Luther's death, and that opprobrium only grew stronger after 1546. The eucharistic controversy had driven the sides apart, long before Calvin even converted from Catholicism.[183] Though Calvin came late to the struggle, he engaged it early in his career. His short treatise of 1538 demonstrated that Calvin believed he could patch up the differences that existed between the Swiss and Germans, differences he believed scandalized the faithful.[184] But such was not to be the case.[185] Calvin's set of formulae for understanding the mode of Christ's communication to the faithful, worked out over decades, earned him little respect from Lutherans. Further, Calvin was motivated by a similar concern to that of Philip of Hesse's at an earlier time, and he sought a doctrinal concord that might allow better military and political alliances against imperial aggression.[186] He worked at finding agreement with the other Swiss first, and was able to come to a compromise with Zurich, the Consensus Tigurinus of 1549.[187] Although the Zurich party saw Calvin as too Lutheran, this agreement with the Zurich church proved to be the final straw for Lutherans.[188] Joachim Westphal published a series of treatises attacking Calvin between 1552 and 1555.[189] He attacked Calvin

---

[183] For the most current and insightful review of the struggle over the Lord's Supper, see Amy Nelson Burnett, *Debating the Sacraments: Print and Authority in the Early Reformation* (Oxford: Oxford University Press, 2019).

[184] Calvini Opera 5.433–60, Petit Traicté de la Saincte Cene de nostre Seigneur Iesus Christ. English translation as *Short Treatise on the Holy Supper of our Lord and only Saviour Jesus Christ*, in *Calvin: Theological Treatises*, edited and translated by J. K. S. Reid (Philadelphia: Westminster Press, 1954), 142–66.

[185] Anthony N. S. Lane, "Was Calvin a Crypto-Zwinglian?" in *Adaptations of Calvinism in Reformation Europe: Essays in Honour of Brian G. Armstrong*, edited by Mack P. Holt (Burlington: Ashgate, 2007), 21–41.

[186] R. Ward Holder, "The Pain of Agreement: Calvin and the Consensus Tigurinus," *Reformation & Renaissance Review* 18 (2016): 85–94. See also Peter Stephens, "The Sacraments in the Confessions of 1536, 1549, and 1566 – Bullinger's Understanding in Light of Zwingli's," *Zwingliana* 37 (2010): 51–76. Philip of Hesse was a German Lutheran prince who called the Colloquy of Marburg in 1529 between the Germans and the Swiss, to create a doctrinal agreement that could be the basis of a military league against the threat of the empire.

[187] The term "Consensus Tigurinus" or "Zurich Consensus" was not used until the nineteenth century. For Calvin's relationships with Zurich and other Swiss cities, see Emidio Campi and Christian Moser, "Loved and Feared": Calvin and the Swiss Confederation," translated by David Dichelle, in *John Calvin's Impact on Church and Society 1509–2009*, edited by Martin Ernst Hirzel and Martin Sallmann (Grand Rapids: Eerdmans, 2009), 14–34.

[188] Stephens, "The Sacraments in the Confessions of 1536, 1549, and 1566," 63.

[189] Esther Chung-Kim, *Inventing Authority: The Use of the Church Fathers in Reformation Debates over the Eucharist* (Waco: Baylor University Press, 2011), 59–77.

and Zwingli as "sacramentarians" who would not accept the reality of the body of Christ, only its sacramental efficacy. Tilemann Hesshusen, a professor at the University of Heidelberg, joined the fight as well, publishing treatises in 1560 and 1561.[190] Calvin had compromised with the Zurich party in order to come to agreement, and he frequently chose silence as a strategy to find accord. However, Calvin's sacrifices in the cause of agreement with other Swiss were quickly exploited as a wedge that split Lutherans and Reformed, rather than as an effort to reach out to his counterparts in other cities and realms. Any forlorn hope for a doctrinal union that would allow military or diplomatic allegiance was lost. In a line almost certainly inspired by Calvinists, if not Calvin himself, *The Formula of Concord* argues that there are two kinds of sacramentarians, the crude sacramentarians who believe that the Supper is nothing other than bread and wine; while the cunning sacramentarians (the most dangerous kind), talk about what happens spiritually, through faith.[191]

In the 1550s, the conflict between some Lutheran defenders of German theologies of the eucharist and Calvin erupted. While Calvin had been willing to approach Luther deferentially, there is scant evidence that he saw the German church as a superior to which he should show deference. Instead, in his natural mode of attacking those who wrote against him, and assuming that a polemic against him equaled an attack on the evangelical ministry, Calvin wrote a series of tracts against his Lutheran detractors.

The Defense of the Sound Doctrine on the Sacraments –1554

The Consensus Tigurinus, agreed upon in 1549 and published in 1551, argued in the twenty-fourth article, "For we deem it no less absurd to place Christ under the bread or couple him with the bread, than to transubstantiate the bread into his body."[192] Westphal saw this as a rejection of Luther's explanation that the body of Christ was with, in, and under the elements. Esther Chung-Kim has noted, in addition, that the influx of "London exiles" escaping the reach of Mary I of England exacerbated the situation, because many of them held a belief in the presence of Christ

---

[190] For more on Hesshusen, see Thilo Krüger, *Empfangene Allmacht: die Christologie Tilemann Heshusens: (1527–1588)* (Göttingen: Vandenhoeck and Ruprecht, 2004).

[191] *Formula of Concord*, quoted in Lane, "Was Calvin a Crypto-Zwinglian?", 25.

[192] Quoted in Chung-Kim, *Inventing Authority*, 61.

in the Supper that more closely aligned with that of the Swiss.[193] In 1552, Westphal published his *Farrago of Confused and Divergent Opinions on the Lord's Supper Taken from the Books of the Sacramentarians.*[194]

Calvin originally believed that the attack was too insignificant to answer, and wrote to Bullinger making that point.[195] But by 1554, with conditions worsening for the London exiles, Calvin put pen to paper and produced *The Defense of the Sound and Orthodox Doctrine on the Sacraments, Their Nature, Power, Purpose, Use and Fruitfulness.*[196] In the treatise, Calvin himself noted that since he was not dealing with adherents to the church of Rome, he should not have to use anything but scripture. But such was not to be the case. The *Defense* was a struggle for the authority and imprimatur of Augustine, more than a simple turn to the orthodox tradition. Calvin began his explicit turn to the orthodox tradition with Augustine, that the Swiss always willingly assented to the North African bishop's teaching that "a sacrament is a kind of visible word."[197] Calvin soon followed that with another citation to Augustine, supporting the idea that the elements become sacraments through the power of the Word that is believed.[198] The Genevan Reformer used this as an authority to support the idea that possession of Christ was granted through the promise, not through the bare elements.

---

[193] The Swiss position was hardly monolithic. The Consensus Tigurinus was an effort to demonstrate those items on which agreement could be stated, without being overly specific so as to raise greater dissension. For a number of articles on the Consensus, see *Reformation and Renaissance Review* 18.1 (March, 2016), dedicated to the theme "Reformation Debates over the Lord's Supper (1536–1560): Sources and Impact of the Consensus Tigurinus."

[194] Joachim Westphal, *Farrago confusanearum et inter se dissidentium opinionum de Coena Domini, ex Sacramentariorum libris congesta* (Magdeburg: Christian Rödlinger, 1552). Westphal followed this the next year with *Recta fides de coena Domini ex verbis apostoli Pauli et evangelistarum demonstrara ac communita*, also published in Magdeburg.

[195] De Greef, *The Writings of John Calvin*, 178.

[196] *Defensio sanae et orthodoxae doctrinae de sacramentis eorumque natura vi fine usu et fructu, quam pastores et ministry Tigurinae ecclesiae et Genevensis antehac brevi consensionis mutuae formula complexi sun tuna com refutatione probrorum quibus eam indocti et clamosi homines infamant.* CO 9.5–36. John Calvin, "Exposition of the Heads of Agreement," in Selected Works of John Calvin: Tracts and Letters vol. 2, edited by Henry Beveridge and Jules Bonnet (Grand Rapids: Baker Book House, 1983), 221–44. Hereafter cited as Defense, with volume and page numbers.

[197] Defense 2.225. CO 9.19. "Quando enim illud Augustini libenter nos amplecti omnes semper professi sumus: sacramentum scilicet quasi visibile esse verbum,"

[198] Defense 2.227. CO 9.21. "Quibus verbis nihil aliud voluimiîíá, quam quod omnium consensus vere et scite Augustinus docet, tum demum ex elementis sacramenta exstare, dum verbum aceedit, non quia profertur, sed quia creditur."

In creating a sacramental doctrine, Calvin turned to Augustine again. He argued that the Swiss had taken from Augustine the idea that "it is Christ alone who baptizes inwardly, and that it is he alone who makes us partakers of himself in the Supper, strongly demonstrating the excellence of both ordinances."[199] The power of the entire sacrament, Calvin argued, was reserved to Christ. None of it was granted to the elements of bread and wine.[200] Calvin continued his assault on Westphal by use of Augustine throughout the brief treatise. He mentioned the bishop of Hippo by name eight times in the short polemic. But that count clearly understates the impact of Augustine in the treatise. For instance, in the middle of the treatise, Calvin turns to Augustine by name, stating, "How much more rightly does Augustine, as became a man well versed in the Scriptures, say that the bread of the Lord was given to Jesus to make him a slave of the devil, just as a messenger of Satan was given to Paul to perfect him in Christ."[201] Calvin did not stop there, but continued discussing Augustine's contributions to sacramental theology for several pages.[202] Calvin's adoption of Augustine was a useful foil in his anti-Lutheran polemic, as Augustine was a favorite of many Lutheran theologians.

Calvin wrote the response to Westphal with the stated intent of being gentle with the Lutheran theologian, as well as bringing an end to the controversy. As so frequently happened with Calvin's polemical corrections of others, his effort at pouring oil on the waters was instead an instance of throwing gasoline on the flames. Westphal would continue to write polemics against Calvin, to which Calvin would continue to respond.

Second Defense – 1556

Calvin quickly produced the *Second Defense of the Pious and Orthodox Faith concerning the Sacraments in Answer to the Calumnies of Joachim*

---

[199] Defense, 2.230. CO 9.23. "Quod autem subiicimus ex Augustino, unum esse Christum qui intus baptizat, item unum eundem esse, qui nos in coena facit sui participes, utriusque mysterii praestantiam summopere commendat."

[200] This chapter and this study are not concerned with the truth of Calvin's arguments, but the manner in which he made them. Thus, for the purposes of this book, I make no evaluations about Westphal's, Calvin's, and Hesshusen's claims.

[201] Defense, 2.234. CO 9.27. "Quanto rectius Augustinus, ut homine probe in scripturis exercitato dignum erat, non secus panem Domini Iudae datum esse docet, quo manciparetur diabolo, quam datum Paulo angelum Satanae, per quem perficeretur in Christo."

[202] Three columns in the CO.

Westphal in 1556.[203] In it, Calvin asserted that Westphal declared that Augustine had claimed that Judas ate the real body of Christ, but could not produce any such passage from the North African bishop.[204] Calvin expanded his polemic by arguing that Westphal was misapplying Augustine's work. He noted that Westphal had quoted Augustine, who had been arguing against the Manichees. This was another significant moment, because Calvin was averring that there had to be a contextual and historical understanding of Augustine, rather than an atomistic sense that drew the bishop's words out of context.[205]

In the *Second Defense*, Calvin took up the history of Berengar of Tours. Berengar was an early medieval theologian (*c.* 999–1088) who had led the cathedral school at Chartres.[206] Berengar engaged in a controversy over the nature of the eucharistic elements – whether they were truly changed in essence – a theory that he denied. His main opponent was Lanfranc of Bec, who attacked him mercilessly. In 1059, Berengar was forced by Pope Nicholas II at Rome to accept a confession of faith that stated that the bread became the true body of Christ that in the sacrament was broken by the hands of the priest and was torn by the teeth of the believers. Consideration of Berengar and the history of eucharistic controversy was already becoming a Reformed tradition – Huldrych Zwingli had discussed the case of Berengar in his *On the Lord's Supper* of 1527. Calvin asserted that Westphal had accused him of the heresy of Berengar, quoting the confession Berengar was forced to recite.[207] Calvin was only too happy to be lumped in with Berengar, because Pope Nicholas and Lanfranc on the other side were the proponents of transubstantiation, before the term was used.

---

[203] John Calvin, *Second Defense of the Pious and Orthodox Faith concerning the Sacraments in Answer to the Calumnies of Joachim Westphal*, in *Selected Works of John Calvin*, vol. 2, edited by Beveridge and Bonnet, 245–345. Hereafter cited as Second Defense, with volume and page numbers. Latin, *Secunda defensio piae et orthodoxae de sacramentis fidei contra Ioachimi Westphali calumnias*, CO 9.41–120.

[204] Second Defense, 2.304–05. CO 9.90.

[205] Second Defense, 2.342–43. CO 9.118.

[206] For more on Berengar, see Charles M. Radding and Francis Newton, *Theology, Rhetoric, and Politics in the Eucharistic Controversy, 1078–1079: Alberic of Monte Cassino against Berengar of Tours* (New York: Columbia University Press, 2003); Peter F. Ganz, R. B. C. Huygens, and Friedrich Niewöhner, *Auctoritas und Ratio: Studien zu Berengar von Tours* (Wiesbaden: Otto Harrassowitz, 1990); and H. E. J. Cowdrey, *Lanfranc: Scholar, Monk, and Archbishop* (Oxford: Oxford University Press, 2003).

[207] Second Defense, 2.260. CO 9.57, "Berengarii haeresim rursus a nobis excitatam esse dicit."

This was an enormously significant moment in the argument between Westphal and Calvin. The Genevan Reformer made an argument that revised the orthodox view of the history of doctrine concerning the presence of Christ in the elements. History was basic to Calvin's view of tradition, and Westphal's evocation of Berengar of Tours as a heretic was a rhetorical blunder that allowed Calvin to make his point. In doing so, Calvin clarified that not all the points of the history of orthodox doctrine would be acceptable in the crafting of a tradition. But the new orthodoxy would require some sense of the hermeneutics of both history and tradition.

Last Admonition of John Calvin to Joachim Westphal – 1557

The next year, he wrote the *Last Admonition of John Calvin to Joachim Westphal*.[208] As with the *Institutes*, one can see an expansion throughout this fight – each of the treatises to Westphal is longer than the previous one. Furthermore, the dependence on and discussion of Augustine grows as well. That was hardly surprising, as Westphal had charged that Calvin had hardly read Augustine.[209] What could be counted as surprising was the fact that both Westphal and Calvin believed that fighting over the mantle of Augustine was well worth their – and their readers' – time.

The Clear Explanation of ... the Holy Supper – 1561

The Eucharistic struggle did not only engage Joachim Westphal. In 1560, Tileman Heshusius published a treatise, *The Presence of the Body of Christ in the Lord's Supper, against the Sacramentarians*.[210] Though Calvin had little regard for Heshusius because he believed him merely to be someone who aped Luther, he obtained a copy and wrote his own treatise in response, published in Geneva in 1561.[211] This was his *The Clear Explanation of Sound Doctrine Concerning the True Partaking*

---

[208] John Calvin, Last Admonition of John Calvin to Joachim Westphal, in *Selected Works of John Calvin*, vol. 2, edited by Beveridge and Bonnet, 2.346–494. Latin, *Ultima Admonitio Ioannis Calvini ad Ioachimum Westphalum*, CO 9.137–252.

[209] De Greef, *The Writings of John Calvin*, 181.

[210] *De praesentia corporis Christi in coena Domini contra sacramentarios*, published in Jena, 1560.

[211] De Greef, *The Writings of John Calvin*, 181.

of the Flesh and Blood of Christ in the Holy Supper.[212] Calvin depended
heavily on the early church's theologians in this treatise. He began with a
consideration of Heshusius' argument, and argued against it from scripture, drawing primarily on Paul. But soon he took up Heshusius' claim
that the Lutheran position was an imitation of the fathers. He wrote:
"It is an intolerable impudence for Heshusius to represent himself as
an imitator of the fathers."[213] Calvin then went on to consider Cyril of
Alexandria and a series of quotations from Augustine.[214]

But that did not end Calvin's consideration of Heshusius' use of the
orthodox tradition. Calvin proceeded to consider how to engage appropriately with the early church, while stating that the Heidelberg theologian had failed to do so in an evenhanded manner. Calvin wrote:

It is rather strange that, while he is ashamed to use the authority of John of
Damascus and Theophylact, he calls them not the least among ecclesiastical
writers. Sound and sober readers will find more learning and piety in a single
commentary on Matthew, which is falsely alleged to be an unfinished work of
Chrysostom, than in all the theology of the Damascene.[215]

Calvin's attack sought to define the correct patristic tradition, that
which was most supportive of learning and piety ("plus doctrinae ac
pietatis"), while condemning Heshusius for cherrypicking his authorities from antiquity.[216] Calvin then went on to consider Justin Martyr,
Irenaeus, Tertullian, Hilary, Cyril, Clement of Alexandria, Cyprian,

---

[212] John Calvin, *The Clear Explanation of Sound Doctrine Concerning the True Partaking
of the Flesh and Blood of Christ in the Holy Supper*, in *Calvin: Theological Treatises*,
edited by J. K. S. Reid (Philadelphia: Westminster Press, 1954), 257–324. Hereafter
cited as Clear Explanation, with page number. CO 9.457–517. *Dilucida explicatio
sanae doctrinae de vera participatione carnis et sanguinis Christi in sacra coena ad dis-
cutiendas Heshusii nebulas.*

[213] Clear Explanation, 280. CO 9.480. "Nec tolerabilis impudentia est, quod in hac fatua
partitione videri vult Heshusius patrum imitator."

[214] Clear Explanation, 280–81. CO 9.480–81.

[215] Clear Explanation, 292. CO 9.490–91. "Mirum autem, quum Ioannis Damasceni et
Theophylacti testimoniis eum uti pudeat, vocare tamen non postremos in scriptori-
bus ecclesiasticis. Atqui plus doctrinae ac pietatis reperient sani et modesti lectores in
uno commentario qui falso inscribitur Opus imperfectum Chrysostomi in Matthaeum,
quam in tota Damasceni theologia." James Kellerman argues that the incomplete commentary on Matthew could not have been written by Chrysostom because it was composed in Latin, it employs apocryphal books that Chrysostom would have been unlikely
to use, and the author quoted the Latin version of Sirach. *Incomplete Commentary on
Matthew (Opus imperfectum)*, translated with introduction by James A. Kellerman,
edited by Thomas C. Oden (Downers Grove: IVP Academic, 2010), xvii–xviii.

[216] Clear Explanation, 293. CO 9.491.

Eusebius, Athanasius, Epiphanius, Basil of Caesarea, Ambrose, Gregory of Nazianzus, Jerome, and Chrysostom, ending with a long consideration of Augustine.[217] Throughout the treatise, both Heshusius and Calvin made clear that it was vitally important to their positions and to their theology to be correctly situated in the orthodox tradition.

Esther Chung-Kim has noted that both Reformed and Lutheran theologians sought to create a new way of doing history, a method of generating authoritative speech, in her analysis of the reliance on the authority of the fathers in the debate between Calvin and the later Lutherans.[218] She writes:

This elaborate, repetitive process of incorporating cues to the church fathers guided Reformers in building up authoritative, albeit contested, confessional traditions. In other words, while interest in the early Christian writers was not new, their works were being recalled in a new way – to provide ancestral roots for a newly consolidated Lutheran or Reformed tradition that could compete simultaneously with the formation of other churches.[219]

Chung-Kim argues that the efforts of Protestant thinkers amounted to a series of efforts to deviate from the late medieval church, and then intensified that series of appeals to the patristic age in their interconfessional strife.[220] She notes that both Luther and Calvin generated models by which they could argue that their concentration on the resources of the orthodox tradition were in effect faithful expositions of scripture. However, neither theologian regularly demonstrated the legitimacy of those claims. As such, they regularly made appeal to the orthodox tradition in order to establish their doctrinal points.

CONCLUSION: CALVIN, POLEMICS, AND TRADITION

John Calvin argued vociferously and frequently, with opponents of a number of confessions. He believed that he was defending the truth of the gospel, making the struggles worth his effort. Examinations of his polemic battles with Lutherans, Catholics, Anabaptists, and Libertines reveal no significant difference in his turn to the orthodox tradition.

---

[217] *Clear Explanation*, 294–307. CO 9.491–504.
[218] Chung-Kim, *Inventing Authority*.
[219] Chung-Kim, *Inventing Authority*, 140.
[220] Chung-Kim, *Inventing Authority*, 141.

He regularly turned to the riches of the ecclesiastical, exegetical, and doctrinal traditions to make his points. Calvin forged an amalgamation of the scripture and tradition in his labors. Chapter 4 will take up the question of whether that was only a feature of his attacks on other confessional groups or was more characteristic of his thought in general.

4

Calvin, Tradition, and Vernacular Works

John Calvin wrote for a diverse set of audiences. He could write for the most learned humanists, or he could seek to arouse the passions of the laity in a French treatise.[1] In point of fact, one could claim that he wrote nothing "for the laity," any more than he wrote things "for Catholics," or "for Lutherans." Many of the categories we call on are theoretical and analytical, thereby allowing for greater clarity but not providing a "thick" historical description of Calvin's reasons for writing.[2] However, Calvin, more than some of his contemporaries, recognized the issue of reaching out to those who were not equipped with a university education. He occasionally wrote treatises in French, some of his polemics were in French, his interpretive work on the Bible was translated into French, and he regularly translated the *Institutes of the Christian Religion* into French. These were significant efforts, requiring much effort to find wording requisite to represent difficult conceptual material in a language that often lacked the technical precision of Latin.[3]

---

[1] The works treated in this chapter do not include those considered in other chapters, such as the Brief Instruction, Against the Libertines, and Apology to the Nicodemites.

[2] Michael Walzer, *Thick and Thin: Moral Argument at Home and Abroad* (Notre Dame: University of Notre Dame Press, 1994). Walzer points out that frequently, groups of people in different countries or societies can agree on the minimalist idea of a concept, such as freedom. That is the "thin definition." But as soon as the discussion includes the implications, providing the "thick" description, agreement becomes exponentially more difficult. This is also the case when the space being transcended is temporal, rather than spatial.

[3] But see Olivier Millet's work demonstrating the shift across Calvin's authorial career in his sense of himself as an author and as an authority in French. Millet, "Calvin's Self-Awareness as Author," translated by Susanna Gebhardt, in *Calvin & His Influence, 1509–2009*, edited by Irena Backus and Philip Benedict (Oxford: Oxford University Press, 2011), 84–101.

Calvin was keenly aware that the reforms he set out to accomplish could not be achieved without the support of a much broader public than the university-trained. This is one of our more clear examples of Calvin's own growth from humanist scholar to evangelical reformer. He had moved beyond the ideal of the scholar writing for scholars, to the evangelical doctor writing for the broader church. He preached in French and learned from that effort to express doctrine in French. He translated his own larger work into French. His efforts were part of the generation of a theological French in the early modern period, a reforming effort that contributed to the essentials of French and Genevan culture in the early modern period.[4]

PROPOSED FRENCH EDITION OF THE SERMONS OF CHRYSOSTOM – 1538–1540

In the years while he was in Strasbourg, Calvin began a project he never completed. He wrote a Latin draft of a preface to a French edition of the sermons of John Chrysostom.[5] The original manuscript exists in Calvin's own handwriting, and forensic and paleographical evidence date it conclusively between 1538 and 1540.[6] This Latin draft demonstrates how tied to Latin Calvin's thought was, and how expressing himself in French did not come easily, especially early in his career. Calvin might have chosen a number of authors to use to guide his readers. In his biblical interpretations,

---

[4] Francis Higman, "The Reformation and the French Language," in *Lire et Découvrir: La circulation des idées au temps de la Réforme* (Geneva: Librairie Droz, 1998), 337.

[5] Two English translations exist. John H. McIndoe provided "John Calvin: Preface to the Homilies of Chrysostom," *Hartford Quarterly*, 5, 2 (1965): 19–26. This version supplies little in the way of commentary or critical apparatus. The preferred translation is that of Ian P. Hazlett, "Calvin's Latin Preface to his Proposed French Edition of Chrysostom's Homilies: Translation and Commentary," in *Humanism and Reform: The Church in Europe, England and Scotland, 1400–1643. Essays in Honour of James K. Cameron*, edited by James Kirk (Oxford: Blackwell, 1991), pp. 129–50. I will offer the Hazlett translation because he had access to manuscripts which supplement the version available in the *Calvini Opera*. Some of this material I have published in "Calvin's Hermeneutic and Tradition: An Augustinian Reception of Romans 7," in *Reformation Readings of Romans*, edited by Kathy Ehrensperger and R. Ward Holder (Edinburgh: T. & T. Clark, 2008), 98–119.

[6] Hazlett, "Calvin's Latin Preface," 133. Irena Backus notes Hazlett and adds that "given Calvin's insistence in the preface on the organisation of the Early Church as model for the Church of his own day, it is not unlikely that it was written in Strasbourg under the influence of Bucer." Backus, "Calvin and the Greek Fathers," in *Continuity and Change: The Harvest of Late Medieval and Reformation History: Essays Presented to Heiko A. Oberman on his 70th Birthday*, edited by Robert J. Bast and Andrew Colin Gow (Leiden: Brill, 2000,), 254.

he frequently considered the opinions of Augustine, Ambrose, Origen, and Jerome, among others.[7] But citations of Chrysostom far outstripped these.[8] In fact, based on the named citations within his Pauline commentaries, we can see that Chrysostom was Calvin's favorite patristic New Testament exegete to consider, surpassing even Augustine. With one exception, Calvin never cited Augustine more than Chrysostom, and frequently his citations to Chrysostom doubled or even trebled the number of citations to Augustine.[9] In the most remarkable difference, in the commentary on II Corinthians, Calvin only named Augustine five times, while he cited Chrysostom twenty-one times. Calvin knew Chrysostom fairly well and seems to have underlined some of Chrysostom's sermons in the 1536 Paris edition of Chrysostom's works.[10] Further, Calvin accepted Chrysostom as a model for both exegesis and practical application of the scripture to Christian life.[11]

What was the substance of Calvin's preface to Chrysostom? First, he pointed out the reasons for producing aids for the reading and understanding of scripture for ordinary Christians, those who could not read

---

[7] Frequently, Calvin's citations to Ambrose are actually Ambrosiaster.

[8] Irena Backus commented that Calvin used Chrysostom as a source for discipline and the use of scripture. "Chrysostom was to Calvin a source of extremely useful information about the discipline of the Early Church, and as such could be adopted wholesale. Moreover, Chrysostom's way of using the Bible held great attraction for the Genevan Reformer ... the Genevan Reformer's use of Chrysostom is remarkably coherent and, in contrast to his use of many other Church Fathers, not primarily oriented by the demands of inter-confessional polemics." Backus, "Calvin and the Greek Fathers," 263. Further, A. N. S. Lane has noted that in the totality of his works, Calvin cited Chrysostom more than any other father, with the two exceptions of Augustine and Jerome. Lane, "Calvin's Knowledge of the Greek Fathers," in *John Calvin: Student of the Church Fathers* (Grand Rapids: Baker Book House, 1999), 72. Richard Gamble observed that Augustine could not be Calvin's model for exegesis, and that Chrysostom probably provides a source for Calvin's exegetical method. Gamble, "'*Brevitas et Facilitas*': Toward an Understanding of Calvin's Hermeneutic," *Westminster Theological Journal*, 47 (1985): 8–9.

[9] Based on the indices supplied by Feld and Calvin's New Testament Commentaries.

[10] Alexandre Ganoczy and Klaus Müller, *Calvins Handschriftliche Annotationen zu Chrysostomus: Ein Beitrag zur Hermeneutik Calvins* (Wiesbaden: Franz Steiner Verlag GMBH, 1981), 111.

[11] Ganoczy and Müller, *Calvins Handschriftliche Annotationen zu Chrysostomus*, 19–20. "Mit dieser Beobachtung stossen wir auf ein eigenartiges Phänomen der Chrysostomusrezeption durch den französischen Reformator. Denn das anhand seiner eigenen Bearbeitung festgestellte paränetische Interesse scheint im Widerspruch zu stehen zu der von ihm ausdrücklich formulierten exegetischen Intention, mit der er dem Kirchenvater begegnete." However, Jeannette Kreijkes has criticized Ganoczy and Müller's conclusions in her "Calvin's Use of the Chevallon Edition of Chrysostom's Opera Omnia: The Relationship Between the Marked Sections and Calvin's Writings," *Church History and Religious Culture* 96 (2016): 237–65.

classical languages. He did so by noting that it is important when reading the scripture to know "what one ought to look for there, to have some sort of goal towards which we may be guided," in order to avoid wandering aimlessly.[12] The Holy Spirit enables the mind of believers to grasp the goal (*scopus*) of scripture, but once believers have received that power, they should also avail themselves of aids to understanding:

The point is, if it is right that ordinary Christians be not deprived of the Word of their God, neither should they be denied prospective resources, which may be of use for its true understanding. Besides, [ordinary Christians] do not have the educational attainment. As this in itself is a considerable privilege, so it is not granted to everyone. It is obvious, therefore, that they should be assisted by the work of interpreters, who have advanced in the knowledge of God to a level that they can guide others as well ... All I have had in mind with this is to facilitate the reading of Holy Scripture for those who are humble and uneducated.

I am certainly well aware of what objection can be made to me in this business. This is that Chrysostom, whom I am undertaking to make known to the public, aimed his studies at the intelligentsia only. But yet, unless both the title [of his work] and [its] style of language deceive, this man specialized in sermons which he delivered to a wide public. Accordingly, he plainly adjusts both [his] approach and language as if he had the instruction of common people in mind.[13]

Calvin set out the necessity of the laity reading the scriptures and the concomitant essential tool of aids to understanding. He would later

---

[12]   Hazlett, "Calvin's Latin Preface," 141. Ioannis Calvini, *Opera Quae Supersunt Omnia.* 59 vols., edited by Wilhelm Baum, Edward Cunitz, and Edward Reuss (Brunswick: Schwetschke and Sons, 1895). Hereafter CO. CO 9.832. "...scire quid illic quaerere oporteat, scopumque aliquem habere ad quem dirigamur." This concern mirrors those which Calvin notes in his prefaces to the *Institutes*. See especially his "John Calvin to the Reader," appended to the 1539 edition of the *Institutes*. Joannis Calvini, *Opera Selecta,* 5 vols., 3rd ed., edited by Peter Barth and Wilhelm Niesel (Munich: Christian Kaiser, 1967). Vol. 3.6.18–31.

[13]   Hazlett, "Calvin's Latin Preface," 141–42. CO 9.832–33. "Iam vero, si aequum est plebem christianam non spoliari Dei sui verbo, neque deneganda sunt ei instrumenta quae ad veram eius intelligentiam usui sint futura. Artes porro et disciplinas non habet: quae ut sunt alioqui non minima subsidia, ita non omnibus conceduntur. Superest ergo ut interpretum opera adiuvetur, qui sic in Dei cognitione profecerunt, ut alios quoque manuducere ad eam possint. ... quo nihil aliud mihi propositum fuit quam ad scripturae sacrae lectionem rudibus ac illiteratis viam sternere.

Equidem non me fugit quid hic obiectari mihi queat: Chrysostomum, quem vulgo hominum publicare instituo, doctis tantum et literarum peritis lucubrationes suas destinasse. At vero, nisi et titulus et orationis compositio mentitur, quos ad universum populum sermones habuit hic complexus est. Ita certe et rerum tractationem et dictionem attemperat, quasi hominum multitudinem instituere velit."

follow this pattern by translating his own commentaries into French. Calvin believed Chrysostom was the best exemplar, in part, because of Chrysostom's ability to accommodate his wisdom and understanding to the abilities of the common people.

Secondly, Calvin defended his choice of Chrysostom. He wrote:

My reason for selecting Chrysostom as the most preferable needs likewise to be dealt with in passing. From the outset, the reader ought to bear in mind the kind of literary genre it is in which I prefer him to others. Although homilies are something which consist of a variety of elements, the interpretation of scripture is, however, their priority. In this area, no one of sound judgement would deny that our Chrysostom excels all the ancient writers currently extant. This is especially true when he deals with the New Testament.[14]

Chrysostom was Calvin's ideal. Calvin's own ideal of interpretation appears when we read his understanding of Chrysostom's principal significance. "The chief merit of our Chrysostom is this: he took great pains everywhere not to deviate in the slightest from the genuine plain meaning of scripture, and not to indulge in any license of twisting the straightforward sense of the words."[15] But we also learn that Calvin believed very early on in his ministry that the orthodox tradition would be helpful to his readers. Unfortunately, Calvin never completed his Chrysostom edition, keeping scholars from analyzing Calvin in another genre. But his aim suggested that Calvin believed that the orthodox tradition would appropriately form Christians, especially those who did not have university educations. The unfinished Chrysostom edition is not like other sources – the entire preface speaks of the value of the tradition. But that is what makes it so valuable.[16]

---

[14] Hazlett, "Calvin's Latin Preface," 144. CO 9.834. "Cur autem Chrysostomum ex omnibus potissimum delegerim, eius quoque rei obiter ostendenda ratio est. Ac primum quidem meminisse lectorem oportet, quale sit scripti genus in quo ipsum aliis praetulerim. Sunt autem homiliae, quae quum variis partibus constent, primum tamen in illis locum tenet scripturae interpretatio, in qua Chrysostomum nostrum vetustos omnes scriptores qui hodie exstant antecedere nemo sani iudicii negaverit. Praesertim ubi novum testamentum tractat."

[15] Hazlett, "Calvin's Latin Preface," 145–46. CO 9.835. "Chrysostomi autem nostri haec prima laus est quod ubique illi summo studio fuit a germana scripturae sinceritate ne minimum quidem deflectere, ac nullam sibi licentiam sumere in simplici verborum sense contorquendo."

[16] See also Jeannette Kreijkes, "The Praefatio in Chrysostomi Homilias as an Indication that Calvin Read Chrysostom in Greek," in *Calvinus Pastor Ecclesiae: Papers of the Eleventh International Congress on Calvin Research*, edited by Herman Selderhuis and Arnold Huijgen (Göttingen: Vandenhoeck & Ruprecht, 2016), 347–54.

TRAITÉ DES RELIQUES – 1543

A more conventional case of Calvin's use of the tradition comes from the *Traité des Reliques*. In 1543, Calvin published a French treatise attacking the veneration of relics. This work, entitled *Advertissement très utile du grand proffit qui reviendroit à la chrestienté, s'il se faisoit inventoire de tous les coups sainctz, et reliques, qui sont tant en Italie, qu'en France, Allemaigne, Hespaigne, et autres royaumes et pays*, is normally given the briefer but less colorful title *Traité des Reliques*.[17] One would expect Calvin to fit his material to his audience by avoiding the witness of the patristic and medieval sources when writing in French for a broad audience that would include the laity, that he would depend not on tradition but on scripture. However, the French *Traité des Reliques* from 1543 does not follow that pattern.[18] In it, Calvin cited Augustine in the first line and sprinkled a relatively brief treatise with a number of patristic allusions and references. This rhetorical practice raised several questions. Did Calvin feel that it is impossible to make his sardonic point without the armor of the fathers? Did he believe that it was somehow more apposite for a treatise on relics than on other topics?

We might expect that Calvin's works that were written for a vernacular audience would be rhetorically fitted for that audience. As Olivier Millet has pointed out, Calvin's forays into vernacular theology represent far more than an effort at translation – he was, in a sense, creating a French theological language.[19] Moreover, Calvin was expanding the theological audience – more people would understand the French of his sermons and of his French treatises than would ever grasp the intricacies of his polished Latin.[20]

---

[17] Calvin, *Advertissement très utile du grand proffit qui reviendroit à la chrestienté, s'il se faisoit inventoire de tous les coups sainctz, et reliques, qui sont tant en Italie, qu'en France, Allemaigne, Hespaigne, et autres royaumes et pays*. CO 6.405–52. See also Francis M. Higman, ed., in *Jean Calvin: Three French Treatises* (London: The Athlone Press, 1970), 47–97; with the text provided by the editors of the *Calvini Opera*, vol. 6. See also the versions in Olivier Millet, ed., *Jean Calvin: Oeuvres choisies* (Paris: Gallimard, 1995); and Irena Backus, ed., *La vrai piété: Divers traités de Jean Calvin et Confession de foi de Guillaume Farel* (Geneva: Labor et Fides, 1986).

[18] Calvin's *Trait des Reliques* was published by Jean Gerard of Geneva in 1543.

[19] Olivier Millet, *Calvin et la dynamique de la parole: Étude de rhétorique réformée* (Paris: H. Champion, 1992).

[20] For more on Calvin's place in theology written for the French laity, see Francis Higman, "Theology for the Layman in the French Reformation 1520–1550," in *Lire et Découvrir: La circulation des idées au temps de la Réforme* (Geneva: Librairie Droz, 1998), 87–106. Higman also examined the impact of French Reformers on the French language in his "The Reformation and the French Language," 337–51.

The argument of the treatise itself was absolutely straightforward.[21] While Calvin's theology of idolatry underlay his attack on relics, he did not go into that in any detail in this treatise.[22] Calvin basically catalogued the relics that were available to be seen in Europe and allowed his readers to draw their own conclusions.[23] For instance, he points out that if John the Baptist did not have multiple heads during his lifetime recorded in the canonical gospels, why would people believe that he had so many after his death? This is the case throughout the brief treatise,[24] along with a recurring theme that many of the stories that animate these relics are not provided in scripture. Calvin ends as we would expect, telling his readers that it is God's providence that caused the liars to be so blind that they failed to deceive skillfully and instead exposed each other.[25]

Calvin makes many patristic references throughout the treatise. By patristic references, I intend only those moments in the text when Calvin

---

[21] For Calvin's use of French and its impact, see Francis Higman, *The Style of John Calvin in his French Polemical Treatises* (Oxford: Oxford University Press, 1967); and "Calvin and the Art of Translation," *Western Canadian Studies in Modern Languages and Literature* 2 (1970): 5–27.

[22] See Carlos M. N. Eire, *War Against the Idols: The Reformation of Worship from Erasmus to Calvin* (Cambridge: Cambridge University Press, 1986). See also Eire, "Early Modern Christianity and Idolatry," in *John Calvin in Context*, edited by R. Ward Holder (Cambridge: Cambridge University Press, 2019), 267–77. For broader context see Lee Palmer Wandel, *Voracious Idols and Violent Hands: Iconoclasm in Reformation Zurich, Strasbourg, and Basel*, rev. ed. (Cambridge: Cambridge University Press, 1999).

[23] Christoph Burger points out that this did not go unnoticed, and that the Carmelite Nikolaus Blanckaert published a tract against the Latin translation of Calvin's treatise, linking Calvin to infamous heretics such as Arius, Eunomius, Wycliffe, and Jan Hus. See his "Der Kölner Karmelit Nikolaus Blanckaert Verteidigt die Verehrung der Reliquien gegen Calvin (1551)," in *Auctoritas Patrum II: Neue Beiträge zur Rezeption der Kirchenväter im 15. und 16. Jahrhundert*, edited by Leif Grane, Alfred Schindler, and Markus Wriedt (Mainz: Verlag Philipp von Zabern, 1998), 27–50.

[24] Forty-three columns in CO.

[25] John Calvin, "An Admonition Showing the Advantages which Christendom Might Derive from an Inventory of Relics," in *Selected Works of John Calvin: Tracts and Letters* vol. 1, edited by Henry Beveridge and Jules Bonnet (Grand Rapids: Baker Book House, 1983), 1.287–341. Hereafter cited as Traite des Reliques, with volume and page number, and French from Higman, with page number. Traite des Reliques, 1.339–340. "Pour faire fin, je prie et exhorte au Nom de Dieu tous lecteurs, de vouloir entendre à la verité, pendant qu'elle leur est tant overtement monstrée, et congnoistre que cela s'est faict par une singuliere providence de Dieu, que ceux qui ont voulu ainsi seduire le povre monde ont esté tant aveuglez, qu'ilz n'ont point pensé à couvrir autrement leurs mensonges; mais comme Madianites, ayans les yeux crevez, se sont dressez les uns contre les autres." Higman, *Three French Treatises*, 94.

explicitly notes a patristic source by the author's name.[26] Given that guideline, there are seventeen instances with which to deal in the text.[27] Of these, only two refer to Calvin's favorite patristic authority, Augustine. Four are to Ambrose, one each to Gregory and Jerome, one each to Socrates and Sozomen, with three each to Theodoret and Eusebius of Caesarea. One more is to Chrysostom, though it is clear that Calvin is not convinced that the commentary in question is actually Chrysostom's.[28] Immediately upon seeing the names and numbers, the reader knows what Calvin is doing: the emphasis on Theodoret and Eusebius with the inclusion of Socrates and Sozomen makes clear that these patristic references are frequently historical sources, not doctrinal authorities. For Calvin, the theological tradition was inseparable from history. The church's memory could not be swayed by hierarchical claims – instead it rested on the clearest possible historical testimonies.

We see this clearly in Calvin's usage of the fathers in the treatise. Writing about the relics of Jesus that came into contact with his body, Calvin started a list. He noted the manger in which Jesus was placed, the cloth in which he was swaddled, the shirt that Mary put him in, and even the altar on which he was placed when he was presented in the temple. Calvin pointed out how long after the death of Jesus these relics were discovered. He then chided the credulous, declaring that "There cannot be anyone of any judgment who does not see that this is folly."[29] To give more evidence for his point, Calvin appealed to the history of the early church. There is not a single word in the gospel history, and nothing is mentioned of these in the time of the apostles.[30] Further, approximately fifty years after Jesus' death, Jerusalem was destroyed.[31] Calvin built a continuation between the history of the Bible and that of the early church.

---

[26] I follow A. N. S. Lane's ideal here, when he states: "But without some objective control discussions of influence can degenerate to a subjective search for parallels. The results of such an approach may sometimes be true, but that would be more by luck than by soundness of method. With the fathers we are helped by Calvin's readiness to cite them." Lane, "Calvin's Use of the Fathers: Eleven Theses," in *John Calvin: Student of the Church Fathers* (Grand Rapids: Eerdmans, 1999), 10.

[27] A fourteenth citation, Higman, *Three French Treatises*, 68, is made to the Jews, but is set aside for our present purposes. Further unnamed sources are mentioned, as in Higman, *Three French Treatises*, 57, "Tant de Docteurs anciens ont escrit depuis…"

[28] Traite des Reliques, 330. Higman, *Three French Treatises*, 87. "…comme celuy qui a escrit le commentaire imparfaict sur sainct Matthieu, qu'on intitule de Chrysostome."

[29] Traite des Reliques, 297. Higman, *Three French Treatises*, 57. "Car il n'y a nul de si petit jugement, qui ne voye la follie."

[30] Traite des Reliques, 297. Higman, *Three French Treatises*, 57.

[31] Traite des Reliques, 297. Higman, *Three French Treatises*, 57.

Though the ancient doctors wrote of some things found or maintained in their age, such as cross and nails, none of them mentioned these other items – the manger, the swaddling cloth, the shirt or altar. Calvin then cited Pope Gregory the Great (r. 590–604), as his source for a testimony that none of these relics existed at Rome at the beginning of the seventh century.[32] The repeated battles and pillaging that Rome suffered after Gregory add to Calvin's point – the preponderance of the historical evidence shows that these late-found relics must be fraudulent. While Calvin frequently cited Gregory in a doctrinal fashion with approval elsewhere, here Calvin simply set him forward as a trustworthy source for the facts at a particular point in time.

Turning to the nails that affixed Jesus to the Cross, Calvin again used the fathers. He turned to Theodoret and Ambrose as his historical sources to make his case for both the number of nails and the difficulty of establishing what became of them. Calvin pointed out that there was presently great controversy over the nails ("plus grand combat"), and notes that even the patristic record was unclear. First, Theodoret stated that Constantine's mother Helena had ordered one of the three nails to be enclosed in her son's helmet (*heaume*), and the other two fitted into his horse's bridle.[33] But Ambrose does not give the same story, instead claiming that one was placed in Constantine's crown (*couronne*), that the second was the material made into his horse's bit ("le mors de son cheval en fut faict"), and that Helena kept the third.[34] Calvin gave these sources to cast light first on the lack of clarity in the patristic testimony, and then to point out that the present situation was gravely confused, with claims of the possession of fourteen of the three nails, made by present-day claimants scattered across three countries, from Milan to Paris.

However, while the Genevan Reformer did use the fathers as early witnesses to facts that might be in question about the provenance or veracity of various relics, that was not the only manner in which he used

---

[32] Traite des Reliques, 297. Higman, *Three French Treatises*, 57.8–10. "Qui plus est, du temps de sainct Gregoire, il n'est point question qu'il y eust rien de tout cela à Rome, comme on voit par ses escritz. Apres la mort duquel Rome a esté plusieurs foys prinse, pillée, et quasi du tout ruynée."

[33] Traite des Reliques, 303. Higman, *Three French Treatises*, 62. "Si les anciens escrivains disent vray, nomméement Theodorite, historien de l'eglise ancienne, Heleine en feit enclaver un au heaume de son filz; des deus autres, elle les mist au mors de son cheval."

[34] Traite des Reliques, 303. Higman, *Three French Treatises*, 62. "Combien que saict Ambroyse ne dit pas du tout ainsi; car il dit que l'un fut mis à la couronne de Constantin; de l'autre, le mors de son cheval en fut faict; le troisiesme, que Heleine le garda."

them. The very first occurrence of a patristic citation is different in kind. The first two words of the treatise are "Sainct Augustin."[35] Calvin gave a longer consideration of Augustine's example on the authenticity of relics. He wrote:

St. Augustine, in a book entitled *On the Labor of Monks*, complained of certain carriers of scraps, who in his time exercised a villainous and dishonest traffic, carrying here and there the relics of martyrs, and he said, "If they even are the relics of Martyrs." By this word, he demonstrated that they committed these abuses and imitation, in making the simple people believe that these bones gathered here and there were actually the bones of saints. But if the origin of this abuse is ancient, it cannot be doubted that in the long time since, the same has only greatly increased until the world has become marvelously corrupted, and has declined to the present time, so that it has reached the point that we now see.[36]

In Calvin's rhetorical hands, Augustine was not only a historical source setting out the practice in Hippo in the early fifth century; he was also an example of the doubt that orthodox thinkers in all ages have cast on the filthy scraps that have been brought by the wandering relic peddlers. Calvin moved directly from Augustine's example to his own theology of the rejection of images. He wrote:

But the first vice, and the root of the evil, was when in place of looking for Jesus Christ in his Word, in his Sacraments, and in his spiritual graces, the world, according to its custom, was more amused with his clothes, his shirts, and his drapings; leaving behind the principal issue in order to chase after the accessory.[37]

Calvin set out the icon-denying ideal that he developed over the next decade.[38] Relics and images were not only false because fraudulent;

---

[35] Traite des Reliques, 289. Higman, *Three French Treatises*, 49.

[36] Traite des Reliques, 289. Higman, *Three French Treatises*, 49. "Sainct Augustin, au livre qu'il a intitulé du labeur des Moynes, se complaignant d'aucuns porteurs de rogatons, qui desja de son temps exerceoyent foyre villaine et deshonneste, portans çà et là des reliques de martyrs, adjouste: Voyre si ce sont reliques de Martyrs. Par lequel mot, il signifie que dez lors il se commettoit de l'abuz et tromperie, en faisant à croyre au simple peuple que dez s recueilliz çà et là estoyent os de sainctz. Puis que l'origine de cest abuz ets si ancienne, il ne faut doubter qu'il n'ayt bien esté multiplié cependant par si long temps : mesmes veu que le monde s'est merveilleusement corrompu depuis ce temps là, et qu'il est decliné tousjours en empirant, jusques à ce qu'il est venu en l'extremité où nous le voyons."

[37] Traite des Reliques, 289. Higman, *Three French Treatises*, 49. "Or, le primier vice, et comme la racine du mal, a esté, qu'au lieu de chercher Jesus Christ en sa Parolle, en ses Sacremens, et en ses graces spirituelles, le monde, selon sa coustume, s'est amusé à ses robbes, chemises, et drappeaux; et en ce faisant a laissé le principal, pour suyvre l'accessoire."

[38] See Calvin's comment on images in his commentary on Galatians 3:1.

they also took the attention of believers away from the principal matters of the faith: Christ's word, Christ's sacraments, and Christ's spiritual graces.

This second pattern of use of a patristic source for doctrinal guidance appeared also in Calvin's citation of Ambrose. Considering the number of relics that had grown up around the adoration of the true cross, Calvin pointed out how numerous those fragments were in early modern Europe. Calling the number of fragments large enough that if they were gathered up they would fill a large ship ("il y en auroit la charge d'un bon grand bateau"), Calvin noted that the gospel testified that the cross was able to be carried by one man.[39] Calvin then related that the supporters of this practice have come up with a supporting belief: the cross can never be reduced no matter how much was taken away from it.[40] This mystical self-filling or completion, much like the Treasury of Merit, Calvin considered beneath contempt, and argued that even superstitious people would see through it. He then noted that beyond the theology of the self-repairing cross, relic supporters have said that the cross is worthy of adoration![41] Calvin called this a diabolical teaching ("doctrine diabolique"), and cited Ambrose as a patristic source who explicitly condemned the practice. Calvin definitely used Ambrose, whom he called "sainct Ambroise" polemically – a departure from his use of Gregory, which was to make a historical point.[42]

In the *Traite des Reliques*, we clearly see two different polemic uses of the patristic witness. The first I term the historical witness polemic. This usage covers the majority of the instances: Calvin merely claimed that Eusebius or Gregory do not record a fact that is in question, or sometimes that they seem to provide historical evidence that a present practice does not stand upon a clear precedent in the patristic age. This kind of polemic represented a practice of history, rather than doctrinal dialectic. We see a second kind of polemic in Calvin's turn to Augustine

---

[39] Traite des Reliques, 301–2. Higman, *Three French Treatises*, 61. "L'Evangile testifie que la croix pouvoit estre portée d'un homme."

[40] Traite des Reliques, 302. Higman, *Three French Treatises*, 61. "Et de faict, ilz ont forgé ceste excuse que, quelque chose qu'on en couppe, jamais elle n'en decroist. Mais c'est une borde si sote et lourde, que mesme les superstitieux la cngnoissent."

[41] Traite des Reliques, 302. Higman, *Three French Treatises*, 61.20–24. "Car ilz n'ont pas esté contens de seduire et abuser les simples, en monstrant du boys commun au lieu du boys de la craoix; mais ilz ont resolu qu'il le faloit adorer, qui est une doctrine diabolique. Et sainct Ambroise nommement la reprouve, comm superstition de Payens."

[42] The popular English translations do not give either "holy Ambrose" or St. Ambrose.

and Ambrose at the beginning of the treatise. This I term the doctrinal witness polemic. As the issues are doctrinal rather than historical, they are naturally more open to debate. But that did not make them more or less significant. Rather, it demonstrated the variety of tasks several of the reformers took on as preacher, humanist, and theologian. When attempting to make a point in a written debate, searching for that doctrinal witness, we may imagine that a writer might seek out a particularly juicy tidbit – he might go to his books, or his friend's books, in order to find a helpful bit of doctrine. But that would be far less likely in his arrangement of historical sources. By their nature, these sources were learned over time, whether in compendia or in full editions, and at least in Calvin's case, the memory was trusted for appropriate recall. Both polemic, but very different in their nature and perhaps different in the manner in which they were obtained.

To set this in its historical context, the *Traite* gives more patristic material than several sections of the 1536 *Institutes*, more than the *Letter to Sadoleto*, almost exactly the same amount as the *Psychopannychia*, which was published in 1542, and much less than the *Bondage and Liberation of the Will*, Calvin's answer to Pighius, which was also published in 1543. But that text has at its heart the question of who "owned" Augustine – it was by nature only about the tradition. Calvin used the patristic witness, in a variety of ways, even when writing a treatise aimed at a less-well-educated audience.

This investigation has also set out two further points. First, while it is intuitively straightforward to see Calvin using the explicit engagement with the Church's tradition, and particularly the patristic witness more in Latin works than in French, that hypothesis does not always prove true. Calvin engaged the patristic witness frequently for his French readers. Audience was a crucial factor for a talented author and did not stop the use of the patristic tradition. Second, this investigation adds further nuance and complexity into the theory that Calvin used patristic testimony for polemic. This single text demands a more nuanced typology for Calvin's argumentative use of the fathers than simply assigning the somewhat pejorative term "polemic." As well, we must ask why Calvin presents a patristic polemic source to a theologically untrained audience. Irena Backus has posited that "the early church constitutes an intrinsic part of Calvin's teaching and has to be seen to do so."[43]

---

[43] Irena Backus, "Calvin and the Church Fathers," in *The Calvin Handbook*, edited by Herman Selderhuis (Grand Rapids: Eerdmans, 2009), 136.

If Calvin could not, or would not, write a popular treatise without recourse to the fathers, that presents a strong indicator of his sense of his theological task as being grounded in the fathers, or at least the orthodox tradition.

TRANSLATIONS OF THE *INSTITUTES* – 1541, 1560

Calvin translated the *Institutes* into French regularly, completing translations of almost every edition. McKee suggests that he began this with the 1536 edition but was unable to complete it because of time pressures.[44] In this consideration, I will examine those translations Calvin published in 1541 and 1560. Though many modern analysts have preferred the fluid character of the 1541 work, the 1560 translation was an improvement according to the stylistic canons of the day. Francis Higman noted that while the 1541 translation formed a unity on a high stylistic level, "the later editions of the Institution have lost this stylistic unity. The 1560 edition is far less homogeneous, owing to the history of its composition; in addition, as we have seen, the stylistic aim of Calvin in the later editions was perceptibly different from that in the first: There is an increase in the popular elements, in the lower levels of style, inspired by the author's experience in writing of his French treatises. The result is something that fits better into the aesthetic requirements of the sixteenth century, which represents more the *propriété* of French; and something which was probably better designed for the immediate task of propagating the ideas of the Reformation, than the 1541 version."[45] Elsie A. McKee, in her introductory essay to her translation of the French 1541 *Institutes*, notes that one particular difference between the Latin edition of 1539 and the French of 1541 are the citations Calvin made. Calvin gave far more patristic and medieval references in the Latin, aimed at university-trained audiences; he made biblical references in the French edition.[46]

So both Higman and McKee found Calvin turning to the use of more accessible elements calculated to reach the readers of French. However, that is not to say that Calvin believed that the tradition was unhelpful for

[44] Elsie A. McKee, translator, *Institutes of the Christian Religion: 1541 French Edition: The First English Version*, "Introduction" (Grand Rapids: Eerdmans, 2009), ix.

[45] Francis Higman, "Calvin and the Art of Translation," in *Lire et Découvrir: La circulation des idées au temps de la Réforme* (Geneva: Librairie Droz, 1998), 389.

[46] McKee, *Institutes of the Christian Religion*, xiv.

the readers of his French translations. Far from it. The French of 1541 only suffers in comparison with the Latin of 1539, in much the same way that the 1560 French translation shows fewer applications of the tradition than the 1559 Latin. Taken simply as works of theology and piety in their own right, both display a continual desire to place the reader of Calvin's theology into the church's tradition, stretching back to the early centuries.

Therefore, we see names of Calvin's favorite theologians in the pages of the French translations. Considering the 1541 edition, those authorities one comes to expect are there: Augustine, Ambrose, Bernard, Chrysostom, Cyprian, Origen, Tertullian, and Jerome all act as Calvin's conversation partners and authorities. Though Calvin reacts negatively at times to the doctrine that individual theologians had taught, when he included an explicit allusion or citation to a patristic or medieval source, in general it was positive. Such was the case with Chrysostom, whom Calvin used as an authority to demonstrate his own fidelity to orthodoxy about the guidance of the Holy Spirit for the church. In the fifteenth chapter, Calvin argued that it was unwise to follow the dictates of reason beyond the Word of God. He averred: "That is why St. Chrysostom's saying is worth noting: 'More than a few,' he says, 'boast of the Spirit; but those who bring something of their own claim him falsely.'"[47] [Pseudo]-Chrysostom's point was that those who add to the testimony of the Spirit, those who add human ideas or wisdom to the scriptures, have no touch of the Spirit.

Calvin turned frequently to Chrysostom throughout the 1541 edition. His first example is negative. While arguing against the freedom of the will, he turned to Chrysostom, a Greek father famous for his support of human freedom of choice. After quoting two passages from Chrysostom and one from Jerome, Calvin wrote, "However much the Greek fathers above others, and among them St. Chrysostom in particular, have exceeded good measure in magnifying human ability,

---

[47] John Calvin, 1541 French translation of the *Institutes of the Christian Religion*. Hereafter cited as 1541 French edition, with page number, and Millet's French edition. 1541 French edition, 640. Jean Calvin, *Institution de la Religion Chrétienne (1541)*, Edition critique par Olivier Millet (Geneva: Librairie Droz, 2008), 1537. "Pourtant la sentence de Chrysostome est notable: Pluseiurs, dit-il, se vantent de l'Esprit; mais ceux qui apportent du leur le parloit point de soymesme." McKee and Millet identify the source as PseudoChrysostom.

nevertheless practically all the early church fathers except St. Augustine are so changeable in this matter, or speak so hesitantly or obscurely, that one can practically not find any certain decision in their writings."[48] Calvin knew that the Greek fathers particularly did not agree with his idea of the bondage of the will. Really, only Augustine was willing to hold a doctrine of the bondage of the will that satisfied Calvin. But instead of attacking Chrysostom and the others, Calvin presented the question as if it were murky in the early church for almost everyone. By doing so, he lessened the harshness of his critique, and preserved the strength of the witness of the early church and the importance of the church's tradition.

That discussion of free will included two citations from Peter Lombard, the author of the *Sentences*, the chief medieval theological textbook. Calvin chided Lombard for using the term free will, but noted: "For finally the master of the *Sentences* stresses that a person is not said to have free will because he is able to think or do the good as well as the evil, but only because he is not subjected to constraint; that freedom is not hindered even if we are wicked and slaves of sin and cannot choose anything but doing evil."[49] Calvin actually agreed with the doctrine that Lombard was posing, but ranted that it should not be called "free will" ("Liberal Arbitre"), preferring to call it the bound will. Making this point, Calvin established both his knowledge of the medieval tradition, and his qualified criticism of it.

The 1541 edition includes dozens of quotations and allusions to Augustine. The only name that appears more often in the index is that of the apostle Paul.[50] Bernard appears very rarely, but Lane and Raitt argue that Calvin would not have yet truly begun studying the

---

[48] 1541 French edition, 59–60. Millet, *Institution de la Religion Chrétienne (1541)*, 274. "Combien que les Docteurs Grecz par dessus les autres, et entre eulx singulierement Sainct Chrysostome ait passé mesure en magnifiant les forces humaines, toutesfois quasi tous les anciens peres, excepté Sainct Augustin, sont tant variables en ceste matiere, ou parlent si doubteusement our obscurement, qu'on ne peut quasi prendre de leurs escritz aucune certaine resolution."

[49] 1541 French edition, 62, *Institution de la Religion Chrétienne (1541)*, 279. "Car finalement le maistre des Sentences prononce que l'homme n'est point dict avoir le Liberal Arbitre pource qu'il soit suffisant à panser our faire le bien autant comme le mal, mais seulement pource qu'il n'est point subject à contraincte; laquelle liberté n'est point empeschée, combien que nous soyons mauvais et serfz de peché, et que nous ne puissions autre chose que mal faire."

[50] 1541 French edition, 713–16.

Cistercian.[51] Augustine appeared early, in an unnamed allusion to the fathers in the dedicatory epistle to François I.[52] The Genevan Reformer would also name Augustine as a source for saying in the Apostles' Creed, "we believe the church," rather than believing "in the church."[53] To Calvin's normal list of fathers he adds Peter Lombard, Thomas Aquinas, and gives two unnamed allusions to Hugh of St. Victor – setting out the medieval church's place in the tradition. But he would use the fathers to criticize that tradition. Calvin quoted Augustine from the Decretals, a set of texts that were basic to canon law collected by the jurist Gratian (flourished mid-twelfth century) in the twelfth century. Attacking the Roman sacramental theory, Calvin wrote: "Have they forgotten what they cite from St. Augustine: that if one separates the word from the water, there remains only water, for it is by the word that it is made a sacrament?"[54] This consideration of the medievals was frequently to censure the Roman church, but it also revealed Calvin's ongoing engagement and correction of the tradition.

Augustine was the most popular father in Calvin's 1541 translation, but he was hardly alone. Calvin argued for a change in the manner of the election of bishops through use of Cyprian. He noted: "St. Cyprian strongly argues that an election is not properly done except by the voices of all the people."[55] Calvin turned to Chrysostom in his exposition of the law to argue against the conclusions of the scholastics, writing: "Who cannot conclude, with St. Chrysostom, that in a matter so necessary

---

[51] Jill Raitt, "Calvin's Use of Bernard of Clairvaux," *Archiv für Reformationsgeschichte* 72 (1981): 98–121; A. N. S. Lane, "Calvin's Use of Bernard of Clairvaux," in *John Calvin: Student of the Church Fathers* (Edinburgh: T. & T. Clark, 1999), 87–114; and Lane, "Calvin's Sources of Bernard of Clairvaux," in *John Calvin: Student of the Church Fathers* (Edinburgh: T. & T. Clark, 1999), 115–50; Luke Anderson, "The Imago Dei Theme in John Calvin and Bernard of Clairvaux," in *Calvinus Sacrae Scripturae Professor: Calvin as Confessor of Holy Scripture*, edited by Wilhelm Neuser (Grand Rapids: Eerdmans, 1994), 178–98; Vincent Brümmer, "Calvin, Bernard and the Freedom of the Will." *Religious Studies* 30 (1994): 437–55; Dennis E. Tamburello, *Union with Christ: John Calvin and the Mysticism of St Bernard* (Louisville: Westminster/John Knox, 1994).

[52] 1541 French edition, 13–14. *Institution de la Religion Chrétienne (1541)*, 1.160–61.

[53] 1541 French edition, 241. *Institution de la Religion Chrétienne (1541)*, 653. Augustine was listed along with Cyprian.

[54] 1541 French edition, 610. *Institution de la Religion Chrétienne (1541)*, 1465. "Ont-ilz oublyé ce qui'ilz alleguent de Saint Augustin, que, si on separe la parolle de l'eaue, il ne restera plus que l'eaue, car c'est par la parolle qu'elle est faicte Sacrement?"

[55] 1541 French edition, 606. *Institution de la Religion Chrétienne (1541)*, 1457. "Sainct Cypryan combat fort que une election n'est pas deuement faicte que par les voix de tout le peuple." Millet supplies Epistle 67, 3–4.

it is clear that these are not exhortations but precepts?"[56] Calvin did not always seek to praise or accept the fathers. In his juxtaposition of Chrysostom and Augustine on the freedom of the will, the Genevan Reformer was engaging in an active process of tradition reception – clarifying for his readers who was correct and who had stumbled on the question of the freedom of human will.[57] Calvin certainly gave fewer allusions to and quotations from the tradition than in his Latin version, but that does not mean that French readers were not also being formed in the sense that the evangelical faith followed the tradition, and the corrected tradition at that.

The 1560 *Institution de la Religion Chrétienne* provides the same character to its readers. While the French translation does not have the same number of citations and allusions to the orthodox tradition as the 1559 Latin version, that does not result in a negligible consideration of the tradition. The index to the two volumes in the *Calvini Opera* for this translation list over two hundred mentions to Augustine in the text. Calvin cites Bernard far more frequently in the final translation than the 1541. Calvin clearly wished to clarify to his French-reading audience points about the use of the tradition. One finds this to be the case when he alluded to both Irenaeus and Tertullian. Calvin was attacking those he believed to be heretical about the Trinity. Calvin wrote:

It should also be noted that the most ancient authorities (Docteurs) taught with all the same agreement and the same voice: so much that it is an impudence as detestable as ridiculous that modern heretics create a shield out of Irenaeus and Tertullian, arguing that both confess that Jesus Christ, who finally appeared visibly, was previously the invisible Son of God.[58]

Calvin would go on to attack Servetus by name, revealing that the struggle for the ownership of the tradition was a very real and important battlefield in early modern polemics.

Calvin's favorite authorities are well represented. Calvin alluded to Augustine by name early in Book I, though without great specificity: "As

---

[56] 1541 French edition, 162. *Institution de la Religion Chrétienne (1541)*, 482. "Qui est-ce qui ne pourra conclurre avec Chrysostome que d'une cause si necessaire, il appert que ce ne sont point exhortations, mais preceptes?"

[57] 1541 French edition, 84. *Institution de la Religion Chrétienne (1541)*, 323.

[58] CO 3.558. "Il est aussi à noter que les plus anciens Docteurs ont tousiours d'un mesme accord et d'une mesme bouche ainsi enseigné: tellement que c'est une impudence aussi detestable que ridicule, en ce que les heretiques modernes font bouclier d'Irenée et Tertullien : veu que tous les deux confessent que Iesus Christ, qui est finalement apparu visible, estoit auparavant Fils invisible de Dieu."

St. Augustine wrote somewhere, because we are able to understand his works, failing to understand God because of his grandeur, we must search out his works to be reformed according to his bounty."[59] Calvin also turned to Augustine to condemn images, writing: "Just as St. Augustine testifies clearly, stating that it is not permissible to have images in high and honored places, because they may be regarded by those who pray and worship, and may attract the senses of the weak, as if they have sense and soul."[60]

Calvin's other favorites appeared as well. Bernard of Clairvaux was particularly well represented in the 1560 French edition. Calvin turned to the French doctor of the church to speak to the conscience. He wrote:

St. Bernard speaks much better, I believe, when he said that the testimony of the conscience, which St. Paul named the glory of the faithful (2 Cor. 1.12), consists of three points. The first is that before all other things it is required to believe that one cannot have remissions of sins without the pure grace of God; secondly, that one can not have any good work unless he [God] himself gives it to you; and thirdly that you cannot merit eternal life by works, if it is not also given to you graciously.[61]

Calvin turned to Cyprian for his doctrine of the church, chided Chrysostom for his doctrine of the freedom of the will; quoted Ambrose to discuss sin and baptism; and turned to Tertullian for a historical attestation on the role of priests in the early church.[62] Calvin regularly used both the fathers as historical witnesses, and as doctrinal sources in the French translation of the *Institutes*, just as he had in the Latin original.

---

[59] CO 3.72. "Et comme S. Augustin advertist quelque part, Pource que nous le pouvons comprendre, defaillans sous sa grandeur, nous avons à regarder à. ses oeuvres pour estre recreez de sa bonté."

[60] CO 3.136–137. "Ce que sainct Augustin tesmoigne clairement, en disant qu'on ne peut colloquer les images en sieges hauts et honnorables, pour estre regardées de ceux qui prient et adorent, qu'elles n'attirent le sens des infirmes, comme si elles avoyent sens et ame."

[61] CO 4.64. "Sainct Bernard parle bien mieux: Ie croy, dit-il, que le tesmoignage de la conscience, lequel sainct Paul nomme La gloire des fideles (2 Cor. 1, 12), consiste en trois poincts. Oar en premier lieu et devant toutes choses, il est requis de croire que tu ne peux avoir remission des pechez, sinon de la pure gratuité de Dieu: secondement, que tu ne peux avoir nulle bonne oeuvre, si luy-mesme ne la te donne: tiercement, que tu ne peux meriter par oeuvres la vie eternelle, si elle ne t'est aussi bien donnée gratuitement."

[62] Cyprian, CO 4.683; 4.692, 4.707; Chrysostom, CO 3.347; Ambrose, CO 4.82; Tertullian, CO 4.930–31.

Calvin's pattern of citing the medieval authorities followed very much his style in the earlier translations. Frequently, Peter Lombard was termed "the master of the Sentences" or "those of the Sorbonne" but was clearly discussed. Similarly, Thomas Aquinas was considered by name for the purpose of disposing with his opinions.[63] Clearly, Calvin sought a critical attitude toward the tradition – but it was never an effort at removing the consideration of the tradition, but rather to demonstrate those moments when it was correct as well as when it had gone astray. While Higman and McKee's basic point that Calvin was less inclined to use allusions to orthodox patristic authors in the French works is sound, one should not conclude that Calvin abandoned the tradition when writing in or translating into French. Far too many citations and allusions, as well as open struggles to demonstrate that Calvin's evangelical faith maintained the true faith passed down through the ages, exist for us to accept a desertion of the tradition in the vernacular texts.

CONCLUSION: CALVIN, THE VERNACULAR AUDIENCE, AND TRADITION

John Calvin needed to pass the faith of true religion on to a much broader audience than he originally considered. His early efforts were written in Latin, the language of the university and the traditional language of theology. But his work in Geneva and Strasbourg brought him face to face with the necessity of creating resources for the wider audience. While the *Institutes* did become much more of a guide for the training of pastors, Calvin realized the necessity of reaching out to laity, whether somewhat learned, or those who had no facility with the subjects that were common in the university curriculum.

The task of making theological resources available in the vernacular, in this case French, was a more difficult endeavor than is sometimes recognized. The language of theology was Latin – in some cases, Calvin had to invent terminology in French to express his dialectical points. Further, the new language did not have the centuries of tradition's weight behind it. Faced with such a task, it would have been easy for Calvin to eschew the allusions to the orthodox sources that were so frequently part of the theological language of the early modern period. Yet that is not what

[63] CO 3.303. CO 4.480.

readers find. Instead, though Calvin might have lessened his reliance on the traditional sources, he did include them. In the case of the Chrysostom edition, planned but never executed, he saw that preparing the traditional resources specifically for vernacular readers was necessary. In seeing this, it is difficult not to conclude that Calvin believed that the tradition was basic to the true religion. For him to pass on the church's teaching necessitated an effort to hand on the riches of the orthodox traditions, both doctrinal and exegetical.

5

Calvin, Tradition, and Doctrine

It has been a long-standing custom to think of the Protestant Reformers as defenders of biblical religion, who set aside the human inventions that had tarnished the clarity of the gospel message in preference for the pure revelation of divine truth.[1] In fact, one could frequently tell the confessional allegiance of the scholar who was writing history prior to the last few decades. If someone spoke of the way in which Luther removed the darkness of human innovations that had obscured the light of the divine gospel, they were a Protestant. If, on the other hand, one spoke of the Reformation as the "Great Schism," you could be sure you were reading a Catholic.[2] One does not go too far to say that always at the heart of the issue were the opposed pair: scripture and tradition. Protestants held for a model of *sola scriptura*, while Catholics had accepted the twofold authority of scripture and tradition.

Three modern movements have made this ideational construction of the Reformation less certain. First, historians have been delving into how the various figures of the era of the Reformations both consciously and unconsciously used the theological tradition in their work.[3] Second, after

---

[1] Some of this material was originally presented as an address at the Annual Church History Lecture at Wheaton College, February 13, 2014.

[2] This has not wholly gone away. I was recently speaking to a Catholic colleague, who is very ecumenical in her outlook, about being on the planning team for some of the remembrances and celebrations of 2017 – the 500th anniversary of the beginning of the Reformation. She immediately asked, "Why would you celebrate that?" To her, at heart, the Reformation remained a scar, a blemish on the church.

[3] See, for instance, Leif Grane, Alfred Schindler, and Markus Wriedt, *Auctoritas patrum: zur Rezeption der Kirchenväter im 15. und 16. Jahrhundert* (Mainz: Verlag Philipp von Zabern, 1993); and *Auctoritas partum II: neue Beiträge zur Rezeption der Kirchenväter*

the postmodern rediscovery of the importance of traditions for communities of discourse, a wide variety of thinkers from liberal Protestant, Roman Catholic, and even Evangelical camps have turned to tradition as a key source for doctrinal considerations. Finally, an increasing professional character to the gild of early modern scholars has reduced the number of historians and theologians who, by training and their own confessional religious stance, saw themselves as existing on one side or the other. The number of scholars studying the early modern period who have no religious commitment has grown over the past half-century. This has contributed to a sense that "taking sides" is a mark of an improper stance toward the subject matter.

In considering tradition, we have not arrived at a firm foundation for doctrinal, ecclesiastical, or cultural analysis and construction. Far too frequently, the modern scholar selects a theory of tradition that fits his or her needs, something that is particularly apposite to the particular problem at hand. While this makes sense in the library, it fails to work for the ecclesial community – whether Reformed, modern Evangelical, or even Roman Catholic. Further, this does not work culturally as creating a set of shared assumptions. So we find both the problem of competing models of tradition and the subsequent problem that any particular given model of tradition may be incompatible with the ecclesiastical needs of a given community or the cultural needs of a given society. Given these problems in the modern age, we may ask what John Calvin was doing in his own use of the theological tradition he inherited.[4] Did his efforts

---

im 15. Und 16. Jahrhundert (Mainz: Verlag Philipp von Zabern, 1998); David C. Steinmetz, "Things Old and New: Tradition and Innovation in Constructing Reformation Theology." *Reformation and Renaissance Review* 19 (2017): 5–18; Esther Chung-Kim, *Inventing Authority. The Use of the Church Fathers in Reformation Debates over the Eucharist* (Waco: Baylor University Press, 2011); Berndt Hamm, "Farewell to Epochs in Reformation History." *Reformation & Renaissance Review* 16 (2014): 211–45; R. Ward Holder, "Calvin and Tradition: Tracing Expansion, Locating Development, Suggesting Authority," *Toronto Journal of Theology* 25.2 (2009): 215–26; Ann-Stephane Schäfer, *Auctoritas Patrum? The Reception of the Church Fathers in Puritanism* (Frankfurt: Peter Lang, 2011); Andreas Merkt, *Das Patristische Prinzip: Eine Studie zur Theologischen Bedeutung der Kirchenväter* (Leiden: Brill 2001); Mathias Mütel, *Mit den Kirchenvätern gegen Martin Luther? Die Debatten um Tradition und auctoritas partum auf dem Konzil von Trient* (Leiden: Ferdinand Schöningh, 2017).

4 The language in the academy has not settled; so Johannes Van Oort wrote of "Calvin's knowledge and use of the church fathers," in a chapter in which he traced Calvin's citations of the patristic writers. Van Oort, "John Calvin and the Church Fathers," in *The Reception of the Church Fathers in the West: From the Carolingians to the Maurists*, edited by Irena Backus (New York, Leiden: Brill, 1997), 661. But Arnoud Visser instead

provide a distant harbinger of the issues we face? Having surveyed the various genres in which and audiences with whom he engaged the tradition, I have established that Calvin used the theological and exegetical traditions as authorities in his own work. While his efforts were at times uneven – and one can see audiences with whom he did not turn to the orthodox tradition as frequently as he did with others – one cannot find a genre or audience in which Calvin wholly eschewed the theological fruit of the tradition. So what was he doing with the doctrinal tradition in his work?

CALVIN: DEPENDING UPON TRADITION

At the beginning of the twenty-first century, it is still possible to find scholars holding on to the idea that Calvin simply read the scriptures as the basic theological method. Whether preaching, commenting upon scripture, or constructing his theological works, both the treatises and the *Institutes of the Christian Religion*, this school of thought claims that Calvin's doctrine came always and only from the Bible. For some, the issue is simply that the Reformers rediscovered the pure Bible. This is the biblicist model of Calvin's use of tradition.

Still a second group of scholars will admit that Calvin frequently took advantage of the storehouse of the tradition. However, these scholars tend to downplay the influence of Calvin's frequent recourse to the fathers and medievals as something that he would reserve for polemic purposes, but not employ in any serious manner of engagement.[5] In other words, Calvin would use the tradition against his enemies, but his basic positive stance was biblical. In this way, the use of tradition is relegated to a secondary function in Calvin's theology in the minds of modern analysts. This is the polemicist model of Calvin's engagement with tradition.

---

describes the "dynamic reception of Augustine of Hippo in the European Reformations." Visser, *Reading Augustine in the Reformation: The Flexibility of Intellectual Authority in Europe, 1500–1620* (Oxford: Oxford University Press, 2011), 5. In that study, Visser examines the editions, the paratextual elements in the editions that sought to guide reading, and the political worlds in which these authorities were used. Both are wonderful studies – but their projects are decidedly different.

[5] Among those who espouse such a position are van Oort, "John Calvin and the Church Fathers," 661–700; and Bernard Roussel, "John Calvin's Interpretation of Psalm 22," in *Adaptations of Calvinism in Reformation Europe: Essays in Honour of Brian G. Armstrong*, edited by Mack Holt (Aldershot: Ashgate, 2007), 9–20.

While both of these positions present a tempting avenue for some as they preserve a customary notion of Protestant biblicism, such positions cannot be maintained in the face of several currents in recent research. A. N. S. Lane has examined the manners in which Calvin used the patristic tradition to argue with a variety of other thinkers.[6] Leif Grane and Markus Wriedt have offered a variety of considerations of how the broader Reformations used the tradition, instead of eschewing it.[7] Richard Muller has researched deeply to demonstrate that Calvin was not averse to scholasticism, and that the burgeoning Reformed tradition regularly used it.[8] In the face of such scholarship, and in light of the broad model of Calvin's use of the tradition demonstrated in the previous chapters, it behooves us to consider exactly what Calvin was doing in his engagement with the tradition. In this chapter, I will demonstrate three points – first, that Calvin used the traditions to help construct the frameworks of his argumentation with both Catholics and Protestants; second, that Calvin used the medieval and patristic tradition as a series of interlocutors and authorities to add tradition's sanction to his own thought; and finally, that Calvin used the traditions for the very substance of his own theological investigations and doctrine.

CALVIN: USING TRADITION FOR THE FRAMEWORK OF HIS ARGUMENTATION

From the late 1530s, Calvin accepted tradition as the proper framework for both interpretation and polemic argumentation. In accepting the necessity of speaking to the authority and issue of tradition, Calvin implicitly accepted its role. Further, his assent to the role of tradition in the rhetorical struggles of the age allowed the tradition subtly to influence his own theological development. His engagement with a variety of Catholic theologians who were only too eager to speak about the tradition and the patristic witness influenced the framework of his theological method and the doctrinal choices he made.

---

[6] A. N. S. Lane, *John Calvin: Student of the Church Fathers* (Grand Rapids: Baker 1999).

[7] Grane, Schindler, and Wriedt, *Auctoritas patrum*; and *Auctoritas partum II*.

[8] Richard Muller, "Scholasticism in Calvin: A Question of Relation and Disjunction," in *The Unaccommodated Calvin: Studies in the Foundation of a Theological Tradition* (Oxford: Oxford University Press, 2000), 39–61. See also Muller, "The Problem of Protestant Scholasticism: A Review and Definition," in *Reformation and Scholasticism: An Ecumenical Enterprise*, edited by Willem J. van Asselt and Eef Dekker (Grand Rapids: Baker Book House, 2001), 45–64.

Calvin loved a good fight, and accepted Sadoleto's challenge, as well as that of Pighius, Trent, Westphal, and Heshusius. In each case, Calvin refused to argue from the scriptural principle alone. Instead, he regularly and with notable skill employed the tradition to make his points. One is hard pressed to find Calvin stating that he preferred the scripture to tradition, and then maintaining that stance. Instead, it was far more common for Calvin to laud the veracity of the Word of God and assert that the orthodox fathers joined him in his opinion.

Instead of forging a model of the sufficiency of scripture to make his case, Calvin accepted the historical nature of the church, and demonstrated that his confession was within the broad stream of that tradition.[9] Calvin turned to history to make his defense. This was neither necessary nor inevitable. The new Genevan reformer could have argued that the Roman case was weaker for its insistence on the tradition of the fathers, instead of the purity of the scripture's witness. He also could have simply denied the relevance of the question. Calvin was a skilled student of rhetorical models and had options.[10] His rhetorical choices should not be passed over without notice.

Another work on which Calvin was laboring in the late 1530s gives further significant insight into the new doctrines he was forming about the church and the true religion. This was his commentary on Romans, published in 1540 in Strasbourg. Romans was the key to the scriptures for Calvin. This would be his first commentary, and for a length of time it stood as his only commentary. The dedicatory epistle to Simon Grynaeus was a brief discussion of both the correct manner of interpreting scripture and Calvin's particular interpretation on Romans. Grynaeus was a scholar teaching in Basel at the time that Calvin would have been finishing the original edition of the *Institutes*. What Calvin may have learned from Grynaeus is an open question, with some modern scholars crediting him as Calvin's Hebrew teacher and others urging

[9] Randall Zachman makes the point that the reformers were all seeking to claim the mantle of catholicity. See "Who is Actually Catholic? How Our Traditional Categories Keep Us from Understanding the Evangelical Reformations," in *Crossing Traditions: Essays on the Reformation and Intellectual History in Honour of Irena Backus*, edited by Maria-Cristina Pitassi and Daniela Solfaroli Camilloci (Leiden: Brill, 2018), 435–46.

[10] For Calvin's consideration of classical rhetoric, see Serene Jones, *Calvin and the Rhetoric of Piety* (Louisville: Westminster John Knox Press, 1995); Kirk Essary, *Erasmus and Calvin on the Foolishness of God: Reason and Emotion in Christian Philosophy* (Toronto: University of Toronto Press, 2017); Olivier Millet, "Docere/movere: les catégories rhétoriques et leurs sources humanistes dans la doctrine calvinienne de la foi," in *Calvinus Sincerioris Religionis Vindex*, edited by Wilhelm Neuser and Brian G. Armstrong (Kirksville: Sixteenth Century Journal Pub, 1997), 35–51.

caution.[11] However, scholars do recognize that Grynaeus would have taught New Testament while Calvin resided in Basel. It would have been normal for the young French humanist to discuss the interpretation of scripture with one of the city's leading scholars on the topic.

Calvin began his dedication by recalling Grynaeus' favored model of interpretation, lucid brevity. He wrote: "Both of us felt that lucid brevity constituted the particular virtue of an interpreter. Since it is almost his only task to unfold the mind of the writer whom he has undertaken to expound, he misses his mark, or at least strays outside his limits, by the extent to which he leads his readers away from the meaning of his author."[12] Having asserted that Romans was the key to the entire scripture, Calvin noted some of the significant commentators who had interpreted Romans in his own time and why and how he differed from them.[13]

That raised the issue of what exactly a commentator should do, and why so many reached differing interpretations from each other. Calvin noted that "God has never so blessed His servants that they each possessed full and perfect knowledge of every part of their subject. It is clear that His purpose in so limiting our knowledge was first that we should be kept humble, and also that we should continue to have dealings with our fellows."[14] The theologian's consideration of biblical interpretation was

---

[11] Richard C. Gamble, "Brevitas et Facilitas: Toward an Understanding of Calvin's Hermeneutic," *Westminster Theological Journal* 47 (1985): 1–17, asserts Grynaeus was Calvin's Hebrew teacher. Max Engammare, "Joannes Calvinus Trium Linguarum Peritus? La Question de L'Hebreu." *Bibliothèque d'Humanisme et Renaissance* 58 (1996): 35–60, does not even list Grynaeus among those who may have taught Calvin Hebrew, suggesting instead Sebastian Münster for Calvin's time in Basel, while noting the lack of clear historical evidence that supports solid conclusions on the question.

[12] Calvin, Commentary on Romans, Dedicatory Epistle to Simon Grynaeus, in *The Epistles of Paul the Apostle to the Romans and to the Thessalonians*, translated by Ross Mackenzie (Grand Rapids: Eerdmans, 1960), 1. *Iohannis Calvini Commentarius in Epistolam Pauli ad Romanos*, edited by T. H. L. Parker (Leiden: Brill, 1981), 1. "Sentiebat enim uterque nostrum, praecipuam interpretis virtutem in perspicua brevitate esse positam. Et sane quum hoc sit prope unicum illium officium, mentem scriptoris, quem explicandum sumpsit, patefacere: quantum ab ea lectores abducit, tantundem a scopo suo aberrant, vel certe a suis finibus quodammodo evagatur."

[13] For a brief overview, see Joel E. Kok, "Heinrich Bullinger's Exegetical Method: The Model for Calvin?" in *Biblical Interpretation in the Era of the Reformation*, edited by Richard A. Muller and John L. Thompson (Grand Rapids: Eerdmans, 1996), 241–54. See also T. H. L. Parker, *Commentaries on Romans: 1532–1542* (Edinburgh: T. & T. Clark, 1986).

[14] Calvin, Commentary on Romans, 4. Parker, Ad Romanos, 3. "Nunquam enim tanto beneficio servos suos dignatus est Deus, ut singuli plena perfectaque omni ex parte intelligentia praediti essent. Nec dubium quin eo consilio, ut nos in humilitate primum, deinde communicationis fraternae studio retineret."

critical, and he stepped back from the confidence in the perspicacity of scripture that had characterized Luther.[15] While Calvin did not say that the scripture itself was not clear, he undoubtedly discerned a serious epistemological problem in it. Because the interpreters could not be trusted to know every part of their subject, they would have to maintain a humility and trust toward each other. While that was true, it did not clarify how to choose between competing interpretations.

Calvin's solution to the problem of scriptural interpretation was to adopt a stance that maintained the orthodox exegetical tradition whenever possible. He wrote: "When therefore, we depart from the views of our predecessors, we are not to be stimulated by any passion for innovation, impelled by any desire to slander others, aroused by any hatred, or prompted by any ambition. Necessity alone is to compel us, and we are to have no other object than that of doing good."[16] This passage alone, attached to Calvin's clearest statement on the method of interpretation of scripture, might well have given historians and theologians pause as they discussed his support of scripture over tradition.[17] Calvin set out a rule that denied ambition, innovation, slander, or hatred.[18]

He continued in this vein as he discussed the teachings of religion. Calvin argued that though one should avoid these vices in the interpretation of scripture, even less liberty was given when teaching religion (*religionis dogmatibus*).[19] As he began the process of commenting upon

---

[15] Susan Schreiner, "'The Spiritual Man Judges all Things': Calvin and the Exegetical Debates about Certainty in the Reformation," in *Biblical Interpretation in the Era of the Reformation: Essays Presented to David C Steinmetz in Honor of his Sixtieth Birthday*, edited by Richard A. Muller and John L. Thompson (Grand Rapids: Eerdmans, 1996), 189–215.

[16] Calvin, Commentary on Romans, 4. Parker, Ad Romanos, 3. "danda est opera ut nuolla novandi libidine incitati, nulla suggillandi alios cupiditate impulsi, nullo instigati odio, nulla ambitione titillati: sed sola necessitate coacti, nec aliud quaerentes quam prodesse, a superioroum sententiis discedamus."

[17] Calvin never wrote a treatise on interpretation of scripture. Gamble points this out in his "Brevitas et Facilitas: Toward an Understanding of Calvin's Hermeneutic," *Westminster Theological Journal* 47 (1985): 1–2. While Melanchthon wrote *Erotematum dialectics, de methodo* and Erasmus contributed his *Ratio verae theologiae*, Calvin gave no sustained consideration of the proper way to proceed.

[18] Bruce Gordon's statement notwithstanding that Calvin was an extraordinary hater. *Calvin* (New Haven: Yale University Press, 2009), vii.

[19] Calvin, Commentary on Romans, 4. "This we should do in the expounding scripture, but in the teachings of religion, in which God has particularly desired that the minds of His people should be in agreement, we are to take less liberty." Parker, Ad Romanos, 4. "deinde ut id fiat in Scripturae expositione: in religionis autem dogmatibus, in quibus praecipue voluit Dominus consentaneas esse suorum mentes, minus sumatur libertatis."

scripture, having just finished the second Latin edition of the *Institutes*, Calvin was evidently considering the difference between teaching religion and interpreting scripture. That is not surprising. What does shock the reader was that Calvin clearly argued that the dogmas of religion were separable from and in some manner independent of the interpretation of scripture. From the argument Calvin made, one can see that the interpretation of scripture would support religious dogmas, but could not simply be those dogmas. The recitation of scripture would not suffice for the true religion, nor would pure interpretive efforts. These insights suggest the independence of a series of traditional teachings from scripture, about which God would allow the smallest degree of liberty.[20]

Calvin would continue to defend the broad orthodox tradition in his polemic against Albert Pighius, published in 1543. Both Pighius and Calvin sought to claim Augustine as their personal theological bulwark in the war over the authority of the fathers. What is fascinating in this treatise is the single-minded effort on Calvin's part to demonstrate the manner in which his favorite theologian, the fount of medieval orthodoxy, supported the evangelical position. The Genevan reformer would go to great lengths to generate a theory of heresy's effect in church history and supply an Augustinian periodization to support it. He would go so far as to abandon some of his own craft as a historian. All of this demonstrated that Calvin was not simply reading the church fathers as a manner of considering their thought in his own work. Instead, he sought to obtain the mantle of orthodoxy from Augustine, one whose immaculate orthodoxy was assumed throughout the early modern period.

We see Calvin continue this pattern. In the *Brief Instruction* – published in 1544, the year after the polemic against Pighius – he denied the possibility of adult baptism and the corollary rejection of infant baptism while claiming that the papal church was not his source. But that claim aside, what could Calvin have been doing other than accepting the model of cooperation between the church and the realm, and doing so in part because of the world in which he had been raised? Calvin continued his dependence

---

[20] Diarmaid MacCulloch offers a significant insight into Calvin's sense of the importance of the Catholic tradition in his "Calvin: Fifth Latin Doctor of the Church?" in *Calvin & His Influence, 1509–2009*, edited by Irena Backus and Philip Benedict (Oxford: Oxford University Press, 2011), 33–45. MacCulloch concentrates upon Calvin's acceptance of the Chalcedonian definition throughout his theological career. While MacCulloch makes it clear that in his opinion Chalcedon was not a triumph, the thrust of his argument and Calvin's ongoing striving for catholicity supports this study's sense of Calvin's overall approach to the orthodox tradition.

on tradition in both the *Brief Instruction* and the *Excuse à Messieurs les Nicodémites* with his claims that Anabaptists were heretics. He called the Anabaptists Cathars and Donatists. He stated that the Nicodemites were Valentinians, Cerdonites, and Marcionites.[21] But in no discussion of these ancient heresies did Calvin work through the biblical reasons that his opponents would be identified as these heretics, nor why these heresies were mistaken in the first place. Calvin accepted the model of hierarchical definition passed down as to orthodoxy and heresy without much consideration.

Finally, it is good to point out how strongly Calvin strove for the Augustinian mantle in his debates with Lutheran pastors over the Lord's Supper. As a conflict between two "Protestant" pastors, the battleground should have been scripture. Calvin pointed that out in his own response. But neither Westphal nor Calvin was willing to surrender the power of Augustine's brand. The authority of the fathers to demonstrate the orthodoxy of the evangelical positions was too weighty to surrender.[22]

Calvin's dialectic has been described in a number of ways. He has been called a biblical theologian, a rhetorical theologian, and an apologetic theologian.[23] But his consideration of the orthodox tradition should make modern readers at least consider whether he was also a theologian of the tradition. Calvin's choice to argue over the correct application of the fathers and their authority demonstrated a keen sense of the historical pattern. He believed that the teachings of true religion were passed down in such a manner as to be carried with the utmost care. But he carefully delineated that from the interpretation of scripture. For Calvin, the gospel truth was given in the first century, and needed to be passed on to each and every age. That is, quite simply, another way to say "tradition."

CALVIN: USING TRADITION TO ADD AUTHORITY
TO HIS THOUGHT

The argument that theological reasoning did not need tradition to have influence was common in the era of the Reformations. Certainly, Calvin

---

[21] Against the Libertines, 190. CO 7.154.
[22] See Chung-Kim's discussion in *Inventing Authority*, especially 59–120.
[23] Millet, "Docere/movere: les catégories rhétoriques," 35–51. William Bouwsma, "Calvinism as *Theologia Rhetorica*," in *Calvinism as Theologia Rhetorica*, edited by Wilhelm Wuellner (Berkeley: Center for Hermeneutical Studies in Hellenistic and Modern Culture, 1986), 1–21; François Wendel, *Calvin: Origins and Development of His Religious Thought*, translated by Philip Mairet (Durham: Labyrinth Press, 1987).

himself made this point a number of times. Modern scholars have echoed him, suggesting that, at most, Calvin supplied readings from the early authorities that agreed with the scriptures.[24] Such a notion preserves the model of Protestant acceptance of the authority of the scriptures and the concomitant avoidance of the power and authority of the tradition.

There are several problems with such a model of the Reformers' consideration of the orthodox traditions. First, the model is ahistorical. Calvin and Luther and Musculus and Melanchthon and Bullinger argued vociferously for the right to claim the tradition. A. N. S. Lane has suggested that this was a calculated move of doctrinal survival, that to accept the very real charge of novelty would have been fatal.[25] Second, this model seems to read back onto the early modern sources a framework that was the outcome of a long process of confessionalization rather than accurately expressing its foundation. Finally, this model demonstrates no predictive capacity. By the late seventeenth century, Protestant faculties of theology no longer saw Catholicism as their main opponent. One would speculate that the use of patristic sources would have greatly decreased because of the lack of need to defend that particular battleground. But nothing of the sort occurs.

Calvin spent an enormous effort throughout his career demonstrating that his theology was orthodox because it agreed with the sound consensus of the fathers. Richard Muller has argued that Calvin did not seek to set forth his own but the church's theology. My argument is that these two statements are functionally identical. The effort to "set out the church's doctrine" could not be done without reference to the orthodox fathers, and a sensitive historian such as Calvin knew it.

Studying what Calvin read has become a cottage industry. Scholars such as David Steinmetz, John Thompson, G. Sujin Pak, and A. N. S. Lane have admirably filled in the modern understanding of what Calvin read, when he read it, and how his reading influenced his thought. Lane has argued that Calvin's citations are not the early modern

---

[24] See Jean Boisset, "La reforme et les Peres de l'Eglise," in *Migne et le renouveau des études patristiques. Actes du colloque de Saint-Flour, 7–8 juillet 1975,* edited by André Mandouze and Joel Fouilheron (Paris: Beauchesne, 1985), 49. Quoted in Scott H. Hendrix, "Deparentifying the Fathers: The Reformers and Patristic Authority," in *Auctoritas patrum,* edited by Grane, Schindler, and Wriedt, 55.

[25] Lane, "Justification in Sixteenth-Century Patristic Anthologies," in *Auctoritas patrum,* edited by Grane, Schindler, and Wriedt, 87–88.

equivalent of modern footnotes and cannot be used to establish the sources he used.[26] He is interested in considering how fair Calvin was in his appropriation of the fathers. He argued that while Calvin was not a modern historian seeking a dispassionate conclusion, the "overwhelming majority accurately represent the father cited and inaccurate interpretation is found more often with writers with whom Calvin had less sympathy (such as Lombard or Gratian) rather than with 'his own' authors (such as Augustine or Bernard)."[27]

But we must ask why Calvin worked so hard to demonstrate his fidelity to the orthodox tradition. We know that he continued to read theological works across his career. Furthermore, at times those works would immediately find their way into his own work. Lane gives the example of material from Bernard of Clairvaux. Certainly, Bernard showed up in Calvin's works. His corpus is one demonstration that Calvin continued to read deeply throughout his life.

It would have been easy for Calvin not to have continued to read deeply in the sources of the orthodox tradition. It would have made perfect sense that one of the busiest men in the sixteenth century would have had little time for reading.[28] He preached four to six times per week, he taught theological and catechetical classes, he led the Company of Pastors in their deliberations, he attended and frequently led the Friday *congrégations* – the weekly Bible studies in Geneva that were open to all.[29] He wrote scores of letters per year, he led the Consistory in its efforts to reform the morals of the Genevans, and all of this before he put pen to paper to write a single word to be printed. We would expect that something had to give, and apparently it did – Calvin was an insomniac who suffered terrible health through much of his mature life.

What did not give, however, was Calvin's continued research in the fathers and medievals. He continued to read broadly in the classical theological sources. He continued to read Augustine, Chrysostom, and Bernard especially. We believe that he continued to read more broadly

---

[26] Lane, "Calvin's Use of the Fathers: Eleven Theses," in *John Calvin*, 1.
[27] Lane, "Calvin's Use of the Fathers and the Medievals," in *John Calvin*, 52–53.
[28] See Max Engammare's "Calvin the Workaholic," translated by Calvin Tams, in *Calvin & His Influence*, edited by Backus and Benedict, 67–83. Engammare makes both the point that Calvin was a workaholic, and that this was fed by his own insecurity.
[29] For more on the schedule of worship in Geneva during Calvin's time, see Elsie Anne McKee, *The Pastoral Ministry and Worship in Calvin's Geneva* (Geneva: Librairie Droz, 2016), especially chapter 4.

than this, but the painstaking work of tracing Calvin's sources has not been done in all cases.[30]

This pattern appears in Calvin's consideration of the practice of infant baptism. He was arguing against those who asserted that only adult baptism was correct and that there was no more reason to give infants baptism than the Lord's Supper. In his expansion of the *Institutes* in 1539, Calvin answered that scripture differentiated between the cases.[31] In 1543, he expanded that with an allusion to Cyprian and Augustine. He wrote: "This permission was indeed commonly given in the ancient church, as is clear from Cyprian and Augustine, but the custom has deservedly fallen into disuse."[32] That was the entirety of his addition to this argument. He delivered the names of two orthodox fathers, to add the patina of patristic authority to his argument, but he neither considered their arguments nor gave the longer consideration that he occasionally did. Calvin's use of the two fathers at this point served to add authority and orthodox weight to his argument, while using them as historical witnesses demonstrated the nature of the orthopraxy he wished to state.

Another instance of a 1543 addition comes from Calvin's discussion of the necessity of remaining with the church even should it have a mixed nature of wheat and tares. He stated that should anyone remain unconvinced by prophets and apostles, let that person yield to the authority of Christ. The rhetorical opening leads the reader to presume that the next statement will be from a gospel account. Instead, it is Cyprian. Calvin wrote:

Cyprian, then, has put it well: "Even though there seem to be tares or unclean vessels in the church, there is no reason why we ourselves should withdraw from the church; rather we must toil to become wheat; we must strive as much as we

---

[30] Sources are a particular and perennial problem in Calvin's writing. This process of tracking sources is further complicated by his ongoing reading and development, clearly visible through the various editions of his *Institutes* and commentaries. On this issue, see Alexandre Ganoczy, *The Young Calvin*, translated by David Foxgrover and Wade Provo (Philadelphia: Westminster Press, 1987) 133–81; R. J. Mooi, *Het Kerk-en Dogmahistorisch Element in de Werken van Johannes Calvijn* (Wageningen: H. Veenman, 1962); A. N. S. Lane, "Calvin's Use of the Fathers and the Medievals," *Calvin Theological Journal* (April 1981): 149–200; Lane, "Calvin's Sources of Saint Bernard," *Archiv für Reformationsgeschichte* 67 (1976):253–83; Alister McGrath, "John Calvin and Late Mediaeval Thought: A Study in Late Mediaeval Influences upon Calvin's Theological Development," *Archiv für Reformationsgeschichte* 77 (1986): 58–78; and Karl Reuter, *Das Grundverständnis der Theologie Calvins: unter Einbezeihung ihrer geschichtlichen Abhangigkeiten* (Neukirchen-Vluyn, 1963).

[31] Calvin, *ICR*, IV.xvi.30. CO 2.997.

[32] Calvin, *ICR*, IV.xvi.30. CO 2.997. "Fuit quidem id in veteri ecclesia factitatum, ut ex Cypriano et Augustino constat; sed merito mos ille obsolevit."

can to be vessels of gold and silver. But the breaking of earthen vessels belongs solely to the Lord, to whom has also been entrusted an iron rod. And let no one so claim for himself what is the Son's alone, that it is enough to winnow the chaff and thresh the straw and by human judgment to separate out all the tares. Proud, indeed, is this stubbornness and impious presumption, which wicked madness takes upon itself," etc.[33]

Though Calvin approves of Cyprian's formulation, the quotation comes from a passage where the Carthaginian bishop strings together a series of insights from and bald allusions to scripture. Further, Calvin begins the passage with an exhortation to yield to Christ's sanction, and then turns to Cyprian, rather than scripture itself. Drawing inferences from patterns of citation and allusion is always tricky, but it seems nigh impossible to argue, without great qualification, that Calvin was freeing himself from the authority of the patristic authors.

Again, in the 1543 *Institutes*, Calvin added material from Jerome, and sought to expand considerably his treatment of the visible church. This was natural given the experience through which he had lived both in Geneva and Strasbourg. Calvin's addition of material from Jerome to material from the 1536 *Institutes* granted authority to the argument he was making. Considering the office of the bishop, he turned to a comment from Jerome on the Paul's letter to Titus, writing: "Thus Jerome, commenting on the letter to Titus, says: 'Bishop and presbyter are one and the same.' And before, by the devil's prompting, dissensions arose in religion and it was said among the people, 'I am of Paul, I of Cephas,' churches were governed by the common counsel of presbyters."[34] Calvin gained the sanction of the creator of the Vulgate to argue for a model of ecclesiology that was more like Geneva's than that of Rome.

A final example from the 1559 *Institutes* appeared in Calvin's arguments about the Trinity. Calvin was arguing against Servetus who sought

---

[33] Calvin, *ICR*, IV.i.19. CO 2.761. "Bene ergo Cyprianus: etsi videntur, inquit, in ecclesia zizania, aut vasa impura, non est tamen cur ipsi de ecclesia recedamus; nobis modo laborandum ut frumentum esse possimus; nobis danda opera et quantum licet innitendum, ut vas aureum vel argenteum simus: caeterum fictilia vasa confringere solius Domini est, cui et virga ferrea data est; nec quisquam sibi quod proprium est soli filio vendicet, ut ad aream ventilandam et purgandam paleam sufficiat, zizaniaque omnia humano iudicio segreganda: superba est ista obstinatio, et sacrilege praesumptio, quam sibi furor pravus assumit, etc."

[34] Calvin, *ICR*, IV.iv.2. CO 2.789. "Ita Hieronymus in epistolam ad Titum: idem, inquit, presbyter qui episcopus. Et antequam diaboli instinctu dissidia in religione fierent, et in populis diceretur, ego Pauli, ego Cephae, communi consilio presbyterorum ecclesiae gubernabantur."

to portray the Son as less than the Father. He noted that he did not agree
with Nestorius and used Augustine to bolster his point. Calvin asserted
that because the first person of the Trinity was called "Father" in the
Old Testament, this demonstrated that the Son existed even in the time
of the Law and the Prophets. At the very end of his argument, he added
Irenaeus and Tertullian, noting: "Besides, the most ancient writers with
one accord testified to this fact so clearly that the shamelessness of those
who dare thrust at us Irenaeus and Tertullian is as ridiculous as it is
detestable. For both of these writers confess that the Son of God was
invisible, but afterward was visibly manifested."[35] Calvin did not use his
patristic authorities as conversation partners, but merely authorities to
demonstrate the feeble nature of his opponents' use of their names.

The notion that Calvin sought the approbation of the patristic witness for the sake of its authority and unimpeachable orthodoxy is not
popular.[36] However, he himself stated that only necessity should compel
leaving their witness. Calvin did not see the church's orthodox tradition
as nearly the problem that ordinary human vices could be. That did not
allow for an inappropriate use of the tradition. Safeguards would have
to be attached. But Calvin's ongoing use of the tradition suggests that
far from seeing it as problematic, he believed it to be a bastion of the
church's truth.

CALVIN: USING TRADITION FOR THE
DEVELOPMENT OF HIS THOUGHT

Many scholars have implicitly argued that Calvin's use of the orthodox
theological tradition was a polemical thrust, rather than a foundational

---

[35] Calvin *ICR*, II.xiv.7. CO 2.359–60. "Adde quod uno ore et consensu vetustissimi quique
scriptores hoc idem tam aperte testate sunt, ut non minus ridicula quam detestabilis sit
eorum impudentia, qui Irenaeum et Tertullianum obiicere nobis audent, quorum uterque invisibilem fatetur fuisse Dei filium, qui postea visibilis apparuit."

[36] Scott H. Hendrix, "Deparentifying the Fathers: The Reformers and Patristic Authority,"
in *Auctoritas patrum*, edited by Grane, Schindler, and Wriedt, 55–68, has argued that
the Reformers were involved in a process of de-parentification, a term borrowed from
family therapy that suggests the Reformers were intentionally reworking their attitudes
toward the patristic figures, especially concerning their authority. Lane, "Calvin's Use of
the Fathers: Eleven Theses," in *John Calvin*, 3, has posited the thesis that "In his commentaries, by contrast, Calvin is less interested in authorities but instead debates with
other interpreters." Lane gives as proof his consideration of the Genesis commentary.
But this is not the case in some of the New Testament commentaries. It may be that
Lane's division of citations into approving, disapproving, and neutral may need greater
intricacy to reflect accurately what Calvin was doing.

move. These scholars adhere to the polemicist model of Calvin's engagement with tradition, making the argument that Calvin's actual positive theology stands on a foundation of the scriptures and Calvin's reasoned consideration of them. Such scholars would take the evidence I have produced so far and relegate it to that category. So we turn to another function: Calvin used the theological tradition for the development of his own thought.

There are at least two questions to consider in examining the influence that Calvin received from the tradition. The first considers whether the various orthodox thinkers exercised a greater inspiration than merely providing a storehouse of allusions and citations. Thomas Torrance offered an important caution when he wrote that "Calvin's indebtedness to their thought cannot be measured simply by the passages where they are mentioned by name, for Calvin's language is often saturated with that of others in such a way that it is clear that they affected him deeply in his early formative years when he was acquiring his primary instruments of thought and speech."[37] Richard Muller went even further, noting that "The 'context' of Calvin's thought includes the works and ideas of individuals whose works Calvin most probably did not read, but whose thought, by way of its impact on the culture, on theology, philosophy or rhetoric, exegesis, method, and so forth, not only stands in the background of Calvin's thought but also frames it significantly."[38] In fact, I believe that it is necessary to expand Torrance's insight. Calvin received the late medieval Christian tradition not only in his early formative years. Quite to the contrary, he continued his love of books and reading throughout his life. We have seen evidence of this and will continue to examine it here.

A second question elevates the issue of worldview or interpretive framework or of *mentalités* that Calvin inherited. How significant was it that he lived in a world that accepted the close harmony of church and realm? How important was it that he seemed to accept without examination many of the factors of medieval life, piety, and citizenship?

A possible example of how Calvin worked within the mental world he received appears in the celebrated case of Michael Servetus, or Miguel de

---

[37] Thomas F. Torrance, *The Hermeneutics of John Calvin* (Edinburgh: Scottish Academic Press, 1988), 81.

[38] Richard A. Muller, "An Approach to Calvin: On Overcoming Modern Accommodations," in *The Unaccommodated Calvin: Studies in the Foundation of a Theological Tradition* (Oxford: Oxford University Press, 2000), 13.

Servet, a Spanish doctor and amateur theologian who was executed for heresy in Geneva on October 27, 1553.[39] Servetus was an anti-Trinitarian who had written books that rejected one of the foundational beliefs of the Christian church as biblically unsupportable. He had a fairly long epistolary quarrel with Calvin, in which the Spanish doctor sought to convince the latter that the Trinity neither existed nor could be exegetically maintained. Calvin eventually ended their correspondence but kept the books that the Spanish doctor had sent him. Servetus was eventually accused of heresy in Vienne, France, and taken into custody there on April 4, 1553. After being imprisoned, he escaped and, against all reason, traveled to Geneva. He was recognized, taken into custody, tried, and found guilty of heresy. During his trial, the Small Council took the counsel of other Protestant cities and thinkers about the appropriate way to deal with Servetus should he be found guilty. The unanimous decision was that Geneva had to execute him or be seen in the court of public opinion to be willing to shelter heresy. Accordingly, the Council handed down a sentence of the usual punishment for heresy, and Servetus was burned at the stake. Calvin provided evidence for the prosecution, though he could do little more as he was not a citizen of Geneva at that time.

Calvin suffers the most attacks for his role in Servetus' trial and death, which many consider sufficient reason, along with his doctrine of double predestination, to hold him in contempt.[40] In the early modern period, Sebastian Castellio, a schoolteacher who had been refused a position as minister in Geneva, wrote two attacks on Calvin. The first, *Concerning Heretics and Whether They Should Be Persecuted*, was published in Basel the year after Servetus was executed. The second, the *Contra libellum Calvini*, was not published until 1612. In both, Castellio argued that it was always wrong to persecute or prosecute someone for issues of dogmatic specifics.

Reading Castellio in the twenty-first century, thoughtful readers nod knowingly, secure in the acceptance of the religious toleration that marks

---

[39] For details, see Gordon, *Calvin*, 229–38. See also Arnold Huijgen, "The Challenge of Heresy: Servetus, Stancaro, and Castellio," in *John Calvin in Context*, edited by R. Ward Holder (Cambridge: Cambridge University Press, 2019), 258–66; Roland Bainton, *Hunted Heretic: The Life and Death of Michael Servetus, 1511–1553* (Boston: Beacon Press, 1953); Hans R. Guggisberg, *Sebastian Castellio, 1515–1563: Humanist and Defender of Religious Toleration in a Confessional Age*, translated by Bruce Gordon (Burlington: Ashgate, 2002).

[40] Kirk Essary, "Calvin's Critics: Bolsec and Castellio," in *John Calvin in Context*, edited by Ward Holder, 336.

out modern liberal democracies. But to read him in such a manner is wholly anachronistic. The mid-sixteenth century still believed in an organic model of society in which heresy was a dangerous cancer, necessitating removal. Castellio's suggestion to Calvin was a post hoc Trojan horse. Had the Genevans displayed mercy to Servetus, it would have cemented Geneva's reputation as a haven for heresy, affecting both the city's reputation and its commerce. Castellio almost certainly would have been able to foresee such a political outcome – his polemic was either a purely ethical model divorced from reality or simply an effort to shame the person whom he blamed for his own lack of employment in Geneva.

It is easy to find such models of traditional thought continuing to influence the thought of the Genevans in general and John Calvin in particular. The question, then, is whether it is possible to demonstrate that Calvin's theological work was influenced by specific models that modern analysts can produce. Can we draw stronger connections than simply arguing that Calvin's doctrine mirrors an earlier thinker's?[41] I will seek to do this in two manners. First, I will consider Calvin's engagement with three particular figures from the patristic and medieval periods – examining his consideration of Bernard of Clairvaux, his attention to John Chrysostom, and his debt to Augustine of Hippo. Each of these thinkers was integral to the development of Calvin's mature theology, and he added both their insights and citations or allusions to their work throughout his corpus.

I will also demonstrate influence by examining Calvin's doctrinal positions on three different doctrinal loci. The first will be his efforts at walking the narrow path between Roman Catholic tradition and Anabaptist biblicism in defending infant baptism. Calvin argued across his career about the necessity of sacraments being founded wholly upon the Word of God. But that left him struggling against the Anabaptists and searching for New Testament witness to infant baptism. Second, I will take up Calvin's consideration of predestination and the influence Augustine exerted on his thought. This locus was given urgency by the polemic with Pighius, but it probably would have been a point of contention in any case – and Calvin had many detractors on this point in his theology. Finally, I will delve into Calvin's Trinitarian doctrine, and how he turned to the tradition in the face of polemical attacks.

---

[41] An excellent example of such a study is Simon G. Burton's "Peter Martyr Vermigli on Grace and Free Choice: Thomist and Augustinian Perspectives," *Reformation & Renaissance Review* 15 (2013): 37–52. Burton traces several points in Vermigli's work to parallels in Gregory of Rimini's work.

These two approaches will demonstrate sufficient grounds to argue that Calvin was regularly if somewhat unconsciously absorbing the orthodox traditions to help to create his theological construct. In using that term, I am seeking to discern a harmony throughout the entirety of his work – a sense of the coherence of the structure of his works that he would have accepted. Calvin believed that his exegetical work, his doctrinal work, his polemical work, and his pastoral work formed a unified whole. That unity was achieved under the influence of the patristic and medieval orthodox traditions, and sought to carry them forward in a new rhetorical stance fit for the middle of the sixteenth century.

Calvin and Bernard of Clairvaux

There is little doubt that Calvin had a positive regard for Bernard that only grew as he gained access to further texts in the Cistercian's corpus. Studies by A. N. S. Lane, Johannes van Oort, and Jill Raitt have made this clear.[42] Van Oort asserted that though Calvin's regard for Gregory the Great declined as he grew older, his appreciation for Bernard continued to grow and flourish.[43]

Lane has demonstrated that Calvin's engagement with the Cistercian father began with his reading of his work in Strasbourg, where he had access to greater libraries during his sojourn there from 1538 to 1541.[44] This new reading was more significant than reading florilegia, and probably reflected Calvin's access to an opera omnia edition of Bernard that Calvin had in Strasbourg.[45] The material affect of the influence of Bernard's theology began to appear specifically in the 1543 *Institutes*.

Calvin inserted one such example in the 1543 *Institutes* as he considered the nature of faith. The passage was long; in that version, it occupies the entirety of the eighteenth paragraph of the fifth chapter. Even in the later 1559 *Institutes*, it remained an entire paragraph. Calvin wrote:

Bernard of Clairvaux reasons similarly when he expressly discusses this question in his Fifth Sermon the Dedication of a Church. "Now when I reflect upon my soul—which by the grace of God I sometimes do—it seems to me that I discover in it, so to speak, two opposite aspects. If I consider it in and of itself, I can say

---

[42] A. N. S. Lane, "Calvin's Sources of Bernard of Clairvaux," in *John Calvin*; van Oort, "John Calvin and the Church Fathers," 694–97; Jill Raitt, "Calvin's Use of Bernard of Clairvaux," *Archive for Reformation History* 72 (1981): 98–121.

[43] Van Oort, "John Calvin and the Church Fathers," 695.

[44] Lane, "Calvin's Sources of Bernard of Clairvaux," 119.

[45] Lane, "Calvin's Sources of Bernard of Clairvaux," 117–21.

nothing more truly of it than that it is reduced to nothing. What need is there now to enumerate the individual miseries of the soul; how it is burdened with sins, enveloped in darkness, enslaved to pleasure, itching with lusts, subject to passions, filled with delusions, always prone to evil, bent to every sort of vice—in a word, full of shame and confusion? To be sure, if all our acts of righteousness, scrutinized in the light of truth, are found to be like 'the rag of a menstruous woman,' then to what will our unrighteous acts be compared? 'If then the light in us is darkness, how great will be the darkness!' What then? Without doubt ... man has been made like unto vanity. Man 'has been reduced to nothing.' Man is nothing. Yet how can he whom God magnifies be utterly nothing? How can he upon whom God has set his heart be nothing? ...

But climbing to a higher watchtower, let us seek the City of God, let us seek his temple, let us seek his house, let us seek his bride. I have not forgotten ... but with fear and reverence ... I say: 'We, I say, are, but in the heart of God. We are, but by his dignifying us, not by our own dignity.'"[46]

This extraordinary passage appears in the midst of Calvin's discussion of faith, and it was added as an entire paragraph along with other

---

[46] *ICR*, III.ii.25. CO 1.463–64. "Nec aliter disserit Bernardus, quum hoc argumentum ex professo tractat, homilia in dedicatione templi quinta. Dei, inquam, beneficio nonnunquam de anima cogitans, videor mihi in ea veluti duo quaedam contraria invenire. Si ipsam, prout in se est, et ex se, intueor: de ea nihil verius dicere possum, quam ad nihilum esse redactam. Quid modo necesse est, singulas eius miserias numerare; quam sit onerata peccatis, offusa tenebris, irretita illecebris, pruriens concupiscentiis, obnoxia passionibus, impleta illusionibus, prona semper ad malum, in vitium omne proclivis, postremo ignominiae et confusionis plena? Nimirum si ipsae quoque iustitiae omnes, ad lumen veritatis inspectae, velut pannus menstruatae inveniuntur: iniustitiae deinceps quales reputabuntur? Si lumen, quod in nobis est, tenebrae sunt: ipsae tenebrae quantae erunt? (Matth. 6, 23.) Quid igitur? sine dubio vanitati similis factus est homo; in nihilum redactus est homo; nihil est homo. Quomodo tamen penitus nihil est, quem magnificat Deus? Quomodo nihil, erga quem appositum est cor divinum? Respiremus, fratres. Etsi nihil sumus in cordibus nostris: forte in corde Dei potest aliquid latere de nobis. O pater misericordiarum, o pater miserorum, quomodo apponis erga nos cor tuum? Cor enim tuum, ubi est thesaurus tuus. Quomodo autem thesaurus tuus sumus, si nihil sumus? Omnes gentes quasi non sint, sic sunt ante te: in nihilum reputabuntur. Nimirum ante te; non intra te. Sic in iudicio veritatis tuae, sed non sic in affectu pietatis tuae. Nimirum vocas ea quae non sunt, tanquam sint. Et non sunt ergo; quia quae non sunt vocas et sunt quia vocas. Licet enim non sint, quantum ad se, apud te tamen sunt, iuocta illud Pauli: non ex operibus iustitiae, sed ex vocante. Deinde mirificam esse hanc connexionem dicit utriusque considerationis. Certe quae inter se connexa sunt, se invicem non destruunt. Quod etiam in conclusione apertius declarat his verbis: iam si utraque consideration diligenter inspexerimus nos, quid sumus; imo in una quam nihil, in altera quam magnificati, puto temperate videtur gloriatio nostra; sed forsan magis aucta est: solidata tamen ut non in nobis, sed in Domino gloriemur. Nimirum si cogitamus, si decreverit salvare nos, statim liberabimur: iam in hoc respirare licet. Sed in altiorem speculam ascendentes quaeramus civitatem Dei, quaeramus templum, quaeramus domum, quaeramus sponsam. Non oblitus sum; sed cum metu et reverentia dico: nos inquam sumus, sed in corde Dei; nos sumus, sed illius dignatione, non nostra dignitate." Calvin was quoting Bernard of Clairvaux, In dedication ecclesiae, sermon 5.

expansions to the material on faith from the 1539 *Institutes*. Calvin did not waste any effort commenting upon Bernard's sermon, nor to consider how the passage supported his own doctrine.

Though the topic of this section of the 1539 and 1543 *Institutes* was faith, the word itself does not appear once in the entire passage from Bernard that Calvin quoted. Instead, the Cistercian father was interested in the character of the soul; that while it contained its own miseries, God loved it. The perspective meant everything in the consideration of the believer. From one frame of reference, humans were nothing. From the other, they were magnified because of God's work. All of this was due to God's granting of dignity to humanity, not from their own work.

Calvin's placement of a passage from Bernard's sermon in his own teaching about faith can only be seen as approval. Furthermore, this approval was so strong that he saw no reason to comment on or discuss the passage – it was appropriate on its own. The quoted instance was not an example in which Bernard seconded what Calvin had already said. Quite to the contrary, Calvin's discussion of faith was related to the soul and its relationship to God, but significantly different. In the preceding passage, he had emphasized the believer's ingrafting in Christ, and the benefits thereby engendered.

Finally, the sheer placement of Bernard's sermon into the *Institutes* accomplished not only the goal of demonstrating authority and orthodoxy, but also development of thought. Calvin's use of Bernard showed that his discussion of faith could be broadened to a consideration of how the soul was loved by God for God's own purposes.

A second passage from 1543 in which Calvin inserted a significant quotation from Bernard appears in III.xv.2. Calvin was discussing merit and the fallacy of depending upon it. He quoted Bernard, from the *Sermons on the Song of Songs*, a favorite of his:

But laying aside the term, let us rather look at the thing itself. Previously, indeed, I cited a statement from Bernard: "As it is sufficient for merit not to presume concerning merit, so to lack merits is sufficient for judgment." But he immediately adds his interpretation, in which he sufficiently softens the harshness of the utterance by saying: "Accordingly, take care to have merits. When you have them, know that they have been given. Hope for fruit, the mercy of God, and you have escaped all peril of poverty, ungratefulness, and presumption. Happy is the church that lacks neither merits without presumption nor presumption without merits." And a little before, he had abundantly shown the godly sense in which he had used the word. "For why," he asks, "should the church concern itself with merits when it has a firmer and more secure reason to glory in God's purpose? God cannot deny himself; he will do what he has promised. Thus you have no reason to ask, 'By what merits may we hope for benefits?' Especially since you hear; 'It is not for your sake ... but for mine.' For merit, it suffices to know that merits do not suffice."[47]

This passage had been in chapter 6 in the 1539 *Institutes* but was moved to chapter 10 in 1543. The quotation of Bernard displays several points. First, Calvin's fondness for Bernard was clear. Though Bernard will speak about merit, Calvin allowed it. This was quite different from his approach to Peter Lombard in the 1541 French translation of the *Institutes*. The issue is the same – Calvin did not like the terminology used, though he approved the underlying doctrinal construct. But Peter Lombard earned Calvin's correction, while Bernard was given a pass because he sufficiently softened his harshness.[48]

Second, by including Bernard's position in his work, Calvin achieved two further purposes. He ameliorated his own position that rejected the terminology of merit root and branch. Though Calvin would hold that scripture proved that human works could not be acceptable to God because of their impurity, Bernard's statement that it was important to take care to have merits stood as a balance.[49] Beyond that, he staked his claim that his own position on merit was within the stream of orthodox Augustinianism.

Calvin's dependence upon Bernard did not end with the 1543 *Institutes*. Even as late as the final Latin edition of the *Institutes* in 1559, Calvin was adding passages from Bernard into the work,[50] including another

---

[47] *ICR*, III.xv.2. CO 1.770. "Dicit quidem alicubi Bernardus : ut ad meritum satis est de meritis non praesumere, sic carere meritis, satis est ad iudicium; sed continuo addita interpretatio duritiem vocis satis emollit, quum dicit: proinde merita habere cures; habita, data noveris; fructum speres Dei misericordiam, et omne periculum evasisti, paupertatis, ingratitudinis, praesumptionis. Felix ecclesia, cui nec merita sine praesumptione, nec praesumptio sine meritis deest. Et paulo ante abunde ostenderat, quam pio sensu uteretur. Nam de meritis, inquit, quid sollicita sit ecclesia, cui de proposito Dei firmior securiorque exsistit gloriandi ratio? Non potest se ipsum negare Deus: faciet quod promisit. Sic non est quod quaeras, quibus meritis speremus bona; praesertim quum audias, non propter vos, sed propter me. Sufficit ad meritum, scire quod non sufficiant merita."

[48] 1541 French edition, 62. "For finally the master of the *Sentences* stresses that 'a person is not said to have free will because he is able to think or do the good as well as the evil, but only because he is not subjected to constraint; that freedom is not hindered even if we are wicked and slaves of sin and cannot choose anything but doing evil.' *Institution de la Religion Chrétienne (1541)*, 279. "Car finalement le maistre des Sentences prononce que l'homme n'est point dict avoir le Liberal Arbitre pource qu'il soit suffisant à panser nostre faire le bien autant comme le mal, mais seulement pource qu'il n'est point subject à contraincte; laquelle liberté n'est point empeschée, combien que nous soyons mauvais et serfz de peché, et que nous ne puissions autre chose que mal faire."

[49] *ICR*, III.xv.3. CO 2.580.

[50] Van Oort, "John Calvin and the Church Fathers," 696.

passage from Bernard's *Sermons on the Song of Songs*. Calvin wrote of the perception ("quae percipiunt") that believers regularly received of God's benefits. He argued that this perception of God's goodwill gave both clarity and assurance to believers. Calvin then wrote:

Bernard speaks to the point on this matter. For after dealing with the reprobate he says: "The decree of the Lord stands firm; his purpose of peace stands firm upon those who fear him, overlooking their evil and rewarding their good actions, so that by a marvelous method of his mercy not only good things but also evil ones work together for good. ... 'Who shall bring any charge against God's elect?' It is sufficient for all righteousness to me to have him alone on my side, against whom alone I have offended. Everything that he has decided not to impute to me is as though it had not been." And a little later: "O place of true repose, which I may not unfitly call by the name 'chamber'! O place in which God is beheld, not, as it were, aroused and in wrath, not as distracted with care, but in which is experienced the influence of his good and favorable and perfect will! That vision does not terrify but soothes; it does not arouse a restless curiosity but allays it; and it does not weary but calms the senses. Here true rest is felt. The God of peace renders all things peaceful, and to behold him at rest is to be at rest."[51]

As Dennis Tamburello noted, this is a passage from a selection from Bernard's *Sermons on the Song of Songs* that Calvin had also quoted earlier in the 1559 *Institutes*.[52] Calvin returned to it here to consider the nature of assurance for believers. Raitt argued, and Tamburello agreed, that Calvin's quotation that elided certain elements was, in a way, misleading:[53] he had left out Bernard's assertion that certain believers could feel a momentary certainty of their election. Both analysts asserted that Calvin's quotation of Bernard at this point, because of the omitted words, created a situation in which Bernard might have felt his words had been misappropriated.[54] Tamburello suggested that

---

[51] *ICR*, III.xxiv.4. CO 2.715. "Qua de re apposite Bernardus. Postquam enim de reprobis loquutus est: stat, inquit, propositum Dei, stat sententia pacis super timentes eum, ipsorum dissimulans mala, et remunerans bona, ut miro modo eis non modo bona, sed et mala cooperentur in bonum. Quis accusabit electos Dei? sufficit mihi ad non fuerit. Et paulo post: o verae quietis locus, et quem non immerito cubiculi appellatione censuerim, in quo Deus non quasi turbatus ira, nec velut distentus cura prospicitur, sed probatur voluntas eius in eo bona et beneplacens et perfecta. Visio ista non terret, sed mulcet; inquietam curiositatem non excitat, sed sedat; nec fatigat sensus, sed tranquillat; hic vere quiescitur; tranquillus Deus tranquillat omnia, et quietum aspicere, quiescere est."

[52] *ICR*, III.xi.22. CO 2.551. Dennis Tamburello, *Union with Christ: John Calvin and the Mysticism of St. Bernard* (Louisville: Westminster John Knox Press, 1994), 62–63.

[53] Raitt, "Calvin's Use of Bernard of Clairvaux," 117–18, discussed in Tamburello, *Union with Christ*, 62–63.

[54] Raitt, "Calvin's Use of Bernard of Clairvaux," discussed in Tamburello, *Union with Christ*, 62.

Calvin's mysticism was more inclusive than Bernard's – the Cistercian suggesting that only a mystic, presumably a monk, could experience such a transport, while Calvin made room for all believers receiving such assurance.[55]

The idea that Bernard would have found his words misused, though possible, is of course an exercise not in history but in speculation. Bernard might also have been excited that people were still reading his work centuries after his death – the point is that such ideas are speculative. More importantly, this theoretical academic exercise aims to narrow the meaning of "influence." In great part, that is related to the goal of this study – to demonstrate and calculate the influence of the orthodox traditions upon the work of John Calvin. But if the analyst begins with a caveat that influence will only be granted should the heir accurately and perfectly replicate the ancestor, this is enormously problematic. A sixteenth-century example should suffice. There is almost universal agreement that Calvin was influenced by Martin Luther.[56] But at almost every point at which Calvin agreed with Luther, he also developed his thought in ways that Luther had not and did not. Calvin believed that his eucharistic teaching was in line with Luther's – Lutherans disagreed. Calvin and Luther both taught a doctrine of election, but Calvin went further in his clear teaching of double predestination. Calvin and Luther both taught the primacy of the scripture, but Calvin did not apply a law-gospel hermeneutic in the same manner as Luther.

Given such facts, should modern analysts reject Luther as an influence on Calvin? To do so would be laughable. There are far too many places wherein Calvin's theology seems to be a further development of inspirations he received from the Wittenberg reformer. If that is the case, why would historians and historical theologians not apply the same models of analysis to Calvin and Bernard, or Calvin and any of the fathers? This broader model of influence, which I argue is the only one that is historically defensible, allows modern eyes to see Calvin taking Bernard's comment, and seeing a further possibility in his own context in Geneva.

---

[55] Tamburello, *Union with Christ*, 63, and chapters 4–5.
[56] See Ganoczy, *The Young Calvin*, 156; R. Ward Holder, ed., *Calvin and Luther: The Continuing Relationship* (Göttingen: Vandenhoeck & Ruprecht, 2013); and Herman J. Selderhuis and Marius J. Lange van Ravenswaay, eds., *Luther and Calvinism: Image and Reception of Martin Luther in the History and Theology of Calvinism* (Göttingen: Vandenhoeck & Ruprecht, 2017).

Calvin and John Chrysostom

John Chrysostom was Calvin's favorite New Testament patristic exegete. Calvin did not always appreciate Chrysostom's doctrine because he considered the Constantinapolitan bishop's appreciation for free will to be wrongheaded. But among interpreters of the scriptures, Calvin's statements about Chrysostom were clear. Calvin made a plan to prepare a French version of Chrysostom's sermons, though he never made significant progress on that project.[57] But given that Calvin never made any other overtures toward preparing an edition or translation of any other patristic author, this is substantial evidence of the effect Chrysostom made upon him.

The great study of the relationship of John Calvin to John Chrysostom still awaits an author. While John Walchenbach wrote a dissertation upon Calvin's use of Chrysostom in his New Testament work, he did not continue that with a deeper study.[58] Other efforts have considered the historical record that Calvin may have left, such as his handwritten notes in the Chevallon edition of Chrysostom, or have considered Chrysostom as a particular case in consideration of another topic such as accommodation in Calvin's thought.[59] But no sustained consideration of Chrysostom's comprehensive influence on Calvin's thought has been written.

Calvin's appreciation for Chrysostom as an exegete has been well established. He turned to him often, and frequently used Chrysostom as

---

[57] Jeannette Kreijkes, "The Praefatio in Chrysostomi Homilias as an Indication that Calvin Read Chrysostom in Greek," in *Calvinus Pastor Ecclesiae: Papers of the Eleventh International Congress on Calvin Research*, edited by Herman J. Selderhuis and Arnold Huijgen (Göttingen: Vandenhoeck & Ruprecht, 2016), 347–354. See also her "Is a Special Faith the Same as Saving Faith? Calvin's Appropriation of Chrysostom's Understanding of a Faith of Miracles," in *More than Luther: The Reformation and the Rise of Pluralism in Europe*, edited by Karla Boersma and Herman J. Selderhuis (Göttingen: Vandenhoeck & Ruprecht, 2019), 165–76.

[58] John Walchenbach, "John Calvin as Biblical Commentator: An Investigation of John Chrysostom as Exegetical Tutor," Ph.D. Dissertation, University of Pittsburgh, 1974. Walchenbach's dissertation was recently published. See John R. Walchenbach, *John Calvin as Biblical Commentator: An Investigation into Calvin's Use of John Chrysostom as an Exegetical Tutor* (Eugene: Wipf & Stock, 2010). Walchenbach's conclusion demonstrates an ideal of influence that approaches repetition. "Our goal has been to propose a plausible explanation to the major question of why Calvin so inadequately represented the full import of Chrysostom's thought on so many occasions" (163).

[59] Alexandre Ganoczy and Klaus Müller, *Calvins Handschriftliche Annotationen zu Chrysostomus: Ein Beitrag zur Hermeneutik Calvins* (Wiesbaden: Franz Steiner Verlag GMBH, 1981); Arnold Huijgen, *Divine Accommodation in Calvin's Theology: Analysis and Assessment* (Göttingen: Vandenhoeck & Ruprecht, 2011).

an authority on how to read the Greek of the passages, especially in contested passages. Readers see this in Calvin's comment on I Corinthians 1.2, where Calvin followed Chrysostom, arriving at a harsh rendering in Latin, but maintaining the Greek construction.[60] Calvin followed Chrysostom again on I Corinthians 9.24, on the signification of οὕτως.[61] But at other moments, Calvin used Chrysostom as a possible example and historical source without approbation. Such a case came in Calvin's discussion of Paul's attack on the Corinthians for their bad behavior in the celebration of the Lord's Supper in the eleventh chapter of I Corinthians. Calvin noted: "But we cannot say for certain what gave rise to this abuse, or what caused it to emerge so quickly." He immediately provided Chrysostom's solution: "Chrysostom thinks that it took its origin in the love-feasts (ἀπὸ τῶν ἀγαπῶν), the situation being that, while the rich had been in the habit of bringing food from their homes, and eating along with the poor, without making any difference between them, they later began to cut the poor out, and to guzzle their delicacies on their own."[62] In such a case, Calvin's dependence on Chrysostom was a type of historical reasoning.

Calvin could also cite Chrysostom approvingly as an authority without much further discussion about the Greek father's thought. Such a case appeared in his comment on I Corinthians 13.2:

Now Paul is his own interpreter (as I have already said), for he limits faith here to miracles. It is what Chrysostom calls 'the faith of signs or miracles,' and we, a 'particular faith,' because it does not lay hold of Christ in His wholeness, but only of his power in effecting miracles. That is why men can sometimes have that, when they do not have the Spirit of sanctification, as was the case with Judas.[63]

Calvin's comment was short, to the point, and approving.[64]

---

[60] John Calvin, *The First Epistle of Paul the Apostle to the Corinthians*, Calvin's New Testament Commentaries, vol. 9, translated by John W. Fraser, edited by David W. and Thomas F. Torrance (Edinburgh: Oliver & Boyd, 1960), 19. CO 49.309.

[61] Calvin, I Corinthians Comm., 198. CO 49.449.

[62] Calvin, I Corinthians Comm., 240. CO 49.482. "Caeterum unde ortus sit hic abusus, aut qua occasione tam cito emerserit, dubium est. Chrysostomus ἀπὸ τῶν ἀγαπῶν fluxisse putat, quod quum divites soliti essent domo afferre unde promiscue cum pauperibus et in commune epularentur: postea exclusis pauperibus soli de suis lautitiis ingurgitare coeperunt."

[63] Calvin, I Corinthians Comm., 275. CO 49.509. "Paulus autem (quemadmodum iam dixi) est sui interpres, qui fidem hic ad miracula restringit. Ea est quam vocat Chrysostomus signorum, nos particularem: quia non apprehendit totum Christum, sed tantum potentiam in edendis miraculis: ideoque interdum in homine esse potest absque spiritu sanctificationis, qualiter fuit in Iuda."

[64] A similar case appeared in his comment upon Galatians 4.22.

An extraordinary passage in which Calvin cited Chrysostom and Ambrose occurred in his comment on Galatians 4.25. Calvin noted that he had been changed, presumably by reading Chrysostom. He wrote: "But why does he compare the present Jerusalem with Mount Sinai? Although I once held the opposite opinion, I now agree with Chrysostom and Ambrose, who expound it of the earthly Jerusalem, and indeed that it had then degenerated into a slavish doctrine and worship. This is why he (Paul) says, *which now is.*"[65] Calvin noted that his own mind had changed, and he leaves the reader to presume that this was because of his study of Chrysostom and Ambrose. He found them to be persuasive interpreters of scripture, and accepted their thought, discarding his own.

One of Calvin's greatest senses of Chrysostom's importance for the church was in his doctrine of the eucharist. After quoting Augustine, Calvin wrote: "And Chrysostom writes the same thing in another passage: 'Christ makes us his body not by faith only but by the very thing itself.' For he means that such good is not obtained from any other source than faith; but he only wishes to exclude the possibility that anyone, when he hears faith mentioned, should conceive of it as mere imagining."[66] The bishop of Constantinople had been turned into a bulwark against the charge of being a mere "sacramentarian." Chrysostom, in Calvin's eyes, denied the possibility of a "mere faith" that was less than the physical substance. Because of the transcendent nature of true doctrine, Calvin could reach back to the fourth-century bishop and find the resources he needed to combat the errors of his own day.

In a remarkable passage that turned to Augustine and Chrysostom, Calvin remarked on the Christian's responsibility to take part in the Lord's Supper regularly. Several points are worthy of notice. First, Calvin set out a sense of the apostolic tradition that he would accept. He added this to the 1543 *Institutes*, stating: "Obviously, by these constitutions holy men meant to retain and protect the frequent practice of

---

[65] Calvin, I Corinthians Comm., 87. CO 50.239. "Verum cur praesentem Ierusalem componit cum monte Sina? Tametsi aliquando fui in contraria opinione, assentior tamen Chrysostomo et Ambrosio, qui de terrena Ierusalem exponunt: et quidem, ut tunc ad servilem doctrinam et cultum degeneraverat. Ideo dicit quae nunc est."

[66] *ICR*, IV.xvii.6. CO 2.1006–07. "Atque id ipsum est quod alicubi scribit Chrysostomus, Christum non fide tantum, sed re ipsa nos suum efficere corpus. Neque enim aliunde quam a fide tale bonum consequi intelligit; sed hoc tantum vult excludere, ne quis, dum fidem nominari audit, nudam imaginationem concipiat."

communion, received, as it was, from the apostles themselves."[67] Calvin noted from both Augustine and Chrysostom that this practice of regular celebration of the Lord's Supper was already falling into disuse in their day. After quoting Augustine, he turned to Chrysostom's Commentary on Ephesians, and quoted him at length:

> It is not said to him who dishonored the banquet, "Why did you recline at Table?" but, "Why did you come in?" Whoever does not partake of the mysteries is wicked and shameless to be present there. I beg of you, if anyone, invited, comes to a banquet, washes his hands, reclines at table, and seems to get ready to eat, and then tastes nothing—does he not dishonor both the banquet and the host? So, when you stand among those who prepare themselves with prayer to receive the most holy food, in the fact that you have not withdrawn, you have confessed that you are one of their number, but at the end you do not partake! Would it not be better for you not to have been present? I am unworthy, you say. Therefore, you were also not worthy of the communion of prayer, which is the preparation for the receiving of the sacred mystery.[68]

In 1215, at the Fourth Lateran Council, the church had required annual partaking of the sacrament as a requirement for believers. As frequently happens in both the history of Christianity and in life, unintended consequences arose. That which had been intended as the minimum had for many lay believers become the maximum. Reformers of various confessional camps believed that this was part of the corruption of the church.

Calvin used Chrysostom to argue against a practice he believed had corrupted the church. The Genevan reformer believed that the church had maintained certain practices from the time of the apostles, and frequent participation in the Lord's Supper was certainly one such practice. The opportunity to use Chrysostom and Augustine as historical witnesses to the phenomenon that even in the early church people were wont to fall away from the discipline of observance certainly helped Calvin's

---

[67] *ICR*, IV.xvii.45. CO 2.1047. "His scilicet constitutionibus volebant sancti viri retinere ac tueri frequentem communionis usum, ab ipsis apostolis traditum, quem fidelibus maxime salutarem esse, vulgi autem negligentia sensim obsolescere videbant."

[68] *ICR*, IV.xvii.45. CO 2.1047. "...non est dictum ei qui convivium dehonestabat, quare recubuisti? sed, quare ingressus es? Quisquis mysteriorum particeps non est, improbus est, et impudens quod hic adstat; quaeso, si quis ad convivium vocatus venerit, manus laverit, discubuerit, visus fuerit se ad edendum comparare, deinde nihil gustet, nonne contumelia et convivium afficiet et convivatorem? sic tu, inter eos stans qui oratione se ad sumendum sacrosanctum cibum praeparant, te unum esse ex eorum numero, eo ipso quod non abscessisti confessus es, tandem non participas: nonne satius foret te non comparuisse? Indignus sum, inquis; ergo nec communione orationis dignus eras, quae est ad sumendum sacrum mysterium praeparatio."

argument. But it also bolstered his belief that the church had a doctrinal and traditional core that transcended historical contingency and the hierarchical church's efforts to define it, and allowed him to assert the church's character in concert with the fathers as he pursued the purification and edification of the church.

Calvin and Augustine

John Calvin's admiration and even love for Augustine of Hippo has been well noted. Van Oort noted that without a doubt Augustine was Calvin's most-cited and most-appreciated patristic authority.[69] Deep studies examining the relationship of the two have been written.[70] In part this should not be noted as a particularly significant relationship between the two. By the sixteenth century, Augustine had achieved such an overwhelming influence in Western Christianity that Jaroslav Pelikan would suggest that the development of medieval theology could be seen as a "series of footnotes to Augustine."[71] Karla Pollmann noted that Augustine was "arguably the most influential Christian writer in the Latin West," and that although many factors contributed to this including his office, his sanctity, and his orthodoxy, "he never would have become the all-surpassing authority he did in fact become if he had not written so many works, and if these had not succeeded in surviving as

---

[69] Van Oort, "John Calvin and the Church Fathers," 689.

[70] See, among others, the articles collected in Benjamin Breckenridge Warfield's *Calvin and Augustine* (Phillipsburg: Presbyterian and Reformed, 1956); the study by Luchesius Smits of Augustine's influence on Calvin's doctrine of election, *Saint Augustin dans l'oeuvre de Jean Calvin* (Assen: Van Gorcum, 1957–58); and the later study by J. Marius J. Lange van Ravenswaay, *Augustinus totus noster: Das Augustinverständnis bei Johannes Calvin* (Göttingen: Vandenhoeck & Ruprecht, 1990). Numerous shorter studies have also been published. Among others, see William Bouwsma, "The Two Faces of Humanism: Stoicism and Augustinianism in Renaissance Thought," in *Itinerarium Italicum: The Profile of the Italian Renaissance in the Mirror of its European Transformations*, edited by Heiko Oberman and Thomas A Brady, Jr. (Leiden: Brill, 1975), 3–60; and Paul Oskar Kristeller, "Augustine and the Early Renaissance," in *Studies in Renaissance Thought and Letters* (Rome: Edizione di storia e letteratura, 1956), 355–372. Augustine's impact was hardly limited to theologians, also having enormous influence over philosophy, music, drama, and art. For an overview of Augustine's influence in the Renaissance, see Meredith J. Gill, *Augustine in the Italian Renaissance: Art and Philosophy from Petrarch to Michelangelo* (Cambridge: Cambridge University Press, 2005); and Karla Pollman and Meredith J. Gill, eds., *Augustine beyond the Book: Intermediality, Transmediality, and Reception* (Leiden: Brill, 2012).

[71] Jaroslav Pelikan, *The Christian Tradition: A History of the Development of Doctrine*, 5 vols. (Chicago: University of Chicago Press, 1971–1989), 1.330.

they have."[72] Alister McGrath argued that the Reformation itself was a response to an important and newly formulated idea, identified as "a new statement of Augustine's ideas on salvation."[73] Of course, in McGrath's statement one can hear the echo of Benjamin Breckenridge Warfield's much earlier conclusion that the Reformation was simply "the ultimate triumph of Augustine's doctrine of grace over his doctrine of the church."[74] Christoph Burger pointed out that one of the great differences between Erasmus and Luther in their struggle over the freedom of the will was the status of Augustine.[75] When Calvin concentrated his attention upon Augustine of Hippo, he himself was continuing a medieval tradition that stretched back to Hugh of St. Victor, called "another Augustine," or Peter Lombard, whose *Sentences* are approximately half comprised of quotations from the North African bishop.

This should be one of the most important issues to consider in examining Augustine's influence on Calvin. When Calvin used Augustine so frequently in his theological works, whether polemical, instructional, or exegetical, he was traveling a very well-trod road. The medieval thinkers who preceded Calvin had done much the same. In fact, they had done it so well and so often that when modern scholars examine the early modern period's reception of Augustine, we are faced with a series of questions.

First, there is the issue of where Calvin learned his Augustine.[76] Karl Reuter has argued that the fount of Calvin's Augustinianism flows from his teacher at the College de Montaigu, John Major.[77] That thesis has been vigorously contested by Alexandre Ganoczy, who denies that Calvin

---

[72] Karla Pollmann, "The Proteanism of Authority: The Reception of Augustine in Cultural History from his Death to the Present, Mapping an International and Interdisciplinary Investigation," in *The Oxford Guide to the Historical Reception of Augustine*, vol. 1, edited by Karla Pollmann and Willemien Otten (Oxford: Oxford University Press, 2013), 3.

[73] Alister McGrath, *The Intellectual Origins of the European Reformation*, 2nd ed. (Oxford: Blackwell, 2004), 167.

[74] Warfield, *Calvin and Augustine*, 322.

[75] Christoph Burger, "Erasmus' Auseinandersetzung mit Augustin im Streit mit Luther," in *Auctoritas patrum*, edited by Grane, Schindler, and Wriedt, 13. "Erasmus ordnet Augustin in die Gruppe der Rechtgläubigen *(orthodoxi)* ein. Doch für ihn ist er nur *eine* gewichtige Autorität unter anderen Autoritäten, während er für Luther als der verlässlichste Ausleger des Paulus eine Sonderstellung einnimmt."

[76] A. N. S. Lane has provided an excellent overview of the issue in "Calvin's Use of the Fathers and Medievals," in *John Calvin: Student of the Church Fathers* (Edinburgh: T. & T. Clark, 1999), 15–66. See especially 16–25.

[77] Reuter, *Das Grundverständnis der Theologie Calvins*.

even studied with Major while at Paris.[78] While others have weighed in, those are the two poles of the argument. McGrath has posited a third option that seeks to avoid the historical issue of provenance. He suggests that Augustinianism was so prevalent that Calvin was bound to absorb it is a kind of "in the air" phenomenon, and that finding the basis of it is probably impractical if not impossible.[79]

Then again, we might ask, what is Augustinianism in the early modern period? Looking not at Calvin but at Martin Luther, David C. Steinmetz discerned five different senses for the term as it is used by historians of late medieval history and theology.[80] He discerned the sense of Augustinianism as simply the "theology of the Latin West in general."[81] While Steinmetz argues convincingly for the meaningfulness of this term, it cannot be analytically helpful. A second sense meant that Augustinian described the "theology of the Augustinian Order."[82] He calls this a descriptive sense that does not necessarily have to do with the doctrines of Augustine of Hippo. Under this sense, one is an Augustinian because of one's membership in the Order, as Luther was. A modern-day equivalent might be to term someone a "Lutheran" theologian because he maintains membership in a Lutheran denomination, regardless of how closely the confession or individual aligned with Luther's actual thought. A third sense of Augustinian, while remaining within the Augustinian Order, is more evaluative, and refers to those with special fealty to St. Augustine. The term is "used evaluatively to describe a party within the Augustinian Order which agrees with St. Augustine on a wide range of disputed issues and at a depth which is more profound than the merely nominal Augustinianism common to all medieval theologians."[83] A fourth sense calls Augustinianism the theological "right wing" of the later medieval period. Steinmetz writes: "Augustinian in this fourth sense is the designation for a sentiment in theology which takes Augustine without ice or water and which translates him into the theological vocabulary of one's own circle without dulling the bracing effect of his thought or deadening the ability of his formulations to jar one loose from one's own

[78] Ganoczy, *The Young Calvin.*
[79] Alister McGrath, *A Life of John Calvin: A Study in the Shaping of Western Culture* (Cambridge: Blackwell Publishers, 1990), 33–47.
[80] David C. Steinmetz, *Luther and Staupitz: An Essay in the Intellectual Origins of the Protestant Reformation* (Durham: Duke University Press, 1980), 13.
[81] Steinmetz, *Luther and Staupitz*, 13.
[82] Steinmetz, *Luther and Staupitz*, 14.
[83] Steinmetz, *Luther and Staupitz*, 14.

comfortable and commonplace way of thinking."[84] Lastly, Steinmetz detects a final sense that adds complexity to the historian's task. This is the sense of Augustinianism as the embodiment of a theological tendency, a tendency that he illustrates in opposition to Pelagianism.[85]

Steinmetz adds the vital caution that the meaning of theological formulations cannot be divorced from context and intention. Theological statements can be taken out of the contingent circumstances that were part of the world that gave them meaning.[86] But to do so is a task that offers both great rewards and great risks. The great risks are somewhat more obvious – modern canons of scholarship decree that one of the more notable sins is that of taking items out of their proper context. However, the great rewards must be acknowledged as well. If Calvin or Luther or Cranmer read Augustine, or Bernard of Clairvaux, or even Paul, and wish to do it with more than antiquarian interest, they must take those words and thoughts and place them into a new world.

William Courtenay brought his own analytical framework to the question when he differentiated between genuine and false forms of Augustinianism.[87] Courtenay argued that almost all religious thought in the West had been received in a process that was attached to Augustine. He asserted a distinction between "Augustinianism" and "the Augustinian school." The first signified Augustine's influence in the strictest sense, while the latter considered the late medieval work of religious attached to the Augustinian hermits.[88] Thus, Augustinianism meant working in the tradition of the bishop of North Africa. The Augustinian school was a group of thinkers who over time had generated their own tradition that used Augustine but also a variety of other influences, including the scholastic tradition of the late medieval universities.

Eric Saak noted Steinmetz's senses of Augustinianism, and added his own consideration on the issue. While granting the significance of Steinmetz's description, Saak pushed for a different route. He wrote that political, philosophical, and theological Augustinianism had been factors in the renewal of the study of Augustine's works, but "one important conduit for the reception of Augustine has not been given its due: the

[84] Steinmetz, *Luther and Staupitz*, 15.
[85] Steinmetz, *Luther and Staupitz*, 15.
[86] Steinmetz, *Luther and Staupitz*, 15.
[87] William J. Courtenay, *Schools and Scholars in Fourteenth Century England* (Princeton: Princeton University Press, 1987).
[88] Courtenay, *Schools and Scholars*, 77.

signification of the term 'Augustinian' not as a doctrinal adjective, but as the historical noun."[89] Saak was making an effort to get back at the religion of Augustine, a theme that he discerns in the writings of the Augustinian hermits such as Alfonsus Vargas.[90] Saak makes clear that he believes that the way to work through the issues of Augustinianism in the late medieval period must be source-critical, leaving behind the doctrinal approach.[91]

One model of considering Augustine's influence has especially been forwarded by Steinmetz. In his classic study of Luther and Staupitz, Steinmetz argued that Luther's own statements that he had received everything that he had from Staupitz were not historically accurate. As historians, we must note down Luther's statements about his own set of influences as historical facts that tell us what Luther was thinking; we should not necessarily take them as indicative of the fact of influence.[92] It is not uncommon for thinkers to be unconscious of influence or for them to attempt intentionally to obscure influence. Steinmetz provides his own cautions about influence, noting that similarity is not influence, and that agreement is not influence – pointing out the importance of negative influence.[93] He argued that the relationship between Staupitz and Luther was significant, but not the kind of doctrinal influence that Luther's own statements led historians to believe. Instead, Steinmetz argued for an "astonishing degree of independence from his teachers that Luther exhibited from the very beginning"[94] and pointed out that the real influence Staupitz had over Luther was pastoral.[95]

Writing later on the same problem, Steinmetz notes that the unresolved problem of the forerunner draws perennial interest.[96] He saw the

---

[89] Eric Leland Saak, "The Reception of Augustine in the Later Middle Ages," in *The Reception of the Church Fathers in the West: From the Carolingians to the Maurists*, edited by Irena Backus (Leiden: Brill, 1997), 375.

[90] Saak, "The Reception of Augustine," esp. 384–397.

[91] Saak, "The Reception of Augustine," 399.

[92] Steinmetz, *Luther and Staupitz*, 3–4, and 142, where Steinmetz characterizes Luther's characterization of his debt to Staupitz as "revisionist historiography." Martin Luther, "Ex Erasmo nihil habeo. Ich hab all mein ding von Doctor Staupitz; der hatt mein occasionem gebe." WA TR I, Nr. 173.

[93] Steinmetz, *Luther and Staupitz*, 7.

[94] Steinmetz, *Luther and Staupitz*, 140.

[95] Steinmetz, *Luther and Staupitz*, 142.

[96] David C. Steinmetz, "Luther and Staupitz: The Unresolved Problem of the Forerunner," in *Ad Fontes Lutheri: Essays in Honor of Kenneth Hagen's Sixty-fifth Birthday*, edited by Timothy Maschke, Franz Posset, and Joan Skocir (Milwaukee: Marquette University Press, 2001), 270–80.

value of shifting the focus from influence to the relationship of context.[97]
Using the example of the history of exegesis, he wrote of the value of
seeing a cloud of forerunners.[98] This shift of emphasis may give us better
understanding – but will it answer the questions posed or simply accept
that they cannot be answered?

In evaluating these various methods, the problem of Augustine's influence stands because of the method employed.[99] In seeking to make head-
way against both the ideas of previous generations of scholarship, and
against the kinds of evidence that the sources will and will not proffer, at
times it seems that we have reached a cul de sac. But what if we shifted
the question? My methodological suggestion is to look not at whether
Calvin was reading Augustine (he was!), but to examine the kind of interpretation that Calvin gave to Augustine. Following Steinmetz, I am arguing for a contextually thick consideration of Calvin's Augustinianism.

The question that we ask of Calvin's reading of Augustine cannot be
as univocal as whether Calvin correctly read Augustine. At a distance of
a thousand years, that would be more than difficult, it would be herculean. But beyond the historical difficulties presented by the very different
contexts in which Calvin and Augustine lived and moved and thought, is
that of the Augustinian tradition itself. Calvin lived in a time and place
when the term "Augustinianism" was close to a synonym for "educated
thought." Further, the various Augustinianisms had branched apart long
before the Luther affair. Writing about her work on the reception of
Augustine, Pollmann argued that "this entire project can be regarded as a
gigantic case study that demonstrates the protean quality of Augustine's
authority, as representative of the nature of authority as such, which can
be evoked, denied, reconstructed, and even (re)invented."[100]

Instead, the argument must be constructed on the basis of how Calvin
was using Augustine. One can argue for more or less successful readings,
but the simplicity of the right or wrong binary will escape the analyst's
grasp. This allows a variety of fruits that this search will yield. First, by

---

[97] Steinmetz, "Problem of the Forerunner," 279.
[98] Steinmetz, "Problem of the Forerunner," 279.
[99] Irena Backus has followed a different method in her *Historical Method and Confessional Identity in the Era of the Reformation (1378–1615)* (Leiden: Brill, 2003), 15. Noting the other issues mentioned earlier, she opts for an examination of treatises on church reform, seeking to break the present impasse. I see this present work as parallel to hers.
[100] Karla Pollmann, "The Proteanism of Authority: The Reception of Augustine in Cultural History from his Death to the Present," in *The Oxford Guide to the Historical Reception of Augustine*, vol. 1, edited by Karla Pollmann and Willemien Otten (Oxford: Oxford University Press, 2013), 3.

concentrating upon Calvin's use of Augustine, we will concentrate upon doctrine. Calvin did occasionally use Augustine as a source of historical witness. But far more frequently, he turned to the North African father as a source of orthodox teaching. Calvin saw Augustine as a way to demonstrate a variety of issues of orthodoxy. First, he saw him as an authority – to be in concert with Augustine was, normally, to be within the boundaries of orthodoxy. Second, he saw Augustine as a historical marker to demonstrate that certain teachings that Calvin promulgated were neither novel nor invented. While that was important, it is also significant to note that Calvin schematized the Christian past for a useful conceptual framework.[101] Finally, Calvin believed that Augustine's doctrine led believers through a process toward the edification of the church.

Calvin's use of Augustine as an authority comes through in many places. One such occurs in the 1559 *Institutes*, when he quoted Augustine to consider the correct way of preaching about predestination. The passage is remarkable for the manner in which Calvin linked passages from Augustine's works together to make his point, rather than providing a single passage from the bishop to fortify his own words. The point of the quotation was the right way to preach about predestination. He stated that it would foster indolence and provide an opening for evil intentions if preachers simply argued that the members of the congregation did not believe because they were divinely destined for damnation. Calvin wrote:

Augustine, therefore, rightly bids such men begone from the church, as foolish teachers or perverse and foreboding prophets. Elsewhere he contends for the opinion that a man benefits by rebuke when he who causes him to do so will profit even without rebuke shows mercy and lends help. But why is it this way with one man, another way with another? Far be it from us to say that judgment belongs to the clay, not to the potter! Afterward he writes: "But when men either come or return into the way of righteousness through rebuke, who works salvation in their hearts but him who gives the increase—regardless of who plants and waters—whom no man's free choice resists when he wills to save him? It is not, then, to be doubted that the will of God—who has done all things that he has pleased in heaven and on earth, and who has also made the things that are to come—cannot be resisted by human wills so as to prevent his doing what he wills, since he does with the very wills of men what he wills." Again: when he would lead men to himself, "Does he bind them by bodily fetters? He acts within; he holds their hearts within; he moves their hearts within; and he draws them by their own wills, which he has wrought within them." But we ought not to omit what he adds immediately thereafter: "For as we know not who belongs to the

---

[101] Backus, *Historical Method and Confessional Identity*, 128.

number of the predestined or who does not belong, we ought to be so minded as to wish that all men be saved. So shall it come about that we try to make everyone we meet a sharer in our peace. But our peace will rest upon the sons of peace. Hence, as far as we are concerned, ... a healthful and severe rebuke should be applied as a medicine to all that they may not either perish themselves or destroy others. It belongs to God, however, to make that rebuke useful to those whom he ... has foreknown and predestined."[102]

Calvin's turn to Augustine was multilayered, and he quoted two of Augustine's later treatises.[103] Calvin's use of the chain of quotations and allusions gave the impression that Augustine agreed with the entire complex of Calvin's thought around issues of predestination, the bondage of the will, and the usefulness of the proclamation of it. Calvin's effort was to show his own maintenance of Augustine's positions, doctrines that were basic to the gospel message. The use of multiple allusions and citations to Augustine in a passage from the *Institutes* demonstrated how Calvin's doctrine was neither novel nor the beginning of a new tradition.

Another key point in Calvin's use of Augustine that too frequently escapes modern analysis is that he was pointing out the usefulness – the edifying quality – of the North African bishop. Augustine was a help to create a pattern of response in a difficult pastoral question. The question

---

[102] *ICR*, III.xxiii.14. CO 2.710–11. "Tales itaque Augustinus non immerito tanquam vel insulsos doctores, vel sinistros et ominosos prophetas ab ecclesia iubet facessere. Tenendum quidem vere alibi contendit, quod tunc correctione proficit homo quum miseretur atque adiuvat qui facit quos voluerit etiam sine correptione proficere. Sed quare isti sic, illi aliter: absit ut dicamus iudicium luti esse non figuli. Item postea: quum homines per correptionem in viam iustitiae seu veniunt seu revertuntur, quis operatur in cordibus eorum salutem, nisi ille qui quolibet plantante et irrigante dat incrementum? cui volenti salvum facere nullum hominis resistit liberum arbitrium. Non est itaque dubitandum, voluntati Dei (qui in coelo et in terra quaecunque voluit fecit, et qui etiam quae futura sunt fecit) humanas voluntates non posse resistere, quominus faciat ipse quod vult; quandoquidem de ipsis hominum voluntatibus quod vult facit Item: quum vult adducere homines, numquid corporalibus vinculis alligat? intus agit, intus corda tenet, intus corda movet, eosque voluntatibus eorum, quas in illis operatus est, trahit. Sed quod continuo subiicit, minime omitti debet: quia nescimus quis ad praedestinatorum numerum pertineat, vel non pertineat, sic nos affici decere ut omnes velimus salvos fieri. Ita fiet ut quisquis nobis occurret, eum studeamus facere pacis consortem; sed pax nostra super filios pacis requiescet. Ergo, quantum ad nos pertinet, omnibus, ne pereant, vel ne alios perdant, salubris et severa, instar medicinae, adhibenda erit correptio: Dei autem erit illis utilem facere quos praescivit et praedestinavit."

[103] The two treatises were *On Rebuke and Grace* and *On the Gift of Perseverance*. *De Dono Perseverantiae* is dated after the *Retractationes* (427), as it quotes it. *De Correptione et Gratia* is one of the last works mentioned in *Retractationes*, so probably is also from 427. Brown lists it in 427. See Peter Brown, *Augustine of Hippo: A New Edition with an Epilogue* (Berkeley: University of California Press, 2000), 380.

was how to continue to preach the gospel message when the message might be seen as frightful. In Calvin's reception, Augustine was a source of good pastoral advice to the company of Reformation-era preachers, leading them to understand both the generous spirit of not attacking the members of their congregations, the practical ministerial advice of treating every member of the body as a sharer in Christ's peace, and the discipline of "healthy and severe rebuke" that would guard both the church's body of believers and the individuals themselves.

Calvin's use of Augustine was so frequent that it is impossible to consider even a small percentage of the citations and allusions to the bishop of Hippo without remaking this study into a consideration of Augustine and Calvin alone. Further, in contested issues, Calvin enjoyed creating a catena of allusions and citations to Augustine. These set out Calvin's reception of Augustine as natural rather than forced. Calvin gave another example of this model of reception and influence in his consideration of the human nature and will after the fall. Calvin began by writing: "Now let us hear Augustine speaking in his own words, lest the Pelagians of our own age, that is, the Sophists of the Sorbonne, according to their custom, charge that all antiquity is against us."[104] He then summarized Augustine's treatise *On Rebuke and Grace*; that the grace of perseverance was given to overcome concupiscence in this life.

Calvin sought to correct the tradition at this point. He wrote: "And so that no one may think that he is speaking of a perfection to come after immortality, as Lombard falsely interprets it, Augustine shortly thereafter removes this doubt."[105] Then he quoted Augustine directly: "Surely the will of the saints is so much aroused by the Holy Spirit that they are able because they so will, and that they will because God brings it about that they so will."[106] Calvin's point was to show that Lombard's consideration of this passage was incorrect, as was his doctrine of the freedom of the will.

Calvin concluded this passage with a statement that was clear in its intent, and the manner that he drew upon the orthodox tradition to form his own doctrine:

[104] *ICR*, II.iii.13. CO 2.222. "Audiamus nunc Augustinum suis verbis loquentem, ne aetatis nostrae Pelagiani, hoc est sorbonici sophistae, totam vetustatem nobis adversam pro suo more criminentur."

[105] *ICR*, II.iii.13. CO 2.223. "Ac ne de futura post immortalitatem perfectione loqui putetur (sicuti perperam Lombardus eo trahit), scrupulum hunc paulo post eximit." Calvin referred to Lombard's Sentences Book II, Distinction 25.

[106] *ICR*, II.iii.13. CO 2.223. "spiritu sancto accenditur voluntas sanctorum; ut ideo possint quia sic volunt, ideo velint, quia Deus operatur ut sic velint."

Now we have from Augustine's own lips the testimony that we especially wish to obtain: not only is grace offered by the Lord, which by anyone's free choice may be accepted or rejected; but it is this very grace which forms both choice and will in the heart, so that whatever good works then follow are the fruit and effect of grace; and it has no other will obeying it except the will that it has made. There are also Augustine's words from another place: "Grace alone brings about every good work in us."[107]

The desire (*volumus*) to obtain this doctrine was clear – Calvin had sought from Augustine the clarity on a question that vexed the sixteenth-century theological world – what should be granted to the free choice of the will? Erasmus and Luther had fought over it; Pighius had attacked Calvin for his position upon it. Calvin believed that he settled the matter by his turn to Augustine.

TRADITION'S INFLUENCES ON CALVIN'S THEOLOGY

The question of Augustine's influence on Calvin is basic to any sense of the orthodox tradition having any sway on Calvin's thought. All the studies that have looked at the relationship between the North African doctor and the Genevan Reformer have concluded that Augustine was the theologian whom Calvin cited and discussed more than any other. Further, the totals were not close – for Calvin, Augustine was not first among equals.

In a significant manner, those issues we gain from Calvin's reading of Augustine teach us about his dependence upon all the orthodox fathers. That is not to say he did not have favorites. Instead, it is to recognize that in Calvin's dependence upon Augustine, he sought to ground his own theology upon the theologian from the early period of the church's history whose orthodoxy was unimpeachable, and whose profundity was unquestioned; and that these methods held true whenever Calvin engaged the orthodox fathers. Further, Augustine's popularity in the early modern period marked Calvin out as a theologian rooted firmly in his own context. To quote Augustine was to show a reverence for learning and for the wisdom passed down from the ages.

---

[107] *ICR*, II.iii.13. CO 2.223. "Habemus nunc Augustini ore testatum quod in primis obtinere volumus, non offerri tantum a Domino gratiam, quae libera cuiusque electione aut recipiatur, aut respuatur; sed ipsam esse, quae in corde et electionem et voluntatem formet: ut quidquid deinde sequitur boni operis, fructus sit ipsius ac effectus, nec aliam habeat sibi obsequentem voluntatem nisi quam fecit. Sunt enim eius quoque verba ex alio loco: omne bonum in nobis opus nonnisi gratiam facere."

However, a significant number of analysts are unwilling to grant that Calvin's constant consideration of Augustine's thought and works, as well as those of other orthodox theologians, amounts to influence. Some prefer a model that argues that Calvin only cited the fathers polemically – the polemicist model. Some argue that the fathers were only conversation partners for Calvin. Because of this ongoing reluctance, it is appropriate at this point to take these issues by the horns and actually deal with them. Though we are discussing Augustine, I will assume that many of these points can be applied to Calvin's relationship to other figures in the orthodox tradition.

In any consideration of Augustine's influence on Calvin, the analysis must take cognizance of Augustine's place in Western Latin thought in 1500. As Courtenay's argument and Pollmann's assertions make clear, Augustinianism at the dawn of the period of the Reformations was another name for intellectually rigorous thought in a variety of topics – neo-platonism, politics, ethics, and theology among them. This makes some sense of McGrath's argument that Calvin would have found his Augustinianism "in the air."

But greater depth can be achieved by considering a number of other vectors of analysis. First, any analysis of Calvin's theology and the foundations on which it rested must take note of Luther. The 1536 *Institutes* was intentionally modeled upon Luther. But Luther himself was a "double Augustinian." He was formed in the Augustinian Friars, an order that revered Augustine. Thus, Luther was an Augustinian in William Courtenay's second sense, because he was a late medieval Augustinian religious. But Luther was also a deep reader of Augustine. He converted Karlstadt to his model of religious thinking through a discussion of Augustine.[108] He turned to Augustine in his own thought. So any theological debt that the young Calvin would owe to Luther would also come with a significant amount of Augustine.[109]

A second trajectory of analysis must examine polemic. I have argued that the number of historical analyses of Calvin's use of Augustine and other fathers as grist for their polemics is an effort to demonstrate that Calvin's use of the patristic heritage was not a matter of substance in his thought, but instead an instrumental use that did not penetrate to the core of his thought, which was biblically based. This is incorrect because it does not grasp the nature of early modern polemic. While

---

[108] Martin Brecht, *Martin Luther: His Road to Reformation 1483–1521*, translated by James L. Schaaf (Philadelphia: Fortress Press, 1985), 49.

[109] Ganoczy, *The Young Calvin*, chap. 14.

Michel Foucault's famous attack on polemic as the enemy of truth has crept into modern and postmodern consciousness, his work fundamentally mistakes the issues at stake for early modern proponents of a wide variety of confessions.[110] For early modern thinkers, the war of words was deadly serious, and polemic had the power "to convict even their most obstinate opponents of God's truth."[111] The Renaissance ideals of the transforming and renewing power of rhetoric undergirded Catholic, Lutheran, Reformed, and Anabaptist thinkers. Calvin's conclusions in polemical contexts usually found its way into his other works, especially the *Institutes*. The demonstrable influence of the doctrine worked out in polemic upon Calvin's later thought casts the idea that the fathers were merely polemic fodder in a strange light. As Amanda Eurich pointed out, "Calvin's lifetime engagement in debate informed and enriched his theological work, especially later editions of the *Institutes*, and reflected his unwavering belief in the power of language to illuminate the Word of God."[112]

A third consideration on Calvin's influence from Augustine comes from the differing ways in which analysts handle scripture and patristic texts. Analysts have a very different understanding of Calvin's use of scripture than of his turn to the fathers. It is normal, and one might even say normative, for a modern analyst of Calvin's work to consider his citations from Paul, or from Acts, or from Daniel, or any other book of scripture, as proof that Calvin was influenced by those scriptural passages.[113] It is very rare that one examines Calvin's exegetical arguments and questions whether they are the substance of his argument or rather the figleaf.[114] But why should that be the case? Especially for modern

---

[110] Michel Foucault, *Essential Works of Foucault 1954–1984*, vol. 1: *Ethics: Subjectivity and Truth*, edited by Paul Rabinow, translated by Robert Hurley (London: Penguin, 2000), 112. As cited in Almut Suerbaum, George Southcombe, and Benjamin Thompson, eds., *Polemic: Language as Violence in Medieval and Early Modern Discourse* (Milton Park: Routledge, 2016), 4. Cited in Amanda Eurich, "Polemic's Purpose," in *John Calvin in Context*, edited by Ward Holder, 215–23.

[111] Eurich, "Polemic's Purpose," 222.

[112] Eurich, "Polemic's Purpose," 222.

[113] See Barbara Pitkin, "Calvin's Reception of Paul," in *A Companion to Paul in the Reformation*, edited by R. Ward Holder (Leiden: Brill, 2009), 267–96; and David M. Whitford, "Robbing Paul to Pay Peter: The Reception of Paul in Sixteenth Century Political Theology, *A Companion to Paul in the Reformation*, edited by R. Ward Holder (Leiden: Brill, 2009), 267–96 and 573–606.

[114] This is so rare that I can only find one such article that discusses this plainly. See Elsie A. McKee, "Calvin's Exegesis of Romans 12:8 – Social, Accidental, or Theological," *Calvin Theological Journal* 23 (1988): 6–18.

historians or historical theologians, the argument that there are significant dividing walls between early canonical and non-canonical texts
has become more difficult to hold.[115] Why should one consider Calvin's
recourse to the fathers so differently from his recourse to Paul, or Isaiah,
or Matthew? There does not seem to be a significant historical reason to
maintain that difference, but there are a host of significant theological
and confessional reasons.

A fourth issue arises from the history of the development of theology.
Bluntly put, later figures put forth claims that earlier figures were orthodox and were on their "side" in arguments or even ecclesiastical clashes
with others. Certainly Matthew Alan Gaumer makes that point about
Augustine himself, arguing that the bishop of Hippo made a concerted
effort to appropriate Cyprian and his authority for the Catholic cause. He
asserted that this reached its pinnacle, not in the Donatist controversy,
but in the Pelagian affair of 411–12.[116] Augustine appropriated Cyprian,
Lombard appropriated Augustine, and the chain of appropriation continued into the middle of the sixteenth century. While appropriation is
not the same as influence, one cannot dismiss the claims of influence so
easily once the fact of appropriation is established.

The consideration of Calvin's use of and dependence upon Bernard,
Augustine, and Chrysostom illustrate Calvin's theology of tradition.
While he would not accept a hierarchically modeled theory that wed the
tradition to the theology of the present hierarchy, Calvin was willing to
engage the orthodox figures in order to demonstrate his own orthodoxy,
and his own handing down of that deposit to the next generation.

CALVIN'S USE OF TRADITION IN FORMULATING
HIS DOCTRINE

Calvin's doctrines present orthodox theology as fashioned to apply in an
evangelical worldview. The Genevan Reformer sought to apply the collected wisdom of the church to his present moment, in order to build up
the church in Christ. This effort produced a conservative character to his
theology – not the opposite of liberal but something that instead achieves

---

[115] See D. H. Williams, "The Patristic Tradition as Canon," *Perspectives in Religious Studies* 32 (2005):357–79. For instance, Williams argued that "This is another way of saying that the first five or six centuries of the church operated *canonically* for the last
millennium and a half."

[116] Matthew Alan Gaumer, *Augustine's Cyprian: Authority in Roman Africa* (Leiden: Brill,
2016), 323.

a balance with innovation.[117] In this section, I will consider Calvin's use of the resources of the tradition to forge his doctrines of infant baptism, predestination, and the Trinity. Each case will illustrate the influence that orthodoxy bore upon Calvin's formulations.

Calvin and Infant Baptism

Baptism was the Achilles heel for the magisterial reformers. It was a clear issue in which their claim to follow the scripture rather than human customs was challenged by the adherents of the Radical Reformation.[118] David Wright pointed out that "Infant baptism was the weightiest constitutive feature of the old church that the magisterial Reformers perpetuated on the basis of tradition rather than explicit scriptural authority."[119] The amount of ink that the magisterial reformers spent on arguing that infant baptism was biblical was a measure of the frantic quality of their response as well as a recognition that the tradition of a child entering into the church through baptism was also a mark of that child entering society. In fact, in Calvin's Geneva, there were no civil birth records, only baptismal records. A key issue for magisterial reform was to avoid being painted with the Anabaptist brush that separated this key moment in a human life from the imprimatur of the church.[120]

Calvin knew this and sought to argue that even though the Roman church had given a plausible example of the power of tradition with

[117] Jaroslav Pelikan spends very little space on Calvin in his history of the development of doctrine, because like Aquinas, Pelikan saw Calvin's efforts as summative rather than innovative. See Pelikan, *The Christian Tradition: A History of the Development of Doctrine*, vol. 4: *Reformation of the Church and Dogma (1300–1700)* (Chicago: University of Chicago Press, 1985).

[118] David F. Wright argued that "the leaders of the Protestant Reformations in the sixteenth century perpetuated a rite which had first come into its own (in the post-Augustinian era) and was sustained for virtually its centuries-long medieval life by doctrinal stipulations which they could no longer endorse." Wright, *Infant Baptism in Historical Perspective: Collected Studies* (Milton Keynes: Paternoster Press, 2007), xxvii. Quoted in Matthew C. Bingham, *Orthodox Radicals: Baptist Identity in the English Reformation* (Oxford: Oxford University Press, 2019), 176.

[119] David Wright, "George Cassander and the Appeal to the Fathers in Sixteenth-Century Debates about Infant Baptism," in *Auctoritas patrum*, edited by Grane, Schindler, and Wriedt, 259.

[120] See Jill Raitt's consideration of Calvin's effort to answer Anabaptist queries in "Three Inter-Related Principles in Calvin's Unique Doctrine of Baptism," *Sixteenth Century Journal* 11 (1980): esp. 59–61. Other helpful studies include Egil Grislis, "Calvin's Doctrine of Baptism," *Church History* 31 (1962): 46–65; and George Hunsinger, "The Dimension of Depth: Thomas F. Torrance on the Sacraments of Baptism and the Lord's Supper," *Scottish Journal of Theology* 54 (2001): 155–76.

regards to infant baptism, that example was nevertheless incorrect.[121] Pedobaptism was enormously important to the Genevans, as the fights with the ministers over names and the role of godparents demonstrated.[122] Because we have considered this at some length earlier, I will seek some brevity at this point in this study.

Calvin's efforts to demonstrate that baptism of infants was both a practice that stretched back to the apostles and was biblical illustrate his deep concern about the practice. The final Latin edition of the *Institutes* placed the defense of infant baptism in IV.xvi. Calvin spends the first twenty-nine paragraphs of the chapter on biblical arguments. His citations and allusions are almost completely aimed at his opponents, those who argued for believer's baptism. In 1543, Calvin added a note to the consideration of infant baptism, which ended up in 1559 at IV.xvi.30, that Cyprian and Augustine's testimony supported him, but this was a brief aside.[123] Calvin then turned his attention to Servetus, answering his charges. The entire chapter exemplified Calvin's ideal as a biblical theologian who turned his back on the tradition.

However, the form of Calvin's argumentation gives another view. Let us look at two closely related passages. The first is Calvin's exegesis of Matthew 19.13–15. The passage reads: "Then little children were being brought to him in order that he might lay his hands on them and pray. The disciples spoke sternly to those who brought them; but Jesus said, 'Let the little children come to me, and do not stop them; for it is to such as these that the kingdom of heaven belongs.' And he laid his hands on them and went on his way."[124] Calvin's exegesis here was expansive – he transformed the experience of Jesus welcoming the children into a form of baptism. Moreover, he did so by arguing that since they are to be received into the Kingdom of Heaven, that it would only be right for them to receive the sign that opened the door of the church.[125] But this was dangerously close

---

[121] See Chapter 2.
[122] See Karen Spierling, *Infant Baptism in Reformation Geneva: The Shaping of a Community, 1536–1564* (Burlington: Ashgate, 2005).
[123] *ICR*, IV.xvi.30. CO 2.997.
[124] Holy Bible, NRSV, Matthew 19.13–15.
[125] *ICR*, IV.xvi.7. "If it is right for infants to be brought to Christ, why not also to be received into baptism, the symbol of our communion and fellowship with Christ? If the Kingdom of Heaven belongs to them, why is the sign denied which, so to speak, opens to them a door into the church, that, adopted into it, they may be enrolled among the heirs of the Kingdom of Heaven?" CO 2.980–81. "Si adduci Christo infantes aequum, est, cur non et ad baptismum recipi, symbolum nostrae cum Christo communionis ac societatis? Si eorum est regnum coelorum, cur signum negabitur, quo velut aditus aperitur in ecclesiam, ut in eam cooptati haeredibus regni coelestis adscribantur?"

to a theory Calvin had relegated to the ash heap, that baptism was the *sine qua non* for entrance into the Kingdom of Heaven.[126] Calvin's argument approaches this pitfall backhandedly – since children are to receive the Kingdom of Heaven, they must be worthy to receive the sign of baptism. But that attaches baptism to heaven, which Calvin rejected.

Similarly, Calvin argued that the lack of explicit scriptural evidence of an infant being baptized in the New Testament was meaningless.[127] He reasoned that such a model would mean that women would be barred from the supper. Similarly, in 1543 Calvin introduced the argument into the *Institutes* that saying that one who could not find biblical warrant for infant baptism in scripture "exhibited the same level of ignorance as believing the Council of Nicaea did not have biblical warrant for declaring that God the Father and God the Son are consubstantial."[128] Of course this method of going beyond the words of scripture denied Calvin's practice when it suited him. But further, Calvin ended his argument by claiming that the church should observe the rule of faith.[129] But the rule of faith is nothing other than the distillation of the common belief of the church – taken from the scripture, but also applied in distinct contexts and

---

[126] *ICR*, IV.xv.20. CO 2.974–975.

[127] *ICR*, IV.xvi.8. CO 2.981–82.

[128] Galen Johnson, "The Development of John Calvin's Doctrine of Infant Baptism in Reaction to the Anabaptists," *Mennonite Quarterly Review* 73 (1999): 809–10. *ICR*, IV.viii.16, CO 2.857. Actually Johnson noted that the Father and the Son are "homoousias," the Greek term for "of the same substance." But Calvin chose the Latin, which is rendered here as "consubstantial." The issue at the time of the Council of Nicaea in 325 CE was whether Christ was truly God or a being created by God. This was the position taught by Arius. The fathers gathered together at Nicaea denied Arius' position, and stated that the Son and the Father were "of the same substance." This became one of the most significant dogmas of the Christian religion – the Triune God. It was also an excellent example of a moment where the church chose to define something with extra-scriptural wording, while arguing that this was merely to clarify, not to change or insert something into the scriptures. This had been settled dogma for centuries, but the upheavals of the humanistic return to the sources had opened the door for a number of (heretical) scholars to raise the question of the necessity of explicit biblical backing for any dogma.

[129] *ICR*, IV. xvi.8. "If such arguments are valid, women should similarly be barred from the Lord's Supper, since we do not read that they were admitted to it in the apostolic age; but here we are content with the rule of faith. For when we weigh what the institution of the Supper implies, it is also easy to judge from this to whom the use of it out to be granted. We observe this also in baptism." CO 2.981. "Si quid valerent id genus argumenta, mulieres pariter coena Domini interdicendae essent, quas apostolorum saeculo ad eam fuisse admissas non legimus. Sed enim hic fidei regula contenti sumus. Dum enim reputamus quid ferat coenae institutio, ex eo etiam, quibus communicandus sit illius usus, facile iudicium est. Quod et in baptism observamus."

growing by the process of accretion that all tradition experiences. Calvin, when faced with a biblical passage that he did not wish to follow, twisted his argument to make the *regula fide* his guide to true belief.

Calvin and Predestination

John Calvin stands in cultural memory as the emblem of predestination. The fact that most hearers do not understand the technical issues inherent in a doctrine of predestination, or the difference between predestination and providence or predestination and pure determinism, is irrelevant. Calvin gained a hated reputation for his desire to have a wrathful God consign billions to the fires of damnation long before they have a chance to speak for themselves. For many modern minds, Calvin is a monster of the early modern period, a picture of what goes wrong when religious fanaticism runs amok.

Of course, the fact that Calvin's acceptance of predestination was neither innovative nor novel has escaped modern culture. Perhaps because of the widespread popularity of the work of Max Weber, Calvin's name became synonymous with predestination in the West. But Calvin's doctrine of double predestination did not differ overly significantly with that of several of his predecessors. In particular, his predestinarian doctrine has significant parallels in the thought of an esteemed Parisian master of the fourteenth century, Gregory of Rimini.[130] Calvin's defense of predestination was always within the broad stream of Augustinian thought.[131]

But in the polemic atmosphere of the middle of the sixteenth century Calvin's claim of Augustine's support for his position was certain to arouse the ire of a host of foes. This would be the pattern, not only on issues of predestination where he was attacked by Albert Pighius, but also on issues of the Lord's Supper, where Lutheran theologians sought to deny him the support of the North African father. Augustine was simply too important in the environment of polemic that characterized the middle of the sixteenth century to leave to one's opponent.

---

[130] See Isabella Mandrella, "Gregory of Rimini," in *A Companion to Responses to Ockham*, edited by Christian Rode (Leiden: Brill, 2016), 197–224; G. R. Evans, *Medieval Commentaries on the Sentences of Peter Lombard, vol. 1, Current Research* (Leiden: Brill, 2002); Gordon Leff, *Gregory of Rimini: Tradition and Innovation in 14th Century Thought* (Manchester: Manchester University Press, 1961).

[131] Charles Raith II, "Predestination in Early Modern Thought," in *John Calvin in Context*, edited by Ward Holder, 249–57; James Halvorsen, *Peter Aureoli on Predestination: A Challenge to Late Medieval Thought* (Leiden: Brill 1998); Christopher David Schabel, *Theology at Paris, 1316–1345: Peter Auriol and the Problem of Divine Foreknowledge and Future Contingents* (Burlington: Ashgate, 2000).

Calvin's continued battles for the mantle of Augustine's authority was a clear marker that he had not abandoned medieval models of doctrinal authority.[132] As with other doctrines in this section, I will not rehearse material already presented – so the struggles with Pighius will remain in Chapter 3. But Calvin continued to consider Augustine's thought as he worked out his own theory of predestination. Further, Calvin turned to Augustine for the broad constellation of other theological loci that were intimately related to predestination, such as the bondage of the will and the denial of human merit. So we see Calvin turning to Augustine to answer Ockham (actually Gabriel Biel), who argued that "grace is denied to no one who does what is in him."[133] In this 1543 addition to the *Institutes*, Calvin wove together a series of statements from Augustine's sermons. He wrote:

> For this reason, Augustine justly derides those who claim for themselves any part of the act of willing, just as he reprehends others who think that what is the special testimony of free election is indiscriminately given to all. "Nature," he says, "is common to all, not grace." The view that what God bestows upon whomever he wills is generally extended to all, Augustine calls a brittle glasslike subtlety of wit, which glitters with mere vanity. Elsewhere he says: "How have you come? By believing. Fear lest while you are claiming for yourself that you have found the just way, you perish from the just way. I have come, you say, of my own free choice; I have come of my own will. Why are you puffed up? Do you wish to know that this also has been given you? Hear Him calling, 'No one comes to me unless my Father draws him.'"[134]

Calvin depended upon Augustine to refute claims of free will and moral movement toward God and earned merit. He turned to Augustine's authority even to make the case that the doctrine of predestination should only be pursued through the scriptures. In 1543, he turned to

---

[132] Backus, *Historical Method and Confessional Identity*, 115. "This does not mean that Calvin, as he explains himself in the rest of the chapter, is at all impressed by Mediaeval doctrines of free will. What it does show, however, is that, contrary to his treatment of ancient philosophers whose works he uses to provide an eclectic conceptual framework, Calvin conserves something of the Mediaeval approach to the fathers."

[133] *ICR*, II.iii.10. CO 2.220. "Qua gratia non quoslibet promiscue dignatur Dominus, quemadmodum vulgo iactatur illud (nisi fallor) occamicum, eam nemini denegari, facienti quod in se est."

[134] *ICR*, II.iii.10. CO 2.220. "Quare merito Augustinus tam eos deridet, qui aliquas volendi partes sibi arrogant, quam reprehendit alios qui putant promiscue dari omnibus quod speciale est gratuitae electionis testimonium. Communis, inquit, omnibus est natura, non gratia; vitreum acumen appellans quod mera vanitate splendet, ubi ad omnes generaliter extenditur, quod Deus quibus vult confert Alibi autem: quomodo venisti? credendo: time ne, dum tibi arrogas quod inventa sit a te via iusta, pereas de via iusta. Veni, inquis, libero arbitrio; voluntate propria veni Quid turgescis? vis nosse quod et hoc praestitum est tibi? ipsum audi vocantem: nemo venit ad me, nisi pater meus traxerit eum."

a long passage from Augustine's commentary on John to make that point:

"We have entered the pathway of faith," says Augustine, "let us hold steadfastly to it. It leads us to the King's chamber, in which are hid all treasures of knowledge and wisdom. For the Lord Christ himself did not bear a grudge against his great and most select disciples when he said: 'I have … many things to say to you, but you cannot bear them now.' We must walk, we must advance, we must grow, that our hearts may be capable of those things which we cannot yet grasp. But if the Last Day finds us advancing, there we shall learn what we could not learn here."[135]

Calvin immediately stated that this concept had to guide the faithful, that their only guide should be the Word of the Lord. The reader finds Calvin using the orthodox tradition to support the necessity of reading scripture – a perplexing necessity.

Calvin turned to Augustine in the next chapter as well, which sought to demonstrate the doctrine from scripture. In material added to the 1559 edition, Calvin turned to the example of Christ to attempt to forestall any discussion of the unfairness of God's choosing. Calvin noted that Christ was conceived a mortal. If he was truly mortal, how could he deserve prior to his birth to be the only begotten Son of God?[136] Unsatisfied with his own consideration of the topic, Calvin turned to Augustine, and wrote, "Augustine wisely notes this: namely, that we have in the very Head of the church the clearest mirror of free election that we who are among the members may not be troubled about it; and that he was not made Son of God by righteous living but was freely given such honor so that he might afterward share his gifts with others."[137] The head of the church was given the honor; he did not earn it. Likewise, Calvin was able to receive the passage, instead of working it out alone.

Later in that same chapter, Calvin turned to the issue of foreknowledge. This had been a significant locus of Reformation-era disputation since

---

[135] *ICR*, III.xxi.2. CO 2.680. "Pervenimus in viam fidei, inquit Augustinus, eam constanter teneamus. Ipsa perducit ad cubiculum regis, in quo sunt omnes thesauri scientiae et sapientiae absconditi. Non enim ipse Dominus Christus suis magnis et selectissimis discipulis invidebat, quum diceret (Ioann. 16, 12): multa habeo vobis dicenda; sed non potestis portare nunc. Ambulandum est, proficiendum est, crescendum est: ut sint corda nostra capacia earum rerum, quas capere modo non possumus. Quod si nos ultimus dies proficientes invenerit, ibi discemus quod hic non potuimus."

[136] *ICR*, III.xxii.1. CO 2.687.

[137] *ICR*, III.xxii.1. CO 2.687. "Hoc prudenter animadvertit Augustinus, in ipso ecclesiae capite lucidissimum esse gratuitae electionis speculum, ne in membris nos conturbet; nec iuste vivendo factum esse filium Dei, sed gratis tanto honore fuisse donatum, ut alios postea faceret donorum suorum consortes."

Erasmus and Luther sparred over it in 1524 and 1525.[138] Both Luther and Calvin rejected the idea that predestination was based in God's foreknowledge of human merit. Calvin started the eighth paragraph by noting that Ambrose, Origen, and Jerome had held this idea.[139] Calvin then noted that Augustine had changed his mind on the point and had instead become a staunch defender of the primacy of grace. Calvin wrote:

Indeed, after having retracted it, in censuring the Pelagians because they persisted in this error, he says: "Who would not marvel that the apostle failed to catch this subtlety? For after he had set forth something amazing concerning persons not yet born (Jacob and Esau), and then confronted himself with the question: 'What then? Is there injustice with God?,' here was the place for him to answer that God foresaw the merits of every man. Still he does not say this but takes refuge in God's judgments and mercy."[140]

This was exactly Calvin's effort – to avoid attempting to find the answers to the mysteries of grace, and he simply praises God for the graceful generosity that is given to humanity. After more passages from Augustine, Calvin himself realized the character of this section and wrote: "If I wanted to weave a whole volume from Augustine, I could readily show my readers that I need no other language than his. But I do not want to burden them with wordiness."[141] Calvin knew that his language, his reasoning, and his doctrine bore the stamp of Augustine's thought. In a different age in which the question of church and scripture were not so tendentious, perhaps Calvin would have explicitly made his arguments on the basis of scripture's and Augustine's authority.

Calvin and the Trinity

The Trinity presented special challenges to the early generations of the era of the Reformations. By then, the Trinity had stood for over a millennium

---

[138] Erasmus, *De Libero Arbitrio: Diatribe sive Collatio*, 1524, Luther, *De Servo Arbitrio*, 1525.

[139] *ICR*, III.xxii.8. CO 2.694. McNeill/Battles note that Ambrose is probably Ambrosiaster and Jerome is probably actually Pelagius.

[140] *ICR*, III.xxii.8. CO 2.694. "Quin et post retractationem, Pelagianos praestringens, quod in eo errore persisterent: quis istum, inquit, acutissimum sensum apostolo defuisse non miretur? nam quum rem stupendam proposuisset de illis nondum natis, et deinde sibi quaestionem obiiceret: quid ergo? numquid est iniquitas apud Deum? erat locus ut responderot, Deum praevidisse utriusque merita; non tamen hoc dicit, sed ad Dei iudicia et misericordiam confugit."

[141] *ICR*, III.xxii.8. CO 2.694. "Si ex Augustino integrum volumen contexere libeat, lectoribus ostendere promptum esset, mihi non nisi eius verbis opus esse; sed eos prolixitate onerare nolo."

as a marker of what the Christian religion meant. As such, it functioned as a *Grenzbegriff*, a boundary marker that demonstrated who was in the Christian communion and who was out. It was a sign of the success of Christianity in the Latin West that this was so rarely challenged, especially by orthodox theologians. The Trinity, especially as defined by the councils of Nicaea and Constantinople, represented the unchanging essence of the faith of the fathers that had been passed down because it was true. The challenges came about because of the efforts of evangelical theologians to maintain their arguments that the truths of the faith were only and always biblical.

The early efforts of the Protestant reformers to find new and more biblically appropriate language to explain the Trinity were halting, and aroused significant consternation.[142] Erasmus left the Johannine Comma (I John 5.7–8) out of his *Novum Instrumentum* of 1516.[143] The resulting furor caused the Prince of the Humanists to replace the material in the 1521 *Novum Testamentum*, though he could not find a Greek manuscript to support it. In the treatise, *Against Latomus*, Luther argued, "What if my soul hates the word homoousion, and I do not wish to use it, I will not be a heretic."[144] Calvin himself said, in the very first edition of the *Institutes*, that "Indeed, I could wish the words were buried, if only among all men this faith were agreed on: that Father and Son and Spirit are one God, yet the Son is not the Father, nor the Spirit the Son, but that they are differentiated by a peculiar quality."[145]

However, that reluctance to use the philosophical-theological terminology that had been worked out through conciliar compromise – and

---

[142] Rebecca Giselbrecht, "Trinitarian Controversies," in *John Calvin in Context*, edited by Ward Holder, 278–86.

[143] David M. Whitford, "Yielding to the Prejudices of His Time: Erasmus and the Comma Johanneum," *Church History and Religious Culture* 95 (2015): 19–40.

[144] LW 32:24, quoted in Giselbrecht, "Trinitarian Controversies," 281.

[145] *ICR*, I.xiii.5, CO 2.92. "Utinam quidem sepulta essent, constaret modo haec inter omnes fides: patrem, et filium, et spiritum esse unum Deum; nec tamen aut filium esse patrem, aut spiritum filium, sed proprietate quadam esse distinctos." Quoted in Giselbrecht, "Trinitarian Controversies," 281. Irena Backus has written that "While it is certain that Calvin could not and would not have conceived elaborating his doctrine of the Trinity in the Institutes without taking Nicene teaching into account, he makes very sure that he grounds the Nicene teaching in the biblical text." Here I both agree and disagree with Backus. First, to argue against her point – Calvin ran into trouble directly for his reluctance to use the language of the Nicene teaching. It was difficult for others to determine whether Calvin was in the orthodox stream when he rejected traditional language. Second, to argue for her point, Backus is basically making my point. It was inconceivable that Calvin would not ground his doctrine of the trinity in Nicene teaching. His effort to demonstrate that as biblical should be seen for what it was – doctrine seeking a biblical warrant, if not prooftext. See Backus, *Historical Method and Confessional Identity*, 111.

had gained tremendous doctrinal weight over the centuries – came at great cost. Calvin ran into this dynamic in the Caroli affair.[146] Pierre Caroli was a difficult person – his constant troubles with both Catholics and Protestants over the course of his adult life makes that clear.[147] But when he arrived in Geneva in 1535, he was also one of the most highly trained theologians resident in the city. He held a doctorate in theology from Paris, having passed his doctoral acts in 1520 under the supervision of Guillaume Duchesne. He had been a member of the Faculty of Theology at Paris, and had lived at the Collége de Sorbonne.[148] He came to Geneva because of suspicions about him and his evangelical tendencies; James Farge notes that the faculty of theology under the leadership of Noel Beda had brought dozens of charges of heresy against him. In 1534, with the Affair of the Placards in Paris, Caroli had to flee. He went first to Geneva, then Basel, then Neuchâtel. He went to the Lausanne Disputation, where Calvin defended the Evangelicals and their reverence for the patristic authorities, and Caroli acquitted himself well.[149] But a charge was brought against him that he had engaged in prayers for the dead. In defending himself, Caroli attacked Guillaume Farel, Pierre Viret, and John Calvin, accusing them of Arianism and spreading the heresy of Servetus. He made this accusation because of the lack of the word "Trinity" in the works of the Genevan ministers, especially the 1536 *Institutes*.[150]

Calvin argued that the Genevans maintained the Trinity, but Caroli denied it and asserted that the Genevans and Calvin should affirm the Nicene and Athanasian Creeds. Gary Jenkins notes that, "Calvin replied

---

[146] See Gary W. Jenkins, *Calvin's Tormentors: Understanding the Conflicts that Shaped the Reformer* (Grand Rapids: Baker Book House, 2018), 17–30. Irena Backus points out that this controversy had a long life that outlived Calvin in pointing out Claude De Sainctes' *Declaration d'aucuns atheismes de la doctrine de Calvin et Bèze contre les premiers fondemens de la chretienté* (Paris: Claude Fremy, 1568). See her *Historical Method and Confessional Identity*, 179–83.

[147] See Olivier Labarthe, *Ioannis Calvini Scripta Didactica et Polemica*, vol. VI, *Ioannis Calvini, Pro G. Farello et Collegis Ejus Adversus Peteri Caroli Theologiastri Calumnias Defensio Nicolai Gallasii*, and *Peteri Caroli, Refutatio Blasphemiae Farellistarum in Sacrosanctam Trinitatem* (Geneva: Droz, 2016); and Jean Calvin, *Défense de Guillaume Farel et de ses collègues contre les calomnies du théologastre Pierre Caroli par Nicolas Des Gallars*, edited by Jean François Gounelle (Paris: Presses Universitaires de France, 1994).

[148] James K. Farge, *Biographical Register of Paris Doctors of Theology, 1500–1536* (Toronto: Pontifical Institute of Medieval Studies, 1980), 66–67.

[149] Jenkins, *Calvin's Tormentors*, 21.

[150] Jenkins, *Calvin's Tormentors*, 22.

that the church has not the power to bind people's consciences. Alexandre Ganoczy ironically notes that while apparently the church catholic has not this power, the church Genevan did."[151] The issue was neither small nor unimportant. The Genevan Small Council could not be represented by ministers whose orthodoxy was suspect on such a basic point of Christian dogma.

Calvin's effort as a callow, if not jejune, theologian to replicate the doctrine of the fathers without the technical vocabulary they had used went extremely poorly. Calvin did not use the terms *essentia*, or *substantia*, or *hypostasis* in the 1536 *Institutes*, except to note how the older orthodox (*veteris orthodoxi*) had written.[152] It is likely that the far more rigorously trained Caroli winced at the lack of the particular formulae and technical vocabulary that had safeguarded dogmatic orthodoxy for centuries. Caroli charged Calvin with denying the eternally begotten nature of the Son in his use of "Jehovah" to signify the Son and his aseity. Caroli claimed that this doctrine denied the Niceno-Constantinapolitan Creed of 381 and had been popularized by Servetus, who had found it in Paul of Samosata.[153]

Jenkins argues that Caroli's attack on Calvin and Farel were part of a turning point for Calvin, where the French Reformer of Geneva shifted from someone willing to use his rhetorical and logical powers to persuade into an authority figure unwilling to brook any suggestion of doctrinal nonconformity to Calvin's view of correct doctrine.[154] But for our purposes, Caroli engendered a far different response. In 1536, Calvin held a position that accepted the Trinity but avoided the technical vocabulary that had been passed down for over a millennium. By steps from 1539 to 1559, Calvin addressed that chink in his armor. He did so through traditional language and through citations and allusions to orthodox fathers.

Interestingly, McNeill's note in the *Institutes* at I.xiii.1, beginning the discussion of the Trinity, states: "Throughout all editions the doctrine of the Trinity stands prior to the analysis of the first article of the Apostles' Creed (the Creator), but up to 1559 it followed immediately the discussion of Christ as the sole object (*scopus*) of faith. Here, with faith deferred to III.ii, under the redeeming work of the Spirit, the doctrine is presented without full epistemological preparation."[155] My contention is

---

[151] Jenkins, *Calvin's Tormentors*, 23, quoting Ganoczy, *The Young Calvin*, 114.
[152] Jenkins, *Calvin's Tormentors*, 24.
[153] Jenkins, *Calvin's Tormentors*, 26–27.
[154] Jenkins, *Calvin's Tormentors*, 29.
[155] *ICR*, I.xiii.1, note 1.

that instead of a lack of epistemological preparation, the new placement of the doctrine represented Calvin's chastened notion of the Trinity and the crucial nature of presenting it at first opportunity.

Calvin, after noting that the discussion of God in human language would of necessity be accommodated, proceeded directly to a defense of the necessity of the use of the language of "persons," in God, and that though distinguished as three persons they share an essence.[156] All of this material is either from 1539 or 1559. Calvin then asserted, in material taken from the 1536 *Institutes* but altered in 1559, that "Now, although the heretics rail at the word 'person,' or certain squeamish men cry out against admitting a term fashioned by the human mind, they cannot shake our conviction that three are spoken of each of which is entirely God, yet that there is not more than one God."[157] The ghost of Caroli probably rolled over, saying "the squeamish man is Calvin!" But winners write not only history but also theology. What is significant for our view is that Calvin added a significant dose of the technical jargon to his description of the Trinity.

Calvin also added a number of citations to the fathers. Those could be almost a cover for his own slow movement toward using this traditional vocabulary. Calvin cited Augustine in *De Trinitate* in the 1559 edition to argue that the word "hypostasis" had been forced on humanity by necessity.[158] In 1543, he brought in the testimony of Augustine to demonstrate that the Holy Spirit was divine.[159] In the 1539 edition of the *Institutes*, he cited Gregory of Nazianzus with pleasure, quoting him first in the Greek and then translating it into Latin.[160] Calvin turned to Augustine in 1559 to clarify the relationship of the Father to the Son, writing, "The whole fifth book of Augustine *On the Trinity* is concerned with explaining this matter. Indeed, it is far safer to stop with that relation which Augustine sets forth than by too subtly penetrating into the sublime mystery to wander through many evanescent speculations."[161] Here, at exactly a

---

[156] *ICR*, I.xiii.2. CO 2.90–91.

[157] *ICR*, I.xiii.3. CO 2.91. "Nunc ut de persona oblatrent haeretici, vel quidam nimis morosi obstrepant, se non admittere hominum arbitrio confictum nomen, quum nobis excutere non possint tres dici, quorum quisque in solidum sit Deus, nec tamen plures esse deos, quaenam est ista improbitas."

[158] I.xiii.5. CO 2.93.

[159] I.xiii.15. CO 2.103.

[160] I.xiii.17. CO 2.104.

[161] *ICR*, xiii.19. CO 2.106. "In huius rei explicatione quintus liber Augustini de Trinitate totus versatur. Longe vero tutius est in ea quam tradit relatione subsistere, quam subtilius penetrando ad sublime mysterium, per multas evanidas speculationes evagari."

locus where Caroli had attacked him, Calvin fortified his doctrine with Augustine, and argued that it was safer to stop with his thought than attempting to penetrate into divine mysteries. The message was clear: the right doctrine was presented by Augustine, and Calvin commended it.

CONCLUSION: MEMORY, HISTORY, AND TRADITION

Calvin sought to ground the foundations of the Christian religion on the clear understanding of the truths of religion, handed down through the ages. This involved him in a significant amount of historical work, as he tried to create a sense of the Christian tradition that was both verifiable and transparent to believers. Calvin was a talented historian, though he did not study history for its own sake. Instead, he believed that he could use history to defend the truth of the Christian church and the orthodox tradition.

This use of history, tradition, and memory faced a problem – both in its own historical context and in the following eras of history that looked back upon it. Did Calvin and other Reformers simply abuse history and historical research for the sake of the conclusions that they believed to be true? This is the problem that Irena Backus engaged, which was set out by the work of Pontien Polman.[162] He had concluded that during the Reformation, history was put at the service of religious controversy. He argued, "At first glance it seems that the fundamental principle of Protestantism, that is the exclusive authority of the Bible, should have stamped the religious controversy of the 16th century with a purely scriptural character. In reality, though in the course of the struggle, Reformers often remind their opponents of this principle, they frequently fail to observe it in practice."[163] Protestant Reformers sought the purity of the Lydian stone of the Bible, but they frequently found themselves reduced to the traditions of the fathers to fill in the significant gaps in the biblical witness.

Polman's model, with or without attribution, has become one of the dominant interpretive frameworks for considering the Reformer's

---

[162] Pontien Polman, *L'element historique dans la controverse religieuse du 16ᵉ siècle* (Gembloux: J. Duculot, 1932).

[163] Polman, *L'element historique*, 539, quoted in Backus, *Historical Method and Confessional Identity*, 2. "A première vue il semble que le principe fondamental du protestantisme, à savoir l'autorité exclusive de la Bible aurait dû imprimer à la controverse religieuse du 16e siècle un caractère purement scripturaire. En réalité, si au course de la lute, les réformateures rappellent souvent ce principe à leurs adversaires, il leur arrive fréquemment de ne pas l'observer en pratique."

consideration treatment of history and tradition. Different from the biblicist and polemicist models that I have noted earlier, Polman argued that history or tradition was a substitute for absent scriptural witness that Reformers used out of necessity. It has been particularly significant for those historians who have aimed to escape the boundaries of confessional history, as it undercut one of the basic tenets of early Protestant thought: the scriptural principle. Readers can see this in a recent study of Puritanism. As Ann-Stephane Schäfer sees it, the issue had to do with the historical development of the Christian religion and defending it in the sixteenth century:

> In general, Protestant reformers faced a dilemma: On the one hand, they emphasized the *sola scriptura* principle, which claimed that the Bible as the only God-authored text was self-sufficient and thus did not require any supplement like, for example, the so-called "unwritten," i.e. non-scriptural, tradition ... in order to be understood properly; on the other hand, it was soon clear that even Protestant theologians would occasionally have to draw on patristic sources if they wanted to be able to defend such central doctrines as the Trinity and the two natures of Christ or infant baptism, which had no clear scriptural foundation, against such heretical movements as Antitrinitarianism and the Anabaptists.[164]

David Wright noted this dynamic for pedobaptism and did so without any sense of needing to argue the point.[165] Andreas Merkt pointed out that Georg Calixt had generated a theory of the first five centuries of Christian history and the purity that they contained.[166] This model is alive and well in the work of a variety of historians and historical theologians who examine the early modern period. The problem with this model is that Polman simply stated that the evangelical or Protestant thinkers failed to observe the scriptural principle, without noting the way that history was a significant motivating factor as well as a replacement for biblicism.

A second model rejects this understanding. This effort at understanding the history of the thought of the Reformers seeks to maintain the basic confessional argument. Protestants grounded their arguments on scripture; Catholics accepted tradition. While the scions of the mainstream academy have relegated such efforts to the dustbins of historiographical irrelevance, such is not the case for certain seminaries, as well as the popular imagination. This model fails to describe adequately what

---

[164] Schäfer, *Auctoritas Patrum?*, 76–77.
[165] David Wright, "George Cassander and the Appeal to the Fathers," 259.
[166] Merkt, *Das Patristische Prinzip*.

Calvin did in writing his theology. The analysis resembles a form of the emperor's new clothes, in which the modern mind intentionally pays no attention to facts that are unpleasant.

A third model seeks to achieve the goals of both previous models. I have noted this earlier, with some frequency; it is the polemicist model. This model of describing the Reformer's efforts with the patristic witness or more specifically Calvin's efforts with that body of material, begins by pointing out the many instances of Calvin's use of the patristic authorities. Thus, it achieves Polman's goal of pointing out the material facts of Calvin's theological method. On the other hand, these analysts argue that Calvin's basic use of the patristic material was polemical. By arguing that point, the idea that Calvin's basic and most substantial doctrinal points are biblically based is maintained. While this is a sophisticated variation of the confessional argument, it does not ultimately arrive at a different conclusion.

All three of these models offer possibilities, but have significant drawbacks as explanations of Calvin's actual practice. First, the Polman model suggests a significant lack of understanding in the early modern period itself. Certainly, both Evangelicals and Catholics believed that the model of theological foundational construction was being changed. However, Calvin and others among his evangelical counterparts were turning to the tradition in serious and significant manners that were demonstrably and doctrinally different from the methodological approaches of their opponents. As well, Polman does not grasp the importance of history in the Protestant theological work of the early modern world. Second, the confessional model maintains a solid underpinning for modern doctrinal concerns. However, that small gain is quickly outweighed by the enormous loss in the inability of this model to come to grips with the evidence that Calvin's corpus provides. The third construct fails at exactly the same point as the second – it is unable to present a predictive or explanatory model for the actual issues that Calvin put forward in his work: whatever else Calvin did, he did not use the fathers or the tradition mainly in his polemic.

Beyond these three options, Irena Backus has suggested a fourth. She wrote: "At no stage does Polman suggest that the 16th century theologians could have been primarily motivated by an interest in history or that they could consider the Bible as a book which determined the course of all subsequent history. I shall show that this view prevailed and that it made recourse to history perfectly consistent with the 'sola Scriptura principle.'"[167] While this is a far better structure on which to build, and I have benefited from many insights from her study, I do not find that Calvin generated this kind of foundational principle that saw the Bible as a determinative factor for all subsequent history. Instead, I believe she is closer to the truth when she wrote: "History was a vital omnipresent force in the Reformation era and theologians of different confession drew different inspiration from it."[168] That insight is closer to Calvin's points about the church's history at a variety of points in his career and in numerous genres of texts he wrote.

From the perspective of social history, Calvin's *Institutes of the Christian Religion* of 1536 marked his entrance onto the theological and ecclesiastical stage. This edition has been termed the "apologetic" edition as it sought to make the case that French Evangelicals were true orthodox Christians and thus represented no threat to the realm, but instead were excellent citizens.[169] Later editions would shift the focus to the training of pastors, but the apologetic character never wholly fell away. Calvin would include the apologetically oriented dedicatory epistle to François I in each of the Latin editions through 1559, long after the monarch's death. At the time of its composition, the apologetic issue was more keenly relevant. Calvin finished the manuscript in 1535, probably by August 23, the date he gave the dedicatory epistle.

Calvin's debut on the world stage was accompanied by his acceptance of the historical nature of the church and the corresponding necessity of defending, receiving, and purifying that historical heritage. At that time, charges were common that the French Evangelicals were no different from Anabaptists, the very same rebels who had been defeated at Münster only months before.[170] The short-lived Kingdom of Münster was a cautionary tale for pastors and princes alike. In 1532, its Lutheran pastor, Bernhard Rothmann, came under the influence of various radical reform ideas, some of which may have come from Melchior Hoffmann. In 1533, Rothmann began to preach radical egalitarianism, that the poor should share in the wealth of the city, even should that require forced redistribution. This attracted Jan Matthjs and Jan of Leiden, two other

---

[167] Backus, *Historical Method and Confessional Identity*, 2.

[168] Backus, *Historical Method and Confessional Identity*, 390.

[169] François Wendel, *Calvin: Origins and Development*, 145–46.

[170] Wulfert de Greef, *The Writings of John Calvin: An Introductory Guide*, expanded edition, translated by Lyle D. Bierma (Louisville: Westminster John Knox Press, 2008), 183. He lists Johannes Cochlaeus, Robert Ceneau, Guillaume Budé, and Jacopo Sadoleto as people making this charge.

disciples of Hoffmann. They entered the city in early 1534 and introduced adult baptism, with large numbers of the population accepting the
rite. Jan Matthjs was quickly elected leader of the city, and he declared
all property held in common. Iconoclastic riots followed, and all who did
not accept the new religion quickly left the city. The prince-bishop Franz
von Waldeck besieged the city in early 1534, and prevented any supplies
from coming into the city. Jan Matthjs, convinced perhaps by a vision of
Jan of Leiden's that he was the new Gideon, led a poorly armed assault
on the besiegers and lost his life. Jan of Leiden declared himself king,
instituted biblical law, including polygamy, and sought to lead the city as
the new Jerusalem. In June 1535, the city fell, and Jan of Leiden as well as
other leaders were executed. The message to all citizens and their princes
was clear: radical religion led to anarchy and the downfall of realms and
their inhabitants.[171]

In a letter to the Protestant German princes dated February 1, 1535,
François I identified the French Evangelicals as Anabaptist rebels, making
the case that they too were dangerous heretics against whom any sovereign must take action.[172] Facing this charge, Calvin naturally sought to
identify evangelical Christianity with orthodoxy throughout the ages. But
in that defense, Calvin also accepted the historical nature of the church
and its traditions. While he would clarify and deepen his understanding
of the church's historical nature and its traditions throughout his career,
his first significant work had already set the course of his work.

John Calvin, as a second-generation Reformer, was still a child of the
Catholic church. Not only did it nurture his early piety, but it also provided him the means of his academic attainment and imparted a sense of
how the Christian religion fitted into the French society in which he had
been brought up. In creating a catechetical model for French evangelical
Christian religion in the 1536 *Institutes*, Calvin sought to preserve the

---

[171] For more on the Kingdom of Münster, see Lowell H. Zuck, *Christianity and Revolution: Radical Christian Testimonies 1520–1650* (Philadelphia: Temple University Press,
1975); James M. Stayer, Helmust Isaak, and Willem De Bakker, "Menno Siomons,
The Blasphemy of Jan van Leiden: When and Why Was It Written?" *The Mennonite
Quarterly Review* 89 (2015): 599–630; R. Po-chia Hsia, "Civic Wills as Sources for the
Study of Piety in Muenster, 1530–1618," *The Sixteenth Century Journal* 14 (1983):
321–48; James M. Stayer, "Anabaptist Münster, 1534–1535: The War Communism of
the Notables," in *German Peasants' War and Anabaptist Community of Goods* (Montreal: McGill-Queen's University Press, 1991), 123–38; and George Huntston Williams,
The Radical Reformation, 3rd ed. (Kirksville: Truman State University Press, 2000),
esp. 589–608.

[172] DeGreef, *The Writings of John Calvin*, 183.

ideals of a public religion in which he had been raised, while transforming it through the application of certain notions of piety, evangelical doctrine, and biblical foundations.

Finding himself in an age of historical consideration, Calvin naturally
turned to the discipline of history insofar as he knew it. By the time
Calvin went to study at Paris, the die was already cast. Martin Luther and
Johann Eck had spent great effort in demonstrating how history proved
the rightness of their causes, Eck by making Luther a modern-day Jan
Hus, and Luther by arguing that the history of the councils of the church
demonstrated that human institutions could not be accorded infallible
authority. Luther would follow that by examining Valla's demolition of
the historical integrity of the Donation of Constantine and ultimately
arguing that the pope was the Anti-Christ.[173]

Calvin continued that model in his debates with Sadoleto, in his dedicatory epistle to the Romans commentary, and throughout his writing
career. Calvin understood that the church, or the Christian religion, was
both a historical object and subject to historical contingencies. The true
religion had been passed down from age to age – and it had taken on
a certain character by its passage through time. Calvin tended to think
of that in terms of doctrine, but he was not unaware of the necessary
historical character. Doctrines did not and could not exist outside the
contingent circumstances of historical contexts. In this consideration of
Calvin's view of history, memory, and tradition, I am not suggesting that
he forged a coherent and normative theory of the first five centuries of the
church's orthodoxy, such as the Lutheran theologian Georg Calixt did.[174]
Calvin was too eclectic in his choices, and would accept figures as late
as Bernard of Clairvaux as serious authorities. However, the historical
contexts in which he tried to place both the biblical figures such as Paul
and the early church authorities such as Augustine influenced the manner
in which Calvin thought about tradition.

For Calvin, it was clear that the truths of the faith were handed on
from generation to generation. That is simply a translation of *tradere*,
the root verb of tradition. Given that fact, Calvin began to articulate a
theory of the tradition that was authoritative, both for his thought and
for the wider ramifications that thought exerted in the Genevan church,
the French evangelical movement, and the network of communities that

---

[173] David M. Whitford, "The Papal Antichrist: Martin Luther and the Underappreciated
Influence of Lorenzo Valla," *Renaissance Quarterly*, 61 (2008): 26–52.
[174] Merkt, *Das Patristische Prinzip*.

made up international Calvinism. He also generated a theoretical model he did not follow, that the tradition had to be apostolic in a strict sense, and could only deal with issues of order, not doctrine. But that would not be what he worked out through his corpus.

Four marks identified Calvin's working theory of tradition. In them, we find a desire to define and navigate a middle road between Roman Catholicism and Anabaptism.[175] First, the tradition would be historical. Calvin rejected out of hand a theory of tradition that would be located in persons or a sole person. Instead, for the church to claim something had been the tradition, it would have to stand up to as rigorous a historical testing as the canons of history in the sixteenth century would allow. This would deny not only outright fabrications, such as the Donation of Constantine, but also pious exaggerations, such as the argument that the idea of purgatory went back to the apostles, or that the church had always held that predestination was incorrect. Calvin sought a model of tradition that could be tested, and its greatest workbench for testing the tradition would be the history that scholars could and would examine.

Second, the tradition would be orthodox. Calvin implicitly and explicitly placed boundaries upon how far the historical testing of received truth would proceed. We have seen one such case in the issue of infant baptism and another in the case of the Trinity. When faced with charges from outside the church catholic – however that was to be defined – Calvin refused to accept the validity of the same historical arguments he would use in other cases. Further, it is clear that Calvin was not simply defining the church by his two marks – there was far more substance than the Word of God rightly preached and heard, and the true administration of the sacraments. Calvin would not allow an unbridled wandering through the forest of scripture – it had to be guided by the true doctrine.

Third, Calvin sought transparency. Even doctors and preachers would have to be able to make their cases that something was or was not part of the orthodox deposit of faith before all believers. Calvin practiced a

---

[175] In his "Who is Actually Catholic?," 435–46, Randall Zachman makes the point that the evangelical Reformers were not fighting against Catholics, they were fighting to be the Catholics. This is analogous to my point in this study that we have misunderstood Calvin and his engagement with the tradition. However, while that point is excellent, it obfuscates one of the basic issues of navigation that Calvin had to perform throughout his life – finding a middle ground between Catholic hierarchical forms of the church on the one hand and Anabaptist primitivism on the other. Whatever we choose to call the figures in that Scylla and Charybdis, that dynamic in great part defined Calvin's life and thought.

sunlight principle insofar as he was able to do so. The historical records that supported the first mark would be insignificant if believers, either trained in universities or simply literate, were unable to see and follow the arguments that something was part of the tradition passed down from their ancestors to them. The hiding away of members of the hierarchy in the ecclesiastical courts to pronounce on truths that would be passed down as time and circumstance demanded was a figment of the past – whether it had ever existed.

Finally, the tradition would be attached to the scriptures themselves. Calvin argued that it beggared belief to accept that the apostles had written the scriptures and then set down an enormous amount of doctrine that regulated and even contradicted the truths placed in the scriptures. For Calvin, the tradition would need always to be in concert with the scriptures. He would argue that the authority of the tradition would only exist to the degree that various figures had explained the scripture clearly, finding the meaning that the original author had in mind. But this was a flexible mark for Calvin, and he was willing explicitly to turn away from the plain sense of scripture on the basis of the rule of faith.

Every history is an effort at coming to terms with the past. But in writing history, every historian creates a vision of the past that highlights its influence in their own day, and thus fashions a "useable history." There is no doubt that Calvin was engaged in just such a process. For every brilliant moment of historical insight such as his realization that the Hypognosticon was not Augustine's, he supplied a believed canard that buttressed the orthodox Christianity he trusted he had received – such as his claim that no father had ever argued against the baptism of infants.

In taking on this task, Calvin was seeking to deliver the church's doctrine. But that effort involved him in a variety of historical and memorial undertakings that undercut the radical form of the scriptural principle while avoiding the sanctification of the status quo ante. In this balancing act, Calvin sought the middle ground, as did many other magisterial Reformers.[176] Calvin wished to avoid the excesses of Rome that in his

---

[176] In "The Reformers and Tradition: Seeing the Roots of a Problem." *Religions* 8 (2017): 1–11, I argued that the magisterial versus Radical historiographical typology might better be replaced by a continuum that considered their engagement with or rejection of the orthodox tradition. For the theologian, this has the added benefit of changing the discussion from the relationship to the state to one of the relationship with the tradition. See also Donald K. McKim, "John Calvin: A Theologian for an Age of Limits," in *Readings in Calvin's Theology*, edited by Donald K. McKim (Grand Rapids: Baker Book House, 1984), 291–310.

eyes had created out of the tradition a nose of wax that could be bent in any direction at the will of the hierarchy. But just as certainly he wished to avoid the immoderation of the return to the scriptures that would jettison the last 1,500 years of belief and practice. So he generated, through practice and definitely not in theory, a programmatic model of considering the tradition as part of the received wisdom of the church. The evidence of that project stands within his work.

6

Tradition as a Historiographical and Cultural Problem

John Calvin faced a problem. It was the basic historical problem of every Christian theologian – how was the gospel's unchangeable core handed down through the centuries to arrive anew and lifegiving in his day? His task, of course, was made much more difficult than many of his historical predecessors', because he had to work this out in a historical setting in which there was great and urgent conflict over the foundations of Christian authority. The Bible and the church were encapsulated in arguments over scripture and tradition.

Calvin's solution was to argue for the necessity of the plain sense of the scriptures as the safe foundation for all Christian doctrine, morality, and worship. But he attached that scriptural foundation to a strong sense of the continuity of much of the tradition, worked out in history under God's providence, across his work.[1] Calvin was clear that he did not innovate for the sake of the new, but he did not clarify that the inherited theological, exegetical, ecclesiastical, and moral traditions functioned for him as a set of subordinate standards that at times overwhelmed any meaningful claim to preserve the purity of the scriptures.

Given that reality, the problem is set – why did later thinkers accept that John Calvin eschewed tradition in favor of a scriptural principle

---

[1] Barbara Pitkin's fascinating study of Calvin's sense of history and its work with scripture, rather than against it, ends with this deep insight. "Calvin's historicizing interpretation of scripture aimed above all else to console his readers and auditors that all history is in God's hands and ultimately meaningful. Because of the difficulty of grasping divine providence in the theater of history, as also in the spectacle of nature, the Bible and history, for Calvin, went hand in hand." Pitkin, *Calvin, the Bible, and History: Exegesis and Historical Reflection in the Era of Reform* (Oxford: Oxford University Press, 2020), 226.

when so much evidence exists to the contrary? The previous three chapters have set out in detail that Calvin's engagement with tradition transcended the use of a simple polemical crutch. Instead, Calvin engaged the tradition in every written form.[2] He used the tradition to debate with a variety of opponents, as well as manipulating it to serve his purposes in persuading a diverse set of audiences, from the popular to the learned. Given all of this, why did a tradition of interpreting Calvin arise and mature that saw his turns to the scripture as legitimate and meaningful but – seemingly intentionally – paid no attention to his turns to the tradition?

In this chapter, I will begin by considering this Reformed tradition of reading Calvin. I will argue that the first cause of this way of reading the Genevan reformer was Calvin himself. Calvin frequently attacked the tradition rhetorically and rarely praised it. I will demonstrate that this model became a standard and a confessional mark. After that is set, I will consider the way this model has influenced historical and historical-theological models into the present. Some of that influence will be the formation of an unhelpful tradition. On the other hand, some will also be reflected in the tools that historians have crafted that unwittingly reinforce the "truths" that analysts knew to exist.

I will then turn to the issue I identified at the beginning of this search enterprise – that the Western intellectual world does not know what tradition is, or how it functions in the foundation of epistemological investigations. I will examine some figures in the modern discussion of tradition, including Terrence Tilley, Kathryn Tanner, Hans-Georg Gadamer, Randall Zachman, and Mark Massa. I will demonstrate how all of these theorists have something to offer in considering a model that would accommodate Calvin's practice. Finally, I will add to these Irena Backus and Reinhold Niebuhr to outline a theory of critical tradition that works in harmony with the scripture, one that I hope will be the subject of further study. This construct will allow historical acceptance of scripture and tradition within a strain of tradition and, in turn, can be used to consider the modern theological task.

---

[2] I am intentionally not counting the speech acts of sermons. First, because sermonic forms rarely use any explicit return to the tradition or authorities other than the scriptures. Second, because Calvin's sermons that we have represent an entirely different type of text than others – they were preached without notes or manuscripts, and transcribed because of the interest of the French refugee community who paid for the scribe to do so. Calvin did review them before publication, but the evidence suggests that his editing was perfunctory.

WHY CALVIN AND TRADITION?

Given the abundance of evidence presented that Calvin used the orthodox Christian tradition as a guide to true religion and as a mantle of orthodoxy for his treatises, commentaries, and the *Institutes*, one can ask, "Why did this division between scripture and tradition arise, either in Calvin's own work or as shorthand for the differentiation between Catholics and Protestants in the early modern period?" At least two answers arise. The first is simple: Calvin himself makes this argument. Time and again, the Genevan Reformer argued that he was following the truth of scripture, that he was founding his doctrine upon scripture, and that traditions or human inventions were either comparatively weak or downright misleading.

Calvin regularly makes these arguments. In the prefatory letter to King François I of France, originally written in 1536 but appended to all future editions of the *Institutes*, Calvin included an attack on custom (*consuetudinem*), and balanced it with the claim to follow the truth.[3] Calvin argued that the abilities of the human mind to find God through true religion rather than delusions of human error were lost – that conventional wisdom simply could not reach the truth about God.[4] Calvin concluded his consideration with a strong condemnation: "Therefore, since either the custom of the city or the agreement of tradition is too weak and frail a bond of piety to follow in worshiping God, it remains for God himself to give witness of himself from heaven."[5] I have already noted his attacks on tradition in his *Canons and Decrees of the Council of Trent with Antidote*, and the *Adultero-German Interim*.

Calvin could occasionally take up the topic of the usefulness or problematic character of human doctrines or human traditions in his commentaries. Two significant opportunities came at I Corinthians 11, and II Thessalonians 2 and 3. In his commentary on I Corinthians, published in 1546, at 11.2, Calvin sharpened his polemical quill. He discussed what Paul meant by παραδόσεις – traditions. Immediately he attacked the Papists (*papistis*), claiming that they had a principle that divided the

---

[3] *ICR*, Prefatory Address to King François I, 23. CO 2.21.
[4] This is what Edward A. Dowey, Jr., meant when he wrote about human inability to find God in his *The Knowledge of God in Calvin's Theology* (New York: Columbia University Press, 1952).
[5] *ICR*, I.v.13. CO 2.51. "Quum ergo nimis infirmum ac fragile sit pietatis vinculum, vel urbis consuetudinem, vel antiquitatis consensum in colendo Deo sequi, restat ut de se testetur e coelo ipse Deus."

teaching of the apostles into two parts, writings and traditions (*partim scriptis, partim traditionibus*). Calvin used this occasion as an opportunity for a frontal assault.

Under this second class they include not only all sorts of absurd superstitious beliefs and childish rites which they have in superabundance, but all sorts of stupid abominations which are contrary to the plain word of God, and finally, tyrannical laws of their own devising which simply torture the consciences of men. Thus there is nothing so foolish, nothing so absurd, in fact nothing so monstrous, that it may not shelter under this umbrella, or, if you like, be tarred with this brush. Therefore, since Paul mentions traditions here, they seize upon this little word in their usual way, in order to make Paul the inventor of all the abominations, which we, on our part, refute by appealing to the clear evidence of Scripture.[6]

Here is the Calvin of the Western imagination – setting himself as the clear opposite of the papists who introduce no end of folly through their anointing of their inventions as "apostolic." This is the Calvin who took up residence in the mental living room of thinkers from his disciple Beza to Karl Barth.

Calvin did try in the I Corinthians commentary to clarify that he accepted some unwritten traditions, but he maintained that these could not be elements of doctrine or have anything to do with those items that were necessary for salvation. Instead, they were items of good order and polity.[7] Calvin unwittingly mildly subverted his theory by citing I Corinthians 14.40 as an example, that everything should be done decently and in order. The problem was logical: this was definitely not an instance where the apostle had provided an unwritten tradition.

In the commentary on II Thessalonians, published in the set of the Pauline epistles by Jean Gerard in 1551, Calvin expanded his sense of tradition, while still attacking Roman theories. First, at 2.15, Calvin noted that the traditions Paul mentioned were more than the simple regulations of polity and order to which he had restricted the word in

---

[6] Comm. I Corinthians 11.2. CO 49.473. "Sub hoc secundo membro includunt non tantum ineptas quaslibet superstitiones et pueriles ritus quibus sunt referti: sed crassas etiam omnes abominationes manifesto Dei verbo contrarias, et tyrannicas suas leges, quae mera sunt conscientiarum tormenta. Ita nihil tam stultum, nihil tam absurdum, denique nihil tam portentosum quod non sub hac umbra lateat et pingatur hoc colore. Quoniam ergo Paulus hic traditionum facit mentionem, verbulum hoc arripiunt suo more, ut Paulum faciant autorem omnium abominationum, quas apertis scripturae testimoniis redarguamus."

[7] Calvin, I Corinthians Comm., 228. CO 49.473.

I Corinthians, and he argued that Paul meant this more broadly in II Thessalonians so as to include doctrine. After extending the meaning of tradition, however, Calvin took up the opportunity to attack the papists for their foolish belief that their traditions should be observed in the same way that Paul's were. Paul's were delivered to him by God, Calvin exclaimed. The final test of all traditions was whether they were in accord with the pure doctrine of the scriptures.[8] Calvin maintained this broader sense of tradition that included doctrine and morality in his comments upon II Thessalonians 3.6.[9] While Calvin could take up the issue of tradition in his scriptural commentary, it was not his style. Perhaps that was because of his desire for lucid brevity, or perhaps the scriptures did not give frequent opportunity to take up these issues.

Calvin concentrated the greatest number of assaults on tradition in his doctrine of the church. Calvin realized early in his career that the manner of considering tradition as part of the church's authority was a basic issue he and other Reformers would have to face. The ideal of an infallible church, protected by the Holy Spirit from making any error, would not allow for any reform. Neither doctrinal nor moral reform could be seriously essayed in such a case. The various social, ecclesiastical, and moral reformers of the sixteenth century had been clamoring for a council to reform the church long before Calvin visited Geneva. However, the argument that the church could not err made an extraordinary impact when that council was finally called at Trent. Calvin's consideration of tradition in ecclesiology would seem wholly fitting, given such a circumstance.

Calvin attacked the presumed power of the church in *Institutes* IV.vii–xi. He recognized the claims of the primacy of the Roman church and the claim he included that its judgments could not be reviewed meant that it was functionally, if not actually, infallible.[10] Calvin's theology did

---

[8] John Calvin, *Commentary on the Second Epistle to the Thessalonians*, translated by Ross Mackenzie, in Calvin's *New Testament Commentaries*, edited by David W. and Thomas F. Torrance, vol. 8 (Edinburgh: Oliver and Boyd Ltd., 1960), 412. Hereafter cited as Calvin, II Thessalonians Comm., with page number. CO 52.207.

[9] Calvin, II Thessalonians Comm., 417. CO 52.212.

[10] *ICR*, IV.vii.19. "But what is most unbearable of all, they leave no jurisdiction on earth to control or restrain their lust if they abuse such boundless power. Because of the primacy of the Roman Church, they say, no one has the right to review the judgments of this see." CO 2.838. "Quod autem omnium maxime intolerabile est, nullum in terris iudicium relinquunt coercendae ac refraenandae suae libidini, si tam immensa potestate abutantur. Nemini, inquiunt, iudicium sedis huius liceat retractare, propter romanae ecclesiae primatum."

not admit of such a hierarchy that would be immune from sin, and the history of the Renaissance popes gave scant reason for him to believe in such persons or institutions. As Calvin examined the claim that the church could depend upon customs or traditions or doctrines that in some manner went further or beyond the warrant of scripture, he stated a rule to avoid this. He argued: "Then here is a universal rule that we ought to heed: God deprives men of the capacity to put forth new doctrine in order that he alone may be our schoolmaster in spiritual doctrine as he alone is true who can neither lie nor deceive. This rule pertains as much to the whole church as to individual believers."[11] This would not be Calvin's final word on the subject.

Calvin scrutinized the claim that the church had to add things to the writings of the apostles or that the apostles left items through the living voice given to the church with a jaundiced eye. He argued that it was too fantastic that the apostles would write epistles and then immediately supply further material they had forgotten to include.[12] Calvin even used Augustine to argue against the use of extra-scriptural traditions, writing, "If they dare attempt it, I shall counter with Augustine's words, that is, 'When the Lord said nothing, who of us may say, "These things are or those things are?" Or if one dare say so, what proof does he provide?'"[13] Modern minds believe Calvin was against the tradition because he said so, loudly and clearly.

Further, this was not a momentary issue – he carried it through to the last Latin edition of the *Institutes*. In IV.xi.8, Calvin attacked the claimed spiritual power of the pope. He wrote: "Indeed, under the term 'spiritual power' I include boldness in formulating new doctrines by which

---

[11] *ICR*, IV.viii.9. CO 2.852. "Deinde universalis est ratio, quam hic respicere convenit: Deum idcirco adimere hominibus proferendi novi dogmatis facultatem, ut solus ipse nobis sit in spirituali doctrina magister; ut solus est verax, qui nec mentiri nec fallere potest. Haec ratio non minus ad totam ecclesiam, quam ad unumquemque fidelium pertinet."

[12] *ICR*, IV.viii.14. "I confess that the disciples were as yet untutored and well-nigh unteachable when they heard this from the Lord. But when they committed their doctrine to writing, were they even then beset with such dullness that they afterward needed to supply with a living voice what they had omitted from their writings through fault of ignorance?" CO 2.856. "Rudes adhuc, fateor, et prope indociles erant discipuli quum istud a Domino audirent, verum hacne tarditate tum etiam tenebantur, quum doctrinam suam scriptis commendarent, ut postea viva voce supplere necesse habuerint, quod in scriptis suis ignorantiae vitio omiserant?"

[13] *ICR*, IV.xiii.14. CO 2.856. "Id si tentare audeant, agam cum ipsis Augustini verbis. Hoc est: quum Dominus tacuerit, quis nostrum dicat, illa vel illa sunt? Aut si dicere audeat, unde probat?"

they have turned the wretched people away from the original purity of God's Word, the wicked traditions with which they have ensnared them, and the pretended ecclesiastical jurisdiction which they exercise through suffragans and officials."[14] Calvin rewrote this section for the 1559 edition, and added the line "the wicked traditions with which they have ensnared them," illustrating his antipathy for this manner of creating ecclesiastical power.

The passages that I have considered do not exhaust Calvin's spleen that he regularly vented toward the church of Rome.[15] When historians and theologians looked for Calvin's stated opinion of traditions and ecclesiastical doctrines, these were the passages they found. Small wonder that Calvin earned the reputation of one who hated the idea of tradition and instead maintained a pure concentration upon the Word of God.

The evidence amassed here and its analysis demands that a greater nuance be granted to Calvin's theology of tradition than he himself was willing to give. It is fair to ask why that is the case. In 1984, Suzanne Selinger published *Calvin Against Himself*, a study that suggested basic issues in Calvin's thought represented unresolved tensions.[16] Among the various critical reviews of the work, beyond the psychoanalytic methodology, were the lack of a sense of Calvin's theology that saw its coherence, and more than that, the coherence of Calvin's own mind.[17] I am not making that case. Instead, I wish to argue that Calvin mistook his own strong but relative rejection of the power and authority of the orthodox theological tradition for an absolute denial. This may have been because of his own sense that his theology was markedly different from that of his opponents. It may have been because of some of his early polemics at Lausanne and against Sadoleto; since he was unwilling to go as far as Cardinal Sadoleto, he may have believed that he was only using scripture for all of his doctrinal foundations. It may have even been the case that he was captured by the logic of the scriptural principle. In any case, his sense of what he was doing was exaggerated in the belief that he did not stray

---

[14] *ICR*, IV.xi.8. CO 2.898. "Ac spiritualis quidem potestatis nomine tum audaciam complector in fabricandis novis doctrinis, quibus miseram plebem a germana verbi Dei puritate averterunt, tum iniquas traditiones quibus ipsam illaquearunt, tum pseudoecclesiasticam iurisdictionem, quam per suffraganeos et officiales exercent."

[15] See also *ICR*, IV.viii.10, IV.viii.15, IV.ix.9, IV.ix.13, and many passages in IV.x.

[16] Suzanne Selinger, *Calvin Against Himself: An Inquiry in Intellectual History* (North Haven: Archon Books, 1984).

[17] See, among others, reviews by Richard Bauckham, *The Journal of Ecclesiastical History* 37 (1986): 501–02; Eric Dean, *Church History* 55 (1986): 523–24; and Robert M. Kingdon, *Journal of the American Academy of Religion* 54 (1986): 191.

from the purity of the Word; that sense also overestimated his abandonment of the medieval tradition.

THE HISTORIOGRAPHICAL TRADITION

I have argued that Calvin's sense of his own and other evangelical reformers' work – as based on scripture rather than tradition – influenced how the modern world looked at Calvin. This is even more significant, however, because it guides the minds of later generations in ways that are both explicit and intentional but also implicit and unpremeditated. Here we come to the second answer, the tradition that stemmed from Calvin and others like him. This is clear when one examines the historiography of the Reformation.[18] This tradition of viewing the events and theology of the period has been affected in ways that have escaped the modern rejection of the confessional paradigm.

Historians of the early modern period frequently note that modern histories of the period and movement or movements rejected the confessional biases of the prior historiography, whether Lutheran, Calvinist, Anglican, or Roman Catholic.[19] However, that effort to leave behind the championing of one church or another has not allowed historians to free themselves from bias entirely. As Carlos Eire noted, "That is not to say that the narratives we have are free of bias. Every historian has to choose an approach to the past, some lens through which to analyze it. Choices have to be made."[20] While Eire wished to consider how an overarching and timeless summation of the Reformations was bound to be wrong because the historian himself could not escape the historical moment in which he lived – and gave Karl Holl as an example – he did suggest a variety of possible frameworks by which to understand the period.[21]

---

[18] The terminology here is not insignificant. Among others, Carter Lindberg, Carlos Eire and I have argued for the use of the term "Reformations" to signify the variety and multivocity of the movements that were happening in epoch of what had been called the "Reformation" until the publication of Lindberg's *The European Reformations* in 1996. See Lindberg, *The European Reformations*, 2nd ed. (Malden: Wiley Blackwell, 2010); R. Ward Holder, *Crisis and Renewal: The Era of the Reformations* (Louisville: Westminster John Knox Press, 2009), and Carlos M. N. Eire, *Reformations: The Early Modern World* (New Haven: Yale University Press, 2017).

[19] Raymond A. Mentzer, "The Deconfessionalization of the Reformations," *The Sixteenth Century Journal* 50 (2019): 43–48.

[20] Eire, *Reformations*, 741.

[21] Eire, Reformations, 741–57.

At this point, I want to illustrate how the ideal of scripture versus tradition worked its way into the thought of historians of the early modern period. I do not suggest in any manner that this is an exhaustive consideration of the surveys of the period. But I do believe that the variety of writers who have included the traditional ways of considering the scripture and tradition is a data point that suggests the ways that historians and other analysts have been influenced about their sense of the term "tradition" and the semantic field it signifies.

An early example from the twentieth century can be taken from Preserved Smith's *The Age of the Reformation*, published in 1920. While Smith sought to write a history that would put the Reformation in its proper relationship to the economic and intellectual revolutions of the sixteenth century, he did import the scripture and tradition paradigm.[22] Smith argued that there was nothing new in Calvin's thought and asserted that, "Recognizing the Bible as his only standard, he interpreted it according to the new Protestant doctors."[23] Interestingly, in Smith's derogatory summary of Calvin's work, he recognized that Calvin was dependent on others. But he maintained that it was only the Protestants – as if Protestant Christianity effected a total break from that which had gone before.

In 1980, Steven Ozment published *The Age of Reform 1250–1550: An Intellectual and Religious History of Late Medieval and Reformation Europe*. Ozment linked a certain scriptural principle to both Swiss and English reforms. He argued that "The test of Scripture became Zwingli's basic reform principle" and "Here the English and Swiss Reformations had something in common. A Scripture principle similar to Zwingli's also inspired William Tyndale more than Luther's doctrine of justification by faith."[24] Ozment followed this up with *Protestants: The Birth of a Revolution*. In this latter volume, Ozment argued for the failure of the Protestant movement, noting that Protestants won battles but never the war. Its greatest asset was the new approach to scripture: "The new test of Scripture gave Protestants a powerful weapon against arbitrary spiritual authority."[25] Without

---

[22] Preserved Smith, *The Age of the Reformation* (New York: Henry Holt and Company, 1920), v.

[23] Smith, *The Age of the Reformation*, 164.

[24] Steven Ozment, *The Age of Reform 1250–1550: An Intellectual and Religious History of Late Medieval and Reformation Europe* (New Haven: Yale University Press, 1980), 324–25.

[25] Steven Ozment, *Protestants: The Birth of a Revolution* (New York: Doubleday, 1992), 216.

noting the words, Ozment accepted without serious question the ideal of scripture versus tradition.

In 1991, Euan Cameron's *The European Reformation* hit booklists. Cameron himself did not accept the model of scriptural principle that I am noting, but he had had little difficulty finding it in other scholars. He criticized another scholar for arguing that people "read the Bible and found that the reformers' teaching derived from it."[26] In 2003, Patrick Collinson's *The Reformation: A History* repeated the clear statement of the scriptural principle. He wrote: "The formulation 'Word of God,' which among Protestants especially became a synonym for the Bible, made the elusive abstraction 'the Word' hard and fast, more concrete, anchoring it in biblical texts, which were given a new and absolute authority: *sola scriptura*. The Church was to be validated by the Bible, not the Bible by the Church."[27] That same year, Diarmaid MacCulloch's *The Reformation: A History*, arrived to popular acclaim. MacCulloch's tome contains assertions of Luther's "insistence on the primacy of the revealed will of God in Scripture," and states that Zwingli and his colleagues were "only too willing to tell Zurich what the Bible said."[28] In his conclusion, MacCulloch considers some of the impacts of the issues that began in the Reformation. He concludes that one of the most significant is that of the critical study of the Bible: "That entails a painful reassessment of sources of authority, which is still convulsing both Protestantism and Catholicism. Although for Protestantism the primary problem has been the authority of the Bible, and for Catholicism the authority of the Church, in both cases the issue at the centre of the conflict has become the same: the Christian attitude to various aspects of sexual behaviour."[29] While MacCulloch's consideration of the present-day situation for both Protestantism and Catholicism may be correct, his assignment of Bible to Protestantism and church to Catholicism seems reflexive.

In 2004, Peter Wallace's *The Long European Reformation* made a similar claim, that Luther's argument rested on his theory of the

---

[26] A.G. Dickens, *The German Nation and Martin Luther* (New York: Harper & Row, 1974), 134, cited in Euan Cameron, *The European Reformation* (Oxford: Oxford University Press, 1991).

[27] Patrick Collinson, *The Reformation: A History* (New York: The Modern Library, 2003), 33.

[28] Diarmaid MacCulloch, *The Reformation: A History* (New York: Penguin Books, 2003), 117, 145.

[29] MacCulloch, *The Reformation*, 705.

unrivalled authority of scripture.[30] In 2007, Hans Hillerbrand's *The Division of Christendom* asserted that the Reformers had insisted "that Scripture and tradition could be at odds, could in fact be in tension with one another."[31] He added:

> Several theological affirmations were shared by all Protestants. They are often identified by their Latin phrases – *sola scriptura, sola gratia, sola fide*, by Scripture alone, by grace alone, by faith alone. It was the modifier *sola* (alone) that constituted the incisive Protestant affirmation, for Catholic theology has, of course, always affirmed Scripture, faith, and grace; the charge that it did not has been Protestant propaganda. Protestants argued a focus solely on Scripture, grace, and faith. The Protestant polemic in the sixteenth century had it that Catholics relied on tradition and minimized the importance of sacred Scripture.[32]

While Hillerbrand would be very careful to note that the Protestant polemic against Catholics was not materially true, he would not cast a wary eye at the claim that Protestants actually did hold for a position of *sola scriptura*.

Three years later, Carter Lindberg's second edition of *The European Reformations* arrived on bookshelves. Lindberg characterized the fight between Zwingli and his followers with the bishop in the following manner: "Here the battle of tradition and Scripture, ecclesiastical authority and gospel authority was joined."[33] The next year, Kenneth G. Appold, in his *The Reformation: A Brief History*, would argue that Luther had been addressed most deeply by the Bible. "In other words, the biblical message spoke to his own faith in a profoundly personal way. Aside from the value of the theological insight itself, this gave him enormous confidence in his reading (he had experienced its truth first-hand), as well as a lasting appreciation for the Bible's ability speak as a 'living voice.'"[34] Appold discussed Luther's consideration of justification and his emphasis on the Word. He wrote of the consequences for Luther's thought, that "wherever a conflict between the church's traditions and the words of Scripture arose, Scriptural

---

[30] Peter G. Wallace, *The Long European Reformation: Religions, Political Conflict, and the Search for Conformity, 1350–1750* (New York: Palgrave MacMillan, 2004), 79. Later in the volume, Wallace described Protestantism as a "Bible-based faith." (122).

[31] Hans J. Hillerbrand, *The Division of Christendom: Christianity in the Sixteenth Century* (Louisville: Westminster John Knox Press, 2007), 279.

[32] Hillerbrand, *Division of Christendom*, 383–84.

[33] Carter Lindberg, *The European Reformations* (Malden, MA: Wiley Blackwell, 2010), 169.

[34] Kenneth G. Appold, *The Reformation: A Brief History* (Malden, MA: Wiley Blackwell, 2010), 62.

authority prevailed. In that sense, one can speak of a 'Scripture principle' in Luther's thought."[35]

In 2017, Alec Ryrie took on Protestantism in its totality in his *Protestants: The Radicals Who Made the Modern World*. While the book necessarily shortens its consideration of the Reformations, Ryrie still sets out the scripture principle clearly: "This is the 'Scripture principle': the conviction that the Bible is the only and absolute source of authority and that all believers are equal before it."[36] The same year, Carlos Eire published *Reformations: The Early Modern World, 1450–1650*. Writing about Calvin, Eire argued that the *Institutes* "provided Calvin and all Reformed clergy with a brilliant means of controlling biblical exegesis among the faithful and of defending the *sola scriptura* principle at the same time."[37]

This catalog of scholarship is not an attack on the scholars gathered here. These are giants of the historical arts, and their scholarship in many cases defines English-speaking consideration of the early modern period. Further, there are others who are not on this list – not because they are unimportant, but because making a comprehensive study would not prove anything further than this shorter survey has. My point is that the model of scripture and tradition or scripture versus tradition, or a scriptural principle, has become such a basic feature of the historiographical landscape as to exist beneath notice. There can be no doubt that Martin Luther lauded the authority of the scripture. One need only read the opening pages of *The Freedom of a Christian* from 1520 to know this. But the idea that the evangelical or Protestant Reformers followed scripture without tradition had to be defended already in the 1520s when other voices of reform started arguing for adult baptism. My point in this brief consideration is to show how widely this model of considering one of the important factors in the Reformations – that of the basis of religious authority – has penetrated into scholarship.

ANALYTICAL MODELS: THE PROBLEM IN BROADER CONTEXT

The issue that I illustrated with histories of the Reformation or Reformations did not neatly stay within the classrooms of those studying the

---

[35] Appold, *The Reformation: A Brief History*, 74.

[36] Alec Ryrie, *Protestants: The Radicals Who Made the Modern World* (London: William Collins, 2017), 29. In his footnote on that page, Ryrie notes that this claim is also common to Alister McGrath, *Christianity's Dangerous Idea* (London: SPCK, 2007); and Brad Gregory, *The Unintended Reformation: How a Religious Revolution Secularized Society* (Cambridge: Harvard University Press, 2012).

[37] Eire, *Reformations*, 292.

early modern period, however that was defined. Instead, it broadened into a problem that affects the way Western thought approaches every question. Simply put, how is knowledge verified? There are a variety of approaches to the question, frequently depending upon the field of study or science involved. Some sciences depend upon a tradition – the scientific method is nothing other than that. Other fields of study depend upon a foundational text – something is true because it is in the Constitution, or in the Bible, or in another authoritative text. This problem is basic to the Western mind, whether considering religion, commerce, science, or any field of thought.

As we noted at the beginning of this study, the editor of the most famous ecclesiastical study in the history of studies of tradition, Yves Congar's *Tradition and Traditions*, suggested that the modern mind does not really know what tradition is. This fact becomes clearer when one examines Terrence Tilley's study of tradition, published in 2000. Tilley argued that the modern world was faced with a series of questions that came about because of historians' study of traditions: "Historians who study traditions have shown that those components of traditions that participants take to be invariant have shifted remarkably over time."[38] He identified the dichotomy as one between the issue of traditions being "made" or "found," and suggested that this was a badly put question. His argument was that "traditions are neither made nor found, yet both constructed and given."[39] Tilley himself recognized the inadequacy of that formulation. While it demonstrated that traditions were neither perfectly rigid nor perfectly malleable, that was a negative characterization that left the positive definition of a tradition adrift.[40] To set out an affirmative ideal of tradition, Tilley argued that "religious tradition is best understood as an enduring practice or set of practices including a vision (belief), attitudes (dispositions, affections), and patterns of action." This model concentrated its power in seeing the tradition not as a groups of doctrines that constituted what the tradition was but as an approach that was fundamentally about how to live in and out of a tradition.[41] Tilley's

---

[38] Terrence W. Tilley, *Inventing Catholic Tradition* (Maryknoll: Orbis Books, 2000), 13. Tilley noted that this was not new, and cited Hans Frei, *The Eclipse of Biblical Narrative: A Study in Eighteenth and Nineteenth Century Hermeneutics* (New Haven: Yale University Press, 1974); Robert M. Grant and David Tracy, *A Short History of the Interpretation of the Bible*, 2nd ed. (Philadelphia: Fortress Press, 1984); and Van A. Harvey, *The Historian and the Believer* (New York: Macmillan, 1966).

[39] Tilley, *Inventing Catholic Tradition*, 15.

[40] Tilley, *Inventing Catholic Tradition*, 44.

[41] Tilley, *Inventing Catholic Tradition*, 45.

model concentrated upon praxis rather than definition.[42] This led to an interesting discussion around the eucharist.

The doctrine of the Real Presence separated Catholics and Protestants, in sixteenth-century and twenty-first-century congregations and councils. But Tilley argued that with his exponentially expanded number of participants in "the tradition," the meaning of the tradition changed. With the changes that came to Roman Catholicism with Vatican II, such as a vernacular service and the priest turning around to face the people, significant modifications occurred in meaning as well. "With changes in action come changes in belief; the Eucharist comes to signify a communal meal more than a sacrifice. The significance of the altar changes; it more signifies the meal table than the place of sacrifice where the human confronts the divine."[43] This was an application of the ancient formulation of *lex orandi, lex credendi*. That which is prayed becomes that which is believed.

Tilley knew that the long pontificate of a theologically and morally conservative pope, John Paul II, offered little support for such a model. But the pope's effort at an imposition of a "language discipline" finally failed because it did not resonate with the beliefs of ordinary Catholics. Tilley wrote:

Transubstantiation may be a "linguistic discipline" to be imposed. But it may well remain *practically* (sic) meaningless as a theology for and of eucharistic practice. It may even acquire a new meaning hardly connected to the tradition sense, for example, that transubstantiation refers to the transformation of the worshiping assembly into the body of Christ in and through reception of the eucharist. The point is that once the term *transubstantiation* is no longer connected with the ritual as traditionally performed, the meaning of the term becomes indeterminate and its significance for the community that use it cannot simply be imposed, even if the term itself is imposed by an institutional authority on a community.[44]

While Tilley was not removing the hierarchical authority of the church, he clearly redefined it in such a manner as to allow greater influence to the *sensus fidelium* – the gathered sensing of the faith of the entire church – than to the pronouncements of the teaching office of the church.[45]

---

[42] Tilley's influences were eclectic: the discussion of the eucharist included figures such as Clifford Geertz, Robert Schreiter, Barbara Myerhoff, and Kathleen Boone.

[43] Tilley, *Inventing Catholic Tradition*, 69.

[44] Tilley, *Inventing Catholic Tradition*, 71–72.

[45] Tilley recognized that he was denying the account of doctrinal or tradition development in John Henry Newman's *Essay on the Development of Christian Doctrine* (81ff). His response was that Newman was seeking to describe the past rather than create a theory that would give significance to those changes yet to come.

Tilley's argument is not only fascinating but also wide-ranging. He established that his theory of tradition is based on participation in the church, and that it does not seek to define the tradition that was passed down, but rather the faithful process of engaging in handing it down. With that in hand, it is possible to consider his conclusion. Tilley argued that "Authority in the Church does not have its foundation outside the Church but arises in the relationships between the communion of saints, the people who practice discipleship, seeking to live a holy life and die a holy death. The Church is not founded on an external authority, whether Jesus or the scriptures."[46] His assertion was the necessity of a community, and membership in that community, for the process of handing down the faith received, is significant for the historian:

Crucial for identity through change is *not* remembering *what* the past said or did. Remembering our forebears is a practice, one of the practices constituent in any living tradition. ... To be faithful members of a religious tradition is to engage in *traditio* faithfully, the practice of passing to the future our inheritance from the past. We cannot and must not merely repeat the past or even its formulations or rubrics.[47]

Tilley's model offers several possibilities for both the secular and Christian worlds. He notes specifically that an enormously significant factor in the tradition is the manner in which the community engages the memory and history from its past, but enculturates those memories in a living present. Tilley was seeking to consider how religious truth could be considered seriously in a postmodern world in which foundational realism was no longer fully rationally acceptable. His solution was that truth was a constructed reality, though he undergirded this with a series of tests to avoid the claim of relativism.

A second model comes about in the reception of the theories of Thomas S. Kuhn, in the work of Mark Massa.[48] Massa explicitly examined the model of a paradigm shift, taken from Kuhn's theory of the manner in which science makes progress.[49] Kuhn argued that scientific progress is not evolutionary, advancing by accretion, but revolutionary. In other words, the idea that science, or any particular field of science, slowly built up by the cumulative observations and minor breakthroughs

---

[46] Tilley, *Inventing Catholic Tradition*, 181.
[47] Tilley, *Inventing Catholic Tradition*, 184.
[48] Mark Massa, SJ, *The Structure of Theological Revolutions: How the Fight Over Birth Control Transformed American Catholicism* (Oxford: Oxford University Press, 2018).
[49] Thomas S. Kuhn, *The Structure of Scientific Revolutions, 50th Anniversary edition with introductory essay by Ian Hacking* (Chicago: University of Chicago Press, 1962, 2012).

over the years to reach ever more perfect descriptions of the world is wrong. Instead, in Kuhn's theory, a particular model or construct organizes scientific research and observation until it is mature. Then, in an unforeseeable revolution, a new model or paradigm replaces the old one, allowing new observations and progress. For Kuhn, it is important to note that the paradigms are incommensurable despite a shared language basis. Mass in Newtonian physics is not the same as mass in Einsteinian physics, though the signifier remains the same.[50] But that paradigm will eventually be replaced by another.

Kuhn argued that the process leading up to a revolution would begin with scientists recognizing the problems with the present model. Research would appear that demonstrated its inability to explain observed phenomena. This could lead to a period of "crisis," in which extraordinary science begins. That would eventually be resolved in one of three manners. First, ordinary science could resolve the questions at hand. Second, problems would resist all approaches and would be set aside for a future generation. Third, the crisis would end with the emergence of "a new candidate for paradigm and with the ensuing battle over its acceptance."[51]

One of Kuhn's examples was the Copernican revolution, occasioned by the publication of Nicholas Copernicus' *On the Revolution of the Celestial Spheres* (*De Revolutionibus Orbium Coelestium*), in 1543. When Copernicus published the book, it was the Ptolemaic system that reigned supreme. This system had been forged in the last two centuries BCE and was still excellent at predicting the paths of the planets. But the system was not as good at predicting the precession of equinoxes, and other issues. By the time of Copernicus, "a man looking at the net result of the normal research effort of many astronomers could observe that astronomy's complexity was increasing far more rapidly than its accuracy and that a discrepancy corrected in one place was likely to show up in another."[52]

Copernicus' theory did not attempt to improve Ptolemy's theory, but abandoned it, replacing it with the heliocentric model of the solar system that schoolchildren learn today. That paradigm shift allowed a significant new set of responses because the new model or construct allowed for different observational and experimental approaches. Kuhn did not stop there, as this was a general theory of scientific progress, but considered the revolutions that came about with the work of Newton, Lavoisier, and Einstein.[53]

---

[50] I owe Nathan Antiel a debt of thanks for his insights on Kuhn at this point.
[51] Kuhn, *The Structure of Scientific Revolutions*, 81–84.
[52] Kuhn, *The Structure of Scientific Revolutions*, 69.
[53] Kuhn, *The Structure of Scientific Revolutions*, 152.

Mark Massa, a Jesuit theological historian working at Boston College, used Kuhn's theory to examine the progress of the natural law tradition within Roman Catholicism, especially as an explanation of its history in the late twentieth century in America. Massa reasoned that as traditionally theology had been the "queen of the sciences," it might be an interesting test case for the application of Kuhn's theory.[54] He argued that this model might help provide a framework and an ideologically neutral method of considering the "micro-tradition of natural law in the Catholic moral theology community."[55] Just as Kuhn had argued against the theory of a continued and linear progress of science, so too Massa was arguing against the theories of John Henry Newman and John Noonan. Further, he rejected them for the same reason, that their ideals of development of Catholic thought were "linear" or based on a notion of "organic extrapolation."[56]

Massa's test case was the promulgation of the papal encyclical, Humanae Vitae.[57] This encyclical, published on July 25, 1968, was the instrument through which the Roman Catholic church banned all artificial means of birth control. Explicitly depending upon its power to interpret the natural law, the church proclaimed that all actions were prohibited "which either before, at the moment of, or after sexual intercourse, [were] specifically intended to prevent procreation – whether as an end or as a means."[58]

The historical background of this encyclical was fraught with theological and moral considerations. A new method of birth control had recently been invented, frequently called "the pill." Ironically, one of the researchers was Dr. John Rock, a devout Catholic.[59] Rock believed that the church would accept his work because it was "natural" in the sense that Catholic moral theology used the term.[60] Adding to the tensions

---

[54] Massa, *The Structure of Theological Revolutions*, 47. Theology as the "queen of the sciences" was a medieval notion, in which theology was frequently seen as the highest science, and the one which required the greatest preparation.

[55] Massa, *The Structure of Theological Revolutions*, 47.

[56] Massa, *The Structure of Theological Revolutions*, 179.

[57] Humanae Vitae, www.vatican.va/content/paul-vi/en/encyclicals/documents/hf_p-vi_enc_25071968_humanae-vitae.html, accessed April 20, 2020.

[58] Humanae Vitae, 14.

[59] Massa, *The Structure of Theological Revolutions*, 56–58.

[60] Massa, *The Structure of Theological Revolutions*, 57: "That is, precisely because the Pill made no use of what Catholic theology called a 'barrier method' – blocking the female or male organic processes by intrauterine devices or prophylactics – Rock believed that the Church would approve his new approach to contraception as in accord with the 'natural law.'"

of the time, the ecumenical council, Vatican II, had only recently concluded in 1965. Called by Pope John XXIII, the council had specifically been charged with the task of "aggiornamento," an "updating" of the church's witness. Many changes had come about, including the vernacular language mass, the acceptance of modern historical-critical methods of biblical research, and the definition of the church as the people of God. Certainly, by 1968, Catholics were wondering what the church's response to this new technology would be.

In the wake of the promulgation of Humanae Vitae, Roman Catholic theologians pointed out the various ways in which it failed both internal coherence and an expression of the faith of the body of believers. A variety of theologians asserted problems with Humanae Vitae, from the right and the left, proposing solutions – paradigms – of their own.[61] Massa concluded:

> Emphasizing that the micro-tradition of natural law was so marked by disjunction and rupture that the phrase 'paradigm revolution' seems warranted is, I understand, a question of calibration and perception. But I do believe that the very question of calibration warrants the use of "paradigm revolutions" when considering the centripetal forces that eventuated in very different models of what "natural law" actually was, the kinds of human behavior that resulted from living in accord with that law, and what the ends of purposes of living such a life in accord with that law brought to a person.[62]

Extrapolating from Massa's work on the "micro-tradition of natural law," this is a significant application of Kuhn's theory to the history of theology. Following this model would suggest that the tradition is not static, that it does not always change in manners that are predictable or linear, or even organic, and that any revolution would generate a variety of new traditions or at least candidates to become the new paradigm.[63] The possible application to the era of the Reformations is obvious, and I will return to this later.

---

[61] Massa discusses Charles Curran, Germain Grisez, Jean Porter, and Lisa Sowle Cahill.

[62] Massa, *The Structure of Theological Revolutions*, 183.

[63] John Henry Newman, in his *An Essay on the Development of Christian Doctrine*, first published in 1845, argued that the development of doctrine was organic, and that the beginnings anticipated its later phases. Newman used various organic models to suggest that it was not possible always to see the later stages at the beginning, such as an acorn and an oak. His model depends upon a hierarchy that can authoritatively assert that some developments are genuine, and some are corruptions. Newman believed that history made this self-evident, but the inability of the famous Catholic historian, Ignaz von Döllinger, to accept the doctrine of papal infallibility, and his consequent excommunication for it, tells a significantly different story. See Thomas Albert Howard, *The Pope and the Professor: Pius IX, Ignaz von Döllinger, and the Quandary of the Modern Age* (Oxford: Oxford University Press, 2017).

A third model analytical model of tradition arises in the rejection of the question by Randall Zachman. Zachman is a historical theologian who worked on the era of the Reformations, writing especially on John Calvin and his thought. In his "Who is Actually Catholic? How Our Traditional Categories Keep Us from Understanding of the Evangelical Reformations," Zachman turned the question of how tradition was maintained by the evangelical Reformers upside down.[64]

Zachman's thesis is straightforward. The parties of the Reformation are conceptually divided into Protestants and Catholics. Luther departed from the Catholic church in order to become a Protestant, and then became a Lutheran.[65] Zwingli followed suit, becoming a Zwinglian or Reformed. Other figures followed, chronologically, if not in Luther's footsteps. Zachman's thesis depends upon the various evangelical reformers' rejection of Rome's claim to be the true church. Instead, they argued that the Lord had maintained in Rome the vestiges of the covenant, especially baptism.[66]

Zachman's point is that when modern historians see a Catholic Reformation and a Protestant Reformation, or Protestant Reformations, they place a construct on the events of the sixteenth century "completely contrary to the self-understanding of the evangelical teachers themselves."[67] The "Protestants" were actually claiming to be the one true Catholic church. This is a key insight in the effects of historiographical models, and their influence on the way we view the early modern period and our own time. However, it is not the final word. While Zachman is correct that one of the tasks of the historian is to create a model of the historical events in which the historical actors could see themselves, modern analysts cannot give the understanding entirely over to each age. To do so is to fail at historical distance and judgment. Calvin himself criticized earlier ages of the church – why should modern historians and historical theologians do any less?

The final model comes from Kathryn Tanner. Tanner has taken on tradition in a number of loci within her work, most especially in her

---

[64] Randall Zachman, "Who is Actually Catholic? How Our Traditional Categories Keep Us from Understanding of the Evangelical Reformations," in *Crossing Traditions: Essays on the Reformation and Intellectual History In Honour of Irena Backus*, edited by Maria-Cristina Pitassi and Daniela Solfaroli Camillocci (Leiden: Brill, 2018), 435–46.

[65] Zachman, "Who is Actually Catholic?," 435.

[66] Zachman, "Who is Actually Catholic?," 444.

[67] Zachman, "Who is Actually Catholic?," 446.

Theories of Culture: A New Agenda for Theology.[68] Tanner's work is brilliant, and offers a number of characteristics that make it helpful for the present project. First, she is clear that the issues of theological tradition have an impact on the culture, and that culture is the field of study for the consideration of tradition. Instead of having to apply Tanner's insights outside their intended purpose, the analyst needs only consider whether she is correct.

Second, Tanner has engaged critically with many of the issues and thinkers that this project has taken up in order to place Calvin in a proper context as well as to use him as an exemplar for broader understandings of tradition and cultural foundations. She has reviewed the work of Terrence Tilley.[69] She engages John Henry Newman and his theory of the development of doctrine as well as Hans-Georg Gadamer and his theories of tradition and the classic.[70]

Third, Tanner has argued this material that I have considered throughout the study is not formally about scripture versus tradition, but that these are actually a subset (and in her eyes one that is past its time) of the issue of tradition:

That issue, most broadly, concerns the evaluation of diversity in Christian belief and practice – diversity in the understanding of what Christianity is all about at any one time and place, as in the context of Reformation Europe itself, or over the course of time, from the earliest apostolic witness to the present, or across geographical regions of the world, with the growing global recognition of cultural plurality. How are such differences in Christian beliefs and practices to be evaluated? Are they all legitimate? If not, how is one to determine which ones are or are not?[71]

The combination of these insights makes her work particularly apposite for this effort. However, her theories do not finally provide a workable model for the analysis of Calvin's efforts.

Tanner has argued that in a postmodern culture, certain models of thinking about tradition are no longer possible. Whether considering a notion of tradition that looks to the treasury of belief that is passed down,

---

[68] Kathryn Tanner, *Theories of Culture: A New Agenda for Theology* (Minneapolis: Fortress, 1997). See also "Self-Critical Cultures and Divine Transcendence," in *Theology After Liberalism: A Reader*, edited by John Webster and George Schner (Malden: Blackwell, 2000), 223–56; and "Postmodern Challenges to Tradition," *Louvain Studies* 28 (2003): 175–93.

[69] Kathryn Tanner, Editorial Symposium, *Horizons* 29 (2002): 303–11.

[70] Tanner, *Theories of Culture*, 130–32.

[71] Tanner, "Postmodern Challenges to Tradition," 176.

the *tradita*, or examining those theories that place confidence in the process of the tradition itself; in both cases Tanner argues that postmodern philosophy and culture see the functional issues as created, rather than discovered.[72] Those signs that demonstrated the transhistorical nature of either the tradition as treasury or the tradition as process, are seen not as facts that are ascertained, but rather issues that are created. She writes: "What these notions of tradition think of as signs manifesting a prior fact of cultural continuity the postmodern interpreter views as contestable proposals for how to arrange the diversity of Christian practices in a continuous fashion."[73] Tanner also makes clear that one of the problems of tradition is moral, that the claim of "tradition" creates a shield for the theologian against certain issues: "Postmodern cultural theory would charge these ... appeals to tradition ... with the same moral difficulty: they hide the way that contestable theological judgements are part and parcel of such appeals. These appeals to tradition therefore keep the theologian from taking responsibility for the theological judgments that are made."[74] Certainly Calvin argued that an unassailable claim of traditional authority could be used in an immoral manner, or even in a way that denied the veracity of the gospel.

While Tanner's criticisms are significant, they introduce new problems. First, she accepts the idea of postmodern philosophical culture as a given. While she goes into great detail about its place in the modern world, she does not make an explicit argument for the necessity of accepting it. Second, and far more significant, once Tanner has accepted postmodern culture as the court in which she judges the rationality or coherence of proposals, she does not maintain those rules. For instance, she argues that postmodernity would see the Christian tradition as invented or constructed, rather than discovered. Her solution to these problems is to argue that Christians find unity not in tradition but in their common reference to God. She writes: "What holds all these different Christian practices together is, instead, their common reference to the God to whom they all hope effectively to witness. They are unified by the effort Christians make to proclaim and to be the disciples of God's Word – a unity of task and not necessarily of accomplishment."[75] This is only acceptable by denying the claim of several postmodern cultural

---

[72] Tanner, *Theories of Culture*, 131–32.
[73] Tanner, *Theories of Culture*, 132.
[74] Tanner, "Postmodern Challenges to Tradition," 83.
[75] Tanner, *Theories of Culture*, 136.

philosophers that God is also a created construct, rather than a deity whose existence does not require the fervent faith of believers.

CALVIN'S THEOLOGY OF TRADITION

John Calvin grew to maturity in a vibrant French Christian culture, complete with foibles, moments of the sublime, weaknesses, and strengths. He went to the best school in France to take up a career that his connections in the church could open up to him. While at Paris, he undoubtedly came in contact with both humanism and evangelicalism. His work in humanistic learning certainly took on a greater focus during his law studies at Bourges, under Alciati. The fruit of this has to be seen in his commentary on Seneca's *De Clementia*.[76]

Calvin's commentary on *De Clementia* was a dismal failure as a commercial venture. However, scholars agree that it was an acceptable effort at commenting upon the great Stoic philosopher's text and was marked by the emphases of the new humanism – history, grammar, and rhetoric. Here Calvin made his first effort at setting out the historical path for both knowledge and morality. The young French scholar set out from his first work to demonstrate the importance of history in understanding the ancient texts.

Calvin would continue to do this in his early career. He denied the charges of innovation in the first edition of the *Institutes*, he argued that the Evangelicals revered the fathers at Lausanne, and he argued to Sadoleto that the Genevan church was closer to the ancient model than Rome. This pattern only strengthened, so much so that Calvin was seen by one analyst as creating his own traditional support for his confession.

Calvin set out to argue that the core message of Christianity transcended the interpretation of the Bible and had to be handed on with the utmost care. To support this, he created a kind of doctrinal-exegetical circle in which the truths of the faith were constantly being considered against the clear voice of scripture, especially in the consensus of the orthodox across the ages and in the present.

Calvin did this because of the world in which he lived, because of the lessons of history, and because of the arguments being arrayed against him and the evangelical cause. The French king believed that the evangelical faith was new. Sadoleto argued that the Genevan ministers were

---

[76] Jean Calvin, *Calvin's Commentary on Seneca's De Clementia*, translated and edited by Ford Lewis Battles and André Malan Hugo (Leiden: Brill, 1969).

crafty men seeking merely to gain some fame. In the 1543 *Institutes*, Calvin noted the Donation of Constantine and how Valla had dispensed with it. But now in his own day, Agustinus Steuchus was attempting to revive a dead fable.[77]

Further, many of his opponents argued that the church's tradition was inextricably bound up in the history of Christianity. The argument from the fathers was also an argument that Rome was the legitimate heir of 1,500 years of history. The efforts to delegitimize Calvin's readings of the fathers was also an effort to claim that the Genevan reform stood upon terra nova, a new and unsteady ground. Calvin could not escape the historical even had he wished to do so.

But Calvin had no wish to escape the truth of history. Instead, he sought to use the canons of historical research for his own purposes. He did this for reasons both empirical and theological. Empirically, Calvin believed that the church of Rome had erred badly in a number of ways. While he could be as harsh in his criticism of abuses as any first-generation Reformer, that was not his primary concern. Instead, it was the manner in which human-devised doctrines and polity had led astray from apostolic models – examples include the primacy of the pope, the sacrifice of the Mass, the invention of Purgatory, and bishops who did not preach.

Theologically, Calvin did not accept the possibility of pure human obedience to God. Anthropologically, he is famous for arguing for the total depravity of humanity. This never meant that humanity was wholly evil. But it did mean that all of humanity – whether in its rationality, its will, or its materiality, was infected by the corrupting power of sin. Thus, Calvin could not and did not believe in the possibility of a church that was so led by the Holy Spirit so as to be wholly pure. This was fundamental to his attack on both Rome and the Anabaptists. Human beings were never so pure as to be trustworthy. The church could not remove itself from the discipline of the magistrate, nor could the church claim to exist above correction.

Thus, Calvin sought a critical engagement with history and the tradition. He recognized that humans were extraordinarily cunning in devising ways to create systems that benefited themselves, rather than redounding to the praise of the living God. He believed that he found the instrument of that critical appropriation in scripture, in the plain sense of it (*sensus*

---

[77] ICR, IV.xi.12. CO 2.901. Steuchus eventually published his defense of the Donation in his *Contra Laurentium Vallam in falsa donation Constantini* (Lyon, 1547).

germanus). Calvin created a model for evaluating the veracity of the tradition by judging it against the truth of the scripture. His model sought a circle of orthodox doctrine and the biblical witness. He simply did not recognize that orthodox doctrine came with an enormous amount of tradition bound into its very marrow.

The problem was that Calvin did not recognize his own situatedness within the tradition into which he was born and which he had received. Instead of judging everything by the scripture's witness, he regularly denied or expanded scripture's license when he needed to do so. This was the case when he sought the "fuller interpretation" instead of the contextually accurate interpretation. It was the case when he denied the plain sense of the scripture for the maintenance of the *regula fide*. It was the case when Calvin rejected the arguments against infant baptism and made his claims on the apostolic tradition that every father had recognized since the first century.

Calvin saw a problem but devised an incomplete solution. The result was that a Calvinistic or Reformed tradition matured without a critical manner of engaging the tradition itself. The problems with this are legion. Keeping one's view merely upon the Reformed tradition, we can see the exploitation of women, both in Calvin's Geneva and in later centuries.[78] In his own city, John Calvin acted as a prosecutor of his sister-in-law in his brother's case against her, refusing to recuse himself from his position of power in the Consistory no matter his conflict of interest.[79] Calvin had much to say about the necessities of modesty for women,

---

[78] See Beth Allison Barr, *The Making of Biblical Womanhood: How the Subjugation of Women Became Gospel Truth* (Grand Rapids: Brazos Press, 2021). While Barr is arguing about the present effects of hyper-masculinized versions of Christianity in the present day White Evangelical world, she is a historian and provides significant material across the millennia of the Christian era to support her case. See also Margaret Bendroth, *Fundamentalism and Gender, 1875 to the Present* (New Haven: Yale University Press, 1993); Merry E. Wiesner-Hanks, *Women and Gender in Early Modern Europe*, 3rd ed. (Cambridge: Cambridge University Press, 2008); and Katherine L. French and Allyson M. Poska, *Women and Gender in the Western Past* (Boston: Houghton Mifflin, 2007).

[79] See Robert M. Kingdon, *Adultery and Divorce in Calvin's Geneva* (Cambridge: Harvard University Press, 1995), 75. See also Robert M. Kingdon, general ed., *Registers of the Consistory of Geneva in the Time of Calvin*, vol. 1: *1542–1544* (Grand Rapids: Eerdmans, 2000), 309ff. Hereafter Consistory Records, with vol. number and page number. *Registres du Consistoire de Genève au Temps de Calvin*, Tome I (1542–44) published by Thomas A. Lambert and Isabella M. Watt under the direction of Robert M. Kingdon with the assistance of Jeffrey Watt (Geneva: Librairie Droz, 1996), 290ff., and Registres IV.140–43.

suggesting that clothing itself could be adulterous.[80] This model of using religion to establish male power has influenced the present, with the novel theology of "complementarianism," which seeks to keep women in their place.[81] The ongoing effects of this tradition have influenced the church's ability to minister to women, as well as denying it many of the talents of women in ministry for generations.

Of course, a power-driven appropriation of the tradition did not only impact the relationships between men and women. Racial relations suffered as well. Several studies have examined the roots of racial slavery.[82] Calvinist ministers supported the imposition of slavery upon Africans, with Robert Lewis Dabney (1820–98) and James Henley Thornwell (1812–62) acting as chief apologists for racial slavery in the American South.[83] This racist theology was not a purely American phenomenon, South African John DeGruchy wrote a powerful description of how Calvinism was basic to apartheid.[84] Allan Boesak noted the manner in

---

[80] See Graeme Murdock, "The Elders' Gaze: Women and Consistorial Discipline in Sixteenth-Century France," in *John Calvin, Myth and Reality: Images and Impact of Geneva's Reformer*, edited by Amy Nelson Burnett (Eugene: Cascade Books, 2011), 69–90.

[81] See, for example, Michael Parsons, *Reformation Marriage: The Husband and Wife Relationship in the Theology of Luther and Calvin* (Edinburgh: Rutherford House, 2005); and a host of online sites. See "Male-Only Ordination is Natural," https://calvinistinternational.com/2019/01/16/male-only-ordination-is-natural-why-the-church-is-a-model-of-reality/, accessed September 16, 2019, as an example. See also Beverly Roberts Gaventa's answer to this ideal of gender-based identity in *Our Mother Saint Paul* (Louisville: Westminster John Knox Press, 2007), 72ff.

[82] The literature is vast. See, among others, David M. Whitford, *The Curse of Ham in the Early Modern Era: The Bible and Justifications for Slavery* (Burlington: Ashgate, 2009); David Brion Davis, *Inhuman Bondage: The Rise and Fall of Slavery in the New World* (Oxford: Oxford University Press, 2006); and Stephen R. Haynes, *Noah's Curse: The Biblical Justification of American Slavery* (Oxford: Oxford University Press, 2002); Katie Geneva Cannon, "Structured Academic Amnesia: As if This True Womanist Story Never Happened," in *Deeper Shades of Purple: Womanism in Religion and Society*, edited by Stacy M. Floyd-Thomas (New York: New York University Press, 2006), 19–27; Cannon, *Katie's Canon: Womanism and the Soul of the Black Community* (New York: Continuum, 1998); Cannon, *Black Womanist Ethics* (Atlanta: Scholars Press, 1988); Delores S. Williams, *Sisters in the Wilderness* (Maryknoll: Orbis, 1993); and Allan Boesak, *A Farewell to Innocence: A Socio-Ethical Study on Black Theology* (Maryknoll: Orbis, 1977).

[83] Thornwell delivered the inaugural sermon to the Presbyterian Church in the Confederate States of America. In it, he expressly denied that the Golden Rule, from Matthew 7.12, applied in any manner to Black slaves.

[84] John DeGruchy, "Calvin(ism) and Apartheid in South Africa in the Twentieth Century: The Making and Unmaking of a Racial Ideology," in *Calvin and His Influence, 1509–2009*, edited by Irena Backus and Philip Benedict (New York: Oxford University Press, 2011), 306–18.

which Calvinist ideology had channeled the biblical interpretation of white South Africans.[85] Willie Jennings gave a searing account of white Dutch Calvinists attempting to evangelize his African American mother, who was a pillar at New Hope Missionary Baptist Church in Grand Rapids, Michigan.[86] The effects still continue, with racially segregated congregations that face almost every pastor in Reformed denominations across the country and around the world. The church's prophetic witness has been muffled, and frequently muzzled by powers of the status quo.

The list continues.[87] The Reformed tradition accepted the exploitation of native peoples, of the planet's resources, and of economic systems designed to maintain the subjugation of the poor, including immigrants. Clear scriptural witness spoke against each example, but traditions – of reading scripture, of doctrine, of the church, and of culture – silenced that witness. Prophetic voices occasionally spoke out – but rarely were able to change the fabric of the society or the church from the patterns of abuse and corruption that had become a basic part of the tradition. Without a critical appraisal and method for passing on the tradition, and some manner of linking it to the scriptures, the likelihood of a changed future remains slim.

REFORMED TRADITION AND SCRIPTURE: A NEW PROPOSAL

Having described Calvin and the way that he arrived at a paradoxical relationship of scripture and tradition, the historian's task is done. But the theologian still must make progress toward a solution. To write the full complement to this volume that gave a Reformed theology of tradition would take another book. But to note those issues that must be addressed and point the way forward is only a small task. I shall now take that up, and seek to point the direction for later efforts, whether my own or that of others.

The problematic areas of a theology of tradition and scripture that takes history seriously have been proffered. Kathryn Tanner points out

---

[85] Allan Boesak, *Black and Reformed: Apartheid, Liberation, and the Calvinist Tradition* (Maryknoll, New York: Orbis Books, 1984).

[86] Willie Jennings, *The Christian Imagination: Theology and the Origins of Race* (New Haven: Yale University Press, 2010), 1–5.

[87] This list is neither inventive nor new. In 1967, the United Presbyterian Church in the United States of America promulgated and ratified a new confession of faith, blandly titled *The Confession of 1967*. In it, the confession lists four areas on which believers must work to be true to their task of being agents of reconciliation in the world. These were poverty, racial relations, the relations between men and women, and peacemaking.

both the problems of postmodernity and the necessity of the critique of tradition. Without a critical appropriation of tradition, later generations of the church can simply act as if there is no possibility of change and can shirk responsibility for that choice. Hans-Georg Gadamer has set out the necessity of seeing oneself within a tradition, and the way that a classic text functions within any reading or interpretive tradition. Terrence Tilley has suggested that the true model for tradition is not to see it as a noun, something that exists, but as a verb, something that is an ongoing activity. He makes it clear that the community that works to hand on the tradition is the entire body of the church. Randall Zachman has demonstrated the necessity of keeping in mind catholicity. Finally, Massa suggests that changes in the tradition happen not through evolutionary but rather revolutionary changes.

I must add to this consideration two further insights. The first is from Irena Backus, who argued in her consideration of the practice of history in the sixteenth century that the key to seeing the theologians of the era of the Reformations as serious historians was to see the manner in which they accepted the Bible as basic to their historical program, and how it transformed their consideration of history. While that is not without problems as the "curse of Ham" demonstrated, this is a key insight in building a theory that addresses the issue of history and the church, scripture and tradition.

Second, a clarifying insight from a modern theologian, Reinhold Niebuhr, on the nature of history, provides a sense of history that is helpful. Niebuhr argued that "Man is, and yet is not, involved in the flux of nature and time. He is a creature, subject to nature's necessities and limitations; but he is also a free spirit who knows of the brevity of his years and by this knowledge transcends the temporal by some capacity within himself."[88] History is both humanity's great prison and its spur to transcendence. Humans are paradoxically both free and bound. Their ability to surpass the natural course of events of birth, life, and death by knowing themselves in history sets them apart from all other creatures.[89] Niebuhr linked human striving to transcend the mortal and the final materiality to a doctrine of God's control of history. Rejecting both cyclical visions of history and the modern sense of an upward trend that

---

[88] Reinhold Niebuhr, *The Nature and Destiny of Man: A Christian Interpretation*. v. 1 Human Nature. 1941. v. 2 Human Destiny. 1943 (Louisville: Westminster John Knox Press, 1996), v. II.1.

[89] Peter B. Josephson and R. Ward Holder, *Reinhold Niebuhr in Theory and Practice: Christian Realism and Democracy in America in the Twenty-First Century* (Lanham: Lexington Books, 2019), 54.

saw the world's history simply bringing better and better human outcomes, Niebuhr asserted that only God could know the end of history,
both as a final moment and as a goal. The true problem of history was
human pretensions both to control history and to be pure in motivation.
He sought this vision in the work of the prophet Amos, who rejected
the national hopes of ancient Israel, even though they were God's elect
people.[90]

Given these elements, it is possible to construct the rudiments of a
model of Reformed engagement with tradition that is broad enough
to encompass Calvin's actual practice and resolve some of the tensions
inherent in his desire for both scripture and tradition. First, the engagement of scripture and tradition will have to be broad. This will require
the church universal to take up this task. Whether theologians or the
insights of textual critics or the analyses of historians, or the lived faith
of particular bodies of believers – all of these will be necessary components for a Reformed theology of tradition. The tradition is broader than
any one person can recognize, and just as Calvin realized that interpreters of the scripture would have to be humble enough to cooperate, that
same dynamic is true as the contemporary world seeks to work at critical
reception and handing down of the tradition.

Second, the engagement will have to be explicit, open, and historically
rational – a kind of sunlight tool. Calvin's caution about the ways that
the Roman hierarchy could use a hidden tool that denied various facts of
history was well taken, but too narrow. He believed that his own use of
those same tools was licit because he argued his answers were scripturally
based. That was one of his greater mistakes. The number of problems in
today's church that could be better had all parties been more transparent
about issues is a caution that this is not a challenge the church or believers have conquered. Calvin's insight was that a hierarchy could not claim
a special place in the knowledge of and engagement with the tradition.
Making that a concrete reality in the postmodern world would be the
foundation of a Reformed theology of tradition.

Third, Christianity should expect that at times the forces of change
will be neither gradual nor gentle. This was true in the first century.
It was true in the sixteenth century. It will be true in the future. The
idea that only incremental change is possible is another way of delegiti-
mizing change. That is true as we seek to continue to hear voices long

---

[90] Josephson and Holder, *Reinhold Niebuhr in Theory and Practice*, 55.

silenced – women, people of color, the poor, the immigrant, all while realizing that there is a rich biblical witness that demands action in the present, rather than a calm that argues that the church's time works in centuries. However, claims for the new paradigms will have to be tested – they cannot simply claim the newness of a reform and reject all scrutiny.

Fourth, the hermeneutical circle of scripture and the tradition must be examined in manners that allow new insights into the scripture such as the advent of the use of original languages, or the historical-critical method to bring forth new insights that transform the tradition. There must be a willingness to have a critical reception of tradition, both because that has always been the case, and because that is necessary for maintaining the vitality of the Christian message in new ages. Finally, this theory must be placed in a context of a vision of history in which humanity is not the center but is instead placed under the providence of God, unknown as that is. With those elements in place, a serious conversation can be held on the topic of scripture and tradition, one that holds a place within Reformed belief, but creates the opportunity to speak to other traditions.

Epilogue

Reading – Texts or Traditions?

John Calvin argued against the use of the doctrinal and ecclesiastical traditions in favor of the purity of the scriptures while simultaneously using those very traditions. The tension between Calvin's rhetoric and his practice is significant – Calvin used a pragmatic approach to the tradition without supplying an overarching theory of how to use the tradition in coherence with his biblical interpretation. Calvin did not even conceive of the need for such a theory.

Because of this tension within his thought, and the manner in which he wrote about it, Calvin contributed to the strains within the foundations of a theological and historiographical tradition. Protestants understood themselves as depending upon scripture instead of scripture and tradition. Catholics understood their own confession as dependent upon scripture and tradition, but just as eagerly defined Protestantism as (defectively) dependent only upon the scripture. This construct became a tradition in its own right, affecting confessional histories as well as the ways that theologians approached the doctrinal task. While I have not traced this through the centuries, its vestiges show in a representative sample of the histories of the Reformations that have been written in the last few decades.

So far, I have been discussing Calvin's influence upon theology and history. But as discussed in the introduction, Calvin contributed to many fields beyond theology and history. In throwing himself into the struggle between scripture and tradition, Calvin participated in a history of questioning the foundations of how humans justify their beliefs. Philosophers call this justification or a branch of epistemology. Societies link such concerns to their ideals of truth. All people, whether those who live in ivory towers or those who neither live there nor wish to do so, care about why something is believable.[1]

The question can be as simply posed as asking, "Why do you believe what you believe?" Does a person believe because it can be supported by a book? Does the person instead believe because of a figure of authority? While any number of volumes have been written upon the topic, the idea of resolving the issue remains illusory. Further, this problem is not simply a matter of religion. This issue of how a person, a community, or a nation supports those ideas that are believed affects all realms of thought and cultural life.

In displaying this tension, Calvin provides an extraordinary exemplar. He enters into our consciousness arguing that he can be believed because his teachings are based upon scripture, even when they demonstrably are not. Thus he becomes a sort of distant mirror, a reflection for the present age that argues about why something may be believed.[2] Calvin's battles about traditions of authority have become ours. We are his distant heirs, frequently battling over the nature of our truth claims. In much the same way as he did, we frequently argue that we have solved the issue, while acting in ways that belie our own anxieties.

I will demonstrate this by looking at two of the greatest venues of textual interpretation that define the American experiment as much as any other: biblical interpretation and Constitutional jurisprudence. Each week in the United States of America, thousands of preachers, priests, deacons, and other religious professionals stand before their communities, whether in virtual space or in person, and give homilies that interpret the Bible.[3] With estimates above 380,000 congregations, a very conservative estimate of the number of sermons produced in an average year

---

[1] John Courtney Murray, SJ, argued that a shared philosophy was made necessary by the American experiment. See his "E Pluribus Unum: The American Consensus," in *We Hold These Truths: Catholic Reflections on the American Proposition* (New York: Sheed and Ward, 1960), 27–43. Murray was arguing that the natural law provided the shared philosophy the nation needed.

[2] With apologies to Barbara Tuchman, who wrote *A Distant Mirror: The Calamitous 14th Century* (New York: Random House, 1978), in part to reflect the nature of the age in which she was living.

[3] A 2017 article in *Christianity Today* quoted Simon Brauer for a figure of 384,000 congregations in the USA in 2012, the last year for which figures are available from the National Congregations Study. See Rebecca Randall, "How Many Churches Does America Have? More Than Expected," *Christianity Today*, September 14, 2017. www.christianityto-day.com/news/2017/september/how-many-churches-in-america-us-nones-nondenomina-tional.html, accessed April 30, 2020.

would approach 20 million.[4] However, even that number of interpretations of scripture is low as it does not account for the various courses in seminaries, universities, divinity schools, and colleges, or the other academic work such as commentaries and articles that are part of the regular academic work of biblical scholars.[5]

While the numbers of congregations and sermons are staggering, they do not outnumber the number of legal decisions made annually. While the federal court system is relatively small, comprising ninety-four district courts, thirteen circuit courts, and the Supreme Court of the United States, all of the other courts across the country act upon principles of jurisprudence that stem from the decisions of the federal system.[6] Over 100 million cases are filed each year in state trial courts, and approximately 400,000 cases in the federal courts.[7] Thus thousands of decisions in state trial courts, appellate courts, and supreme courts, are made every week that are influenced by the interpretation of the Constitution.

Both the interpretation of the Constitution and the Bible raise the same basic question that Calvin's struggle with scripture's relationship to tradition presented: In generating an interpretation, can the text stand alone, or must it be read within a tradition? In modern North American biblical communities, this is frequently termed the question of biblical literalism versus some tradition of reading, whether ecclesiastical or academic. In the United States jurisprudence, this conflict is normally termed constitutional originalism versus living constitutionalism. In both cases, ecclesiastical and juridical, the basic issue is text versus tradition.

---

[4] 380,000 multiplied by 52 Sundays per year = 19,760,000 sermons or homilies per year. But that number is almost certainly too low, as some congregations hold multiple services per Sunday, as well as multiple services per week.

[5] In 2018, the Society for Biblical Literature listed over 8,300 members. This would not capture all the members of other Bible societies, such as the Catholic Biblical Association. Nor would it capture the other religious scholars who write and speak about the Bible, but define themselves as scholars of religion or theologians or ethicists and do not hold membership in either society. See the Society for Biblical Literature website for details. www.sbl-site.org/assets/pdfs/sblMemberProfile2019.pdf, accessed April 30, 2020.

[6] "Introduction to the Federal Court System." www.justice.gov/usao/justice-101/federal-courts, accessed April 30, 2020. My thanks to Professor Timothy Gatton of Oklahoma City University School of Law for pointing me in the right direction for the scope of the number of legal decisions handed down annually.

[7] "FAQs: Judges in the United States," https://iaals.du.edu/sites/default/files/documents/publications/judge_faq.pdf?fbclid=IwAR0FCwf-xeXx7LPgQ-Z66K6i8MlmvY17VAfL-18WXzyzFci9FfCJk4jAyMug, accessed August 25, 2020. See also Bureau of Justice Statistics, State Court Caseload Statistics, www.bjs.gov/index.cfm?ty=tp&tid=30&fbclid=IwAR2rhrWdoAfzD2bmWwKbMFHsOFAdtgvmcijTfcosr5SVyItPuf5gxXsWTV8, accessed August 25, 2020.

The demonstration of the persistence of the problem Calvin faced suggests that learning from his example, as well as trying to find the solutions to the problems he faced, is incumbent upon this age.

BIBLICAL INTERPRETATION: THE LITERAL READING AND READING IN A TRADITION

In the mainline world, especially in the halls of the academy, it is easy to forget that reading in a tradition is not always accepted.[8] "Mainline" is a term that refers to Protestant churches that were clustered along the Philadelphia railroad line that ran through the wealthy and prestigious suburbs, and normally refers to the United Methodist Church, the Evangelical Lutheran Church in America, the Presbyterian Church (USA), the Episcopal Church, the American Baptist Church, the Disciples of Christ, and the United Church of Christ.[9] These denominations dominated white middle- and upper-class Christianity through the first three-quarters of the twentieth century in the United States of America.[10]

These denominations had a set of doctrinal norms that, while not identical, were close enough in character and witness that it was legitimate

---

[8] See Kathryn Tanner, "Postmodern Challenges to Tradition," *Louvain Studies* 28 (2003): 176. "There is a growing convergence between Protestants and Catholics on this issue, with most Protestants understanding scripture to be the product of Christian tradition, and many Catholics recognizing the priority within the Christian tradition of the apostolic witness. But more importantly, most Christian appeals to tradition nowadays are not functioning within Protestant-Catholic polemics, and therefore simply do not concern the relative weighting of scripture or tradition. They are instead intra-Protestant or intra-Catholic affairs, directed at opponents within one's own communion, who are therefore likely to share one's judgment about the relative weighting of scripture and tradition but perhaps not much else!" Tanner implies that issues between Protestants and Catholics have dropped away. Ten years after this, Robert Sungenis published the second edition of *Not By Scripture Alone: A Catholic Critique of the Protestant Doctrine of sola scriptura* (Goleta, CA: Queenship Publishing, 2013). In the introduction, Peter Kreeft argued that the solution to this problem would allow Protestants and Catholics to reunite. Further, Tanner seems to suggest that all Christians accept some form of a tradition.

[9] At any given point in history, these denominations might have different names. For instance, prior to 1988, the American Lutheran Church and the Lutheran Church in America were separate denominations though closely related, but somewhat geographically distinct. The two denominations joined in 1988 to form the Evangelical Lutheran Church in America.

[10] Robert P. Jones, *The End of White Christian America* (New York: Simon & Schuster, 2016), especially Chapter 1, "Who Is White Christian America?"

to speak of "mainline" or "mainstream" theology.[11] By the 1950s, all of these denominations generally accepted a historical-critical method of reading the scriptures. This would function for them as a "tradition," though almost no scholar would have used that language in the middle of the last century.[12]

Further, scholars with ties to these denominations dominated theological and religious education through most of the twentieth century. Schools such as Harvard Divinity School, Union Theological Seminary, Yale Divinity School, Princeton Theological Seminary, Andover Newton Theological School, Boston University School of Theology, Vanderbilt Divinity School, Candler School of Theology, the University of Chicago Divinity School, and Perkins School of Theology – all were founded by and for much of the last century staffed by overwhelmingly white, mainline Christians.[13] Further, smaller, regional, denominational seminaries were staffed by faculties who were trained by the scholars at these larger divinity schools and seminaries. The academic hegemony of such mainline scholarship was achieved to such a degree that some sociologically focused studies have discerned a difference between the pastors and the parishioners in their churches.[14]

---

[11] The literature on mainline Protestantism is vast. See, among others, Stephen Ellingsen, *The Megachurch and the Mainline: Remaking Religious Tradition in the Twenty-first Century* (Chicago: University of Chicago Press, 2007); Jason Lantzer, *Mainline Christianity: The Past and Future of America's Majority Faith* (New York: New York University Press, 2012); Margaret Lamberts Bendroth, *The Last Puritans: Mainline Protestants and the Power of the Past* (Chapel Hill: University of North Carolina Press, 2015); Randall Balmer, *Grant Us Courage: Travels Among the Mainline of American Protestantism* (New York: Oxford University Press, 1991); George Marsden, *The Soul of the American University: From Protestant Establishment to Established Nonbelief* (New York: Oxford University Press, 1994); Roger Finke and Rodney Stark, *The Churching of America, 1776–1990: Winners and Losers in Our Religious Economy* (New Brunswick: Rutgers University Press, 1992); Martin E. Marty, *The Public Church: Mainline, Evangelical, Catholic* (New York: Crossroad, 1981).

[12] The careful reader will have noted that I have written this about White Mainline Christians and White Evangelical Christians. That is purposeful, both because Black Christians have been systematically excluded from the power structures of these two groups, and because Black Christians in both the mainline and evangelical worlds act differently from their White counterparts.

[13] For a helpful overview of a number of the significant theological voices at these schools, see Gary Dorrien's *The Making of American Liberal Theology*, vol. 2 "Idealism, Realism, and Modernity, 1900–1950," and vol. 3 "Crisis, Irony, and Postmodernity, 1950–2005" (Louisville: Westminster John Knox Press, 2001–06).

[14] See, for instance, results of the Presbyterian Panel surveys by Presbyterian Mission Agency Research Services, www.presbyterianmission.org/ministries/research-services/, accessed May 1, 2020.

The hegemony of these denominations among white Christian America in the twentieth century concealed the enormous numerical strength of another group of white Christians in America in the twentieth century: the Evangelicals.[15] They came sharply into focus in the late twentieth century with the work of the Rev. Jerry Falwell and the Moral Majority, as well as other figures who used the new technological tools of Christian broadcasting and the culture wars to gain overwhelming pride of place in the mind of mainstream media.[16] This part of white Christian America has been one of the main foci of study of American Christianity since 1976, when *Newsweek* magazine declared that year to be the "Year of the Evangelical."[17] This has been true in both scholarly and popular offerings.[18]

American evangelicalism is a broad phenomenon, which ranges from conservative Christianity to an "identity politics marker" for certain white cultural Christians who rarely if ever attend church.[19] For "religious evangelicals," the definition that is most frequently used is the "Bebbington quadrilateral." Helpfully, this set of characteristics is also accepted by the National Association of Evangelicals.[20] These include

---

[15] That hegemony also masked the growing numerical and cultural power of American Catholicism. For the purposes of this study, I am not including them.

[16] For an excellent recent study of white evangelicalism, see Kristin Kobes Du Mez' *Jesus and John Wayne: How White Evangelicals Corrupted a Faith and Fractured a Nation* (New York: Liveright, 2020).

[17] Jon Meacham, "The Editor's Desk," *Newsweek*, November 12, 2006. www.newsweek .com/editors-desk-106637, accessed January 5, 2020.

[18] Among the studies that are frequently considered, see George Marsden, ed. *Evangelicalism and Modern America* (Grand Rapids: Eerdmans, 1984); Randall Balmer, *Mine Eyes Have Seen the Glory: A Journey into the Evangelical Subculture in America* (New York: Oxford University Press, 1989); David Bebbington, *Evangelicalism in Modern Britain: A History from the 1730s to the 1980s* (London: Unwin Hyman, 1989); Randall Balmer, *Thy Kingdom Come: How the Religious Right Distorts the Faith and Threatens America: An Evangelical's Lament* (New York: Basic Books, 2006); Frances Fitzgerald, *The Evangelicals: The Struggle to Shape America* (New York: Simon & Schuster, 2017); Thomas S. Kidd, *Who is an Evangelical? The History of a Movement in Crisis* (New Haven: Yale University Press, 2019); Mark Noll, *The Scandal of the Evangelical Mind* (Grand Rapids: Eerdmans, 2010); Mark Noll, David Bebbington and George Marsden, *Evangelicals: Who They Have Been, Are Now, and Could Be* (Grand Rapids: Eerdmans, 2019); Kathleen M. Sands, *America's Religious Wars: The Embattled Heart of Our Public Life* (New Haven: Yale University Press, 2019); and Du Mez, *Jesus and John Wayne*.

[19] Thomas S. Kidd, *Who is an Evangelical? The History of a Movement in Crisis* (New Haven: Yale University Press, 2019), 154.

[20] National Association of Evangelicals, www.nae.net/what-is-an-evangelical/, accessed May 3, 2020.

biblicism, crucicentrism, conversionism, and activism.[21] Biblicism refers to the centrality of the Bible and a literal approach to it in the life of Evangelicals.[22] Crucicentrism denotes the importance of the cross for Evangelicals, who will speak of the necessity of being washed in Jesus' blood. Conversionism is a concentration upon a conversion experience, normally able to be dated, with an invitation of Jesus into an evangelical's heart and life. Activism is the most diffuse and can mean evangelical witness that seeks to convert others, or it can mean activity in the community that seeks to follow the gospel or that seeks to make the society more Christian. Thus, this covers evangelism, acts of charity, and political work. In biblicism, many Evangelicals argue that their positions come from a literal acceptance of the words and authority of the Bible. Darryl Hart points this out, and the effect it has upon evangelical ecclesiastical authority and communal life.[23]

My argument here is not that biblical literalism is wrong, but that the idea of a biblically literal community is in itself a tradition. Every "biblically literal" community of faith decides subconsciously that certain passages are not meant literally, or that they should be glossed over or not considered. Proving this is fairly easy. Jesus said, "If your right eye causes

---

[21] Bebbington, *Evangelicalism in Modern Britain*, 2–17. The four characteristics were a concentration on the authority of the Bible, frequently read literally; a concentration on the salvific work of Jesus Christ; a concentration on conversion, frequently with a call for a dated moment of "accepting Jesus"; and the belief that the entire world should be brought to Christ. These are termed biblicism, crucicentrism, conversionism, and activism. While this is useful, it does not cover the breadth of American evangelicalism in the present day. Kristen Kobes Du Mez has argued that a better sense of White evangelicalism in the United States would be found through examining its consumer culture and militant masculinity. Du Mez, *Jesus and John Wayne: How White Evangelicals Corrupted a Faith and Fractured a Nation* (New York: Liveright, 2020.)

[22] It is important to point out that what Calvin meant by the "plain sense," was never pure literalism, and in fact many analysts have pointed out that his "plain sense" included a variety of senses of signification. See, among others, R. Ward Holder, *John Calvin and the Grounding of Interpretation: Calvin's First Commentaries* (Leiden: Brill, 2006); Gary Neal Hansen, "John Calvin and the Non-Literal Interpretation of Scripture," Ph.D. diss., Princeton Theological Seminary, 1998; Randall C. Zachman, "Expounding Scripture and Applying It to Our Use: Calvin's Sermons on Ephesians." *Scottish Journal of Theology* 56 (2003): 481–507; Zachman, "'Do You Understand What You Are Reading?': Calvin's Guidance for the Reading of Scripture." *Scottish Journal of Theology* 54 (2001): 1–20; Hans-Joachim Kraus, "Calvins exegetische Prinzipien," *Zeitschrift fur Kirchengeschichte* 79 (1968): 329–41.

[23] Darryl G. Hart, "No Creed but the Bible, No Authority without the Church: American Evangelicals and the Errors of Inerrancy," in *Interdisciplinary Perspectives on the Authority of Scripture: Historical, Biblical, and Theoretical Perspectives*, edited by Carlos Bovell (Eugene: Wipf & Stock, 2011), 3–27.

you to sin, tear it out and throw it away; it is better for you to lose one of your members than for your whole body to be thrown into hell. And if your right hand causes you to sin, cut it off and throw it away; it is better for you to lose one of your members than for your whole body to go into hell."[24] But attending an evangelical church, whether in Massachusetts or California, Alaska or Alabama, will not produce a greater number of one-eyed believers, or amputees, than the wider population.

Of course, the argument will immediately be made that Jesus meant this metaphorically, or state that this is a *reductio ad absurdum*. So it is important to deal with passages that Evangelicals agree are not meant metaphorically. I shall consider three. The first has to do with women's ordination. The second concerns the acceptance of homosexuals who continue to practice their homosexuality in committed relationships and, since 2015 with the Supreme Court decision in Obergefell versus Hodges, in marriages.[25] The third deals with evangelical ideals of Christianity and the nation. In each case, to avoid the creation of a straw man, I will discuss a particular example from a specific theologian.

The first example involves the Rev. Dr. Timothy Keller, founder of Redeemer Presbyterian Church in Manhattan.[26] Keller was noted as one of the most significant preachers in American Christianity prior to his retirement.[27] While he was known for his winsome style, Keller had no room for women in ministry. He argued this in a blog post in 2008, entitled "Women in Ministry."[28] In it, Keller laments the divisions in evangelical Christianity and sets forth the foundations for women in ministry at Redeemer. Keller turns to 1 Corinthians 11.3, and in it, links

---

[24] Matthew 5.29–30, *The New Oxford Annotated Bible, New Revised Standard Version*, edited by Bruce M. Metzger and Roland E. Murphy (New York: Oxford University Press, 1991). All further citations to this version by book, chapter, and verse.

[25] Thus proving Diarmaid MacCulloch right that the issue of the Bible is being stressed by issues of sexuality in the modern era. See Diarmaid MacCulloch, *The Reformation: A History* (New York: Penguin Books, 2003), 705.

[26] Timothy Keller website, https://timothykeller.com/author, accessed May 3, 2020. Keller's denomination is called Presbyterian, but definitely is not part of the mainline. His work was within the Presbyterian Church of America, a conservative and evangelical denomination that traced its roots to the fundamentalist-modernist debates in the early twentieth century.

[27] Kate Shellnutt, "Tim Keller, John Piper, and Andy Stanley Among the 12 'Most Effective' Preachers," *Christianity Today*, May 2, 2018. www.christianitytoday.com/news/2018/may/tim-keller-john-piper-andy-stanley-most-effective-preachers.html, accessed May 3, 2020.

[28] https://blogs.thegospelcoalition.org/scottysmith/2008/08/14/titleitems/, accessed May 3, 2020.

the question of women in ministry to "the Trinitarian Pattern." In expositing his complementarian theology, Keller argues that biblical headship involves voluntary, respectful submission between equals. Using the model of the Trinity, he points out that the Father and the Son are equal in all regards. However, the Son voluntarily took on a subordinate role in obedience to the Father for our salvation.[29]

Thus, Keller concludes that "headship" is something granted by one to another, and that in this relationship both are equal. The "head" has real and final authority but uses it only to serve and please and build up the giver. He links this to Paul's way of thinking about the relationship between men and women and says that since Paul argues that it is in the order of creation, it cannot ever be changed. The office of elder is forbidden to women. Keller balances this with women being able to take a variety of roles in society, which he fully endorses.

Keller turns to two common objections that evangelical feminists raise in answer to his exposition of Paul. The first is that Paul was writing to specific occasions that no longer apply. The second is more radical: Paul was in error about women in ministry. Keller disposes with the first by pointing out that Paul's letters are actually letters, that they are always to specific occasions that in some sense must be applied outside their original context. He takes up the second point with a set of stories that taken together make the case that if the exegete is able to note that Paul is wrong, the entire enterprise of biblical literalism – which is the heart of evangelicalism – falls apart. He ends his consideration with a conclusion that there can be no actual evangelical feminism.

One could argue with Keller by claiming the importance of Galatians 3.28, but that would not move the discussion further. Instead, it is important to concentrate upon Keller's own arguments to demonstrate their character as a tradition rather than a simple recourse to the text. First, Keller denies the possibility of dividing between the timeless and the occasional or specific messages in Paul's writings. He argues that to do so would be to derive a canon within the canon, which is to fail to listen to all of God's revelation. Second, he argues that Paul cannot be judged to be in error – Christians must live in submission to the scripture and cannot choose to reject parts of it.

---

[29] Beth Allison Barr points out that strictly speaking, this was heretical – because it placed one of the persons of the Trinity in a subordinate role to another. See *The Making of Biblical Womanhood: How the Subjugation of Women Became Gospel Truth* (Grand Rapids: Brazos Press, 2021), 191–97.

Therefore, it is important either to demonstrate that Keller has divided between timeless and timebound messages, or one must argue that Paul was in error. I will do the first, though Paul being in error is involved. The passage to discuss comes directly after 1 Corinthians 11.3–8, on which Keller had concentrated in his blog post. One pertinent question is: Why stop there? There seem to be several things that Paul wrote they don't obey. The most obvious is the continuation of the passage of which Keller approved – about the husband being the head of the wife, in 1 Corinthians 11.3. When readers proceed further in the passage, they find:

Any man who prays or prophesies with something on his head disgraces his head, but any woman who prays or prophesies with her head unveiled disgraces her head – it is one and the same thing as having her head shaved. For if a woman will not veil herself, then she should cut off her hair; but if it is disgraceful for a woman to have her hair cut off or to be shaved, she should wear a veil. For a man ought not to have his head veiled, since he is the image and reflection of God; but woman is the reflection of man.[30]

Paul became more specific about the order of nature – one of Keller's top priorities – in verses 13–15. "Judge for yourselves: is it proper for a woman to pray to God with her head unveiled? Does not nature itself teach you that if a man wears long hair, it is degrading to him, but if a woman has long hair, it is her glory? For her hair is given to her for a covering."[31]

The history of Reformed interpretation of this passage offers an interesting response to Keller. Calvin's 1546 commentary on 1 Corinthians, published by Wendelin Rihel in Strasbourg, took on this particular passage. In a comment upon v. 14. Calvin wrote:

Paul again sets nature before them as the teacher of what is proper. Now, he means by 'natural' what was accepted by common consent and usage at that time, certainly as far as the Greeks were concerned. For long hair was not always regarded as a disgraceful thing in men. Historical works relate that long ago, i.e., in the earliest times, men wore long hair in every country. Thus the poets are in the habit of speaking about the ancients and applying to them the well-worn epithet "unshorn." In Rome, they did not begin to use barbers until a late period, about the time of Africanus the Elder. When Paul was writing these words, the practice of cutting hair had not yet been adopted in Gaul and Germany. Yes, and more than that, indeed, it would have been a disgraceful thing for men, just as much as women, to have their hair shaved or cut. But since the Greeks

---

[30] 1 Corinthians 11.4–8.
[31] 1 Corinthians 11.13–15.

did not consider it very manly to have long hair, branding those who had it as effeminate, Paul considers that their custom, accepted in his own day was in conformity with nature.[32]

Calvin went out of his way to demonstrate that even though Paul was factually incorrect, he had good reasons for believing that the customs of his day (*morem*) were actually the order of nature.[33] But Calvin was also clear that this was not the order of nature – not something decreed by God. Keller's principles make clear that he cannot accept Calvin's solution – because Paul cannot be wrong.

Keller's practice, and the practice at Redeemer, however, demonstrate that this is an example of a passage that must be handled by a reading tradition. This is not a passage that should be considered for edification. In fact, the websites of the Redeemer congregations demonstrate time and again women in staff positions who have cut their hair short. This is also true of the members. The fact is that Keller's interpretive principles about women are not sustained through a single chapter in Paul.

The great majority of biblically based Christians would define this entire discussion as "adiaphora," meaning things that are indifferent. This was a significant issue in the era of the Reformations, when battles were fought over what elements of worship and doctrine actually were indifferent as to a believer's salvation. But Keller, having said that nothing in Paul can be either wrong or culturally conditioned, cannot make that point.

Still, some readers will reject this discussion of women's hair and the order of nature as beneath the dignity of a truly theological discussion. Therefore, it is worthwhile to consider an issue that has been at the forefront of American evangelical attention since well before 2015 – the possibility of homosexual marriage. Since 2015, with the Supreme Court

---

[32] John Calvin, *Commentary on I Corinthians*, CNTC 9.235. CO 49.478. "Iterum naturam illis decori magistram proponit. Quod autem omnium consensu et consuetudine receptum tunc erat, et quidem apud Graecos, vocat naturale: nam viris non semper fuit coma dedecori. Olim ubique viros fuisse comatos, hoc est, primis sacculis, referunt historiae. Unde et poetae vocare solent intonsos veteres trito epitheto. Sero tonsoribus Romae uti coeperunt, circa aetatem Aphricani superioris. Et quo tempore scribebat haec Paulus, nondum in Galliis et Germania invaluerat tondendi usus. Quin potius deforme fuisset non minus viris quam mulieribus, radi aut tonderi: sed quoniam in Graecia parum virile erat alere comam, ut tales quasi effeminati notarentur: morem iam confirmatum pro natura habet."

[33] See Holder, *John Calvin and the Grounding of Interpretation*, 106–07.

decision of Obergefell versus Hodges, gay marriage has been legal in the United States. But this legality has not influenced the mainstream of evangelical considerations of the question. An example comes from the Rev. Dr. Gordon Hugenberger.

Gordon Hugenberger was pastor at one of the most celebrated evangelical pulpits in America, Park Street Church in Boston, serving as senior pastor from 1997 to 2017. He earned a baccalaureate degree from Harvard, a Master's of Divinity from Gordon Conwell, and a doctorate in Old Testament from the College of St. Paul and St. Mary in Cheltenham, England, and also studied at the Oxford Centre for Postgraduate Hebrew Studies in Oxford, England. Park Street Church is a historic congregational church, dating back to 1804, and has supplied an extraordinary amount of leadership not only to Boston's Evangelicals but also the evangelical movement across the United States.[34]

In 2004, Hugenberger set out why Park Street Church did not accept homosexual practice (which he consistently differentiated from homosexual orientation).[35] Hugenberger framed the theological opinion as an answer to a question.[36] He began by noting that all evangelical denominations of which he was aware, as well as a great variety of evangelical institutions, were unanimous in rejecting homosexual practice. Hugenberger then dealt with Paul, including his pronouncement in Romans 1 about sinners being given up to degrading passions. While the arguments that Hugenberger made were well recognized by those who have followed this issue, he deployed them skillfully.

Then Hugenberger turned to the Old Testament. Hugenberger quoted Leviticus 18.22: "Do not lie with a man as one lies with a woman; that is detestable."[37] Hugenberger pointed out the universality of the

---

[34] The Rev. Dr. Harold Ockenga, pastor from 1936 to 1969, also served as the founding President of Fuller Theological Seminary from 1947 to 1954, and the founding president of Gordon-Conwell Theological Seminary from 1969 to 1979. The Rev. Dr. Hugenberger served as a faculty member at Gordon-Conwell.

[35] https://web.archive.org/web/20121223042151/http://www.parkstreet.org/qa_homosexuality, accessed May 4, 2020.

[36] "Dear Gordon, We love the fact that Park Street Church stresses the Gospel of Christ, but it doesn't get stressed out about so many of the secondary issues which seem to divide Christians (baptism, Charismatic gifts, style of worship, etc.). We sense, however, that there is not a similar openness to various points of view about the ethics of homosexuality. Why? Isn't this an issue over which sincere Christians disagree? After all, Jesus never condemned homosexuality, and Paul only condemned heterosexuals who engaged in homosexual acts, which were 'unnatural' for them. Sincerely, Puzzled."

[37] Hugenberger cited the form above. Leviticus 18.22, NRSV states: "You shall not lie with a male as with a woman; it is an abomination."

prohibition, covering both promiscuity and long-term committed relationships. Hugenberger cited a number of statistics to promote the idea
that one could be healed of homosexual practice, and began his conclusion with the statement that "Finally, although I probably don't need to
say this, I do want to emphasize that I do NOT consider homosexuality
to be worse than any of the zillion sins I commit every day." Hugenberger
emphasized that he would minister to homosexual and heterosexual persons, and that his position was necessary in a culture that increasingly
allowed only one side to be heard.[38]

Of course, Hugenberger's position was not as welcoming as he suggested. Park Street Church does not permit homosexual marriages, nor
does it support ministries to help heterosexual men and women depart from
problematic heterosexual practices. But most important was Hugenberger's
acceptance of the passage from Leviticus. This is early in Leviticus 17–27,
which is called the Holiness Code.[39] Hugenberger's use of it means that
he believes that the Holiness Code is binding upon Christians. He will
not make a Pauline move, that Christ has abolished the law in order that
believers might be saved by faith, to evade the ceremonial law.

This is highly problematic for any theologian trying to generate a literal hermeneutic for the Old Testament. To read the Holiness Code literally, the following would have to be put in place. All wages for anyone
would have to be paid daily.[40] No garments made of two different materials could be worn.[41] No tattoos could be worn.[42] No aliens could be
oppressed, but must be loved as oneself.[43] The penalty for adultery must
be death.[44] Those who own land must allow it to lie fallow as a sabbath
every seventh year.[45] Doctrinal positions that draw a distinction between
the works of the law and faith allow a way out of this conundrum, but

---

[38] Hugenberger's statement of necessity represents a political gambit in white evangelicalism in America in the early twenty-first century. Though white evangelicals are part of
the majority culture, with all the privileges that entails, they define any expansion of
rights for those who have customarily been marginalized as an attack on their freedom
of religion and freedom of speech. See Gerardo Martí, "The Unexpected Orthodoxy
of Donald J. Trump: White Evangelical Support for the 45th President of the United
States," *Sociology of Religion: A Quarterly Review* 80 (2019): 1–8; for a discussion of
this phenomenon.

[39] Samuel E. Balentine, *Leviticus* (Louisville: Westminster John Knox Press, 2002), 141–209.

[40] Leviticus 19.13.

[41] Leviticus 19.19.

[42] Leviticus 19.28.

[43] Leviticus 19.33–34.

[44] Leviticus 20.10.

[45] Leviticus 25.3–4.

Hugenberger's position did not. If his position that homosexuality was to be seen as no worse a sin than all of these others, then Park Street Church should have been hosting efforts to save people from tattoos, or wool clothing with leather adornment. There would have to be an outreach to aliens that saw them as the children of God, rather than a political problem and wedge issue.

Again, the point of this exercise is not to determine whether Gordon Hugenberger's theology was sufficient. Instead, it is to draw out evidence that leads to the conclusion that the biblicism or biblical literalism practiced at Park Street Church is a tradition in its own right. Those experienced in the tradition know to look to the Holiness Code only for certain passages, and allow others to fade into the history of the children of Israel. That is the mark of a reading or interpretive tradition.

One concluding example may suffice. While MacCulloch's theory that authority was being broken over issues of human sexuality has some cogency, it is not wholly sufficient to explain the model of breakdown in communication and understanding between the different segments of Christianity as the end of the second decade of the third millennium of the Christian era arrives. Another has to do with economic distribution of goods or distributive justice. In the presidential campaign of 2016 in the United States, Donald Trump faced Hillary Clinton. On October 7, the *Washington Post* released a video and article about Trump's behavior in 2005 during a taping of *Access Hollywood*.[46] During the ensuing uproar, evangelical theologian Wayne Grudem retracted an earlier blog post that opined that voting for Donald Trump was a morally good choice. On October 9, Grudem retracted his first post and put up another, "Trump's Moral Character and the Election."[47] But after Trump excused the language as "locker-room talk," and said it had never actually happened in a televised debate, Grudem removed his second post, replaced it with the first, and added a third, titled, "If You Don't Like Either Candidate, Then Vote for Trump's Policies."[48]

---

[46] David Farenthold, "Trump Recorded Having Extremely Lewd Conversation about Women in 2005" *Washington Post*, October 8, 2016 www.washingtonpost.com/politics/trump-recorded-having-extremely-lewd-conversation-about-women-in-2005/2016/10/07/3b9ce776-8cb4-11e6-bf8a-3d26847eeed4_story.html, accessed May 4, 2020.

[47] Wayne Grudem, *Townhall*, October 9, 2016. https://townhall.com/columnists/waynegrudem/2016/10/09/trumps-moral-character-and-the-election-n2229846, accessed May 4, 2020.

[48] Wayne Grudem, *Townhall*, October 19, 2016. https://townhall.com/columnists/waynegrudem/2016/10/19/if-you-dont-like-either-candidate-then-vote-for-trumps-policies-n2234187, accessed May 4, 2020.

Wayne Grudem is a significant voice in American white evangelicalism. He was educated at Harvard, with an M.Div. from Westminster Theological Seminary in Philadelphia, and a doctorate in New Testament from Cambridge. He has taught at Trinity Evangelical Divinity School in Deerfield, Illinois, and now teaches at Phoenix Seminary. He co-founded the Council on Biblical Manhood and Womanhood with John Piper. The purpose of that council is the promulgation of complementarian views of men and women. Grudem has written and published *Systematic Theology: An Introduction to Biblical Doctrine*, a best-seller in evangelical seminaries. His blog posts were seen and considered by a significant portion of White Evangelicals.

In his listing of the reasons why Christians should vote for Trump, Grudem included a consideration of Trump's desired tax policy. He wrote: "Trump has pledged to cut taxes significantly, while Clinton wants to raise them. Trump is advocating a 15% tax rate for corporations rather than the current 35%. Lower corporate taxes would lead to business expansion and a massive increase in available jobs and higher pay levels."[49] He ended that section with a wave toward the correct size of government: "Tax rates are also a good indicator of government control. Higher tax rates mean greater government control of our lives, while lower tax rates indicate greater freedom."[50] But the New Testament does not speak about the proper size of taxes, only that Jesus said his disciples should pay them.[51] Neither does the New Testament speak about the right kind of government, only that believers should obey it.[52]

Grudem added to his list of issues by arguing that believers should vote for Trump because "Trump has promised to rapidly rebuild our depleted military forces, but Clinton would continue the liberal policy of eviscerating them through denying funding."[53] Jesus specifically said, "My kingdom is not from this world."[54] Jesus directed his followers not

---

[49] Grudem, "If You Don't Like Either Candidate."
[50] Grudem, "If You Don't Like Either Candidate."
[51] Matthew 22.21. See also Romans 13.6–7.
[52] Romans 13.1–7.
[53] Grudem, "If You Don't Like Either Candidate." Du Mez points out that Grudem grew more political during the Obama administration, publishing *Politics – According to the Bible: A Comprehensive Resource for Understanding Modern Political Issues in Light of Scripture* (Grand Rapids: Zondervan Publishing, 2010). In it, Grudem attacked immigration, both legal and illegal, and embraced military strength for the United States. See Du Mez, *Jesus and John Wayne*, 239–40.
[54] John 18.36.

to fight, but to turn the other cheek.[55] Grudem could make the argument that many Christian realist political theologians might make, that since the United States' enemies will not lay down their weapons, the country is obliged to make preparation for war. But Christian realists recognize that the way in which they are reading the scripture participates in a very specific tradition, rather than merely representing a literal rendering. Grudem has made no such claim, because to do so would overturn one of the most basic points of evangelical authority.

My point throughout these three examples has not been to attempt to win a theological or cultural battle. Instead, it has been to identify the reading or interpretive tradition that is at the root of evangelical theology. Instead of the simple appeal to the scripture, purified of any outside influence, evangelical theology regularly sets out a collection of presuppositions that illustrate the manner in which evangelical appeals to the literal scripture occur from within a tradition.[56] This is true of matters that would seem to be morally indifferent – such as the length of women's hair, as well as matters of great cultural and moral significance – such as whom people may love.

CONSTITUTIONAL INTERPRETATION: ORIGINALISM AND LIVING CONSTITUTIONALISM

Though Protestant biblical interpretation has, in the modern era, settled into a number of camps that are confessionally based, Constitutional interpretation is not divided in the same manner. Constitutional law affects the entire community or nation; various segments of the country, different though they may be, are all affected by the same courts. The closest analog to the mainline versus evangelical differentiation would be the delineation of the different circuit courts – that have reputations as liberal or conservative. But this is not the same at all: Liberal citizens who live under the jurisdiction of the 5th Circuit Court of Appeals cannot go to a different court and pay no attention to the interpretation of the law from that court, no matter how conservative it might appear.[57]

---

[55] Matthew 5.39.

[56] In attempting to illustrate this point briefly, several key points have been left out. Most urgent among these are the manners in which "literal reading" has been used to support racism, sexism, colonialism, globalism, and xenophobia.

[57] Emma Platoff, "Trump-Appointed Judges are Shifting the Country's Most Politically Conservative Circuit Court further to the Right," *Texas Tribune*, August 30, 2018 www.texastribune.org/2018/08/30/under-trump-5th-circuit-becoming-even-more-conservative/, accessed May 5, 2020; Andreas Broscheid, "Comparing Circuits: Are Some U.S. Courts of Appeals More Liberal or Conservative Than Others?" *Law & Society Review* 45 (2011): 171–94.

However, once one steps over that difference, one realizes that the interpretation of the Constitution, and thus the backbone of legal theory, in many ways mirrors the differences in biblical exegesis. The most widely espoused theory of interpretation among conservative legal scholars and judges is called originalism. This is balanced by a theory that is sometimes called living constitutionalism. In point of fact, a wide variety of interpretive theories exist, including textualism, originalism, judicial precedent, pragmatism, and moral reasoning.[58] But the greatest issue is between originalism, which argues that it is a textually based theory, and something that is usually called living constitutionalism.[59] In part this is because of the importance of the conservative Federalist Society and its influence in choosing justices for the federal courts.[60] The Federalist Society members are almost all proponents of originalism.

Originalism's chief proponent in the last few decades has been Associate Supreme Court Justice Antonin Scalia (1936–2016). Scalia spoke often on the virtues of originalism, and the flaws in the opposing position, which he called "non-originalism." Justice Scalia was not an ivory tower academic and saw little advantage to engaging in academic reserve in his rhetoric. He wrote:

It may surprise the layman, but it will surely not surprise the lawyers here, to learn that originalism is not, and had perhaps never been, the sole method of constitutional exegesis. It would be hard to count ... the opinions that have in fact been rendered not on the basis of what the Constitution originally meant, but on the basis of what the judges currently thought it desirable for it to mean.[61]

Scalia believed that only originalism could be the kind of legal interpretation that saw the Constitution as a set of laws. His contempt for other forms of legal interpretation was clear, he wrote about those who did not support originalism:

If the law is to make any attempt at consistency and predictability, surely there must be general agreement not only that judges reject one exegetical approach (originalism) but also that they adopt another. And it is hard to discern any emerging consensus among the nonoriginalists as to what this might be. Are the

---

[58] Brandon J. Murrill, "Modes of Constitutional Interpretation," *Congressional Research Service*, March 15, 2018.

[59] David A. Strauss, *The Living Constitution* (New York: Oxford University Press, 2010).

[60] Carl Hulse, "Appeals Court Vacancy Is Under Scrutiny Ahead of Contested Confirmation Hearing," *New York Times*, May 4, 2020. www.nytimes.com/2020/05/04/us/politics/senate-confirmation-justin-walker.html, accessed May 5, 2020.

[61] Hon. Antonin Scalia, "Originalism: The Lesser Evil," *University of Cincinnati Law Review* 57 (1989): 849–65.

'fundamental values' that replace original meaning to be derived from the philosophy of Plato, or of Locke, or Mills, or Rawls, or perhaps from the latest Gallup poll?[62]

Because of its significance at the federal court level, and its notoriety in the public imagination, large numbers of articles have been written about originalism in the popular press.[63] This has been mirrored in the legal community as well, with the consideration of a large number of legal scholars who have engaged originalism in law review articles.[64] Originalism is a textual epistemological effort, much like biblical literalism. Keith Whittington wrote:

At its most basic, originalism argues that the discoverable public meaning of the Constitution at the time of its original adoption should be regarded as authoritative for purposes of later constitutional interpretation. The text of the Constitution itself, including its structural design, is a primary source of that public meaning, but extrinsic sources of specifically historical information might also

---

[62] Scalia, "Originalism."

[63] A small sample could include Aaron Blake, "Neil Gorsuch, Antonin Scalia and Originalism, Explained," *Washington Post*, February 1, 2017, www.washingtonpost.com/news/the-fix/wp/2017/02/01/neil-gorsuch-antonin-scalia-and-originalism-explained/, accessed May 5, 2020; Will Baude, "Does Originalism Constrain Conservative Judges?" *Washington Post*, August 28, 2017 www.washingtonpost.com/news/volokh-conspiracy/wp/2017/08/28/does-originalism-constrain-conservative-judges/, accessed May 5, 2020; Eric J. Segall, "Does Originalism Matter Anymore?" *New York Times*, September 10, 2018 www.nytimes.com/2018/09/10/opinion/kavanaugh-originalism-supreme-court.html, accessed May 5, 2020.

[64] A small sample of the last decade would include David A. Strauss, "Can Originalism Be Saved?" *Boston University Law Review* 92 (2012): 1161–70; Ernest A. Young, "Dying Constitutionalism and the 14th Amendment," *Marquette Law Review* 102 (2019): 949–78; Jack M. Balkin, "Nine Perspectives on Living Originalism," *University of Illinois Law Review* (2012): 815–76; Mitchell N. Berman and Kevin Toh, "On What Distinguishes New Originalism from Old: A Jurisprudential Take," *Fordham Law Review* 82 (2013): 545–76; James E. Fleming, "Living Originalism and Living Constitutionalism as Moral Readings of the American Constitution," *Boston University Law Review* 92 (2012): 1171–85; Keith E. Whittington, "Originalism: A Rationalization for Conservatism or a Principled Theory of Interpretation?: Is Originalism Too Conservative?" *Harvard Journal of Law and Public Policy* 34 (2011): 29–41; S. L. Whitesell, "The Church of Originalism," *University of Pennsylvania Journal of Constitutional Law* 16 (2014): 1531–68; Logan E. Sawyer III, "Principle and Politics in the New History of Originalism," *American Journal of Legal History* 57 (2017): 198–221; Peter J. Smith and Robert W. Tuttle, "Biblical Literalism and Constitutional Originalism," *Notre Dame Law Review* 86 (2011): 693–762; William Baude, "Is Originalism Our Law?," *Columbia Law Review* 115 (2015): 2349–408; Thomas B. Colby, "The Sacrifice of the New Originalism," *Georgetown Law Journal* 99 (2011): 713–78; and Lawrence B. Solum, "Originalism versus Living Constitutionalism: The Conceptual Structure of the Great Debate," *Northwestern University Law Review* 113 (2019): 1243–95.

elucidate principles embodied in the text of the Constitution. Each textual provision must necessarily bear the meaning attributed to it at the time of its own adoption."[65]

The text of the Constitution, understood at the time of its writing and ratification, presents the truth that judges should find. Originalist scholars and judges offer derogatory considerations of other methods of interpretation. Associate Supreme Court Justice Clarence Thomas stated that "there are really only two ways to interpret the Constitution – try to discern as best we can what the framers intended or make it up."[66]

The most important issue for the analysis of this study is the notion that originalism is a claim that textual truth outweighs all other claims to the truth. Context, other than the context of the original thinkers who created the Constitution or the Congress that passed an amendment or a law, is meaningless, as are the consequences of the positions taken.[67] Much like biblical literalism, the originalist constitutional advocates argue that adding anything such as the ethos of the nation to the text and original meaning of the Constitution introduces not only errors but also chaos.

But do the advocates of constitutional originalism stay within the narrow boundaries of the text of the Constitution? To consider that, I will discuss three Supreme Court cases with opinions and votes that came from self-avowed constitutional originalists. Again, these are cases chosen to demonstrate that this issue is not a phantasm of fevered minds, but an issue that impacts judicial decision-making. I will consider the issue of campaign spending and free speech, the idea that corporations have the rights of persons, and the issue of the free exercise of religion. The outcome of these will suggest, though not prove in such a brief consideration, that constitutional originalism is itself a reading tradition, with a certain specific tradition of rules and expansions that arrive at a set of desired outcomes.

---

[65] Keith E. Whittington, "Originalism: A Critical Introduction," *Fordham Law Review* 85 (2013): 377–78.

[66] The Honorable Clarence Thomas, "Judging in a Government by Consent," 2008 Wriston Lecture to the Manhattan Institute, quoted by Segall, "Does Originalism Matter Anymore?"

[67] Thus denying the preferred approach of Associate Justice Stephen Breyer, who argued in favor of an interpretation that took heed of consequences. See the Honorable Stephen Breyer, "Our Democratic Constitution," in the *New York University Law Review* 77 (2002): 245–72. Breyer wrote, "At the same time, my discussion will illustrate an approach to constitutional interpretation that places considerable weight upon consequences – consequences valued in terms of basic constitutional purposes" (246–47).

In considering the freedom of speech, one thorny question has been whether the expenditure of money is speech that is protected or bribery that is illegal. In 2010, in Citizens United versus FEC, the court struck down the longstanding doctrine that corporations could not spend unlimited sums in the political process. Arguing that money was speech and that corporations were, for political purposes, people with rights, the majority struck down most restrictions upon corporate donations. Justice Antonin Scalia, the leading polemicist for originalism, argued against the dissent of Justice John Paul Stevens. But Scalia's argument is odd for an originalist. He wrote:

Even if we thought it proper to apply the dissent's approach of excluding from First Amendment coverage what the Founders disliked, and even if we agreed that the Founders disliked founding-era corporations; modern corporations might not qualify for exclusion. Most of the Founders' resentment towards corporations was directed at the state-granted monopoly privileges that individually chartered corporations enjoyed. Modern corporations do not have such privileges, and would probably have been favored by most of our enterprising Founders – excluding, perhaps, Thomas Jefferson and others favoring perpetuation of an agrarian society.[68]

Scalia's argument may be correct logically.[69] But it mangles originalist principles – what the Founders believed is exchanged for what they may have believed had they known about the benefits of modern corporations. Further, Scalia made it clear that one of the founders, Jefferson, clearly did not accept his reasoning. But given the societal goods that Scalia saw from the majority opinion, the founder's reasoning had to be set aside. That is simply another way of saying "living constitutionalism."

In 2014, in McCutcheon versus FEC, the court made a move toward seeing all spending of money as free speech. The court, on April 2, 2014, handed down a decision that held that Section 441 of the Federal Election Campaign Act, which imposed limits on contributions an individual can make over a two-year period to national party and federal candidate committees, is unconstitutional. The decision was 5–4, and

[68] Honorable Antonin Scalia, Citizens United v. Federal Election Comm'n, 558 U.S. 310 (2010) https://supreme.justia.com/cases/federal/us/558/310/#tab-opinion-1963048, accessed May 6, 2020.

[69] Segall notes, "But Scalia did not make any effort in Citizens United, or anywhere else, to demonstrate that anyone living in 1791 would have privileged corporate political speech over legislative efforts to combat corruption." Eric J. Segall, "The Constitution According to Justices Scalia and Thomas: Alive and Kickin'." *Washington University Law* Review 91 (2014): 1665.

the five assenting justices were Roberts, Scalia, Alito, and Kennedy, with Thomas voting with the majority but writing a separate opinion. Justice Thomas wrote that "the Founding Fathers thought that political speech was vitally important and needed special protection under the First Amendment."[70] That makes perfect sense: the First Amendment in the Bill of Rights enshrines the freedom of speech. However, Thomas made no effort to claim that in 1790, when the Constitution was being ratified, that the framers believed in the necessity of large sums of money being given to political action committees or candidates. Absent that clear statement in the text, Thomas seems to have filled in the gap with his own sense of what was proper. In both cases, the originalist position is exchanged for something that fits the context and conventions of the modern world.

Another constellation of issues arises when the court takes up the freedom of religion. Again, there is no doubt that the establishment clause protects the freedom of religious belief and practice. But how far that could go has long been a controverted point. Does Jefferson's "wall of separation between Church and State," from his letter to the Danbury Baptists of 1802, truly set out what the framers intended? The court has regularly had to consider this. One such case was Trinity Lutheran Church of Columbia, Inc. versus Comer, Director, Missouri Department of Natural Resources. Justice Gorsuch joined Justice Thomas and the other conservative members of the court in striking down a nineteenth-century section of the Missouri State Constitution that prohibited public money from going directly to religious institutions. Their broadly worded concurring opinion did not even reference the original meaning of the First Amendment's "free exercise" clause.[71] Both Justice Sotomayor and Justice Ginzburg argued that providing funds directly to a church violated the Establishment Clause.[72]

---

[70] Segall, "The Constitution According to Justices Scalia and Thomas," 1665.

[71] Trinity Lutheran Church of Columbia, Inc. v. Comer, 582 U.S. ___ (2017), https://supreme.justia.com/cases/federal/us/582/15-577/#tab-opinion-3752808, accessed May 6, 2020.

[72] Honorable Justice Sonia Sotomayor, Trinity Lutheran Church of Columbia, Inc. v. Comer, 582 U.S. ___ (2017) dissent. https://supreme.justia.com/cases/federal/us/582/15-577/#tab-opinion-3752808, accessed May 6, 2020. "Properly understood then, this is a case about whether Missouri can decline to fund improvements to the facilities the Church uses to practice and spread its religious views. This Court has repeatedly warned that funding of exactly this kind – payments from the government to a house of worship – would cross the line drawn by the Establishment Clause."

Neither Thomas nor Gorsuch could suggest that the Establishment Clause in its original meaning, that "Congress shall make no law respecting an establishment of religion, or prohibiting the free exercise thereof," supported the state making a direct payment to a church for its ministry of any kind. This was certainly not Jefferson's understanding in 1802 when he wrote to the Danbury Baptists, which was certainly a more contemporaneous account of the matter than discussing Missouri's constitution. But in any case, the point is not that I am setting out to argue that originalism is wrong or living constitutionalism is correct. Instead, I am arguing that the manners in which originalism is continually deployed suggest that instead of a literalism dependent on the text of the Constitution, it is a tradition of reading that hinges on a variety of other factors that are no less historically contingent than the living constitutionalist values.

Finally, even famous proponents of originalism cannot agree on originalism. A perfect example arose in the summer of 2020. In Bostock versus Clayton County, the justices had what seemed a perfect opportunity for originalism to strike down a creeping liberal extension of protections.[73] All agreed that the original framers of the law, in this case Title VII of the Civil Rights Act of 1964, did not define "sex" to include sexual orientation. But the case was decided in support of civil rights protections for LGBTQ+ people.[74] Further, one of the most prominent supporters of originalism, Associate Justice Neil Gorsuch, argued that originalism forced him to side with the majority. Conservative sources howled that he had botched the job.[75] Associate Justice Samuel Alito argued that originalism demanded that no such protections be extended.[76] The argument over what an originalist argument could be signaled that the simple textual originalism that originalists claim to have was chimerical.

[73] Bostock v. Clayton County, Georgia. www.supremecourt.gov/opinions/19pdf/17-1618_hfci.pdf, accessed August 20, 2020.

[74] Adam Liptak, "Civil Rights Law Protects Gay and Transgender Workers, Supreme Court Rules," *New York Times*, June 15, 2020. www.nytimes.com/2020/06/15/us/gay-transgender-workers-supreme-court.html, accessed June 16, 2020.

[75] Tony Perkins, "Justice Gorsuch botched Bostock v. Clayton County ruling on homosexual and transgender 'rights,'" *The Washington Times*, June 19, 2020. www.washingtontimes.com/news/2020/jun/19/justice-gorsuch-botched-bostock-v-clayton-county-r/, accessed August 24, 2020.

[76] Marcia Coyle, "Gorsuch, Alito, and Kavanaugh Tangle over Textualism in Major Win for LGBT Workers," *The National Law Journal*, June 15, 2020. www.law.com/nationallawjournal/2020/06/15/gorsuch-alito-and-kavanaugh-tangle-over-textualism-in-major-win-for-lgbt-workers/?slreturn=20200724174800, accessed August 24, 2020.

Further examples could be multiplied. In the summer of 2021, the court handed down its decision in Brnovich versus Democratic National Committee. At issue was whether Arizona's new restrictions on voting violated the Voting Rights Act and its updates. The court decided for Arizona's more restrictive regulations, by a 6–3 vote that mirrored the Republican versus Democratic-appointed justices on the bench. Justice Elena Kagan attacked the majority specifically for its rejection of what Congress intended. Nicholas Stephanopoulos, Harvard Law Professor, wrote about the decision:

Today's conservative judges pride themselves on being textualists. When interpreting a statute, they always start with the law's text. Unless the law is ambiguous, they end with the text, too. As Justice Samuel A. Alito Jr. put it just last year, the courts' focus must never waver from what a statute's "words were understood to mean at the time of enactment." Any other approach, even one that "sails under a textualist flag," Alito lectured, is "like a pirate ship" – inappropriate and illegitimate.

So it was a shock to see the Supreme Court, in an opinion authored by none other than Alito, stacking one extra-textual constraint after another onto Section 2 of the Voting Rights Act. That provision prohibits any "standard, practice, or procedure" that makes it disproportionately harder for minority citizens to vote. In that situation, voting isn't "equally open" to citizens of all races, and minority citizens "have less opportunity" to vote.

But Alito, and the five conservative justices who joined his opinion in Brnovich v. Democratic National Committee, were unwilling to heed this clear textual command. They invented several limits that will make it harder for plaintiffs to win future Section 2 cases — and that appear nowhere in Section 2's language.

One of these is a requirement that a law imposes more than the "usual burdens of voting," before being struck down. But Section 2 states that it applies to any "denial or abridgment" of the right to vote. The court qualified that broad language, effectively inserting the word "substantial" before "abridgment," with no basis in the text.[77]

Stephanopoulos' and Kagan's points are clear; the "originalist" justices could not find in the text of the statute what they needed for the outcome they desired. Originalist justices do not bind themselves to the text when it does not present the outcome they wish. That strongly suggests that originalism, like literalism, is a reading tradition with far more rules than the names imply.

---

[77] Nicholas Stephanopoulos, "The Supreme Court showcased its 'textualist' double standard on voting rights," *The Washington Post*, July 1, 2021. www.washingtonpost.com/opinions/2021/07/01/supreme-court-alito-voting-rights-act/, accessed July 19, 2021.

The argument that originalism either is or is not the correct manner in which to interpret the Constitution is politically fraught. Originalism has become bonded to the cause of conservatism in American politics. Consequential or living constitutional approaches have been attached to liberal American political efforts. This study is not the platform on which to decide those issues. However, it is the place to make some observations. First, originalism does not always and only look to the Constitution as the framers intended, examining its text and the meaning of it in the history of the moment when it was ratified or amended. Second, the proponents of originalism frequently avoid some of its conclusions in favor of other arguments when making decisions. This leads to a conclusion – that originalism is a reading tradition, like other reading traditions. It has its strengths and weaknesses and is wielded by those who have learned to deploy it according to the canons of that tradition.

CONCLUSION: LIVING AS HEIRS OF A DIVIDED TRADITION

John Calvin sought a secure and immoveable foundation for his thought and his church. Because he was able to see the ways in which the claims of tradition had been abused and the dangers that were inherent in a tradition that was received uncritically, he argued for a clear and different standard: the purity of the scriptures. But Calvin was also a conservative. His stances relied on the history and traditions of the Christian movement, both for issues to be avoided and those to be lauded. He did not wish to reinvent Christianity in a new form, nor could he have done so and survived in the rough and tumble world of the early modern era. So he mistook his relatively greater dependence upon scripture as an absolute standard, even when evidence in his own doctrine makes it clear that this was actually not the case.

The depictions of history and tradition that figures such as Tanner, Gadamer, Adorno, and Nora have wrought remind us that Calvin could no more escape his own tradition than he could climb out of his own skin. It is no failure on Calvin's part that he was motivated by the traditions he inherited. In fact, there is no failure at all. The point is that Calvin engaged a community in the belief of a foundation that was wholly biblical. In doing so, he strengthened a claim to a model of Christianity that was impotent to see its own life in tradition. Because of that impotence, the tradition could not be critically received, but could only be accepted. That has had horrible consequences, and far more than I have catalogued.

Calvin has also strengthened the division between traditions of reading and ideals of literalism. The modern (or postmodern!) Western world is the heir to that history that he nourished. This can be seen in our struggles over epistemology, in the ways that we still argue that we can successfully make foundational arguments based entirely on textuality. Like the emperor wearing his fine new clothes, we stride out in public and credit those who would smirk as either evil or benighted.

But this study also suggests that we have the possibility of learning from these moments and coming to a better understanding of the traditions that we receive and are handing on to later generations. In doing so, we can begin to create practices for receiving them critically, whether in concert with the scripture in theological circles, or in explicitly setting out the multiple foundations of the legal arguments we make. In these and many other cases, the world will be better for the recognition, and the newfound abilities able to make small steps of progress.

Bibliography

PRIMARY WORKS

John Calvin: Original Language Editions

Calvin, Jean. *Calvin's Commentary on Seneca's De Clementia*. Translated and edited by Ford Lewis Battles and André Malan Hugo. Leiden: Brill, 1969.

Calvin, Jean. *Défense de Guillaume Farel et de ses collègues contre les calomnies du théologastre Pierre Caroli par Nicolas Des Gallars*. Edited by Jean François Gounelle. Paris: Presses Universitaires de France, 1994.

Calvin, Jean. *Institution de la religion Chrétienne (1541)*. 2 volumes. Edited by Olivier Millet. Geneva: Librairie Droz, 2008.

Calvin, Ioannis. *Ioannis Calvini Commentarii in Secundam Pauli Epistolam ad Corinthios*. Edited by Helmut Feld. Geneva: Librairie Droz, 1994.

Calvin, Ioannis. *Ioannis Calvini: Scripta Didactica et Polemica. Vol. I*. Edited by Mirjam van Veen. Geneva: Librairie Droz, 2005.

Calvin, Ioannis. *Ioannis Calvini: Scripta Didactica et Polemica. Vol. III, Defensio Sanae et Orthodoxae Doctrinae de Servitute et Liberatione Humani Arbitrii*. Edited by Anthony N. S. Lane, assisted by Graham Davies. Geneva: Librairie Droz, 2008.

Calvin, Ioannis. *Ioannis Calvini Scripta Didactica et Polemica. Vol. VI, Ioannis Calvini, Pro G. Farello et Collegis Ejus Adversus Peteri Caroli Theologiastri Calumnias Defensio Nicolai Gallasii, and Peteri Caroli, Refutatio Blasphemiae Farellistarum in Sacrosanctam Trinitatem*. Edited by Olivier Labarthe. Geneva: Librairie Droz, 2016.

Calvin, Ioannis. *Iohannis Calvini Commentarius in Epistolam Pauli ad Romanos*. Edited by T. H. L. Parker. Leiden: Brill, 2016.

Calvin, Iean. *Jean Calvin: Oeuvres choisies*. Edited by Olivier Millet. Paris: Gallimard, 1995.

Calvin, Iean. *Jean Calvin: Three French Treatises*. Edited by Francis M. Higman. London: Athlone Press, 1970.

Calvin, Ioannis. *Opera Quae Supersunt Omnia.* 59 volumes. Edited by Wilhelm Baum, Edward Cunitz, and Edward Reuss. Brunswick: C.A. Schwetschke & Son, 1895.

Calvin, Ioannis. *Opera Selecta.* 5 volumes. 3rd ed. Edited by Peter Barth and Wilhelm Niesel. Munich: Christian Kaiser, 1967.

John Calvin: Translations

Calvin, John. "Apology of John Calvin, to Messrs the Nicodemites upon the Complaint That They Make of His Too Great Rigour (1544)," translated by Eric Kayayan. *Calvin Theological Journal* 29 (1994): 346–63.

Calvin, John. *Calvin: Theological Treatises,* edited and translated by J. K. S. Reid. Philadelphia, PA: Westminster Press, 1954.

Calvin, John. *Commentaries on the Book of the Prophet Daniel,* translated by Thomas Myers. Grand Rapids: Baker Book House, 1979.

Calvin, John. *The Epistle of Paul the Apostle to the Romans.* Translated by Ross Mackenzie, edited by David W. Torrance and Thomas F. Torrance. In *Calvin's New Testament Commentaries,* vol. 8. Edinburgh: Oliver and Boyd Ltd., 1960.

Calvin, John. *Genesis.* Translated by John King. Carlisle: Banner of Truth Trust, 1965.

Calvin, John. *Institutes of the Christian Religion.* 2 volumes. Translated by Ford Lewis Battles, edited by John T. McNeill. Philadelphia: Westminster Press, 1960.

Calvin, John. *Institutes of the Christian Religion: 1536 Edition.* Translated and annotated by Ford Lewis Battles. Grand Rapids: Eerdmans, 1975.

Calvin, John. *The Second Epistle of Paul the Apostle to the Corinthians.* Translated by T. A. Smail, edited by David W. Torrance and Thomas F. Torrance. In *Calvin's New Testament Commentaries,* vol. 10. Edinburgh: Oliver and Boyd Ltd., 1960.

Calvin, John. *Selected Works of John Calvin: Tracts and Letters.* 7 volumes. Translated by Beveridge, edited by Henry Beveridge and Jules Bonnet. Grand Rapids: Baker Book House, 1983.

Farley, Benjamin Wirt, ed. *Treatises Against the Anabaptists and Against the Libertines.* Grand Rapids: Baker Book House, 1982.

Hazlett, Ian P. "Calvin's Latin Preface to his Proposed French Edition of Chrysostom's Homilies: Translation and Commentary." Edited by James Kirk. In *Humanism and Reform: The Church in Europe, England and Scotland, 1400–1643. Essays in Honour of James K. Cameron.* Oxford: Blackwell, 1991, 129–50.

Lane, Anthony N. S., ed. *The Bondage and Liberation of the Will: A Defence of the Orthodox Doctrine of Human Choice against Pighius.* Translated by Graham Davies. Grand Rapids: Baker, 1996.

McIndoe, John H. "John Calvin: Preface to the Homilies of Chrysostom." *Hartford Quarterly* 5 (1965): 19–26.

McKee, Elsie Anne, translator. *Institutes of the Christian Religion: 1541 French Edition: The First English Version.* Grand Rapids: Eerdmans, 2009.

Olin, John C., ed. *A Reformation Debate: Sadoleto's Letter to the Genevans and Calvin's Reply.* San Francisco: Harper Torchbook, 1966.

Other Authors

Augustine. *Confessions*. Translated and edited by Henry Chadwick. Oxford: Oxford University Press, 1991.

Burleigh, John H. S., ed. *Augustine: Earlier Writings*. Philadelphia: Westminster Press, 1953.

Clavis Patrum Latinorum: Qua in Corpus Christianorum Edendum Optimas quasque Scriptorum Recensiones a Tertulliano ad Bedam. Edited by Eligius Dekkers and Emil Gaar. Steenbrugis: Abbot of St. Peter, 1995.

D. Aurelii Augustini Hipponensis Episcopi, Omnium Operum. In 10 volumes. Paris: Claude Chevallon, 1531. In Yale Divinity School Library.

D. Martin Luthers Werke [Weimar Ausgabe]. Weimar: Böhlau, 1883–1993.

Incomplete Commentary on Matthew (Opus imperfectum). Translated with introduction by James A. Kellerman, edited by Thomas C. Oden. Downers Grove: IVP Academic, 2010.

Kingdon, Robert M., general editor. *Registers of the Consistory of Geneva in the Time of Calvin*, vol. 1, 1542–44. Grand Rapids: Eerdmans, 2000, 309ff.

Kramer, Fred, translator. *Philip Melanchthon Commentary on Romans*, 2nd ed. St. Louis: Concordia Publishing, 2010.

Migne, Jacques-Paul, and A. G. Hamman. *Patrologiae cursus completus, sive biblioteca universalis, integra, uniformis, commoda, oeconomica, omnium SS. Patrum, doctorum scriptorumque eccelesiasticorum qui ab aevo apostolico ad usque Innocentii III tempora floruerunt … [Series Latina, in qua prodeunt Patres, doctores scriptoresque Ecclesiae Latinae, a Tertulliano ad Innocentium III]*. Paris: Apud Garnier, 1844–64.

Registres du Consistoire de Genève au Temps de Calvin, Tome I (1542–1544) published by Thomas A. Lambert and Isabella M. Watt under the direction of Robert M. Kingdon with the assistance of Jeffrey Watt. Geneva: Librairie Droz, 1996.

Schleitheim Brotherly Union. "Brüderlich Vereinigung etlicher Kinder Gottes, siben Artikel betreffend," vol. 2, part 3. Edited by Otto Clemen. In *Flugschriften aus den ersten Jahren der Reformation*. Leipzig: Halle, 1907–11.

Schleitheim Brotherly Union. English translation. *The Legacy of Michael Sattler*. Edited by Yoder, John Howard. Scottdale: Herald Press, 1973, 172–80.

Vincentius of Lerins. *The Commonitorium of Vincentius of Lerins*. Edited by Reginald Stewart Moxon. Cambridge: Cambridge University Press, 1915.

SECONDARY SOURCES

Adams, Gwenfair Walters, ed. *Romans 1–8 (Reformation Commentary on Scripture)*. Downers Grove: IVP Academic, 2019.

Adorno, Theodor W. "On Tradition." *Telos* 94 (1992): 75. Collaborative translation based on text in Theodor W. Adorno, *Gesammelte Schriften* (Frankfurt: Suhrkamp Verlag, 1977), Vol. X, Pt. 1, 310–20.

Adorno, Theodor W. "The Meaning of Working Through the Past." In *Critical Models: Interventions and Catchwords*, translated by Henry W. Pickford. New York: Columbia University Press, 2005, 89–103.

Amelang, James S. *Parallel Histories: Muslims and Jews in Inquisitorial Spain.* Baton Rouge: Louisiana State University Press, 2013.

Anderson, Luke. "The Imago Dei Theme in John Calvin and Bernard of Clairvaux." In *Calvinus Sacrae Scripturae Professor: Calvin as Confessor of Holy Scripture*, edited by Wilhelm Neuser. Grand Rapids: Eerdmans, 1994, 178–98.

Appold, Kenneth G. *The Reformation: A Brief History.* Malden: Wiley Blackwell, 2010.

Arce, Marina Torres. "Swimming against the Tide: The Entry of Jews in Spain. Religious Mobility, Social Control and Integration at the End of the Ancien Régime." In *Religious Diaspora in Early Modern Europe: Strategies of Exile*, edited by Timothy G. Fehler, Greta Grace Kroeker, Charles H. Parker, and Jonathan Ray. London: Pickering and Chatto, 2014, 19–29.

Armogathe, J. R. "Les vies de Calvin au XVIe et XVIIe siècle." In *Historiographie de la Réforme*, edited by Philippe Joutard. Paris: Delachaux et Niestle, 1977, 45–59.

Auerochs, Bernd. "Gadamer Uber Tradition." *Zeitschrift für philosophische Forshung* 49 (1995): 294–311.

Awad, Najeeb George. "Should We Dispense with Sola Scriptura? Scripture, Tradition and Postmodern Theology." *Dialog: A Journal of Theology* 47 (2008): 64–79.

Backus, Irena. "Calvin and the Church Fathers." In *The Calvin Handbook*, edited by Herman Selderhuis. Grand Rapids: Eerdmans, 2009, 125–36.

Backus, Irena. "Calvin and the Greek Fathers." In *Continuity and Change: The Harvest of Late Medieval and Reformation History: Essays Presented to Heiko A. Oberman on His 70th Birthday*, edited by Robert J. Bast and Andrew Colin Gow. Leiden: Brill, 2000, 253–76.

Backus, Irena. *Historical Method and Confessional Identity in the Era of the Reformation (1378–1615).* Boston, Leiden: Brill, 2003.

Backus, Irena. *La vrai piéte: Divers traités de Jean Calvin et Confession de foi de Guillaume Farel.* Geneva: Labor et Fides, 1986.

Backus, Irena. *The Reception of the Church Fathers in the West: From the Carolingians to the Maurists.* 2 vols. Leiden: Brill, 1997.

Bainton, Roland. *Hunted Heretic: The Life and Death of Michael Servetus, 1511–1553.* Boston: Beacon Press, 1953.

Balentine, Samuel E. *Leviticus.* Louisville: Westminster John Knox Press, 2002.

Balkin, Jack M. "Nine Perspectives on Living Originalism." *University of Illinois Law Review* 2012 (2012): 815–76.

Balmer, Randall. *Grant Us Courage: Travels Among the Mainline of American Protestantism.* New York: Oxford University Press, 1991.

Balmer, Randall. *Mine Eyes Have Seen the Glory: A Journey into the Evangelical Subculture in America.* New York: Oxford University Press, 1989.

Balmer, Randall. *Thy Kingdom Come: How the Religious Right Distorts the Faith and Threatens America: An Evangelical's Lament.* New York: Basic Books, 2006.

Barr, Beth Allison. *The Making of Biblical Womanhood: How the Subjugation of Women Became Gospel Truth.* Grand Rapids: Brazos Press, 2021.

Battles, Ford Lewis. "God Was Accommodating Himself to Human Capacity." *Interpretation* 31 (1977): 19–38.

Bauckham, Richard. "Review of Suzanne Selinger, Calvin Against Himself: An Inquiry in Intellectual History." *The Journal of Ecclesiastical History* 37 (1986): 501–02.

Baude, Will. "Does Originalism Constrain Conservative Judges?" *Washington Post*, August 28, 2017. www.washingtonpost.com/news/volokh-conspiracy/ wp/2017/08/28/does-originalism-constrain-conservative-judges/.

Baude, William. "Is Originalism Our Law?" *Columbia Law Review* 115 (2015): 2349–408.

Bebbington, David. *Evangelicalism in Modern Britain: A History from the 1730s to the 1980s*. London: Unwin Hyman, 1989.

Bendroth, Margaret Lamberts. *Fundamentalism and Gender, 1875 to the Present*. New Haven: Yale University Press, 1993.

Bendroth, Margaret Lamberts. *The Last Puritans: Mainline Protestants and the Power of the Past*. Chapel Hill: University of North Carolina Press, 2015.

Benin, Stephen. *The Footprints of God: Divine Accommodation in Jewish and Christian Thought*. Albany: SUNY Press, 1993.

Berman, Mitchell N. and Toh, Kevin. "On What Distinguishes New Originalism from Old: A Jurisprudential Take." *Fordham Law Review* 82 (2013): 545–76.

Bingham, Matthew C. *Orthodox Radicals: Baptist Identity in the English Revolution*. Oxford: Oxford University Press, 2019.

Blacketer, Raymond A. "Calvin as Commentator on the Mosaic Harmony and Joshua." In *Calvin and the Bible*, edited by Donald McKim. Cambridge: Cambridge University Press, 2006, 30–52.

Blacketer, Raymond A. *The School of God: Pedagogy and Rhetoric in Calvin's Interpretation of Deuteronomy*. Dordrecht: Springer, 2006.

Blackmore, Josiah. "Imaging the Moor in Medieval Portugal." *Diacritics* 36 (2006): 27–43.

Blake, Aaron. "Neil Gorsuch, Antonin Scalia and Originalism, Explained," *Washington Post*, February 1, 2017. www.washingtonpost.com/news/the-fix/ wp/2017/02/01/neil-gorsuch-antonin-scalia-and-originalism-explained/.

Bloom, Harold. "The Necessity of Misreading," *The Georgia Review* 29 (1975): 267–88.

Boersma, Hans. "Anchored in Christ: Beyond the Scripture-Tradition Divide." *Christian Century* 128 (February 8, 2011): 26–31.

Boesak, Allan. *A Farewell to Innocence: A Socio-Ethical Study on Black Theology*. Maryknoll: Orbis, 1977.

Boesak, Allan. *Black and Reformed: Apartheid, Liberation, and the Calvinist Tradition*. Maryknoll: Orbis Books, 1984.

Boisset, Jean. "La reforme et les Peres de l'Eglise." In *Migne et le renouveau des études patristiques. Actes du colloque de Saint-Flour, 7–8 juillet 1975*, edited by André Mandouze and Joel Fouilheron. Paris: Beauchesne, 1985, 39–51.

Bostock v. Clayton County, Georgia. www.supremecourt.gov/opinions/19pdf/ 17-1618_hfci.pdf.

Bouwsma, William. *Calvin: A Sixteenth Century Portrait*. Oxford: Oxford University Press, 1988.

Bouwsma, William. "Calvinism as Theologia Rhetorica." In *Calvinism as Theologia Rhetorica*, edited by Wilhelm Wuellner. Berkeley: Center for Hermeneutical Studies in Hellenistic and Modern Culture, 1986, 1–21.

Bouwsma, William. "The Two Faces of Humanism: Stoicism and Augustinianism in Renaissance Thought." In *Itinerarium Italicum: The Profile of the Italian Renaissance in the Mirror of its European Transformations*, edited by Heiko Oberman and Thomas A. Brady, Jr. Leiden: Brill, 1975, 3–60.

Boyle, Marjorie O'Rourke. *The Human Spirit: Beginnings from Genesis to Science*. University Park: The Pennsylvania State University Press, 2018.

Braude, Benjamin. "The Sons of Noah and the Construction of Ethnic and Geographical Identities in the Medieval and Early Modern Periods." *William and Mary Quarterly* 54 (1997): 103–42.

Brecht, Martin. *Martin Luther: His Road to Reformation 1483–1521*, translated by James L. Schaaf. Philadelphia: Fortress Press, 1985.

Brewer, Brian C. "'Those Satanic Anabaptists': Calvin, Soul Sleep, and the Search for an Anabaptist Nemesis." In *Calvin and the Early Reformation*, edited by Brian C. Brewer and David M. Whitford. Leiden: Brill, 2020, 125–54.

Breyer, Stephen. "Our Democratic Constitution." *New York University Law Review* 77 (2002): 245–72.

Broscheid, Andreas. "Comparing Circuits: Are Some U.S. Courts of Appeals More Liberal or Conservative Than Others?" *Law & Society Review* 45 (2011): 171–94.

Brown, Peter. *Augustine of Hippo: A New Edition with an Epilogue*. Berkeley: University of California Press, 2000.

Bru, Vincent. "La notion d'accommodation divine chez Calvin: Ses implications theologiques et exegetiques." *La Revue Reformee* 49 (1998): 79–91.

Brümmer, Vincent. "Calvin, Bernard and the Freedom of the Will." *Religious Studies* 30 (1994): 437–55.

Bultmann, Rudolf. "New Testament and Mythology." In *New Testament & Mythology and Other Basic Writings*, selected, edited, and translated by Schubert M. Ogden. Philadelphia: Fortress Press, 1984, 1–44.

Bureau of Justice Statistics, State Court Caseload Statistics. www.bjs.gov/index .cfm?ty=tp&tid=30&fbclid=IwAR2rhrWdoAfzD2bmWwKbMFHsOFAdtgv mcijTfcosr5SVyItPuf5gxXsWTV8.

Burger, Christoph. "Der Kölner Karmelit Nikolaus Blanckaert Verteidigt die Verehrung der Reliquien gegen Calvin (1551)." In *Auctoritas Patrum II: Neue Beiträge zur Rezeption der Kirchenväter im 15. und 16. Jahrhundert*, edited by Leif Grane, Alfred Schindler, and Markus Wriedt. Mainz: Verlag Philipp von Zabern, 1998, 27–50.

Burger, Christoph. "Erasmus' Auseinandersetzung mit Augustin im Streit mit Luther," in *Auctoritas patrum: zur Rezeption der Kirchenväter im 15. und 16. Jahrhundert*, edited by Leif Grane, Alfred Schindler, and Markus Wriedt. Mainz: Verlag Philipp von Zabern, 1993, 1–13.

Burnett, Amy Nelson. *Debating the Sacraments: Print and Authority in the Early Reformation*. Oxford: Oxford University Press, 2019.

Burton, Simon G. "Peter Martyr Vermigli on Grace and Free Choice: Thomist and Augustinian Perspectives." *Reformation & Renaissance Review* 15 (2013): 37–52.

Büsser, Fritz. "Bullinger as Calvin's Model in Biblical Exposition: An Examination of Calvin's Preface to the Epistle to the Romans." In *In Honor of John Calvin, 1509–64*, edited by E. J. Furcha. Montreal: Faculty of Religious Studies, McGill University, 1987, 64–95.

Butterfield, Herbert. *Christianity and History.* New York: Scribner, 1950.

Calcagno, Antonio. "The Force of the Embodied Individual: De Beauvoir and Gadamer on Interpretive Understanding." In *Relational Hermeneutics: Essays in Comparative Philosophy*, edited by Paul Fairfield and Saulius Geniusas. London: Bloomsbury, 2018, 39–51.

Cameron, Euan. "Calvin the Historian: Biblical Antiquity and Scriptural Exegesis." In *Calvin and the Book: The Evolution of the Printed Word in Reformed Protestantism*, edited by Karen E. Spierling. Göttingen: Vandenhoeck & Ruprecht, 2015, 77–94.

Cameron, Euan. *The European Reformation.* Oxford: Oxford University Press, 1991.

Campi, Emidio and Moser, Christian. "Loved and Feared": Calvin and the Swiss Confederation," translated by David Dichelle. In *John Calvin's Impact on Church and Society 1509–2009*, edited by Martin Ernst Hirzel and Martin Sallmann. Grand Rapids: Eerdmans, 2009, 14–34.

Cannon, Katie Geneva. *Black Womanist Ethics.* Atlanta: Scholars Press, 1988.

Cannon, Katie Geneva. *Katie's Canon: Womanism and the Soul of the Black Community.* New York: Continuum, 1998.

Cannon, Katie Geneva. "Structured Academic Amnesia: As if This True Womanist Story Never Happened." In *Deeper Shades of Purple: Womanism in Religion and Society*, edited by Stacy M. Floyd-Thomas. New York: New York University Press, 2006, 19–27.

Chenu, M. D. *Nature, Man, and Society in the Twelfth Century: Essays on New Theological Perspectives in the Latin West*, translated by Lester K. Little. Chicago: University of Chicago Press, 1968.

Chisholm, John Edward. *The Pseudo-Augustinian Hypomnesticon against the Pelagians and Celestinans.* Fribourg: The University Press, 1967.

Chung-Kim, Esther. *Inventing Authority: The Use of the Church Fathers in Reformation Debates over the Eucharist.* Waco: Baylor University Press, 2011.

Clanton, J. Caleb. *The Philosophy of Alexander Campbell.* Knoxville: University of Tennessee Press, 2013.

Cohen, Jeremy. ed. *From Witness to Witchcraft: Jews and Judaism in Medieval Christian Thought.* Wiesbaden: Otto Harrassowitz, 1996.

Cohen, Mark R. *Under Crescent and Cross: The Jews in the Middle Ages.* Princeton: Princeton University Press, 1994.

Colby, Thomas B. "The Sacrifice of the New Originalism." *Georgetown Law Journal* 99 (2011): 713–78.

Colish, Marcia. *Medieval Foundations of the Western Intellectual Tradition, 400–1400.* New Haven: Yale University Press, 1997.

Collinson, Patrick. *The Reformation: A History.* New York: The Modern Library, 2003.

Comerford, Kathleen M. "The Council of Trent and the Augsburg Interim." In *John Calvin in Context*, edited by R. Ward Holder. Cambridge: Cambridge University Press, 2019, 190–197.

Congar, Yves, OP. *Tradition and Traditions: The Biblical, Historical, and Theological Evidence for Catholic Teaching on Tradition*, translated by Michael Naseby and Thomas Rainborough. New York: Simon and Schuster, 1997.

Courtenay, William J. *Schools and Scholars in Fourteenth Century England.* Princeton: Princeton University Press, 1987.

Cowdrey, H. E. J. *Lanfranc: Scholar, Monk, and Archbishop.* Oxford: Oxford University Press, 2003.

Coyle, Marcia. "Gorsuch, Alito, and Kavanaugh Tangle over Textualism in Major Win for LGBT Workers." *The National Law Journal*, June 15, 2020. www.law.com/nationallawjournal/2020/06/15/gorsuch-alito-and-kavanaugh-tangle-over-textualism-in-major-win-for-lgbt-workers/?slreturn=20200724174800.

Davis, David Brion. *Inhuman Bondage: The Rise and Fall of Slavery in the New World.* Oxford: Oxford University Press, 2006.

Dawson, Jane. *John Knox.* New Haven: Yale University Press, 2015.

De Gruchy, John. "Calvin(ism) and Apartheid in South Africa in the Twentieth Century: The Making and Unmaking of a Racial Ideology." In *Calvin and His Influence, 1509–2009*, edited by Irena Backus and Philip Benedict. New York: Oxford University Press, 2011, 306–18.

De Gruchy, John W. "Transforming Traditions: Doing Theology in South Africa Today." *Journal of Theology for Southern Africa* 139 (2011): 7–17.

Dean, Eric. Review of Suzanne Selinger, *Calvin Against Himself: An Inquiry in Intellectual History. Church History* 55 (1986): 523–24.

Dickens, A. G. *The German Nation and Martin Luther.* New York: Harper & Row, 1974.

Dingel, Irene. *Politik und Bekenntnis: Die Reaktionen auf das Interim von 1548.* Leipzig: Evangelische Verlag-Anst, 2006.

Dingel, Irene, Lies, Jan Martin, and Schneider, Hans-Otto, eds. *Der Adiaphoristische Streit (1548–1560).* Göttingen: Vandenhoeck & Ruprecht, 2012.

Dipple, Geoffrey. *Just as in the Time of the Apostles: Uses of History in the Radical Reformation.* Kitchener: Pandora Press, 2005.

Dorrien, Gary. *The Making of American Liberal Theology*, Vol. 2: *Idealism, Realism, and Modernity, 1900–1950*, and Vol. 3: *Crisis, Irony, and Postmodernity, 1950–2005.* Louisville: Westminster John Knox Press, 2001–06.

Dowey, Edward A. Jr. *The Knowledge of God in Calvin's Theology.* 3rd ed. Grand Rapids: Eerdmans, 1994.

Dreyer, Wim A. "Karl Barth's Römerbrief: A Turning Point in Protestant Theology," *Studia Historiae Ecclesiasticae* 43 (2017): 1–15.

Duby, Georges. *The Three Orders: Feudal Society Imagined*, translated by Arthur Goldhammer. Chicago: University of Chicago Press, 1980.

Du Mez, Kristin Kobes. *Jesus and John Wayne: How White Evangelicals Corrupted a Faith and Fractured a Nation.* New York: Liveright, 2020.

Eire, Carlos M. N. "Early Modern Christianity and Idolatry." In *John Calvin in Context*, edited by R. Ward Holder. Cambridge: Cambridge University Press, 2019, 267–77.

Eire, Carlos M. N. *Reformations: The Early Modern World.* New Haven: Yale University Press, 2017.

Eire, Carlos M. N. *War Against the Idols: The Reformation of Worship from Erasmus to Calvin.* Cambridge: Cambridge University Press, 1986.

Eliot, T. S. "Tradition and the Individual Talent," 1919, published in *The Sacred Wood: Essays on Poetry and Criticism.* London: Methuen, 1920, 42–53.

Ellingsen, Stephen. *The Megachurch and the Mainline: Remaking Religious Tradition in the Twenty-first Century.* Chicago: University of Chicago Press, 2007.

Engammare, Max. "Calvin the Workaholic," translated by Calvin Tams. In *Calvin & His Influence, 1509–2009,* edited by Irena Backus and Philip Benedict. Oxford: Oxford University Press, 2011, 67–83.

Engammare, Max. "Joannes Calvinus Trium Linguarum Peritus? La Question de L'Hebreu." *Bibliothèque d'Humanisme et Renaissance* 58 (1996): 35–60.

Engammare, Max. *On Time, Punctuality and Discipline in Early Modern Calvinism,* translated by Karin Maag. Cambridge: Cambridge University Press, 2009.

Essary, Kirk. *Erasmus and Calvin on the Foolishness of God: Reason and Emotion in Christian Philosophy.* Toronto: University of Toronto Press, 2017.

Essary, Kirk. "Calvin's Critics: Bolsec and Castellio." In *John Calvin in Context,* edited by R. Ward Holder. Cambridge: Cambridge University Press, 2019, 336–44.

Eurich, Amanda. "Polemic's Purpose." In *John Calvin in Context,* edited by R. Ward Holder. Cambridge: Cambridge University Press, 2019, 215–23.

Evans, G. R. *Medieval Commentaries on the Sentences of Peter Lombard, Vol. 1: Current Research.* Leiden: Brill, 2002.

Evans, G. R. *Problems of Authority in Reformation Debates.* Cambridge: Cambridge University Press, 1992.

Evans, Robert. *Reception History, Tradition and Biblical Interpretation: Gadamer and Jauss in Current Practice.* London: Bloomsbury T&T Clark, 2014.

FAQs: Judges in the United States." https://iaals.du.edu/sites/default/files/documents/publications/judge_faq.pdf?fbclid=IwAR0FCwf-xeXx7LPgQ-Z66K6i8MlmvY1 7VAfL18WXzyzFci9FfCJk4jAyMug.

Faulkner, William. *Requiem for a Nun.* New York: Random House, 1951.

Farenthold, David. "Trump Recorded Having Extremely Lewd Conversation about Women in 2005." *Washington Post,* October 8, 2016. www.washingtonpost.com/politics/trump-recorded-having-extremely-lewd-conversation-about-women-in-2005/2016/10/07/3b9ce776-8cb4-11e6-bf8a-3d26847eeed4_story .html.

Farge, James K. *Biographical Register of Paris Doctors of Theology, 1500–1536.* Toronto: Pontifical Institute of Medieval Studies, 1980.

Fea, John. *Was America Founded as a Christian Country?: A Historical Introduction,* rev. ed. Louisville: Westminster John Knox, 2016.

Febvre, Lucien. *The Problem of Unbelief in the Sixteenth Century, The Religion of Rabelais,* translated by Beatrice Gottlieb. Cambridge, MA: Harvard University Press, 1982.

Fehleison, Jill. *Boundaries of Faith: Catholics and Protestants in the Diocese of Geneva.* Kirksville: Truman State University Press, 2011.

Ferguson, Everett. *The Early Church at Work and Worship, Vol. 2: Catechesis, Baptism, Martyrdom and Eschatology.* Cambridge: James Clark and Company, 2014.

Finke, Roger and Stark, Rodney. *The Churching of America, 1776–1990: Winners and Losers in Our Religious Economy.* New Brunswick: Rutgers University Press, 1992.

Fitzgerald, Frances. *The Evangelicals: The Struggle to Shape America.* New York: Simon & Schuster, 2017.

Fleming, James E. "Living Originalism and Living Constitutionalism as Moral Readings of the American Constitution." *Boston University Law Review* 92 (2012): 1171–85.

Forstman, H. Jackson. *Word and Spirit: Calvin's Doctrine of Biblical Authority.* Stanford: Stanford University Press, 1962.

Foucault, Michel. *Essential Works of Foucault 1954–1984, Vol. 1: Ethics: Subjectivity and Truth*, edited by Paul Rabinow, translated by Robert Hurley. London: Penguin, 2000.

Fox, Robin Lane. *Augustine: Conversions to Confessions.* New York: Basic Books, 2015.

Franzmann, Majella. *Jesus in the Manichaean Writings.* Edinburgh: T. & T. Clark, 2003.

Frei, Hans. *The Eclipse of Biblical Narrative: A Study in Eighteenth and Nineteenth Century Hermeneutics.* New Haven: Yale University Press, 1974.

French, Katherine L. and Poska, Allyson M. *Women and Gender in the Western Past.* Boston: Houghton Mifflin, 2007.

Froehlich, Karlfried. "The Fate of the Glossa Ordinaria in the Sixteenth Century." In *Die Patristik in der Bibelexegese des 16. Jahrhunderts*, edited by David C. Steinmetz. Wiesbaden: Harrassowitz Verlag, 1999, 19–47.

Gadamer, Hans-Georg. *Hermeneutik I: Wahrheit und Methode. Grundzüge einer Philosophischen Hermeneutik (1960)*, 1986, *Vol. 1: Gesammelte Werke.* Tübingen: J.C.B. Mohr [Paul Siebeck], 1986.

Gadamer, Hans-Georg. *Truth and Method*, 2nd revised ed., edited and translated by Joel Weinsheimer and Donald G. Marshall. New York: Continuum, 2004.

Gamble, Richard. "'Brevitas et Facilitas: Toward an Understanding of Calvin's Hermeneutic." *Westminster Theological Journal* 47 (1985), 1–17.

Ganoczy, Alexandre. *Le Jeune Calvin: genèse et evolution de sa vocation réformatrice.* Wiesbaden: Steiner, 1966.

Ganoczy, Alexandre. *The Young Calvin*, translated by David Foxgrover and Wade Provo. Philadelphia: Westminster Press, 1987.

Ganoczy, Alexandre and Müller, Klaus. *Calvins Handschriftliche Annotationen zu Chrysostomus: Ein Beitrag zur Hermeneutik Calvins.* Wiesbaden: Franz Steiner Verlag GMBH, 1981.

Ganz, Peter F.; Huygens, R. B. C.; and Niewöhner, Friedrich; eds. *Auctoritas und Ratio: Studien zu Berengar von Tours.* Wiesbaden: Otto Harrassowitz, 1990.

Gaumer, Matthew Alan. *Augustine's Cyprian: Authority in Roman Africa.* Leiden: Brill, 2016.

Gaventa, Beverly Roberts. *Our Mother Saint Paul.* Louisville: Westminster John Knox Press, 2007.

George, Timothy. "Calvin's Psychopannychia: Another Look." In *In Honor of John Calvin, 1509–1564*, edited by E. J. Furcha. Montreal: McGill University Press, 1987, 297–329.

George, Timothy. *Reading Scripture with the Reformers*. Grand Rapids: IVP Academic, 2011.

Georgini, Sara. *Household Gods: The Religious Lives of the Adams Family*. Oxford: Oxford University Press, 2019.

Gilmont, Jean-François. *John Calvin and the Printed Book*, translated by Karin Maag. Kirksville: Truman State University Press, 2005.

Gill, Meredith J. *Augustine in the Italian Renaissance: Art and Philosophy from Petrarch to Michelangelo*. Cambridge: Cambridge University Press, 2005.

Giselbrecht, Rebecca. "Trinitarian Controversies." In *John Calvin in Context*, edited by R. Ward Holder. Cambridge: Cambridge University Press, 2019, 278–86.

Gordon, Bruce. *Calvin*. New Haven: Yale University Press, 2009.

Gordon, Bruce. *John Calvin's Institutes of the Christian Religion: A Biography*. Princeton: Princeton University Press, 2016.

Grane, Leif, Schindler, Alfred, and Wriedt, Markus, eds. *Auctoritas Patrum: Contributions on the Reception of the Church Fathers in the 15th and 16th Centuries*. Mainz: Verlag Philipp von Zabern, 1993.

Grane, Leif, Schindler, Alfred, and Wriedt, Markus eds. *Auctoritas Patrum II: neue Beiträge zur Rezeption der Kirchenväter im 15. und 16. Jahrhundert*. Mainz: Verlag Philipp von Zabern, 1998.

Grant, Robert M. and Tracy, David. *A Short History of the Interpretation of the Bible*, 2nd ed. Philadelphia: Fortress Press, 1984.

Gray, John. "What Scares the New Atheists," *The Guardian*, March 3, 2015. www.theguardian.com/world/2015/mar/03/what-scares-the-new-atheists.

Greef, Wulfert De. *The Writings of John Calvin: An Introductory Guide*, expanded edition, translated by Lyle D. Bierma. Louisville: Westminster John Knox Press, 2008.

Gregory, Brad. *The Unintended Reformation: How a Religious Revolution Secularized Society*. Cambridge, MA: Harvard University Press, 2012.

Grislis, Egil. "Calvin's Doctrine of Baptism." *Church History* 31 (1962): 46–65.

Grudem, Wayne. "If You Don't Like Either Candidate, Then Vote for Trump's Policies." *Townhall*, October 19, 2016. https://townhall.com/columnists/waynegrudem/2016/10/19/if-you-dont-like-either-candidate-then-vote-for-trumps-policies-n2234187.

Grudem, Wayne. *Politics – According to the Bible: A Comprehensive Resource for Understanding Modern Political Issues in Light of Scripture*. Grand Rapids: Zondervan Publishing, 2010.

Grudem, Wayne. "Trump's Moral Character and the Election." *Townhall*, October 9, 2016. https://townhall.com/columnists/waynegrudem/2016/10/09/trumps-moral-character-and-the-election-n2229846.

Guggisberg, Hans R. *Sebastian Castellio, 1515–1563: Humanist and Defender of Religious Toleration in a Confessional Age*, translated by Bruce Gordon. Burlington: Ashgate, 2002.

Haidt, Jonathan. *The Righteous Mind: Why Good People Are Divided by Politics and Religion*. New York: Pantheon Books, 2012.

Halbwachs, Maurice. "The Reconstruction of the Past." In *On Collective Memory*, edited, translated, and with an introduction by Lewis A. Coser. Chicago: University of Chicago Press, 1992, 46–51.

Hall, David D. *The Puritans: A Transatlantic History*. Princeton: Princeton University Press, 2019.

Halvorsen, James. *Peter Aureoli on Predestination: A Challenge to Late Medieval Thought*. Leiden: Brill 1998.

Hamm, Berndt. "Farewell to Epochs in Reformation History." *Reformation & Renaissance Review* 16 (2014): 211–45.

Hansen, Gary Neal. "Door and Passageway: Calvin's Use of Romans as a Hermeneutical and Theological Guide." In *Reformation Readings of Romans*, edited by Kathy Ehrensperger and R. Ward Holder. Edinburgh: T. & T. Clark, 2008, 77–94.

Hansen, Gary Neal. "John Calvin and the Non-Literal Interpretation of Scripture." Ph.D. Dissertation, Princeton Theological Seminary, 1998.

Harnack, Adolf von. *Marcion: das Evangelium vom fremden Gott*. Leipzig: J.C. Hinrichs, 1921; translated by John E. Steely and Lyle D. Bierma, *Marcion: The Gospel of an Alien God*. Durham: Labyrinth Press, 1990.

Hart, Darryl G. "No Creed but the Bible, No Authority without the Church: American Evangelicals and the Errors of Inerrancy." In *Interdisciplinary Perspectives on the Authority of Scripture: Historical, Biblical, and Theoretical Perspectives*, edited by Carlos Bovell. Eugene: Wipf & Stock, 2011, 3–27.

Harvey, L. P. *Muslims in Spain, 1500–1614*. Chicago: University of Chicago Press, 2005.

Harvey, Van A. *The Historian and the Believer*. New York: Macmillan, 1966.

Hatch, Nathan. *The Democratization of Christianity*. New Haven: Yale University Press, 1989.

Haynes, Stephen R. *Noah's Curse: The Biblical Justification of American Slavery*. Oxford: Oxford University Press, 2002.

Headley, John M. "The Reformation as Crisis in the Understanding of Tradition." *Archiv für Reformationsgeschichte* 78 (1987): 5–23.

Hendrix, Scott H. *Tradition and Authority in the Reformation*. Aldershot: Variorum, 1996.

Hendrix, Scott H. "Deparentifying the Fathers: The Reformers and Patristic Authority." In *Auctoritas Patrum: zur Rezeption der Kirchenväter im 15. und 16. Jahrhundert*, edited by Leif Grane, Alfred Schindler, and Markus Wriedt. Mainz: Verlag Philipp von Zabern, 1993, 55–68.

Heng, Geraldine. "England's Dead Boys: Telling Tales of Christian-Jewish Relations Before and After the First European Expulsion of the Jews." *MLN* 127, *Comparative Literature Issue: De Theoria: Early Modern Essays in Memory of Eugene Vance* (2012): S54–S85.

Higman, Francis. "Calvin and the Art of Translation." *Western Canadian Studies in Modern Languages and Literature* 2 (1970): 5–27.

Higman, Francis. "Calvin Polémiste." In *Lire et Découvrir: La Circulation des Idées au Temps de la Réforme*. Geneva: Librairie Droz, 1998, 403–18.

Higman, Francis. "I Came Not to Send Peace, but a Sword." In *Lire et Découvrir: La Circulation des Idées au Temps de la Réforme*. Geneva: Librairie Droz, 1998, 419–33.

Higman, Francis. "Les Genres de la Littérature Polémique Calviniste au XVIe Siècle." In *Lire et Découvrir: La Circulation des Idées au Temps de la Réforme*. Geneva: Librairie Droz, 1998, 437–48.

Higman, Francis. "The Reformation and the French Language." In *Lire et Découvrir: La Circulation des Idées au Temps de la Réforme*. Geneva: Librairie Droz, 1998, 337–52.

Higman, Francis. *The Style of John Calvin in his French Polemical Treatises*. Oxford: Oxford University Press, 1967.

Higman, Francis. "Theology for the Layman in the French Reformation, 1520–1550." In *Lire et Découvrir: La Circulation des Idées au Temps de la Réforme*. Geneva: Librairie Droz, 1998, 87–106.

Hillerbrand, Hans J. *The Division of Christendom: Christianity in the Sixteenth Century*. Louisville: Westminster John Knox Press, 2007.

Holder, R. Ward, ed. *Calvin and Luther: The Continuing Relationship*. Göttingen: Vandenhoeck & Ruprecht, 2013.

Holder, R. Ward. "Calvin and Tradition: Tracing Expansion, Locating Development, Suggesting Authority." *Toronto Journal of Theology* 25 (2009): 215–26.

Holder, R. Ward. "Calvin as Commentator on the Pauline Letters." In *Calvin and the Bible*, edited by Donald McKim. Cambridge: Cambridge University Press, 2006, 224–56.

Holder, R. Ward. "Calvin's Hermeneutic and Tradition: An Augustinian Reception of Romans 7." In *Reformation Readings of Romans*, edited by Kathy Ehrensperger and R. Ward Holder. Edinburgh: T. & T. Clark, 2008, 98–119.

Holder, R. Ward. *Crisis and Renewal: The Era of the Reformations*. Louisville: Westminster John Knox Press, 2009.

Holder, R. Ward. *John Calvin and the Grounding of Interpretation: Calvin's First Commentaries*. Leiden: Brill, 2006.

Holder, R. Ward. ed. *John Calvin in Context*. Cambridge: Cambridge University Press, 2019.

Holder, R. Ward. "Of Councils, Traditions, and Scripture: Calvin's Antidote to the Council of Trent." In *Calvinus Pastor Ecclesiae. Papers of the Eleventh International Congress on Calvin Research*, edited by Herman Selderhuis and Arnold Huijgen, Göttingen: Vandenhoeck and Ruprecht, 2016, 305–17.

Holder, R. Ward. "The Pain of Agreement: Calvin and the Consensus Tigurinus." *Reformation & Renaissance Review* 18 (2016): 85–94.

Holder, R. Ward. "The Reformers and Tradition: Seeing the Roots of a Problem." *Religions* 8 (2017): 1–11.

Hovda, Bjørn Ole. *The Controversy over the Lord's Supper in Danzig 1561–1567: Presence and Practice—Theology and Confessional Policy*. Göttingen: Vandenhoeck & Ruprecht, 2018.

Howard, Thomas Albert. *The Pople and the Professor: Pius IX, Ignaz von Döllinger, and the Quandary of the Modern Age*. Oxford: Oxford University Press, 2017.

Howell, Kenneth J. *God's Two Books: Copernican Cosmology and Biblical Interpretation in Early Modern Science*. South Bend: Notre Dame University Press, 2002.

Hugenberger, Gordon. "Questions and Answers on Issues Related to Homosexuality and Same-Sex Marriage." https://web.archive.org/web/20121223042151/www.parkstreet.org/qa_homosexuality.

Huijgen, Arnold. "The Challenge of Heresy: Servetus, Stancaro, and Castellio." In *John Calvin in Context*, edited by R. Ward Holder. Cambridge: Cambridge University Press, 2019, 258–66.

Huijgen, Arnold. *Divine Accommodation in Calvin's Theology: Analysis and Assessment*. Göttingen: Vandenhoeck & Ruprecht, 2011.

Hulse, Carl. "Appeals Court Vacancy Is Under Scrutiny Ahead of Contested Confirmation Hearing." *New York Times*, May 4, 2020. www.nytimes .com/2020/05/04/us/politics/senate-confirmation-justin-walker.html.

Humanae Vitae. www.vatican.va/content/paul-vi/en/encyclicals/documents/hf_p-vi_enc_25071968_humanae-vitae.html.

Hunsinger, George. "The Dimension of Depth: Thomas F. Torrance on the Sacraments of Baptism and the Lord's Supper." *Scottish Journal of Theology* 54 (2001): 155–76.

Huntley, Frank L. "Macbeth and the Background of Jesuitical Equivocation." *PMLA* 79 (1964): 390–400.

Ingram, Kevin, ed. *The Conversos and Moriscos in Late Medieval Spain and Beyond, Vol. 1: Departures and Change*. Leiden: Brill, 2009.

"Introduction to the Federal Court System." www.justice.gov/usao/justice-101/ federal-courts.

Jaeger, Werner. *Paideia: The Ideals of Greek Culture*, 3 vols., translated by Gilbert Highet. Oxford: Oxford University Press, 1939–1945.

Jedin, Hubert. *Kardinal Caesar Baronius: der Anfang der katholischen Kirchengeschichtsschreibung im 16. Jahrhundert*. Münster: Aschendorff, 1978.

Jenkins, Gary W. *Calvin's Tormentors: Understanding the Conflicts that Shaped the Reformer*. Grand Rapids: Baker Book House, 2018.

Jennings, Willie. *The Christian Imagination: Theology and the Origins of Race*. New Haven: Yale University Press, 2010.

Johnson, Galen. "The Development of John Calvin's Doctrine of Infant Baptism in Reaction to the Anabaptists." *Mennonite Quarterly Review* 73 (1999): 803–23.

Jones, Robert P. *The End of White Christian America*. New York: Simon & Schuster, 2016.

Jones, Serene. *Calvin and the Rhetoric of Piety*. Louisville: Westminster John Knox Press, 1995.

Josephson, Peter B. and Holder, R. Ward. *Reinhold Niebuhr in Theory and Practice: Christian Realism and Democracy in America in the Twenty-First Century*. Lanham: Lexington Books, 2019.

Joyce, James. *Ulysses*. New York: Random House, 1961.

Junker-Kenny, Maureen. *Religion and Public Reason: A Comparison of the Positions of John Rawls, Jürgen Habermas, and Paul Ricoeur*. Berlin: Walter De Gruyter, 2014.

Jürgens, Henning. "Intra-Protestant Conflicts in 16th Century Poland and Prussia—The Case of Benedict Morgenstern." In *Calvin and Luther: The Continuing Relationship*, edited by R. Ward Holder. Göttingen: Vandenhoeck & Ruprecht, 2013, 143–64.

Kamen, Henry. *The Spanish Inquisition: A Historical Revision*. New Haven: Yale University Press, 1998.

Kant, Immanuel. "What is Enlightenment?" in *Basic Writings of Kant*. New York: Modern Library, 2001, 133–42.

Kaplan, Benjamin. "Remnants of the Papal Yoke: Apathy and Opposition in the Dutch Reformation." *Sixteenth Century Journal* 25 (1994): 653–69.

Kaplan, M. Lindsay. "Jessica's Mother: Medieval Constructions of Jewish Race and Gender in 'The Merchant of Venice.'" *Shakespeare Quarterly* 58 (2007): 1–30.

Keller, Timothy. Website, https://timothykeller.com/author.

Keller, Timothy. "Women in Ministry." https://blogs.thegospelcoalition.org/scottysmith/2008/08/14/titleitems/.

Kidd, Thomas S. *Who is an Evangelical? The History of a Movement in Crisis.* New Haven: Yale University Press, 2019.

Kingdon, Robert M. *Adultery and Divorce in Calvin's Geneva.* Cambridge, MA: Harvard University Press, 1995.

Kingdon, Robert M. *Geneva and the Coming of the Wars of Religion in France, 1555–1563.* Geneva: Librairie Droz, 1956.

Kingdon, Robert M. Review of Suzanne Selinger, *Calvin Against Himself: An Inquiry in Intellectual History. Journal of the American Academy of Religion* 54 (1986): 191.

Klepper, Deanna. "Historicizing Allegory: The Jew as Hagar in Medieval Christian Text and Image." *Church History: Studies in Christianity and Culture* 84 (2015): 308–44.

Kok, Joel E. "Heinrich Bullinger's Exegetical Method: The Model for Calvin?" In *In Biblical Interpretation in the Era of the Reformation: Essays Presented to David C. Steinmetz in Honor of his Sixtieth Birthday*, edited by Richard A. Muller and John L. Thompson. Grand Rapids: Eerdmans, 1996, 241–54.

Kraus, Hans-Joachim. "Calvins exegetische Prinzipien." *Zeitschrift für Kirchengeschichte*, 79 (1968): 329–41.

Kreijkes, Jeannette. "Calvin's Use of the Chevallon Edition of Chrysostom's Opera Omnia: The Relationship Between the Marked Sections and Calvin's Writings." *Church History and Religious Culture* 96 (2016): 237–65.

Kreijkes, Jeannette. "Is a Special Faith the Same as Saving Faith? Calvin's Appropriation of Chrysostom's Understanding of a Faith of Miracles." In *More than Luther: The Reformation and the Rise of Pluralism in Europe*, edited by Karla Boersma and Herman J. Selderhuis. Göttingen: Vandenhoeck & Ruprecht, 2019, 165–76.

Kreijkes, Jeannette. "The Praefatio in Chrysostomi Homilias as an Indication that Calvin Read Chrysostom in Greek." In *Calvinus Pastor Ecclesiae: Papers of the Eleventh International Congress on Calvin Research*, edited by Herman Selderhuis and Arnold Huijgen. Göttingen: Vandenhoeck & Ruprecht, 2016, 347–54.

Kristeller, Paul Oskar. "Augustine and the Early Renaissance." In *Studies in Renaissance Thought and Letters*, Vol. 1. Rome: Edizione di storia e letteratura, 1956, 355–72.

Kruger, Stephen F. "Medieval Christian (Dis)Identifications: Muslims and Jews in Guibert of Nogent." *New Literary History* 28 (1997): 185–203.

Krüger, Thilo. *Empfangene Allmacht: die Christologie Tilemann Heshusens: (1527–1588).* Göttingen: Vandenhoeck and Ruprecht, 2004.

Kuhn, Thomas S. *The Structure of Scientific Revolutions.* Chicago: University of Chicago Press, 1962.

Lamberigts, Matthijs and Leo Kenis, eds. *L'Augustinisme à l'ancienne Faculté de théologie de Louvain*. Louvain: Peeters; Leuven University Press, 1993.

Lane, A. N. S. "Calvin and the Fathers in his Bondage and Liberation of the Will." In *John Calvin: Student of the Church Fathers*. Grand Rapids: Baker 1999, 151–78.

Lane, A. N. S. "Calvin's Knowledge of the Greek Fathers." *In John Calvin: Student of the Church Fathers*. Grand Rapids: Baker Book House, 1999, 67–86.

Lane, A. N. S. "Calvin's Sources of Bernard of Clairvaux." *In John Calvin: Student of the Church Fathers*. Grand Rapids: Baker Book House, 1999, 115–50.

Lane, A. N. S. "Calvin's Use of Bernard of Clairvaux." *In John Calvin: Student of the Church Fathers*. Grand Rapids: Baker Book House, 1999, 87–114.

Lane, A. N. S. "Calvin's Use of the Fathers: Eleven Theses." In *John Calvin: Student of the Church Fathers*. Grand Rapids: Baker Book House, 1999, 1–14.

Lane, A. N. S. "Did Calvin Use Lippoman's Catena in Genesim?" In *John Calvin: Student of the Church Fathers*. Grand Rapids: Baker Book House, 1999), 191–204.

Lane, A. N. S. *John Calvin: Student of the Church Fathers*. Grand Rapids: Baker Book House, 1999.

Lane, A. N. S. "Justification in Sixteenth-Century Patristic Anthologies." In *Auctoritas Patrum: zur Rezeption der Kirchenväter im 15. und 16. Jahrhundert*, edited by Leif Grane, Alfred Schindler, and Markus Wriedt. Mainz: Verlag Philipp von Zabern, 1993, 69–95.

Lane, A. N. S. "The Sources of the Citations in Calvin's Genesis Commentary." *In John Calvin: Student of the Church Fathers*. Grand Rapids: Baker Book House, 1999, 205–38.

Lane, A. N. S. "Was Calvin a Crypto-Zwinglian?" In *Adaptations of Calvinism in Reformation Europe: Essays in Honour of Brian G. Armstrong*, edited by Mack P. Holt. Burlington: Ashgate, 2007, 21–41.

Lange van Ravenswaay, J. Marius J. *Augustinus totus noster: Das Augustinverständnis bei Johannes Calvin*. Göttingen: Vandenhoeck & Ruprecht, 1990.

Lantzer, Jason. *Mainline Christianity: The Past and Future of America's Majority Faith*. New York: New York University Press, 2012.

LeClercq, Jean. *The Love of Learning and the Desire for God: A Study in Monastic Culture*. New York: Fordham University Press, 1961.

Leff, Gordon. *Gregory of Rimini: Tradition and Innovation in 14th Century Thought*. Manchester: Manchester University Press, 1961.

Lindberg, Carter. *The European Reformations*, 2nd ed. Malden: Wiley Blackwell, 2010.

Liptak, Adam. "Civil Rights Law Protects Gay and Transgender Workers, Supreme Court Rules." *New York Times*, June 15, 2020. www.nytimes.com/2020/06/15/us/gay-transgender-workers-supreme-court.html.

Loades, David ed. *John Foxe and the English Reformation*. Brookfield: Scolar Press, 1997.

Lotito, Mark. *The Reformation of Historical Thought*. Leiden: Brill, 2019.

Lubac, Henri de. *The Sources of Revelation*. New York: Herder and Herder, 1968.

MacCulloch, Diarmaid. "Calvin: Fifth Latin Doctor of the Church?" In *Calvin & His Influence, 1509–2009*, edited by Irena Backus and Philip Benedict. Oxford: Oxford University Press, 2011, 33–45.

MacCulloch, Diarmaid. *The Reformation: A History*. New York: Penguin Books, 2003.

McGrath, Alister. *A Life of John Calvin: A Study in the Shaping of Western Culture*. Cambridge: Blackwell Publishers, 1990.

McGrath, Alister. *Christianity's Dangerous Idea*. London: SPCK, 2007.

McGrath, Alister. *The Intellectual Origins of the European Reformation*, 2nd ed. Oxford: Blackwell, 2004.

McGrath, Alister. "John Calvin and Late Mediaeval Thought: A Study in Late Mediaeval Influences upon Calvin's Theological Development." *Archiv für Reformationsgeschichte* 77 (1986): 58–78.

McKee, Elsie Anne. "Calvin's Exegesis of Romans 12:8—Social, Accidental, or Theological." *Calvin Theological Journal* 23 (1988): 6–18.

McKee, Elsie Anne. "Les Anciens et l'Interpretation de 1 Tm 5, 17 chez Calvin: Une Curiosite dans l'Histoire de l'Exegese." *Revue de Theologie et de Philosophie* 120 (1988): 411–17.

McKee, Elsie Anne. *The Pastoral Ministry and Worship in Calvin's Geneva*. Geneva: Librairie Droz, 2016.

McKim, Donald K., ed. *Calvin and the Bible*. Cambridge: Cambridge University Press, 2006.

McKim, Donald K. "John Calvin: A Theologian for an Age of Limits." In *Readings in Calvin's Theology*, edited by Donald K. McKim. Grand Rapids: Baker Book House, 1984, 291–310.

McNamara, Jo Ann. "Canossa and the Ungendering of the Public Man." In *Medieval Religion: New Approaches*, edited by Constance Huffman Berman. New York: Routledge, 2005, 92–110.

McNutt, Jennifer Powell. "Calvin Legends: Hagiography and Demonology." In *John Calvin in Context*, edited by R. Ward Holder. Cambridge: Cambridge University Press, 2020, 383–92.

Madigan, Kevin. *Medieval Christianity: A New History*. New Haven: Yale University Press, 2015.

"Male-Only Ordination is Natural," https://calvinistinternational.com/2019/01/16/male-only-ordination-is-natural-why-the-church-is-a-model-of-reality/.

Malloch, Archibald Edward. "Father Henry Garnet's Treatise of Equivocation." *Recusant History* 15 (1981): 387–95.

Mandrella, Isabella. "Gregory of Rimini." In *A Companion to Responses to Ockham*, edited by Christian Rode. Leiden: Brill, 2016, 197–224.

Margolf, Diane C. "The French Wars of Religion." In *John Calvin in Context*, edited by R. Ward Holder. Cambridge: Cambridge University Press, 2019, 50–58.

Marsden, George, ed. *Evangelicalism and Modern America*. Grand Rapids: Eerdmans, 1984.

Marsden, George. *The Soul of the American University: From Protestant Establishment to Established Nonbelief*. New York: Oxford University Press, 1994.

Martí, Gerardo. "The Unexpected Orthodoxy of Donald J. Trump: White Evangelical Support for the 45th President of the United States." *Sociology of Religion: A Quarterly Review* 80 (2019): 1–8.

Marty, Martin E. *The Public Church: Mainline, Evangelical, Catholic.* New York: Crossroad, 1981.

Massa, Mark S., SJ. *The Structure of Theological Revolutions: How the Fight Over Birth Control Transformed American Catholicism.* Oxford: Oxford University Press, 2018.

May, Gerhard; Greschat, Katharina; and Meiser, Martin; eds. *Marcion und seine kirchengeschichtliche Wirkung/Marcion and his Impact on Church History: Vorträge der Internationalen Fachkonferenz zu Marcion, gehalten vom 15–18. August 2001.* Berlin: Walter de Gruyter, 2002.

Matteoni, Francesca. "The Jew, the Blood and the Body in Late Medieval and Early Modern Europe." *Folklore* 119 (2008): 182–200.

Meacham, Jon. "The Editor's Desk," *Newsweek*, November 12, 2006. www.newsweek.com/editors-desk-106637.

Mentzer, Raymond A. "French Christianity in the Early 1500s." In *John Calvin in Context*, edited by R. Ward Holder. Cambridge: Cambridge University Press, 2019, 17–24.

Mentzer, Raymond A. "The Deconfessionalization of the Reformations." *The Sixteenth Century Journal* 50 (2019): 43–48.

Merkt, Andreas. *Das Patristische Prinzip: Eine Studie zur Theologischen Bedeutung der Kirchenväter.* Leiden: Brill, 2001.

Meyerson, Mark D. *A Jewish Renaissance in Fifteenth-Century Spain.* Princeton: Princeton University Press, 2004.

Meyerson, Mark D. "The Survival of a Muslim Minority in the Christian Kingdom of Valencia (Fifteenth-Sixteenth Centuries)." In *Conversion and Continuity: Indigenous Christian Communities in Islamic Lands Eighth to Eighteenth Centuries*, edited by Michael Gervers and Jibran Bikhazi. Toronto: Pontifical Institute of Medieval Studies, 1990, 365–80.

Millet, Olivier. *Calvin et la dynamique de la parole: Etude de rhétorique réformée.* Paris: Librairie Honoré Champion, 1992.

Millet, Olivier. "Docere/movere: les catégories rhétoriques et leurs sources humanistes dans la doctrine calvinienne de la foi." In *Calvinus Sincerioris Religionis Vindex Calvin as Protector of the Purer Religion*, edited by Wilhelm H. Neuser and Brian G. Armstrong. Kirksville: Sixteenth Century Essays and Studies, 1997, 35–51.

Millet, Olivier. "Calvin's Self-Awareness as Author," translated by Susanna Gebhardt. In *Calvin & His Influence, 1509–2009*, edited by Erena Backus and Philip Benedict. Oxford: Oxford University Press, 2011, 84–101.

Mooi, R. J. *Het Kerk-en Dogmahistorisch Element in de Werken van Johannes Calvijn.* Wageningen: H. Veenman, 1965.

Moore, R.I. *The Formation of a Persecuting Society: Authority and Deviance in Western Europe, 950–1250.* Cambridge: Cambridge University Press, 1987.

Mootz, Francis J. III, ed. *Gadamer and Law.* Farnham: Ashgate, 2007.

Moser, Christian. "Heinrich Bullinger's Efforts to Document the Zurich Reformation: History as Legacy." In *Architect of Reformation: An Introduction to*

Heinrich Bullinger, 1504–1575, edited by Bruce Gordon and Emidio Campi. Grand Rapids: Baker Academic Publishing, 2004, 201–14.

Muller, Richard A. "An Approach to Calvin: On Overcoming Modern Accommodations." In *The Unaccommodated Calvin: Studies in the Foundation of a Theological Tradition*. Oxford: Oxford University Press, 2000, 3–18.

Muller, Richard. "The Problem of Protestant Scholasticism: A Review and Definition." In *Reformation and Scholasticism: An Ecumenical Enterprise*, edited by Willem J. van Asselt and Eef Dekker. Grand Rapids: Baker Book House, 2001, 45–64.

Muller, Richard. "Scholasticism in Calvin: A Question of Relation and Disjunction." In *The Unaccommodated Calvin: Studies in the Foundation of a Theological Tradition*. Oxford: Oxford University Press, 2000, 39–61.

Murdock, Graeme "The Elders' Gaze: Women and Consistorial Discipline in Sixteenth-Century France." In *John Calvin, Myth and Reality: Images and Impact of Geneva's Reformer*, edited by Amy Nelson Burnett. Eugene: Cascade Books, 2011, 69–90.

Murray, John Courtney SJ. "E Pluribus Unum: The American Consensus." In *We Hold These Truths: Catholic Reflections on the American Proposition*. New York: Sheed and Ward, 1960, 27–43.

Murrill, Brandon J. "Modes of Constitutional Interpretation." Congressional Research Service, March 15, 2018.

Mütel, Matthias. *Mit den Kirchenvätern gegen Martin Luther? Die Debatten um Tradition und auctoritas patrum auf dem Konzil von Trient*. Leiden: Ferdinand Schöningh, 2017.

Muttitt, Andrew. "John Calvin, 2 Samuel 2:8–32 and Resistance to Civil Government: Supreme Equivocation or Mastery of Contextual Exegesis?" *KOERS – Bulletin for Christian Scholarship* 82 (2017): 1–10.

Newman, John Henry. *An Essay on the Development of Christian Doctrine*. South Bend, Indiana: University of Notre Dame Press, 1994.

Niebuhr, Reinhold. *The Nature and Destiny of Man: A Christian Interpretation*. v. 1 Human Nature. 1941. v. 2 Human Destiny. 1943. Louisville: Westminster John Knox Press, 1996.

Nirenberg, David. *Communities of Violence: Persecution of Minorities in the Middle Ages*. Princeton: Princeton University Press, 1996.

Nirenberg, David. "Conversion, Sex, and Segregation: Jews and Christians in Medieval Spain." *The American Historical Review*, 107 (2002): 1065–93.

Nissimi, Hilda. "Religious Conversion, Covert Defiance and Social Identity: A Comparative View." *Numen* 51 (2004): 367–406.

Noble, Ivana. "The Tension between an Eschatological and a Utopic Understanding of Tradition: Tillich, Florovsky, and Congar." *Harvard Theological Review* 109 (2016): 400–21.

Noll, Mark. *The Scandal of the Evangelical Mind*. Grand Rapids: Eerdmans, 2010.

Noll, Mark; Bebbington, David; and Marsden, George. *Evangelicals: Who They Have Been, Are Now, and Could Be*. Grand Rapids: Eerdmans, 2019.

Nora, Pierre. *Realms of Memory: Rethinking the French Past*, translated by Arthur Goldhammer, in 3 vols. New York: Columbia University Press, 1996.

Nora, Pierre. *Zwischen Geschichte und Gedächtnis*. Berlin: Verlag Klaus Wagenbach, 1990.

Nosál, Martin. "The Gadamerian Approach to the Relation Between Experience and Language." *History and Theory* 54 (2015): 195–208.

Nozick, Robert. *The Nature of Rationality*. Princeton: Princeton University Press, 1993.

Oberman, Heiko A. "Quo Vadis, Petre? Tradition from Irenaeus to Humani Generis." *Scottish Journal of Theology* 16 (1963): 225–55.

Odenstedt, Anders. *Gadamer on Tradition-Historical Context and the Limits of Reflection*. New York: Springer, 2017.

Olay, Csaba. "Die Überlieferung Der Gegenwart und Die Gegenwart Der Überlieferung. Heidegger und Gadamer Über Tradition." *International Yearbook for Hermeneutics* 12 (2013): 196–219.

Olbricht, Thomas H. "Exegetical and Theological Presuppositions in Nineteenth-Century American Commentaries on Acts." In *Scripture and Traditions: Essays on Early Judaism and Christianity in Honor of Carl R. Holladay*, edited by Patrick Gray and Gail R. O'Day. Leiden: Brill, 2008, 359–86.

O'Malley, John W. SJ. "The Hermeneutic of Reform: A Historical Analysis." *Theological Studies* 73 (2012): 517–46.

O'Malley, John W. SJ. "Tradition and Traditions: Historical Perspectives." *The Way* 27 (1987): 163–73.

Oort, Johannes van. "John Calvin and the Church Fathers." In *The Reception of the Church Fathers in the West: From the Carolingians to the Maurists*, edited by Irena Backus. New York, Leiden: Brill, 1997, 661–700.

Ozment, Steven. *The Age of Reform 1250–1550: An Intellectual and Religious History of Late Medieval and Reformation Europe*. New Haven: Yale University Press, 1980.

Ozment, Steven. *Protestants: The Birth of a Revolution*. New York: Doubleday, 1992.

Pabel, Hilmar. *Herculean Labors: Erasmus and the Editing of St. Jerome's Letters in the Renaissance*. Leiden: Brill, 2008.

Painter, Borden W. Jr. *The New Atheist Denial of History*. New York: Palgrave Macmillan, 2014.

Pak, G. Sujin. "John Calvin's Life." In *John Calvin in Context*, edited by R. Ward Holder. Cambridge: Cambridge University Press, 2019, 9–16.

Pak, G. Sujin. *The Judaizing Calvin: Sixteenth-Century Debates over the Messianic Psalms*. Oxford: Oxford University Press, 2010.

Pak, G. Sujin, *The Reformation of Prophecy: Early Modern Interpretations of the Prophet & Old Testament Prophecy*. Oxford: Oxford University Press, 2018.

Parker, T. H. L. *Calvin's Old Testament Commentaries*. Edinburgh: T. & T. Clark, 1986.

Parker, T. H. L. *Commentaries on Romans 1532–1542*. Edinburgh: T. & T. Clark, 1986.

Parry, Mary Elizabeth. "Between Muslim and Christian Worlds: Moriscas and Identity in Early Modern Spain." *Muslim World* 95 (2005): 177–98.

Parsons, Michael. *Reformation Marriage: The Husband and Wife Relationship in the Theology of Luther and Calvin*. Edinburgh: Rutherford House, 2005.

Payton, James R., Jr. "Calvin and the Legitimation of Icons: His Treatment of the Seventh Ecumenical Council." *Archiv für Reformationsgeschichte* 84 (1993): 222–41.

Payton, James R. "Calvin and the Libri Carolini." *Sixteenth Century Journal* 28 (1997): 467–80.

Payton, James R. "History as Rhetorical Weapon: Christian Humanism in Calvin's Reply to Sadoleto, 1539." In *In Honor of John Calvin, 1509–64*, edited by E. J. Furcha. Montreal: Faculty of Religious Studies, McGill University, 1987, 96–132.

Pelikan, Jaroslav. *The Christian Tradition: A History of the Development of Doctrine*, 5 vols. Chicago: University of Chicago Press, 1971–89.

Pelikan, Jaroslav. *The Christian Tradition: A History of the Development of Doctrine, Vol. 4: Reformation of the Church and Dogma (1300–1700)*. Chicago: University of Chicago Press, 1985.

Perkins, Tony. "Justice Gorsuch botched Bostock v. Clayton County ruling on homosexual and transgender 'rights.'" *The Washington Times*, June 19, 2020. www.washingtontimes.com/news/2020/jun/19/justice-gorsuch-botched-bostock-v-clayton-county-r/.

Pettegree, Andrew. "Calvin and Luther as Men of the Book." In *Calvin and the Book: The Evolution of the Printed Word in Reformed Protestantism*, edited by Karen E. Spierling. Göttingen: Vandenhoeck & Ruprecht, 2015, 17–32.

Phelan, Owen M. "Horizontal and Vertical Theologies: 'Sacraments' in the Works of Paschasius Radbertus and Ratramnus of Corbie." *Harvard Theological Review* 103 (2010): 271–89.

Pitkin, Barbara. "Calvin's Reception of Paul." In *A Companion to Paul in the Reformation*, edited by R. Ward Holder. Leiden: Brill, 2009, 267–96.

Pitkin, Barbara. *Calvin, the Bible, and History: Exegesis and Historical Reflection in the Era of Reform*. Oxford: Oxford University Press, 2020.

Platoff, Emma. "Trump-Appointed Judges are Shifting the Country's Most Politically Conservative Circuit Court further to the Right." *Texas Tribune*, August 30, 2018 www.texastribune.org/2018/08/30/under-trump-5th-circuit-becoming-even-more-conservative/.

Pollmann, Karla. "The Proteanism of Authority: The Reception of Augustine in Cultural History from his Death to the Present, Mapping an International and Interdisciplinary Investigation." In *The Oxford Guide to the Historical Reception of Augustine*, Vol. 1, edited by Karla Pollmann and Willemien Otten. Oxford: Oxford University Press, 2013, 3–14.

Pollman, Karla and Gill, Meredith J. eds. *Augustine beyond the Book: Intermediality, Transmediality, and Reception*. Leiden: Brill, 2012.

Pollmann, Karla and Otten, Willemien, eds. *The Oxford Guide to the Historical Reception of Augustine*, Vol. 1 Oxford: Oxford University Press, 2013.

Polman, Pontien. *L'element historique dans la controverse religieuse du 16e siècle*. Gembloux: J. Duculot, 1932.

Popper, Karl. *The Open Society and Its Enemies*. London: Routledge, 1945.

Pullapilly, Cyriac. *Caesar Baronius: Counter-Reformation Historian*. South Bend: University of Notre Dame Press, 1975.

Radding Charles M. and Newton, Francis. *Theology, Rhetoric and Politics in the Eucharistic Controversy, 1078–1079: Alberic of Monte Cassino against Berengar of Tours.* New York: Columbia University Press, 2003.

Räisänen, Heikki. "Marcion." In *A Companion to Second-Century "Heretics,"* edited by Antti Marjanen and Petri Luomanen. Leiden: Brill, 2005, 100–24.

Raith, Charles II. "Predestination in Early Modern Thought." In *John Calvin in Context,* edited by R. Ward Holder. Cambridge: Cambridge University Press, 2019, 249–57.

Raitt, Jill. "Calvin's Use of Bernard of Clairvaux." *Archiv für Reformationsgeschichte* 72 (1981): 98–121.

Raitt, Jill. "Three Inter-Related Principles in Calvin's Unique Doctrine of Baptism." *Sixteenth Century Journal* 11 (1980): 51–61.

Randall, Rebecca. "How Many Churches Does America Have? More Than Expected." *Christianity Today,* September 14, 2017. www.christianitytoday.com/news/2017/september/how-many-churches-in-america-us-nones-nondenominational.html.

Ratzinger, Joseph. *Principles of Catholic Theology: Building Stones for a Fundamental Theology,* translated by Frances McCarthy. San Francisco: Ignatius Press, 1987.

Ray, Jonathan. "Chaos and Community: 1492 and the Foundation of the Sephardic Diaspora." In *Religious Diaspora in Early Modern Europe: Strategies of Exile,* edited by Timothy G. Fehler, Greta Grace Kroeker, Charles H. Parker, and Jonathan Ray. London: Pickering and Chatto, 2014, 153–66.

Refini, Eugenio. *The Vernacular Aristotle: Translation as Reception in Medieval and Renaissance Italy.* Cambridge: Cambridge University Press, 2008.

Reuter, Karl. *Das Grundverständnis der Theologie Calvins: unter Einbeziehung ihrer geschichtlichen Abhangigkeiten.* Neukirchen-Vluyn: Neukirchener Verlag des Erziehungsvereins, 1963.

Rice, Eugene F. *Saint Jerome in the Renaissance.* Baltimore: Johns Hopkins University Press, 1988.

Ricoeur, Paul. "Existence and Hermeneutics." In *The Philosophy of Paul Ricoeur: An Anthology of His Work,* edited by Charles E. Reagan and David Stewart. Boston: Beacon Press, 1978, 97–108.

Ricoeur, Paul. "Hermeneutics and the Critique of Ideology." In *The Hermeneutic Tradition: From Ast to Ricoeur,* edited by Gayle L. Ormiston and Alan D. Schrift. Albany: SUNY Press, 1990, 298–324.

Ricoeur, Paul. *Hermeneutics and the Human Sciences,* edited and translated by J. B. Thompson. Cambridge: Cambridge University Press, 1981.

Rooy, H. F. van. "Calvin's Genesis Commentary—Which Bible Text Did He Use?" In *Our Reformational Tradition. A Rich Heritage and Lasting Vocation,* edited by B. J. van der Walt. Potchefstroom: Potchefstroom University for Higher Education, 1984, 203–16.

Rorty, Richard. *Contingency, Irony, and Solidarity.* Cambridge: Cambridge University Press, 1989.

Roussel, Bernard. "John Calvin's Interpretation of Psalm 22." In *Adaptations of Calvinism in Reformation Europe: Essays in Honour of Brian G. Armstrong,* edited by Mack Holt. Aldershot: Ashgate, 2007, 9–20.

Rudolph, Kurt. *Gnosis: The Nature and History of Gnosticism*, translated by R. Wilson. San Francisco: Harper & Row, 1983.

Rummel, Erika. *Biblical Humanism and Scholasticism in the Age of Erasmus*. Leiden: Brill, 2008.

Rummel, Erika. *The Humanist-Scholastic Debate in the Renaissance and Reformation*. Cambridge, MA: Harvard University Press, 1995.

Ryrie, Alec. *Protestants: The Radicals Who Made the Modern World*. London: William Collins, 2017.

Ryrie, Alec. "Scripture, the Spirit and the Meaning of Radicalism in the English Revolution." In *Radicalism and Dissent in the World of Protestant Reform*, edited by Bridget Heal and Anorthe Kremers. Göttingen: Vandenhoeck & Ruprecht, 2017, 100–17.

Saak, Eric Leland. "The Reception of Augustine in the Later Middle Ages." In *The Reception of the Church Fathers in the West: From the Carolingians to the Maurists*, edited by Irena Backus. Leiden: Brill, 1997, 661–700.

Sands, Kathleen M. *America's Religious Wars: The Embattled Heart of Our Public Life*. New Haven: Yale University Press, 2019.

Sawyer, Logan E. III. "Principle and Politics in the New History of Originalism." *American Journal of Legal History* 57 (2017): 198–221.

Scalia, Antonin. Citizens United v. Federal Election Commission, 558 U.S. 310 (2010). https://supreme.justia.com/cases/federal/us/558/310/#tab-opinion-1963048.

Scalia, Antonin. "Originalism: The Lesser Evil." *University of Cincinnati Law Review* 57 (1989): 849–65.

Schabel, Christopher David. *Theology at Paris, 1316–1345: Peter Auriol and the Problem of Divine Foreknowledge and Future Contingents*. Burlington: Ashgate, 2000.

Schäfer, Ann-Stephane. *Auctoritas Patrum? The Reception of the Church Fathers in Puritanism*. Frankfurt: Peter Lang, 2011.

Schmidt, Lawrence K. "Gadamer and the Philosophy of Science." In *Hermeneutics and Phenomenology: Figures and Themes*, edited by Saulius Geniusas and Paul Fairfield. London: Bloomsbury, 2018, 149–62.

Scholl, Hans. "Karl Barth as Interpreter of Calvin's Psychopannychia." In *Calvinus Sincerioris Religionis Vindex: Calvin as Protector of the Purer Religion*, edited by Wilhelm H. Neuser and Brian G. Armstrong. Kirksville: Sixteenth Century Essays and Studies, 1997, 291–308.

Schreiner, Susan. "'The Spiritual Man Judges All Things': Calvin and the Exegetical Debates about Certainty in the Reformation." In *Biblical Interpretation in the Era of the Reformation: Essays Presented to David C Steinmetz in Honor of his Sixtieth Birthday*, edited by Richard A. Muller and John L. Thompson. Grand Rapids: Eerdmans, 1996, 189–215.

Scott, William O. "Macbeth's – and Our – Self-Equivocations." *Shakespeare Quarterly* 37 (1986): 160–74.

Segall, Eric J. "The Constitution According to Justices Scalia and Thomas: Alive and Kickin'." *Washington University Law Review* 91 (2014): 1663–72.

Segall, Eric J. "Does Originalism Matter Anymore?" *New York Times*, September 10, 2018. www.nytimes.com/2018/09/10/opinion/kavanaugh-originalism-supreme-court.html.

Selderhuis Herman J. and Lange van Ravenswaay, J. Marius J., eds. *Luther and Calvinism: Image and Reception of Martin Luther in the History and Theology of Calvinism*. Göttingen: Vandenhoeck & Ruprecht, 2017.

Selinger, Suzanne. *Calvin Against Himself: An Inquiry in Intellectual History*. Hamden: Archon Books, 1984.

Shagan, Ethan. *The Birth of Modern Belief: Faith and Judgment from the Middle Ages to the Enlightenment*. Princeton: Princeton University Press, 2018.

Shellnutt, Kate. "Tim Keller, John Piper, and Andy Stanley Among the 12 'Most Effective' Preachers." *Christianity Today*, May 2, 2018. www.christianityto-day.com/news/2018/may/tim-keller-john-piper-andy-stanley-most-effective-preachers.html.

Smalley, Beryl. *The Study of the Bible in the Middle Ages*. South Bend: University of Notre Dame Press, 1964.

Smith, Peter J. and Tuttle, Robert W. "Biblical Literalism and Constitutional Originalism." *Notre Dame Law Review* 86 (2011): 693–762.

Smith, Preserved. *The Age of the Reformation*. New York: Henry Holt and Company, 1920.

Smits, Luchesius. *Saint Augustin dans l'oeuvre de Jean Calvin*. Assen: Van Gorcum, 1957–58.

Solum, Lawrence B. "Originalism versus Living Constitutionalism: The Conceptual Structure of the Great Debate." *Northwestern University Law Review* 113 (2019): 1243–95.

Sotomayor, Sonia. Trinity Lutheran Church of Columbia, Inc. v. Comer, 582 U.S. ___ (2017) dissent. https://supreme.justia.com/cases/federal/us/582/15-577/#tab-opinion-3752808.

Spierling, Karen. *Infant Baptism in Reformation Geneva: The Shaping of a Community, 1536–1564*. Burlington: Ashgate, 2005.

Spohnholz, Jesse. *The Convent of Wesel: The Event that Never Was and the Invention of Tradition*. Cambridge: Cambridge University Press, 2017.

Stayer, James M. "Anabaptist Münster, 1534–1535: The War Communism of the Notables." In *German Peasants' War and Anabaptist Community of Goods*. Montreal: McGill-Queen's University Press, 1991, 123–38.

Stayer, James M. "The Contours of the Non-Lutheran Reformation in Germany, 1522–1546: The Distinction between the Bible-Centred Meeting Places and the Altar-Centred Churches." *Church History and Religious Culture* 101 (2021): 167–74.

Stayer, James M.; Isaak, Helmut; and Bakker, Willem De. "Menno Siomons, The Blasphemy of Jan van Leiden: When and Why Was it Written?" *The Mennonite Quarterly Review* 89 (2015): 599–630.

Steinmetz, David C. "Calvin Among the Thomists: Exegesis of Romans 9." In *Biblical Hermeneutics in Historical Perspective*, edited by Mark Burrows and Paul Rorem. Grand Rapids: Eerdmans, 1991, 198–214.

Steinmetz, David C. "Calvin as an Interpreter of Genesis." In *Calvin as Protector of the Purer Religion*, edited by Wilhelm Neuser and Brian Armstrong. Kirksville: Sixteenth Century Journal Publishers, 1997, 53–66.

Steinmetz, David C. *Calvin in Context*, 2nd ed. Oxford: Oxford University Press, 2010.

Steinmetz, David C. *Luther and Staupitz: An Essay in the Intellectual Origins of the Protestant Reformation*. Durham, NC: Duke University Press, 1980.

Steinmetz, David C. "Luther and Staupitz: The Unresolved Problem of the Forerunner." In *Ad Fontes Lutheri: Essays in Honor of Kenneth Hagen's Sixty-fifth Birthday*, edited by Timothy Maschke, Franz Posset, and Joan Skocir. Milwaukee: Marquette University Press, 2001, 270–80.

Steinmetz, David C. "Things Old and New: Tradition and Innovation in Constructing Reformation Theology." *Reformation and Renaissance Review* 19 (2017): 5–18.

Stephanopoulos, Nicholas. "The Supreme Court Showcased its 'Textualist' Double Standard on Voting Rights," *The Washington Post*, July 1, 2021. www.washingtonpost.com/opinions/2021/07/01/supreme-court-alito-voting-rights-act/.

Stephens, Peter. "The Sacraments in the Confessions of 1536, 1549, and 1566—Bullinger's Understanding in Light of Zwingli's." *Zwingliana* 37 (2010): 51–76.

Strauss, David A. "Can Originalism Be Saved?" *Boston University Law Review* 92 (2012): 1161–70.

Strauss, David A. *The Living Constitution*. New York: Oxford University Press, 2010.

Strom, Jonathan. *German Pietism and the Problem of Conversion*. University Park: Penn State University Press, 2017.

Stuhlmacher, Peter. *Historical Criticism and Theological Interpretation of Scripture*, translated by Roy A. Harrisville. Philadelphia: Fortress Press, 1977.

Suerbaum, Almut; Southcombe, George; and Thompson, Benjamin; eds. *Polemic: Language as Violence in Medieval and Early Modern Discourse*. Milton Park: Routledge, 2016.

Sungenis, Robert. *Not by Scripture Alone: A Catholic Critique of the Protestant Doctrine of sola scriptura*, 2nd ed. Goleta: Queenship Publishing, 2013.

Surtz, Ronald E. "Morisco Women, Written Texts, and the Valencia Inquisition." *Sixteenth Century Journal* 32 (2001): 421–33.

Taglia, Kathryn. "Delivering a Christian Identity: Midwives in Northern French Synodal Legislation, c. 1200–1500." In *Religion and Medicine in the Middle Ages*, edited by Peter Biller and Joseph Ziegler. Rochester: York Medieval Press, 2001, 77–90.

Tamburello, Dennis E. *Union with Christ: John Calvin and the Mysticism of St Bernard*. Louisville: Westminster/John Knox, 1994.

Tanner, Kathryn. "Postmodern Challenges to Tradition." *Louvain Studies* 28 (2003): 175–93.

Tanner, Kathryn. "Self-Critical Cultures and Divine Transcendence." In *Theology After Liberalism: A Reader*, edited by John Webster and George Schner. Malden: Blackwell, 2000, 223–56.

Tanner, Kathryn. *Theories of Culture: A New Agenda for Theology*. Minneapolis: Fortress, 1997.

Tardieu, Michel. *Manichaeism*, translated by M. B. DeBevoise. Champaign: University of Illinois Press, 2008.

Taylor, George H. "Understanding as Metaphoric, Not a Fusion of Horizons." In *Gadamer and Ricoeur: Critical Horizons for Contemporary Hermeneutics*, edited by Francis J. Mootz, III, and George H. Taylor. London: Continuum, 2011, 104–18.

Tavard, George W. *The Starting Point of Calvin's Theology*. Grand Rapids: Eerdmans, 2000.

Thiel, John. *Senses of Tradition: Continuity and Development in Catholic Faith*. Oxford: Oxford University Press, 2000.

Thiselton, Anthony C. *New Horizons in Hermeneutics: The Theory and Practice of Transforming Biblical Reading*. Grand Rapids: Zondervan, 1992.

Thompson, John L. *Writing the Wrongs: Women of the Old Testament among Biblical Commentators from Philo through the Reformation*. Oxford: Oxford University Press, 2001.

Tilley, Terrence. *Inventing Catholic Tradition*. Maryknoll: Orbis Books, 2000.

Tillich, Paul. *Systematic Theology III: Life and the Spirit, History and the Kingdom of God* Chicago: University of Chicago Press, 1963.

Todd, Margo. *The Culture of Protestantism in Early Modern Scotland*. New Haven: Yale University Press, 2002.

Torrance, Thomas F. *The Hermeneutics of John Calvin*. Edinburgh: Scottish Academic Press, 1988.

Trinity Lutheran Church of Columbia, Inc. v. Comer, 582 U.S. ___ (2017). https://supreme.justia.com/cases/federal/us/582/15-577/#tab-opinion-3752808.

Tuchman, Barbara. *A Distant Mirror: The Calamitous 14th Century*. New York: Random House, 1978.

Turner, Victor and Turner, Edith. *Image and Pilgrimage in Christian Culture*. New York: Columbia University Press, 1978.

Turpin, Pascaline. "'Ceci est mon corps, ceci est mon sang': comment le haut Moyen Âge lit-il la Cène?" *Mélanges de Science Religieuse* 71 (2014): 41–51.

Vanhoozer, Kevin. *First Theology: God, Scripture, and Hermeneutics*. Downers Grove: IVP, 2002.

Veen, Mirjam van. "Supporters of the Devil: Calvin's Image of the Libertines." *Calvin Theological Journal* 40 (2005): 21–32.

Verhey, Allen. "Calvin's Treatise 'Against the Libertines,'" Introduction by Allen Verhey, translated by Robert G. Wilkie and Allen Verhey. *Calvin Theological Journal* 15 (1980): 190–219.

Verkruyse, Peter. *Prophet, Pastor, and Patriarch: The Rhetorical Leadership of Alexander Campbell*. Tuscaloosa: University of Alabama Press, 2005.

Visser, Arnoud. *Reading Augustine in the Reformation: The Flexibility of Intellectual Authority in Europe, 1500–1620*. Oxford: Oxford University Press, 2011.

Wabuda, Susan. "Equivocation and Recantation During the English Reformation: The 'Subtle Shadows' of Dr. Edward Crome." *Journal of Ecclesiastical History* 44 (1993): 224–42.

Walchenbach, John R. "John Calvin as Biblical Commentator: An Investigation of John Chrysostom as Exegetical Tutor." Ph.D. Dissertation, University of Pittsburgh, 1974.

Walchenbach, John R. *John Calvin as Biblical Commentator: An Investigation into Calvin's Use of John Chrysostom as an Exegetical Tutor*. Eugene: Wipf & Stock, 2010.

Wallace, Peter G. *The Long European Reformation: Religions, Political Conflict, and the Search for Conformity, 1350–1750*. New York: Palgrave Macmillan, 2004.

Walzer, Michael. *Thick and Thin: Moral Argument at Home and Abroad*. Notre Dame: University of Notre Dame Press, 1994.

Wandel, Lee Palmer. *Voracious Idols and Violent Hands: Iconoclasm in Reformation Zurich, Strasbourg, and Basel*, rev. ed. Cambridge: Cambridge University Press, 1999.

Warfield, Benjamin Breckenridge. *Calvin and Augustine*. Phillipsburg: Presbyterian and Reformed, 1956.

Warnke, Georgia. "Experiencing Tradition Versus Belonging To It: Gadamer's Dilemma." *The Review of Metaphysics* 68 (2014): 347–69.

Webster, John. "Purity and Plenitude; Evangelical Reflections on Congar's Tradition and Traditions." *International Journal of Systematic Theology* 7 (2005): 399–413.

Wendel, François. *Calvin: Origins and Development of His Religious Thought*, translated by Philip Mairet. Durham, NC: Labyrinth Press, 1987.

Westphal, Merold. *Whose Community? Which Interpretation? Philosophical Hermeneutics for the Church*. Grand Rapids: Baker Book House, 2009.

Whitesell, S. L. "The Church of Originalism." *University of Pennsylvania Journal of Constitutional Law* 16 (2014): 1531–68.

Whitford, David M. *The Curse of Ham in the Early Modern Era: The Bible and Justifications for Slavery*. Burlington: Ashgate, 2009.

Whitford, David M. "The Papal Antichrist: Martin Luther and the Underappreciated Influence of Lorenzo Valla." *Renaissance Quarterly* 61 (2008): 26–52.

Whitford, David M. "Robbing Paul to Pay Peter: The Reception of Paul in Sixteenth Century Political Theology." In *A Companion to Paul in the Reformation*, edited by R. Ward Holder. Leiden: Brill, 2009, 573–606.

Whitford, David M. *Tyranny and Resistance: The Magdeburg Confession and the Lutheran Tradition*. St. Louis: Concordia Pub. House, 2001.

Whitford, David M. "Yielding to the Prejudices of His Time: Erasmus and the Comma Johanneum." *Church History and Religious Culture* 95 (2015): 19–40.

Whittington, Keith E. "Originalism: A Critical Introduction." *Fordham Law Review* 85 (2013): 375–409.

Whittington, Keith E. "Originalism: A Rationalization for Conservatism or a Principled Theory of Interpretation?: Is Originalism Too Conservative?" *Harvard Journal of Law and Public Policy* 34 (2011): 29–41.

Wiedenhofer, Siegfried. "Tradition-History-Memory: Why Do We Need a Complex Theory of Tradition?" translated by John Cochrane. In *Tradition and Tradition Theories: An International Discussion*, edited by Thorsten Larbig and Siegfried Wiedenhofer. Münster: LIT-Verlag, 2006, 375–98.

Wiesner-Hanks, Merry E. *Women and Gender in Early Modern Europe*, 3rd ed. Cambridge: Cambridge University Press, 2008.

Wilcox, Pete. "Calvin as Commentator on the Prophets." In *Calvin and the Bible*, edited by Donald McKim. Cambridge: Cambridge University Press, 2006, 107–30.

Williams, D. H. "The Patristic Tradition as Canon." *Perspectives in Religious Studies* 32 (2005): 357–79.

Williams, Delores S. *Sisters in the Wilderness*. Maryknoll: Orbis, 1993.

Williams, George Huntston. *The Radical Reformation*, 3rd ed. Kirksville: Truman State University Press, 2000.

Woo, Kenneth. "Nicodemism and Libertinism." in *John Calvin in Context*, edited by R. Ward Holder. Cambridge: Cambridge University Press, 2019, 287–95.

Wright, David F. "Accommodation and Barbarity in John Calvin's Old Testament Commentaries." In *Understanding Prophets and Poets: Essays in Honor of George Wishart Anderson*, edited by A. Graeme Auld. Sheffield: Journal for the Study of the Old Testament Press, 1993, 413–27.

Wright, David F. "Calvin's Accommodating God." *Calvinus Sincerioris Religionis Vindex*, edited by Wilhelm Neuser and Brian Armstrong. Kirksville: Sixteenth Century Journal Publishers, 1997, 3–20.

Wright, David F. "Calvin's Pentateuchal Criticism: Equity, Hardness of Heart, and Divine Accommodation in the Mosaic Harmony Commentary." *Calvin Theological Journal* 21 (1986): 33–50.

Wright, David F. "George Cassander and the Appeal to the Fathers in Sixteenth-Century Debates about Infant Baptism." In *Auctoritas Patrum: zur Rezeption der Kirchenväter im 15. und 16. Jahrhundert*, edited by Leif Grane, Alfred Schindler, and Markus Wriedt. Mainz: Verlag Philipp von Zabern, 1993, 257–280.

Young, Ernest A. "Dying Constitutionalism and the 14th Amendment." *Marquette Law Review* 102 (2019): 949–78.

Zachman, Randall C. "Calvin as Commentator on Genesis." In *Calvin and the Bible*, edited by Donald McKim. Cambridge: Cambridge University Press, 2006, 1–29.

Zachman, Randall C. "'Do You Understand What You Are Reading?': Calvin's Guidance for the Reading of Scripture." *Scottish Journal of Theology* 54 (2001): 1–20.

Zachman, Randall C. "Expounding Scripture and Applying It to Our Use: Calvin's Sermons on Ephesians." *Scottish Journal of Theology* 56 (2003): 481–507.

Zachman, Randall C. "Who is Actually Catholic? How Our Traditional Categories Keep Us from Understanding the Evangelical Reformations." In *Crossing Traditions: Essays on the Reformation and Intellectual History In Honour of Irena Backus*, edited by Maria-Cristina Pitassi and Daniela Solfaroli Camilloci. Leiden: Brill, 2018, 435–46.

Zimmerman, Jens. "Phenomenology, Hermeneutics, and Religion: Restoring the Fullness of Knowing." In *Hermeneutics and Phenomenology: Figures and Themes*, edited by Saulius Geniusas and Paul Fairfield. London: Bloomsbury, 2018, 163–74.

Zuck, Lowell H. *Christianity and Revolution: Radical Christian Testimonies 1520–1650*. Philadelphia: Temple University Press, 1975.

Index